LAW OFFICE PROCEDURES
A Practical Guide

LAW OFFICE PROCEDURES
A Practical Guide

JUDY A. LONG
Rio Hondo College

West Publishing Company
Minneapolis/St. Paul   New York   Los Angeles   San Francisco

NOTICE TO THE READER

Publisher does not warrant or guarantee any of the products described herein or perform any independent analysis in connection with any of the product information contained herein. Publisher does not assume, and expressly disclaims, any obligation to obtain and include information other than that provided to it by the manufacturer.

The reader is expressly warned to consider and adopt all safety precautions that might be indicated by the activities herein and to avoid all potential hazards. By following the instructions contained herein, the reader willingly assumes all risks in connection with such instructions.

The Publisher makes no representation or warranties of any kind, including but not limited to, the warranties of fitness for particular purpose or merchantability, nor are any such representations implied with respect to the material set forth herein, and the publisher takes no responsibility with respect to such material. The publisher shall not be liable for any special, consequential, or exemplary damages resulting, in whole or part, from the readers' use of, or reliance upon, this material.

Production Credits
Composition: Parkwood Composition
Text Design: Maureen McCutcheon
Cover Image: Liz Monson
Cover Design: Maureen McCutcheon
Proofreader: Lynn Reichel
Production, Prepress, Printing, and Binding by West Publishing Company

Library of Congress Cataloging-in-Publication Data
Long, Judy A.,
    Law office procedures: a practical guide / Judy A. Long.
        p.   cm.
    Includes index.
    ISBN 0-314-09238-2 (pbk.)
    1. Law offices—United States.   I. Title.
    KF318.L66   1997
    340'.068—dc20

DEDICATION

To My Children—Danielle and Jeffrey

BRIEF CONTENTS

CONTENTS

PREFACE

The law office environment is somewhat different from the traditional business world. The goal of this text is to present an overview of the structure and functions of the law office while providing the student with an opportunity to learn about different specialty areas of the law and to assist in the solution of real-life problems. *Law Office Procedures: A Practical Guide* includes both the theoretical and the practical aspects of the practice of law. The book focuses on the roles of the paralegal and the legal secretary.

Practical Approach

To draw students into the material and involve them in the procedures of a law office, a simulated law office is presented in the Introduction. The student is addressed throughout the text as a paralegal or legal secretary employed for the firm. Practical projects at the end of each chapter ask students to perform tasks for an attorney in this hypothetical firm, utilizing skills and applying material discussed in the chapter. Students are encouraged to develop a comprehensive Notebook that can be used in employment interviews and as an on-the-job reference.

In addition, the following practical features are included:

- A description of the various individuals employed in a law office.

- A discussion of the functions of the paralegal and legal secretary in different specialty practices.

- A detailed summary of the trial process.

- A description of the administrative operations of the law office.

- An appendix on job search techniques to assist students in finding employment.

Learning Aids

Each chapter in *Law Office Procedures: A Practical Guide* contains the following learning aids:

- **Chapter Objectives** at the beginning of each chapter emphasize the primary concepts of the chapter.

- **Exhibits** throughout each chapter illustrate formats for various pleadings and other legal documents. Selected exhibits are designated with a notebook logo indicating that students should copy these forms and include them in their Notebook for future reference.

- **State Specific Information** boxes are included where appropriate in each chapter. These boxes provide space for students to write down information on rules and procedures specific to their own state.

- **Key Terms** are printed in boldface and defined in the margin where they first appear within the chapter. For easy review, the key terms are also listed at the end of the chapter.

- **Chapter Summaries** at the end of each chapter provide a brief review of the main concepts covered.

- **Self-Tests** at the end of each chapter help students review the main concepts discussed. Answers to the self-test questions are included in Appendix B to enable students to identify any areas that they may not have addressed thoroughly.

- **Review Questions** in short-answer format also appear at the end of each chapter to provide additional review of chapter concepts.

- **Projects** at the end of each chapter provide students with practical experience in performing the tasks of legal secretaries and paralegals, including proofreading, drafting and preparing documents, and filling out forms. Selected Projects are preceded by a Notebook logo, indicating that students should place the document or form created in the Project in their Notebooks.

Support Material

This text is accompanied by support material that will aid instructors in teaching and students in learning. The following supplements accompany this text:

- An *Instructor's Manual* prepared by Judy Long is designed to help instructors present the material in an organized and comprehensive manner. The *Instructor's Manual* includes a detailed summary of each chapter, lesson plans (including suggestions for field trips and guest speakers), answers to the Review Questions, and suggestions for additional Projects. A comprehensive test bank contains more than 200 objective test questions and answers. In addition, the manual includes transparency masters for use in lecture. The text of the *Instructor's Manual* is also provided on disk in ASCII format.

- A data disk contains selected documents in WordPerfect 5.1 format that can be used to complete certain end-of-chapter Projects. Projects that can be completed using the data disk are marked in the text with the following logo:

- *Strategies and Tips for Paralegal Educators,* a pamphlet by Anita Tebbe of Johnson County Community College, presents teaching strategies designed for legal educators. It concentrates on how to teach and is organized in three parts: the *who* of legal education—students and teachers; the *what* of legal education—goals and objectives; and the *how* of legal education—methods of instruction, methods of evaluation, and other aspects of teaching. A copy of this pamphlet is available to each adopter.

- West's Video Library includes a variety of videos on topics such as ethics, legal research, and trial procedures. Qualified adopters can select and exchange tapes for use in the classroom. Ask your local representative for details on the titles included in this video library.

Acknowledgments

Many individuals provided assistance in the preparation of this textbook. I would like to thank Elizabeth Hannan (editor) and Patty Bryant (developmental editor) for their numerous suggestions and considerable assistance. I would also like to thank Jayne Lindesmith (production editor) and Carrie Kish and Karen Laird (promotion managers) for their assistance in producing and marketing the final text.

The following individuals provided very valuable suggestions and recommendations in their reviews of the text:

Vicky B. Alexandra
Utica School of Commerce, NY

Nancy L. Barnett
National Education Center, CA

Allison Colvin
Career College of Northern Nevada

Randall N. Forsythe
Sawyer College, IN

Loretta A. Gannon
Chubb-Keystone School, PA

Sandy Gravunder
Chippewa Valley Technical College, WI

Dolores A. Hofmann
Bryant and Stratton Business Institute, NY

Judy Johnson
Rasmussen Business College, MN

Karen Krych
St. Cloud Business College, MN

Melody Lawhon
Empire College of Business and Law, CA

Joyce Marchione-Traina
American Business Academy, NJ

Barbara Martucci
Tri-State Business Institute, PA

Evelyn Riyhani
University of California, Irvine

Laura St. George
Champlain College, VT

Michael Ryan Sheehan
Virginia Beach, VA

Jacqueline Forest Sichel
Empire College, CA

Vicki L. Steel
Business Skills Training Center, TX

Hazel M. Tordiff
Washington Business School, VA

Of particular assistance was Vicky Alexandra who offered many helpful suggestions and ideas for sample forms and documents, some of which were included in the final text.

I sincerely appreciate the considerable assistance I received from the following attorneys whom I met on America On Line. These individuals assisted not only by providing materials for the text, but also by contributing their expertise in their specialty areas. A very special thanks to:

- Fred Hadley from Indiana for his extraordinary assistance in Civil Litigation and his numerous documents and pleadings.

- Kenneth Celli from California for his Criminal Law materials and advice on Criminal Law and also for his valuable assistance in reviewing the Criminal Law chapter in its entirety.

- Marc Shapiro of New York for his advice and assistance in the Real Property chapter and for providing Real Estate Closing materials.

- Jonathan Washburn from South Carolina for his Real Property materials and his wonderful sense of humor when I felt guilty about asking for his help "just one more time."

I would also like to thank the following colleagues and friends who furnished material for the text:

- Rachel Sotelo of Relief Paralegal Services for her landlord/tenant materials.

- Frankie E. Wade of Jackson, Tennessee, for the Divorce Complaint in Chapter 8.

- John Callinan for his charts of the court structure.

- Dana Zupanovich for her Corporate Law documents.

- Stan Ross for reviewing chapters of the text, for providing material for the Real Property chapter, and for his constant encouragement.

Thanks to Steve Standeven for his computer expertise as he got me out of several difficult situations and helped me find materials that I thought were lost forever. A very special thanks to my Law Office Procedures students, many of whose names are used in the text, for allowing me to use my early drafts of the text for experimentation purposes and for their assistance in making this book user-friendly.

Thanks to all of those individuals whose names have been inadvertently omitted.

Judy A. Long

LAW OFFICE PROCEDURES
A Practical Guide

Introduction

Welcome to the law office of Michaels & Williams. This general practice law firm is located at 1122 Main Street, Your Town, Your State. The senior partners are Kimberly A. Michaels and Jeffrey M. Williams. You are employed as a paralegal (legal assistant) or legal secretary for Mr. Williams. You will be working for this firm for the duration of this course. In each chapter, you will complete various projects simulating the tasks performed in a law office. All projects and documents should be prepared for Mr. Williams.

NOTEBOOK

One of the features of this text is that it will help you prepare a reference notebook that will be useful not only during this course but later as well. A 📖 logo beside documents and projects in the text indicates that they should be placed in your notebook. To prepare your notebook, you will need a three-ring binder with dividers and tabs. Each section in the notebook will coincide with a chapter in the text. You should prepare your "skeleton" notebook before beginning the assignments in the chapters.

As you study each chapter, whenever you come to a document or form with a notebook logo, add a copy to your notebook along with any instructions in the text for preparing the document. Whenever your instructor gives you specific instructions on the way a document is prepared, served, or filed, add these directions to your notebook along with a sample of the document. All checklists in the text should be included in your notebook under the appropriate subject heading. Each chapter concludes with a series of projects that require you to work with the documents and forms in the chapter. When you receive your projects back from your instructor, place them in your notebook under the appropriate heading. At the end of the course, your instructor may check your notebook to make sure you have included all the appropriate documents and projects.

Keep adding to your notebook as you take more courses in your paralegal or legal secretarial program. Some of the material you will encounter in subsequent courses will fit under the headings you establish for this course. In some cases, though, you will need to add new headings as you progress through your course of study.

Your notebook will also prove valuable after you graduate because most employers of paralegals and legal secretaries ask for a writing sample to be submitted with the employment application. The assignments you have filed in your notebook can be used as writing samples. The notebook will also help you learn organizational skills and will provide you with models to use when you must prepare similar documents later, either in other classes or in a law office setting. Since documents prepared in law offices tend to be repetitive in nature, you can often follow the format of a document in your notebook and simply fill in the names and other new information.

After you are "on the job," you should continue to add to your notebook whenever you prepare something new or different. Include both the new item and instructions for its preparation. You should continue to add to your notebook throughout your legal career. Former students have extolled the benefits of a notebook after several years in the legal profession. Instructors are encouraged to use this "notebook approach" throughout the course of study in the paralegal or legal secretarial programs.

PROJECT

1. Purchase a three-ring binder and make a tab divider for each chapter of the text-book. Copies of all forms and projects should be inserted in the notebook under the appropriate headings. Subsequent projects should be inserted under the appropriate chapter heading. Prepare a Table of Contents and add to it as new material is inserted. The Table of Contents should be organized as follows:

Chapter Number	Subject	Page Number

Under "Chapter Number, " list the number of the chapter from which the material in your textbook was obtained. Under "Subject," list the name of the document, check-list, or instructions. The "Page Number" is the number of the page in your notebook. Since you will be adding material under each topic throughout this course and later, number the pages consecutively by chapter. For example, the number of the first page under Chapter 5 in your notebook would be 5-1.

Law Office Structure

CHAPTER OBJECTIVES

As a result of studying this chapter, you will learn the following material:

1. ***Public and Private Law Firms***   The structure of law firms will be described. You will become familiar with the differences between public-sector and private law offices.
2. ***Law Office Personnel***   The functions of various law office personnel, including the attorney, paralegal, legal secretary, law clerk, and receptionist, will be described. You will learn the main duties involved in each position.
3. ***Free-Lance Paralegals***   The role of the free-lance paralegal in the legal structure will be examined.
4. ***Legal Specialties***   Various legal specialty areas will be described. You will learn the differences between civil and criminal practice and what corporate law, family law, and estate planning entail.
5. ***Corporate Law Departments***   The structure of the corporate law department will be discussed. You will learn the functions of the paralegal and legal secretary in the corporate setting.
6. ***Government Law Offices***   The various state and federal offices will be described. You will learn the functions of the paralegal and legal secretary in the government setting.
7. ***Professional Organizations***   The professional organizations available to law office personnel will be discussed. You will learn how these organizations can be helpful to your career.

THE LAW FIRM

There are several different types of law offices. One distinction is between private law firms and public-sector (government) law offices. Private law firms may be organized as individual proprietorships, partnerships, or professional corporations, as will be described more fully in Chapter 11. All law offices, however, whether private or public, employ much the same personnel. This section will describe the many different individuals who comprise the law office team. The chart in Exhibit 1.1 shows the organization of a typical law office.

Lawyers/Attorneys

The terms **lawyer** and **attorney** are used interchangeably and have the same meaning. To be able to use the title "lawyer" or "attorney," a person must pass the Bar

EXHIBIT 1.1   Law Office Organization Chart

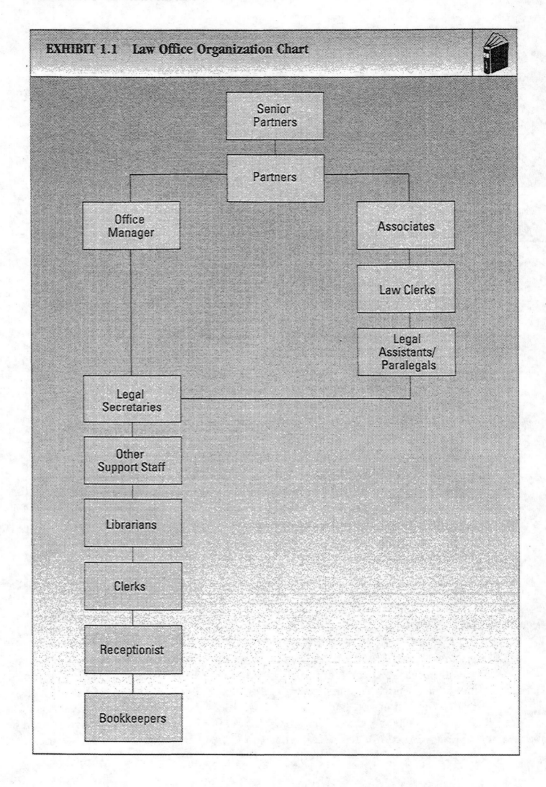

Examination for the state in which her practice is located and be formally admitted to that State's Bar. To practice law in another state, the individual must pass the Bar Examination for that state, even though she has already been admitted to practice in the first state. To become eligible to take the Bar Examination, individuals typically spend four or more years in college to earn a Bachelor's Degree and approximately three years in law school to earn a Law Degree.

Large law firms may have lawyers at many different levels, including senior partners, partners, junior partners, senior associates, associates, and junior associates. In general, the larger the law firm, the more levels of titles its attorneys will have.

Partners are the actual owners of the firm and receive a percentage of its profits. **Senior partners** generally have a greater ownership interest than other partners and are often the founders of the firm. **Associates** are paid a salary and are not allocated an ownership interest in the law firm. Nor do they share in the profits. New associates are called junior associates in some law offices.

Attorneys with the title **Of Counsel** act in an advisory capacity to the firm, often in a given specialty area. They generally do not have an ownership interest in the firm and do not share in the profits.

Paralegals/Legal Assistants

Most law firms use the job titles **paralegal** and legal assistant interchangeably and assign the same tasks to both. A few offices, however, distinguish between the paralegal and the legal assistant by giving more responsibility to the paralegal.

Paralegals are trained professionals who usually have either a four-year Bachelor's Degree and a paralegal certificate or a two-year Associate Degree in Paralegal Studies. Some colleges and universities offer a Bachelor's Degree in Paralegal Studies. Paralegals assist lawyers in many areas, including drafting documents, discovery, interviewing clients and witnesses, legal research, and investigation. Depending on the lawyer's specialty, the paralegal may also be involved in other activities. Generally, the paralegal's duties are diverse and vary considerably with the type of law practiced by the attorney.

Free-Lance Paralegals

Free-lance paralegals work independently in their own businesses and are not permanent employees of a particular law firm, although they may work for a firm on a temporary basis. These paralegals work in many areas of law, including probate, domestic relations, worker's compensation, immigration, and landlord/tenant law.

Free-lance paralegals work either for attorneys on an as-needed basis or directly with their own clients, who appear in court without attorney representation (persons who appear in court without an attorney are said to be appearing "in propria persona," often shortened to "pro per" or "pro se"). Paralegals who work independent of attorneys and have their own clients have received much criticism in recent years as many states have become concerned that unlicensed individuals are engaging in the unauthorized practice of law. Some states are considering requiring paralegals to be certified or licensed in certain specialty areas to alleviate this problem.

Free-lance paralegals working without attorney supervision may not give a client legal advice. They must inform the client that they are paralegals and not attorneys. They may help the client complete the forms and/or documents required by the court for a particular case; however, they may not advise the client about whether to litigate

lawyer
An individual who has attended law school and passed the State Bar Examination; an **attorney**.

attorney
An individual who has attended law school and passed the State Bar Examination; a **lawyer**.

partner
An attorney who is one of the owners of a law firm and receives a percentage of its profits.

senior partner
An attorney who is one of the major owners of a law firm and has a larger ownership interest than an ordinary partner has; often one of the firm's founders.

associate
A lawyer in a private law firm who is paid a salary and does not share in the firm's profits.

Of Counsel
A title used for an attorney who acts in an advisory capacity to a law firm and does not have an ownership interest or share in the profits.

paralegal
A legal assistant; an assistant to an attorney; may not practice law but may perform tasks under the attorney's supervision.

an action, what settlement is realistic, or any other issues that require them to give legal advice or do anything that might be considered the practice of law and exercise of independent legal judgment. The client, and not the paralegal, signs the forms and documents. Free-lance paralegals should consult with an attorney when they require legal advice for the client or other information that they might not have available.

Some states are restricting the ability of paralegals to practice on a free-lance basis and to operate their own offices. It is important to check the rules of your own state to determine the requirements for free-lance paralegals. Record the requirements in the State Specific Information box.

STATE SPECIFIC INFORMATION	The rules for free-lance paralegals in the state of _____ are: _____ _____ _____ _____

Legal Secretary

legal secretary
A secretary to a lawyer or a law firm.

A good **legal secretary** is a tremendous asset to a law firm. The legal secretary handles incoming telephone calls, mail, docket control, calendaring, scheduling appointments, filing, and typing correspondence and documents. Many legal secretaries may also perform paralegal functions, particularly in small law offices.

Although some legal secretaries enter the legal field upon graduation from high school, most attend legal secretarial programs at community colleges, adult education programs, or proprietary schools. Since law offices use word processing software packages, it is imperative that the prospective legal secretary receive computer training.

Law Office Manager/Managing Attorney

law office manager
An individual who handles the administrative functions in a law firm; may also be the **managing attorney.**

managing attorney
An attorney who handles the administrative and management functions of a law firm.

While many firms employ a **law officer manager** to perform the administrative and management functions of the organization, in some law offices an attorney, called the **managing attorney,** performs this job. Large firms may have both positions and divide the responsibilities between them. Some offices also have additional levels of management under the direction of the law office manager, including such positions as personnel manager, file manager, library coordinator, accounting officer, and other specialized administrative positions. Some firms have separate Word Processing Departments with their own manager. Large law offices may also employ a paralegal supervisor or coordinator.

Generally, the law office manager is a senior paralegal with training in that area, an attorney, or an individual with a degree in Business who has had law firm experience. This person is responsible for all of the administrative and support functions of the law office, including general administration, personnel, employee benefits, file room, duplicating services, library, equipment, word processing, and purchasing. This position carries a tremendous amount of responsibility and requires talent in a broad range of administrative functions.

Receptionist

Some lawyers consider the **receptionist** to be one of the most critical employees in the firm. Whether a prospective client approaches the firm by telephone or in person, his first contact is with the receptionist; therefore, this person must be very personable, courteous, and professional at all times. A cheerful smile and friendly manner are "musts" for the law firm receptionist. The receptionist should also know how to handle difficult clients and/or situations. Since the secretaries may sometimes ask the receptionist to help with overflow typing and word processing, good keyboarding skills are also needed.

receptionist
The person who greets callers to the law office and answers the telephone.

Law Librarian

The **law librarian** is in charge of the library and usually has a degree in Library Science or, sometimes, paralegal training. In some very small law firms, the law librarian may be a law clerk in the firm. Most law librarians have also been trained in computerized legal research systems, such as WESTLAW, LEXIS, or CD-ROM databases. Other responsibilities may include keeping track of volumes, ordering books, doing computerized research, updating volumes, and generally maintaining the library. The larger the law firm, the larger the law library. Therefore, in very large firms, several individuals may be assigned to the library.

law librarian
An individual working in a law office or law library with responsibility for the law books.

Law Clerks

Law clerks are law school students who are working part-time either in a law office or for a judge. Judges at all levels, including Supreme Court Justices, employ law clerks. Usually, law clerks must have completed their second or third year of law school. Their responsibilities include doing legal research, investigating cases, and drafting pleadings and other documents. In some firms, law clerks may also file documents with the court and run errands for the attorneys. Sometimes their work may include responsibilities similar to those of the paralegal or law librarian.

    Law clerks are gaining valuable experience in the "real world" environment of the law firm that will help them practice law after they graduate and pass the Bar Examination. A law clerk's assignment is usually temporary, but it may turn into a permanent job as an attorney once the law clerk graduates and passes the Bar Examination.

law clerk
A law student working in a law firm part-time while attending law school.

Bookkeeper/Payroll

Even small firms employ a **bookkeeper,** an individual who keeps the books, prepares the payroll, and bills individual clients after compiling data from the timesheets of the attorneys, paralegals, and other legal support staff. The bookkeeper may also pay all of the firm's bills. In larger law offices, these tasks may require several employees.

bookkeeper
An individual who is employed by a law firm to pay bills and keep accounting records.

Legal Specialties

Law firms generally specialize in one or more areas. Small firms may have one specialty or may be **"general practices."** Much like a doctor, an attorney may choose to be a general practitioner or a specialist.

    The most common specialties are civil litigation and criminal law. **Civil practice** includes lawsuits by individuals or corporations. The firm may specialize in automobile

general practice
A law firm that practices all areas of law and does not specialize.

civil practice
A law practice that deals with private lawsuits that are brought to enforce a right or gain payment for a wrong. One individual or company sues another, usually for money damages.

criminal law
The area of law dealing with crimes and illegal conduct under which individuals accused of crimes are brought to trial and punished if convicted.

family law
The branch of law dealing with divorce, support, custody, adoption, and related matters.

corporate law
A legal specialty dealing with setting up corporations, securities, and corporate mergers.

estate planning
The area of law that deals with ways to pass property upon one's death; includes wills, trusts, and probate.

real property
The area of law dealing with real estate transactions and landlord/tenant relations.

in-house counsel
Attorneys employed by a corporation. They are employees of the corporation on salary.

corporate law department
The department of a corporation that handles its legal matters.

accident cases, defective products litigation, or any other cases where people or companies sue one another. In private law firms, **criminal law** involves defending individuals accused of crimes. In the public sector, District Attorneys or Prosecuting Attorneys prosecute these same individuals for the State or County.

Other common specialties are included in the following list. Each will be discussed in detail later in the text.

1. *Family Law.* Attorneys in this area deal with divorce (or dissolution of marriage), child custody, support, and other issues related to marriage and children. Adoptions, surrogate parenting, and guardianships are also included in this area.

2. *Corporate Law.* Attorneys specializing in this field set up corporations, maintain corporate record books, and handle securities cases, antitrust suits, acquisitions, corporate mergers, liquidations, and dissolutions.

3. *Estate Planning.* Attorneys who specialize in estate planning write wills, prepare trusts, and handle the probate of estates.

4. *Real Property.* Attorneys working in this area deal with real estate transactions, as well as with landlord and tenant problems.

Some other specialty areas include worker's compensation, environmental law, intellectual property, bankruptcy, immigration, labor, and consumer law.

THE CORPORATE LAW DEPARTMENT

Most large corporations have their own law departments. Attorneys in these departments are called **in-house counsel**. A **corporate law department** employs paralegals and legal secretaries, librarians, file clerks, and other legal support personnel. However, it does not include bookkeepers and similar administrative personnel because they are available in other departments of the corporation. For instance, the corporation may have its own Human Resources and Payroll Departments, which will perform those functions for the law department.

Employment responsibilities in a corporate law department are as diverse as the corporation's products or services. Most corporations, however, have a litigation section because litigation crosses all specialty areas. The following are some of the other areas that arise in a corporation's legal department:

1. Worker's compensation

2. Corporate

3. Contracts

4. Real estate

5. Patents

6. Industrial relations

7. Insurance

8. Environmental law

Usually, the corporate law department's only client is the corporation itself; therefore, contacts with clients are limited to contacts with other employees. Some individuals like the pace of a corporate law department better than a law firm. With only one client, the position may not be as hectic or stressful as in a private firm. On the other hand, those who prefer working in private firms find corporate work dull or boring and miss the fast pace and constant deadlines of the private firm.

GOVERNMENT LAW OFFICES

Many government agencies at the federal, state, county, and local levels employ paralegals and legal secretaries. A number of job opportunities involve criminal law from the prosecutorial side. Government agencies also employ paralegals and legal secretaries in family law, consumer law, and probate. Most counties have domestic violence programs that utilize paralegals, under attorney supervision, to help victims obtain restraining orders. Probate paralegals and secretaries are employed by the Probate Department of the court. Many counties have consumer protection agencies that hire paralegals as counselors and investigators.

Government paralegals and legal secretaries usually have a standard workweek of thirty-five to forty hours, receive excellent benefits packages (such as paid vacation, sick leave, and medical insurance), and are given regular salary reviews and opportunities for advancement. Duties and responsibilities tend to be quite varied, depending on the area of government in which the paralegal is employed.

The Federal Government

The U.S. Department of Justice, which has branch offices in most major cities, is one of the largest employers of paralegals in the country. Agencies within the Justice Department that employ paralegals and legal secretaries include the Drug Enforcement Administration, the Office of the Solicitor General, and the Office of Personnel Management. Other federal government departments that employ paralegals and legal secretaries include the military, Civil Rights Commission, Equal Employment Opportunity Commission (EEOC), Transportation Department, U.S. Postal Service, Federal Deposit Insurance Corporation (FDIC), Commerce Department, Labor Department, and the Securities and Exchange Commission (SEC), to name only a few.

Some paralegals and legal secretaries in the federal government are involved in investigating criminal cases, examining case files, preparing documents, doing legal research and analysis, analyzing statutes, interviewing witnesses, developing evidence for the prosecution, gathering documents, and preparing material for trial. Depending on the department, cases may involve prosecutions of drug dealers, employment discrimination, courts-martial, or stock fraud.

State and County Governments

Many state and county departments employ paralegals and legal secretaries in the criminal area for both the prosecution and the defense. Paralegals and legal secretaries in these departments help prepare cases for trial, do legal research, find and prepare witnesses for trial, and investigate cases. A paralegal or legal secretary who works for the defense, usually called the Public Defender, may spend time interviewing accused persons and investigating their background. Working for the Prosecutor (or District Attorney) may involve the investigation of prior convictions, legal research, and preparation of cases for trial. Usually, much of the investigation of prior convictions is performed using a computer.

County governments also employ paralegals and legal secretaries in various other capacities. Duties in departments, such as Consumer Affairs, may include preparation of documents and pleadings for consumer fraud cases along with consumer counseling and investigation of consumer complaints. Working for the County Counsel entails handling lawsuits against the county.

Local governments are increasingly becoming involved with environmental matters. Some government agencies prosecute individuals and businesses that violate the laws related to air and water pollution. Individuals interested in environmental law should contact their county and local governments to learn what positions are available in this area.

PROFESSIONAL ORGANIZATIONS

It is important for paralegals and legal secretaries to join the appropriate organization for their profession. Most organizations offer less expensive student memberships that provide students the opportunity to attend meetings, meet individuals already employed in the profession, and network for future employment. The following is a partial listing of the major national organizations in several areas:

Attorneys	American Bar Association (ABA) 750 N. Lakeshore Drive Chicago, IL 60611-4497
Paralegals	National Association of Legal Assistants (NALA) 1601 S. Main Street Tulsa, OK 74119
	National Federation of Paralegal Associations (NFPA) 104 Wilmot Road Suite 201 Deerfield, IL 60011
Law office managers	Association of Legal Administrators 175 E. Hawthorn Parkway Suite 325 Vernon Hills, IL 60061-1428
Legal secretaries	National Association of Legal Secretaries (NALS) 2250 E. 73rd Street Suite 550 Tulsa, OK 74136-6864

Local chapters or local professional organizations should also be investigated. A good place to start a search is with the local or county bar association in your city. Some localities also have branches of the national organizations listed above.

SUMMARY

Law offices in the private and public sectors have different structures, but both employ the same or similar types of individuals, including lawyers, paralegals, legal secretaries, law clerks, law librarians, and bookkeepers. Corporate law departments work differently from law firms in that their only client is the corporation. Independent paralegals are becoming more widespread in today's society as clients look for low-cost legal services.

Government law offices also employ paralegals and legal secretaries. Many government departments at the county, state, and federal level have law departments. Paralegals and legal secretaries in government law offices may work in criminal law for either the prosecution or the defense, consumer protection, or pollution control, to name only a few possibilities.

Many specialty areas exist in the law. Among the more common specialties are civil litigation, family law, corporate law, real property, and criminal law.

KEY TERMS

Associate 5	Law librarian 7
Attorney 3	Law office manager 6
Bookkeeper 7	Lawyer 3
Civil practice 7	Legal secretary 6
Corporate law 8	Managing attorney 6
Corporate law department 8	Of Counsel 5
Criminal law 8	Paralegal 5
Estate planning 8	Partner 5
Family law 8	Real property 8
General practice 7	Receptionist 7
In-house counsel 8	Senior partner 5
Law clerk 7	

SELF-TEST

A.   Match the positions on the left with their functions or definitions on the right:

_1_ a. paralegal   1. drafts documents

_4_ b. legal secretary   2. manages administration

_2_ c. law office manager   3. maintains library

_3_ d. law librarian   4. schedules meetings

_5_ e. bookkeeper   5. pays bills

B.   Indicate whether the following statements are true (T) or false (F):

_F_ 1. Free-lance paralegals may give legal advice to their clients.

_F_ 2. Corporate law departments have many more clients than private law firms.

_F_ 3. The professional organization for paralegals is NALS.

_T_ 4. The professional organization for legal secretaries is NALS.

C.   Fill in the blanks:

1. The managing attorney performs the administrative functions of the

_____ in the law firm.

2. The _____ paralegal has his own clients.

3. In order to call herself an attorney, a person must have passed the

_____ for the state in which she practices.

4. The individual who greets the clients as they arrive at the law office is called

the _____ .

D.   Return to the positions listed on the left in Question A1 above, and indicate
which position is responsible for each of the following functions. Positions may
be used more than once.

_____ 1. updating books in the library

_____ 2. running errands for the attorney

_____ 3. sending bills to clients

_____ 4. typing documents

_____ 5. drafting documents

_____ 6. negotiating settlements with insurance companies

_____ 7. hiring paralegals

_____ 8. appearing in court on behalf of the client

_____ 9. giving the client legal advice

_____10. answering the firm's telephone

_____11. finding new offices for the firm

REVIEW QUESTIONS

1.   List four departments of the federal government that employ legal secretaries and

paralegals. _____

_____

_____

2. Describe the functions of a free-lance or independent paralegal.

_____

_____

3. What is the difference between a partner and an associate in a law firm?

_____

_____

4. Explain the differences between a private law firm and a corporate law department.

_____

_____

PROJECTS

1. Is there a federal Office of Personnel Management in your city? If not, where is the closest office?

2. Does your state allow free-lance paralegals to have their own offices? What are the rules governing free-lance paralegals in your state?

Administrative Functions

CHAPTER OBJECTIVES

As a result of studying this chapter, you will learn the following material:

1. **Calendaring**   All systems of maintaining office calendars will be presented. You will learn how to develop an individualized system, as well as how to maintain tickler files and docket control.

2. **Timekeeping and Billing**   The methods of charging time to clients will be discussed. You will learn how to keep "billable hours." Different billing methods will also be discussed.

3. **Telephone Techniques**   Various methods of communicating by telephone will be discussed. You will learn how to answer telephones, make appointments, take messages, and communicate with clients by telephone.

4. **Records Management**   Various methods of maintaining client files will be outlined. You will also be introduced to the law library.

5. **Computers**   A general outline of how computers are used in a law office will be presented. You will be introduced to some standardized computer systems, as well as to other standard office equipment.

6. **Legal Correspondence**   The preparation of correspondence for the law office will be discussed. You will learn proper forms of address and a standard format for writing letters.

7. **Format of Legal Documents**   Standard formats for legal documents will be presented. You will learn about legal cap, writing citations, and other practices unique to law offices.

CALENDARING

Calendaring or keeping track of deadlines and appointments is an important part of the paralegal's and legal secretary's responsibilities. Many offices have computers with the capability of performing this function. For a computer system to operate properly, however, someone has to key in the correct information, such as dates, times, and names. Generally, the secretary will keep the attorney's calendar. The paralegal should keep her own calendar of appointments and due dates.

Each piece of mail that comes into the law office should be read and logged onto a **mail log.** Any required action should also be noted. The date a response is due should be noted on the calendar, whether it is a manual or computer system. A notation about two weeks ahead of the due date should also be made on the calendar,

calendaring
The process of keeping track of appointments and deadlines on a desk or office calendar.

mail log
A record of incoming mail.

another should be made one week ahead, and another three days ahead. In this way, you can avoid the "last minute crunch" of having to prepare documents and/or correspondence on the anticipated due date. Usually, the product is better if sufficient time is allowed to prepare it properly. Calendaring items properly will help to avoid the problem of malpractice suits against the attorney for missed deadlines.

A good tool for keeping the attorney "on track" is to prepare a daily schedule each morning of items that are coming due within the next week. This schedule can be printed and given to the attorney with the mail each morning so that the day can be planned efficiently. Paralegals should develop a procedure for using their own computers for making daily schedules. With the systems now available, the day's activities can be called up on the computer screen at the beginning of each day by using a simple code. Then, as more items come into the office and additional cases are filed, the schedule can be updated.

Whenever a document is served on a client through the law office, the paralegal and legal secretary should note on the calendar when an answering document is due. Again, make a note two weeks ahead, one week ahead, three days ahead, and one day ahead. Many documents require further research before they can be prepared. Therefore, the paralegal should plan the amount of time needed for doing the research and preparing the document. A date for preparation before the due date should be noted on the calendar. Many law offices call this procedure a "tickler system."

Many manual systems are available for individuals who do not wish to use computers for calendaring. A desk calendar and/or diary may be used. Another option is a card file set up with months and dates. Booklets with separate headings for months and dates are also available. The computer performs this function quickly, however, and is easy to use.

Pocket Calendars

Recently, many manufacturers have produced pocket calendars in the form of a minicomputer. You may key in appointments, due dates, reminders, and telephone numbers and even prepare short memoranda. These devices are particularly useful for individuals who make appointments while away from the office and need to record and use telephone numbers quickly. Of course, regular paper calendars and pocket address books are available for this purpose.

Court Dockets

The court docket lists scheduled court dates, along with the times, cases, and attorneys involved. These documents are particularly useful in a large law firm where many attorneys are appearing in different courtrooms. These firms may have a docket control clerk who prepares and verifies the dockets.

Exhibit 2.1 shows a sample docket slip for the fictional firm of Weiss & Richardson, which includes ten attorneys.

Computerized Docketing/Calendaring Programs.   Many law firms use computerized docket control programs that are specifically developed to help track important deadlines and dates. These programs are useful for keeping track of court appearances and filing deadlines, as well as client appointments and firm meetings.

Many paralegals and legal secretaries also use docket control programs for self-imposed deadlines. For instance, suppose a paralegal has been asked to draft a com-

EXHIBIT 2.1   A Sample Docket Slip

SUPERIOR COURT DOCKET SLIP

Weiss & Richardson

June 23, 199x

TIME	CASE	COURTROOM	ATTORNEY
9:00 a.m.	Wilson v. Beck	B22, North Superior Court	Evans
9:00 a.m.	Sanchez v. Johns	D44, Hadley Municipal Court	Richardson
2:00 p.m.	Alter v. Rio	B25, North Superior Court	Michaels
3:00 p.m.	Stand v. Ross	C44, North Superior Court	Richardson

plaint. Although the final complaint is not due for three weeks, the paralegal might set a personal deadline of one week in which to complete the first draft of the complaint. This self-imposed deadline can be entered into the computer along with the other dates.

Most computerized docket control programs have a built-in reminder, or tickler, system to provide advance notice of an approaching deadline or appointment. For instance, look at Exhibit 2.2, which shows a sample monthly display screen from a calendaring program. The identifier at the top of the screen indicates that this is the January 1995 schedule for an individual with the initials "RSS." Now look at the square for January 18, 1995. The screen shows three numbers: 1, 1, and 1. This means that RSS has one appointment, one critical deadline, and one self-imposed deadline. For specific information on these deadlines, the user would position the cursor on the square for January 18 and press the ENTER key. A more detailed summary then appears at the bottom of the screen.

Docket control programs also allow users to print a variety of reports. For example, the paralegal or legal secretary could print a list of events for a particular day or a list of all appointments or deadlines related to a specific client's case. Exhibit 2.3 is a sample printout of a weekly calendar for Courtney C. Richards. Note that on Tuesday, March 19, the second entry has an asterisk next to it. The asterisk indicates that this entry is a reminder of a future deadline or appointment, in this case, a trial date.

Tickler Files

This same computer-generated calendar may also be used to maintain a tickler file, or reminder of what must be done on a given day. Title the calendar entry "tickler file" and key in the material that has to be prepared that day instead of the appointments. Alternatively, the space at the bottom of the calendar page can be used for reminders of items that must be completed on a given day. Exhibit 2.4 shows a sample calendar page with a tickler file for the following items:

EXHIBIT 2.2   A Sample Screen from a Calendaring Program

SUN	MON	TUE	WED	THU	FRI	SAT
1	2	3	4	5	6	7
8	9	10	11	12	13	14
15	16	17	18	19	20	21
22	23	24	25	26	27	28
29	30	31				
				APPOINT-MENTS	CRITICAL DEADLINES	SELF-IMPSD DEADLINES

```
Enter day to display, ← for last month, → for next month: _

             Summary for RSS on Wednesday January 18, 1995

ITEM   TIME    ACCOUNT/CLIENT                  SERVICE/INFO.

1      10:30 AM   00010000                     Discuss Tax Evasion Charges
                  Joseph Trimble

2    * C 02:00 PM 00011537                      Trial - Hilltop v. Triple K
                  Hilltop Auto Sales            Judge Berry, Room 306

3      S          00011024                      Amend Complaint
                  Avery International           Add Defendants

Press ← for yesterday, press → for tomorrow.

Enter ITEM no., PgDn for more items, Home to start over, or Ins to add:
```

SOURCE: Courtesy of MicroCraft, Inc., Docket ® by MicroCraft, Inc.

1. Interrogatories must be prepared in the *Flannery v. Keyes* case.
2. The complaint in the *Becka* case must be filed with the Superior Court before 5:00 P.M.

ATTORNEY FEES

attorney fees
The fees that the attorney charges the client.

There are several different types of **attorney fees** including hourly fees, contingency fees, and fees by the particular project. Some firms use a combination of these methods. To avoid fee disputes with the client, all fee agreements should be in writing and signed by both the attorney and the client at the initial client interview. Many states require that all fee arrangements with clients be written and signed by the attorney and the client.

Hourly Fees

If the firm bills the client hourly, the attorney will charge a specified amount for each hour spent working on the client's case. Generally, a lower hourly fee is charged for paralegal time than for attorney time. In most states, secretarial time is not billed to the client unless the secretary is performing paralegal tasks. In firms that charge hourly

EXHIBIT 2.3   A Sample Printout of a Weekly Calendar

COMPULAW, LTD.
WEEK AT A GLANCE
Page 1

Report for Courtney C. Richards
For the week beginning March 18, 1996

Monday 18	Tuesday 19	Wednesday 20	Thursday 21	Friday 22
9:00 a.m. Case Tools Corporation CTC v. Bren Industries, Inc. 10056.003 Hearing Los Angeles Superior Court Defendant's motions to dismiss. 1:00 p.m. to 4:00 p.m. Apex Construction Company v. Jones APEX-001 Meeting: Client Office Discuss settlement offer.	9:30 a.m. to 12:00 p.m. Apex Construction Company v. Jones APEX-001 Deposition Office Depo of Lawrence G. Smith at the offices of West & Rains, 1400 West North Street, 21st floor. *Due on 05/28/1996 No Time Acme Refrigeration Acme vs. The March Group ACME-001 Trial and Pretrial Dates Santa Monica Superior Court THE DATE THAT THIS CASE IS SET FOR JURY OR NONJURY TRIAL.	No Time Precision Parts, Inc. v. United Systems, Inc. PREC-001 Discovery Office LAST COURT DAY FOR RESPONSE TO INTERROGATORIES TO BE SERVED. See Document #11. 10:00 a.m. Precision Parts, Inc. v. United Systems, Inc. PREC-001 Deposition Opposing counsel's office Depo. of Lois West at the offices of Smith, Jones, Adams & Johnson, 21st floor. 5:00 p.m. Acme Refrigeration Acme v. The March Group ACME-001 Discovery Santa Monica Superior Court LAST COURT DAY TO SERVE (BY MAIL) REQUESTS	No Time Apex Construction Company v. Jones APEX-001 Discovery Office LAST COURT DAY FOR RESPONSE TO INTERROGATORIES TO BE SERVED. 12:00 p.m. Case Tools Corporation CTC v. Bren Industries, Inc. 10056.003 Meeting: Client Restaurant: Business Lunch with Howard Jones of CTC. Wong Chu Chinese Restaurant, 444 East April Lane. 5:00 p.m. Bell Computer Products Bell v. Delta Chips of GA 100092.001 Last day to file this action Los Angeles Superior Court Last court day to apply for correction of award.	8:30 a.m. to 10:00 a.m. Office Administration Meetings 0000-001 Meeting: Office Related Office Meeting to discuss the great new features of our calendar program. The new WEEK AT A GLANCE report can be printed in landscape format. We have the option to print the TRI-CAL on top or bottom. Quick review should make it very easy for attorneys to look at their schedules. 5:00 p.m. Acme Refrigeration Acme v. The March Group ACME-001 Trial and Pretrial Dates Santa Monica Superior Court LAST COURT DAY TO FILE AND SERVE (BY HAND) NOTICE

EXHIBIT 2.3   A Sample Printout of a Weekly Calendar *Concluded*

Monday 18	Tuesday 19	Wednesday 20	Thursday 21	Friday 22
		FOR THE PRO-DUCTION OF DOCUMENTS. *** BE SURE TO ALLOW ENOUGH TIME TO MAKE A MOTION TO COMPEL.	CCP 1284.	OF MOTION FOR SUMMARY JUDGMENT. *** CHECK CURRENT LAW AND MOTION CALEN-DAR TO ASSURE AVAILABILITY OF HEARING DATE.

* Reminders.
SOURCE: Courtesy of CompuLaw, Ltd.

February 1996						
S	M	T	W	T	F	S
				1	2	3
4	5	6	7	8	9	10
11	12	13	14	15	16	17
18	19	20	21	22	23	24
25	26	27	28	29		

March 1996						
S	M	T	W	T	F	S
					1	2
3	4	5	6	7	8	9
10	11	12	13	14	15	16
17	18	19	20	21	22	23
24	25	26	27	28	29	30
31						

April 1996						
S	M	T	W	T	F	S
	1	2	3	4	5	6
7	8	9	10	11	12	13
14	15	16	17	18	19	20
21	22	23	24	25	26	27
28	29	30				

billable hours
The hours that are billed to the client.

fees, it is imperative that the paralegal keep track of **billable hours** (the total time spent on the client's case), so that the client can be charged appropriately.

Contingency Fees

contingency fees
Attorney fees that represent a percentage of the award received by the client in a civil action.

Contingency fees are used in plaintiffs' cases in civil litigation, such as personal injury and accident cases. This fee is a percentage of the award that the client receives from the defendant. For instance, if the attorney is charging the client a 40 percent contingency fee and the client receives an award of $40,000, the attorney would receive $16,000 and the client would receive $24,000. Contingency fees are not allowed in divorce, dissolution, or criminal actions. In most worker's compensation cases, however, contingency-type fees are required, although generally at a lower percentage. In some states, the attorney's fee in worker's compensation cases is set by a worker's compensation commissioner.

advance fees
Fees paid before the services are performed.

retainer fees
Fees paid in advance to obtain the attorney's services as needed.

Many law firms use a combination of **advance** or **retainer fees,** which are deducted from the contingency fee settlement. Law firms that use contingency fees usually do not require that paralegals keep track of billable hours since each hour is not billed individually to the client.

Project Fees

project fees
Fees charged by an attorney for an individual project such as a will, trust, or divorce.

Many law offices charge their clients **project fees,** which are flat fees based on the project to be undertaken. For instance, some attorneys have a set fee for preparing a

---

EXHIBIT 2.4   A Sample Printout of a Weekly Calendar with Tickler File

---

Monday 18

9:00 a.m.
    Case Tools
    Corporation
    CTC v. Bren
    Industries, Inc.
    10056.003
    Hearing
    Los Angeles
    Superior Court
    Defendant's
    motions to
    dismiss.

1:00 p.m. to 4:00 p.m.
    Apex
    Construction
    Company v.
    Jones
    APEX-001
    Meeting: Client
    Office
    Discuss settle-
    ment offer.

TICKLER FILE:
1. Interrogatories—
    Flannery v. Keyes
2. Complaint—
    Becka case—
    file with Superior
    Court before
    5:00 p.m.

SOURCE: Courtesy of
CompuLaw, Ltd.

---

simple will, establishing a living trust, or setting up a corporation. Many of these documents are available on the computer, and the lawyer merely adds individual client information to adapt the documents to the client's specifications.

Attorney fees for probating an estate are established by statute. The fees are based on the size of the estate and represent a percentage of its assets. In unusual situations that take extraordinary amounts of time, the attorney may petition the court to obtain fees greater than those set by statute. Recent cases have allowed attorneys to ask the court for extraordinary fees for paralegal time when the paralegal actually worked on the probate.

TIMEKEEPING AND BILLING

Some law firms require their paralegals to keep track of the amount of time they spend on each client's case. Several devices are available for performing this function.

In most law offices, time spent working on a project is recorded on a timesheet (see Exhibit 2.5 for a sample timesheet). Usually, the name of the client, the amount of time spent, and the task performed are recorded on the timesheet. Firms using this system require that their attorneys and paralegals keep track of their billable hours so the client can be billed for their time. Usually, a firm requires its attorneys and paralegals to generate a minimum number of billable hours per year. Some firms use the number of billable hours spent by a given paralegal when computing bonuses and/or salary increases.

nonbillable hours
Hours spent working in a law office that cannot be billed directly to a client.

Nonbillable hours are the hours spent working in the law office that cannot be billed directly to a client. For instance, you may be asked to perform legal research on the hours that may be billed to a client, or you may be asked to inventory the volumes in the law library to determine what additions are needed. Generally, this time is billed under a special administrative code.

It is important to keep track of *all* time spent working on each client's case. Sometimes paralegals are reluctant to complete a timesheet for a ten-minute telephone call. But if you spend much time on the telephone during the day, you may come up very short on billable hours if all calls are not noted. Consider that ten ten-minute calls in a day equal one hour and forty minutes that should be billed to clients. New paralegals are also often reluctant to note the actual time spent preparing a document for the first time because they are afraid that the attorney will think they spent too long on that project. Obviously, though, preparing a given type of document for the first time will take longer than preparing it for the fifth time. The attorney is aware of this, and the firm may reduce the amount of time charged to the client. Therefore, all time spent on each client's case should always be noted on the timesheet.

Hours are usually recorded on the timesheet in tenths; that is, every six minutes equals .1 hour. Thus, if the paralegal spends an hour interviewing a client, it is recorded as 1.0 hours. If the paralegal spends six minutes talking with the client on the telephone, that time is billed as .1 hour. Uneven amounts are rounded up to the next tenth. Therefore, if fifteen minutes are spent on a telephone call to a client, the time is billed as .3 hour.

Some firms utilize paralegals to perform functions that are not billable to a client. For instance, suppose you are the Supervising Paralegal and have a personnel problem with two employees. You call the employees into your office to discuss the situation. In this case, no client will be billed because this would be considered an administrative or personnel function. Generally, the timesheet code for administrative or personnel functions would be utilized in such cases.

Billing for Expenses

In some firms, the paralegal has an expense account for business expenditures. For instance, if the paralegal is required to travel to a remote location to retrieve documents, the travel expenses will be paid by the firm and usually charged to the client. Exhibit 2.6 shows a sample travel expense account for reimbursement based on the following fact pattern:

FACTS: Our client, Steven P. Standeven, is suing Robert R. Becka for damages incurred when Mr. Becka breached a contract with Mr. Standeven. You are

---

EXHIBIT 2.5   A Sample Timesheet

Time Record

Name: Jane Martinez, Paralegal   Date: October 25, 1996

CLient Number	Client/Case	File Number	Description of Services	Time Hours	Tenths
PI99544	J. Roberts Personal injury	45678	Draft Interrogatories	1	3
PV4444	M. Martinson Probate matter	19999	Draft Petition to Distribute	2	2
YV23458	S. Stanford Contract	15876	Draft Contract	2	2
PI3333	L. Lawson Auto accident Lawson v. Stanford	45777	Summarize Deposition	2	4
			Total time:	8	1

required to travel to Chicago to Mr. Becka's business office to obtain documents related to the contract under a Request for Production. Your expense account appears in Exhibit 2.6.

TELEPHONE TECHNIQUES

Often a prospective client's first impression of the law office comes from the voice on the other end of the telephone. Therefore, you should make a special effort to be

---

EXHIBIT 2.6   A Sample Expense Account

EXPENSE ACCOUNT OF JULIE R. ALTERIO

Case: Standeven v. Becka, No. C-45501

6/23	Plane fare—Pittsburgh to Chicago and return	$301.00
	Meals	35.00
	Airport shuttle	35.00
	Hotel—Airport Hilton	100.00
6/24	Return to Pittsburgh	
	Meals	20.00
	Total Expenses	$491.00

---

friendly and courteous at all times when answering the telephone. Even when you are preparing a "rush job" and the telephone has been ringing all day, you should try to "keep a smile in your voice." Your voice will either encourage or discourage prospective clients from employing the law firm. You must convey through your voice that you and the firm are friendly, helpful, professional, and responsive to the caller's needs.

Incoming Calls

Incoming calls should be answered by the third ring. If you are the first person to answer the call, you should identify the firm and your name:

- "Good afternoon, Rhodes and Kowalski, Ms. Robertson speaking."

If someone else has answered the incoming call and transferred it to your office, you should identify yourself:

- "Mr. Kowalski's office, Ms. Adams speaking."

or

- "Ms. Adams speaking."

Voice Mail

In most offices, voice mail enables you to be away from your desk while the machine answers your calls. You should leave a brief, courteous message on your voice mail, such as the following:

> You have reached the office of John Roberts, Ms. Pappas's paralegal. I am away from my desk now, but will return by two P.M. Please leave a message at the sound of the tone and I will return your call.

You should change your messages frequently so that callers will know the approximate time you will return. If you will be out of the office for several days, then say that on your message.

Telephone Conversations

Listening carefully is the key to good communications. Although you may be involved in several projects when the telephone rings, pay attention to what the caller has to say. Concentrate on that caller as though you had nothing else to do. Try to listen without interrupting. Ask appropriate questions to obtain correct information. Address the caller by name.

Sometimes clients call frequently for what you may think are unimportant reasons. It is important to be courteous to these individuals, but if the conversation becomes too lengthy, you may need to find a polite way to end it. Each individual has his own style of ending a call. Be sure that you are not abrupt or rude. For example, you may tell the client that you have another call or that you will get the information he requested and return the call.

Copies of messages from clients should go in the client's file, as well as the time (or times) you called them or attempted to return their calls. Any specific information received from the client should be noted.

Telephone Tag

With the increased use of voice mail, many of us spend a considerable amount of time playing "telephone tag." You call his voice mail; he calls your voice mail back; you call his voice mail back. This may continue for several days before you reach the person.

To alleviate this problem, establish a specific time of day to return the individual's call. Leave a message stating when you will be in the office and say that if the person is not available at that time, you will call him at a specified time. You might leave the following message:

> I will be in and out of the office all afternoon. I will call you back between four and five P.M. this afternoon.

or

> I will be in my office from one to four P.M. this afternoon for your return call. Otherwise, you may reach me tomorrow between nine and eleven A.M.

Returning Telephone Calls

Many clients complain that their attorneys do not return their telephone calls. If the attorney is involved in a trial, deposition, or meetings, the telephone messages can pile up quickly. Some attorneys have tried to alleviate the problem by advising their clients that they will be in the office at a certain time each day to receive telephone calls. During that period, they talk to clients or others who call in.

Another way to get back to clients is to ask the paralegal to be available to take calls when the attorney is not in the office. Many situations that arise can be handled by the paralegal as long as she does not give legal advice to the client. Any time the paralegal or legal secretary finds herself saying, "I would advise you to do . . .," legal advice is being disseminated, and this is not allowed.

What Not to Say

Each client feels that her problem is the most important case in the office. Therefore, when told by the secretary that the attorney is with another client, she may want to interrupt the attorney to take her call. It is better to say that the attorney is in a meeting or out of the office. Do not give information on the telephone about the attorney's whereabouts unless you know the situation is a genuine emergency or unless you have received prior authorization from the attorney.

Sometimes the attorney may decide to have a luncheon meeting with a client or another attorney. If the attorney is not back to the office by three P.M., it is not appropriate to tell the client that the attorney is "still out to lunch." Similarly, if the attorney took the afternoon off to play golf with a client, you should not tell the caller that the attorney "took the afternoon off."

Taking Messages

Keep a telephone message pad next to your telephone. If you are taking a message for someone else, be sure that you spell the caller's name correctly. Spell the name back to the caller if you have any question about the spelling. Note the time and date of the call. Ask for the area code and telephone number, along with a brief message. If the individual wants to be called back, ask the time when he will be at that number. Be sure to repeat the telephone number back to be sure you have noted it correctly. Ask whether the call is urgent and the essence of the urgency.

Automatic carbon telephone pads are useful for recording telephone numbers and the date and time of the call and for proving or disproving certain facts. Attorneys or paralegals may use the carbon copies for completing their daily timesheets. Exhibit 2.7 shows an example of a telephone message form.

Knowing Where People Are

Legal secretaries sometimes complain that the attorney leaves the office and does not say where she is going or when she will return. It is important to keep track of the attorney so that you can answer telephone calls efficiently and accurately. Therefore, when an attorney is leaving the office, ask where she is going and when she will return. If you ask the question often enough, the attorney will form the habit of telling the secretary her whereabouts.

As a paralegal, you should always let your secretary know when you are leaving the office for a period of time and approximately when you will return. If you have voice mail, indicate on the message when you will be returning to the office.

Appointment Setting

When you are setting up an appointment with a client, be sure to write a letter of confirmation showing the date, time, and place of the appointment. If it is an initial appointment, the client should be informed whether the consultation is free. Don't schedule too many appointments back to back in case one takes longer than expected. In your confirmation letter, indicate the purpose of the meeting and list any materials that the individual should bring to the meeting. To save time, you can compose form letters on your computer to be used for this purpose.

Telephone Numbers

Various methods can be used to keep track of frequently called telephone numbers. You may use a card file, rotary file, or your computer for this purpose. The following information should appear for each individual in the directory:

EXHIBIT 2.7   Sample Telephone Message Form

To _____

Date _____   *Time* _____

WHILE YOU WERE OUT

_____

of _____

Phone _____

STOPPED BY		PLEASE RETURN CALL	
TELEPHONE		WILL CALL AGAIN	
RETURNED YOUR CALL		PLEASE PAGE	

Message_____

_____

_____

Message received by _____

---

1. Name
2. Position
3. Address with zip code
4. Telephone number with area code
5. Fax number
6. Time zone (if the person or firm is in another part of the country, e.g., EST +2 would indicate that the time in the zone where the person lives is two hours later than in your city)

Directories of court personnel and attorneys should be kept on your desk if they are available for your state. Some of these directories are available on disk so that you may keep the file in your computer.

RECORDS MANAGEMENT

Record keeping is an important part of the function of the paralegal and the legal secretary. Client confidentiality must be maintained as a part of the function.

Client Files

Depending on the size of the firm, files may be maintained by the secretary or in a central file room. To keep all client matters confidential, a numerical filing system should be used.

Whenever you are working on documents for a client, keep the material in a closed folder. Do not leave papers scattered around your desk. Remember that if a client comes in for an appointment and sees other clients' files on your desk, he may worry that his file will also be left open for others to read. Client confidentiality should always be of paramount importance when you are expecting someone for an appointment.

One solution to this problem is to conduct client interviews in a conference room instead of your office. If your firm uses this procedure, be sure to bring all materials you will need for the interview to the conference room. These will include the client's file and any forms the client must complete, along with your own interview form and enough paper, pens, and pencils. Interrupting the interview so that you can retrieve items from your office can be very distracting and stressful for the client.

The Law Library

Large law firms have established procedures for maintaining the law library. You should always follow these procedures when removing books. Be sure to prepare an "out" card when taking a book from the library. Record your name and office room number.

Some small firms have very loose procedures for the removal of books from the library. You may want to institute a system by which individuals who take books must prepare an "out" card and place it on the shelf where the book was located.

Sometimes paralegals or legal secretaries are assigned the task of updating the books with supplements or inserts. In this case, explicit instructions will be given regarding which pages to remove and which to insert into the "looseleaf service" books. Other books have "pocket parts" in the back that are updated annually. Remove the old pocket part and insert the new one. Although updating books is a tedious and time-consuming task, it must be done regularly so that current editions of the books are available at all times.

LAW OFFICE EQUIPMENT

To work effectively in a law office, you will need to become familiar with various types of equipment. Fax machines, copiers, shredders, and computers are among the most important equipment used by law firms.

fax machines
Machines that can be used to transmit information and written material instantly from one location to another.

Fax (Facsimile) Machines

Most law offices use **fax machines** to transmit and receive written materials via a telephone line. A separate telephone line should be used for fax transmissions. Protection of confidential information is critical when using fax equipment. The firm's letterhead and the business cards of members of the firm should include the firm's fax number.

Copy Equipment

Many different types of copy machines are on the market. Since documents produced in law offices are quite lengthy, the ability to collate pages is an important feature. Depending on its size, the office may have several machines dispersed throughout the firm or a single machine in a central location. If clients are charged for copies, an electronic counting device can be used to keep track of the number of copies made for each client.

The newer copy machines are easy to operate and reproduce material quickly. Directions will be included on the machine itself. Purchasing or leasing a good-quality machine will save considerably on maintenance costs and delays while equipment is repaired. Many companies offer maintenance contracts for a time period beyond the expiration of the warranty.

Shredders

Since most documents and correspondence prepared in a law office are confidential, these materials should be destroyed very carefully. Shredders that cut paper into strips are available for this purpose.

All confidential paperwork should be shredded when it is no longer needed to avoid problems that may arise if the confidentiality of this material is compromised. For example, if a draft copy of a document is prepared, changed, and redone, the draft should be shredded. It is not unusual to find recycled paper cut into scratch paper for public organizations, such as schools. The reverse side of a student's scratch paper may contain confidential information about a client's case. Therefore, any paper that is to be destroyed should be put through the shredder.

Computers

Law offices use computers extensively. Since much of the documentation prepared in an attorney's office is repetitive in nature, many specialized legal software systems have been developed. Large offices may use **networks** that connect many computers so that employees can communicate with each other electronically.

network
A series of computers connected together so that users can communicate electronically.

Computer Hardware.   Computerized systems require certain hardware to operate. This hardware includes the central processing unit, monitor, and keyboard (see Exhibit 2.8). Most systems also have floppy disk drives so that the user can transfer data from one computer to another or print the material at another location.

The Central Processing Unit.   The central processing unit (CPU) is the "brain" of the computer system. It takes the information that is entered on the keyboard and stores it either on the hard drive in the computer or on floppy disks that can be removed. The CPU performs all of its functions based on commands given to it via a mouse or the keyboard. Information can be transferred from the CPU to a printer to create a hard copy.

EXHIBIT 2.8   Computer Hardware

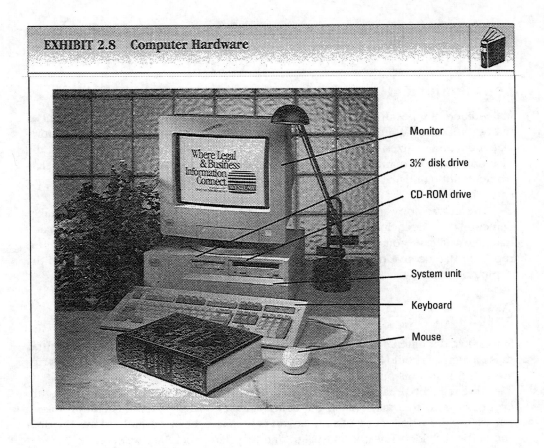

The Monitor.   The monitor looks like a television screen. It displays information based on what the operator types in on the keyboard. Monitors display information in color, black and white, or both. Color monitors are more expensive and may not be necessary unless sophisticated color charts and graphics are used regularly.

The Keyboard.   A computer keyboard is similar to a typewriter keyboard but also includes a numeric keypad and function keys (see Exhibit 2.9). By using the function keys, the operator may perform various operations, such as saving a document or printing it. These operations vary with the software package being used.

The Mouse.   A mouse is a pointing device that enables the user to move the cursor around the screen to perform various operations. It is used with menu-driven programs, that is, programs with pull-down menus showing the function that can be performed. The user moves the cursor to the appropriate location and clicks the cursor on the operation to be executed. Most of the newer computer applications systems can use a mouse. The mouse is particularly userful with the Windows program, which shows pictures on the screen to represent the applications being used (see Exhibit 2.10).

The Trackball.   A trackball operates on the same principle as a mouse but takes up less desk space. Instead of moving the device around the desktop, the user rotates

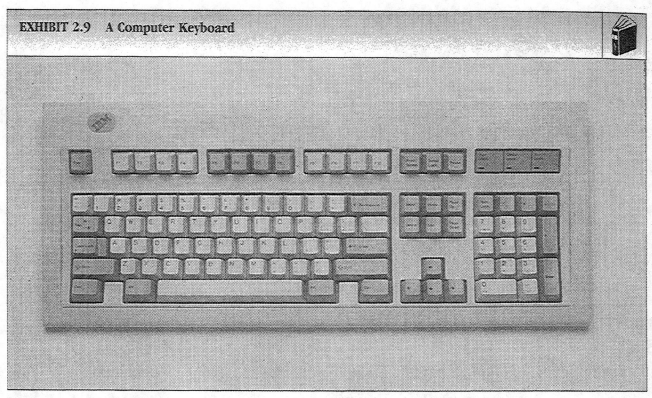

EXHIBIT 2.9   A Computer Keyboard

the ball to move the cursor on the screen. Some users prefer the versatility of the track-ball and find that it is easier to operate than a mouse.

Laser Printers

Most law offices use laser printers that are connected to a computer. Although laser printers are the most expensive printers, they are also the fastest and produce the best-quality hard copies. Extra trays may be purchased to accommodate pleading paper, letterhead, envelopes, and plain paper.

Modems

A **modem** is a device that connects one computer with other computers at remote locations via the telephone lines. Modems can operate as fax machines if material being keyboarded must be sent to another location. The user merely sends the material over the telephone line to the recipient's fax number.

Both the sender and the receiver must use modems with the same baud rate. Modems used with today's sophisticated computers have baud rates ranging from 9,600 up to 28,800 (for the newest machines). Older modems, which are considerably slower, have baud rates of 2,400. The faster the baud rate, the faster the material will be transmitted over the telephone lines.

modem
A machine that uses telephone lines to connect one computer with another at a remote location; may operate as a fax machine for material prepared on a computer.

EXHIBIT 2.10   A Typical Windows Screen

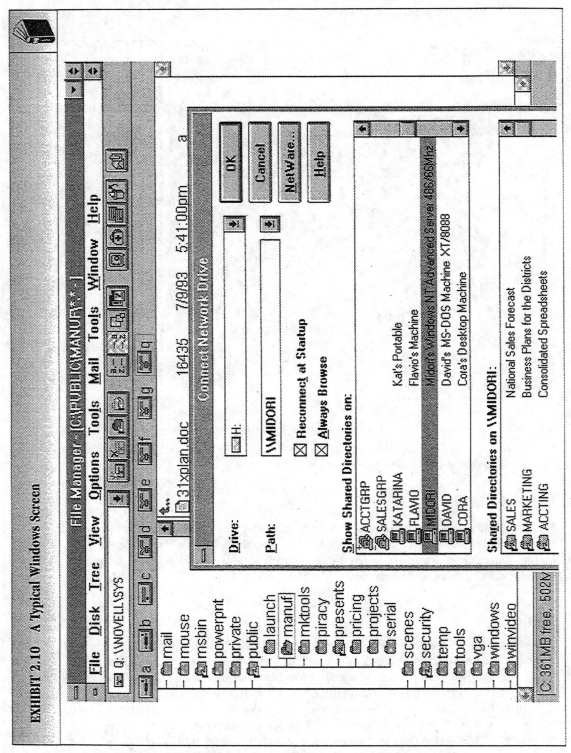

Internal modems are connected inside the computer itself and cannot be removed. External modems are connected to the computer on the outside and can be removed. Most systems use internal modems, although they may be more expensive.

A modem is needed to connect your computer with the computerized legal research systems. The CD-ROM systems are self-contained, however, and do not require access to a remote database. Both computerized research systems and CD-ROMs are discussed later in the chapter.

Computer Networks

If the office has many computers that share data, a network is an excellent investment. Individuals whose computers are connected to the network can communicate with each other and share information. Networks are also useful for doing legal research, particularly if the office has purchased any CD-ROM materials.

Word Processing

Word processing systems allow the user to create, store, and retrieve documents on the computer. Correspondence and documents may be prepared quickly and efficiently. Corrections and changes can be made easily by inserting the revised material. Proficiency in using these systems is essential for the paralegal and legal secretary. Sophisticated printers that reproduce material quickly are also available.

Word processing programs also allow documents and correspondence to be stored for later use. Then these documents can be retrieved and revised as needed without having to retype the entire document. Repetitive documents in particular can be retrieved and revised quickly.

Word processing programs also offer a variety of other features including the following:

1. Automatic centering of headings
2. Ability to change type styles and size of printing fonts
3. Margin and tabulation changes within the document
4. Automatic page numbering
5. Spell check
6. Style feature that prints pleading paper
7. Thesaurus for finding words with similar meanings
8. Merge and insert operations for the merging of two documents or the insertion of additional material

With modern word processing programs, composing letters or documents at the computer is relatively simple even for those who lack good typing ("keyboarding") skills. An attorney or paralegal may draft correspondence or a document at the computer workstation, go back and edit very quickly, and then copy it to a floppy disk for the secretary to print.

In a networked system, a message may be sent via E-mail to the secretary advising of the document's status for final printing. This method is much faster than preparing an outline, dictating the material into a machine, having the secretary type it, editing and making changes, and then having the secretary retype the document to incorporate the changes. Always remember to "back up" a copy of important material being keyboarded on the computer so that the material will not be lost in the event of an electrical or other breakdown. Data should always be copied onto a floppy disk to use as a backup.

Because law offices require many repetitive documents, a number of programs on the market offer master copies of documents, along with different clauses that may be used for different clients. For instance, will preparation programs allow the user to choose clauses based on whether the client is married, has children, owns real property, and so on. Other programs allow the user to make different types of documents for the same client. For instance, suppose the client for whom the will was prepared wishes to set up a corporation. With the use of a few simple codes, the information stored in the client's file on the computer can be used to prepare the articles of incorporation without having to type any documents.

COMPUTERIZED LEGAL RESEARCH SYSTEMS

WESTLAW
A computerized legal research system.

LEXIS
A computerized legal research system.

Sophisticated computerized legal research systems have been developed by many companies; two of the most popular are **WESTLAW** and **LEXIS.** Although these systems cannot replace manual legal research entirely, they are so much faster than manual research that many law offices are installing them. Cases, statutes, and documents can be found in a few minutes with a computerized system, whereas finding these materials manually might take several hours.

With a computerized research system, your computer will be connected to a centralized database ("library") via a modem, which uses telephone lines to connect to the central "library." To conduct a search, you must formulate a search request using combinations of words, phrases, and codes. The law office is billed for the minutes it is "on line" to the database. Therefore, it is important to frame the issues and search requests carefully and fully before connecting to the central database.

A printer will be connected to the computer so that you can make a copy of pertinent cases, statutes, and documents that are found. Because of the expense involved, some firms have specialized research paralegals or librarians who perform these searches. In many firms, however, all paralegals are trained to perform research on these systems.

CD-ROM

Some legal publishers have put their books on CD-ROM, which operates much like the compact discs (CDs) that play music. In this case, however, the CDs contain vast libraries of information that can be found quickly and easily via your computer. A significant advantage of CD-ROM materials is that with a network, many people can use the same library simultaneously, whereas with the computerized research systems, each computer must be connected to the system individually by modem. Since no telephone lines are used, the CD-ROM systems may be less expensive.

OFFICE MANUAL

Many large firms have policies and procedures manuals. If one is not available in your firm, you might offer to write one. Such manuals usually include the following items:

1. Organization chart of the firm or company

2. Billing procedures

3. Expense account information

4. Format for documents and correspondence

5. Personnel policies

6. Library and filing room procedures

7. Mailing information

LEGAL CORRESPONDENCE

Paralegals and legal secretaries prepare much of the correspondence in a law office. Some items are different from the ordinary business letter. Exhibit 2.11 shows a typical letter format, and the next paragraphs explain each part of the letter. You should check the files in your own office to determine whether it uses a different format.

Letterhead

All law offices have letterhead paper for preparing correspondence. The letterhead includes the name, address, telephone number, and fax number of the law firm. Some firms list all partners of the firm, while others list all attorneys employed by the firm. Paralegals may be listed, but must be identified by title so that no one reading the letterhead will infer that a paralegal is an attorney because no title is given. Various state bar associations have said that paralegals may be listed on a firm's letterhead as long as their title appears after their name.

Date

The current date must be included on the letter. Be sure the year is correct, particularly at the beginning of the year when many people tend to use the previous year's date.

Inside Address

The name, title, and full address of the recipient should be included; the address should include the proper state abbreviation and zip code. Attorneys may be referred to as "Carl H. Jensen, Esq." or in two lines as "Mr. Carl H. Jensen, Attorney at Law." Never refer to an attorney as Mr. and Esq. at the same time. A judge of a trial court is addressed as "Judge Juan Carrerra," while a justice of an appellate court is addressed as "Justice Anna Romero." Try to limit the inside address to four lines if possible.

Re (Subject) Line

In legal offices, the subject line is called the "Re line." This line usually includes the name of the case or client and the case number. However, if a different topic is the subject of the letter, that information is used instead.

EXHIBIT 2.11   A Sample Letter from a Law Office

LETTERHEAD HERE
NAME AND ADDRESS OF FIRM
PHONE NUMBER AND FAX NUMBER
NAMES OF ATTORNEYS HERE   PARALEGAL HERE

Today's Date

Judge Robin Baynes
Superior Court Dept. C-3
459 Sherwood Avenue
Troy, VA 11111

RE: Format for Legal Correspondence

Dear Judge Baynes:

Here is an example of the manner in which we handle legal correspondence using the block format. Some offices use the modified block format, where the paragraphs start with a five-space indention from the left margin.

Reference initials are always used; they include the writer's and typist's initials. Any enclosures are noted, as well as carbon copies. If you don't want the recipient of the letter to know another person is getting a carbon copy, then "bcc" goes on the copies only and not the original. An ordinary carbon copy is noted on the original, such as is the case here.

Very truly yours,

LONG AND MARIN

Judy A. Long

JAL:jal
cc: Kenneth P. Carbone

Salutation

The salutation should use the same form of address used in everyday conversation. Therefore, if you usually address Mr. Jensen as Carl, the salutation would be "Dear Carl." However, if you do not address Mr. Jensen by his first name in conversation, the proper salutation would be "Dear Mr. Jensen." The following are other appropriate forms of address:

> Dear Judge Parker:

> Dear Justice Madrid:

> Dear Doctor Rodriquez:

Body

The body of the letter should be as brief as possible. The recipient may not read an inordinately long letter. If a request is being made, the due date should be included in the last paragraph of the letter. As in any other writing, the following format should be used:

1. Introduction
2. Body
3. Conclusion or request

Closing

Most law offices use "Very truly yours" as the closing. However, if you are writing to a friend who is also an associate or colleague, "Sincerely yours" would be appropriate. Again, consult the office files to determine the closing used in your firm.

Signature Line

The name of the law firm is used in the signature line, as well as your name and title. The following are typical signature lines for a paralegal and a legal secretary:

> Very truly yours,
>
> LONG AND MARIN
>
>
> JANET R. KIEFER
> Paralegal

> Very truly yours,
>
> LONG AND MARIN
>
>
> JOHN R. MARTIN
> Secretary to Judy A. Long

FORMAT OF LEGAL DOCUMENTS

Most offices use the same basic format for all their legal documents. For the appropriate heading for your state, check your office's files. The general format may best be described in terms of legal cap.

Legal cap is lined and numbered paper that is required for most documents filed with the courts. It is available as a "Style" in Wordperfect. If you are using Wordperfect for Windows, just click on Layout, Styles, Pleading Paper, and begin typing the document. Although it will not appear on the screen, the document will be generated on pleading paper (legal cap). If you want to be sure this is so, then go into "Print Preview" and zoom into 100 percent of the document. It should appear on pleading paper.

In most states, Lines 1–4 are reserved for the name and address of the law firm. Many firms have their letterhead printed on pleading paper so that this information does not have to be keyboarded (typed). On Line 8, the name of the court and its address could be centered in all capital letters. The caption begins on Line 11; it includes the name of the parties, case number, and document name. An example is shown in Exhibit 2.12.

legal cap
Lined and numbered paper that must be used for most documents filed with a court.

YOUR NOTEBOOK

As the introduction explained, you should begin preparing your own notebook to take with you to the law office during your first year in the program. Whenever you create a new document, include it in your notebook. Keep any textbooks from school that show practical applications of the material you have learned. It is advisable to keep all textbooks to use for reference purposes. When your instructor gives you a handout that may be useful, put it in your notebook. As you move from one office to the next, make copies of all new items that you prepare, being sure to remove confidential client information. This notebook will prove to be invaluable to you as you pursue your career as a paralegal or legal secretary.

To make the material in your notebook easier to find, identify the documents in each section with tabs in alphabetic or subject order. You may also wish to include an index and/or table of contents as the notebook grows. Develop a Forms File and Legal Documents section for these items.

SUMMARY

One of the most important tasks of the paralegal and legal secretary is calendaring. Since most matters in the law office have deadlines, it is imperative that items be noted on the calendar and/or tickler file. Billable hours are the hours that are charged to the client. The paralegal must record all time spent working on a case so the client can be billed properly. Various billing methods are used, including hourly fees, project fees, and contingency fees.

Computers are used extensively in law offices for word processing, docket control, preparation of documents, and legal research. Many law offices have computerized research systems, such as WESTLAW or LEXIS. Some offices have CD-ROM systems.

It is imperative that the legal secretary and paralegal maintain good telephone techniques when speaking with clients. Messages must be taken accurately. Appointments must be noted on both the attorney's and the secretary's calendar.

EXHIBIT 2.12   A Standard Format for Legal Documents

1	Steven P. Evans
2	Attorney at Law
3	2500 Orbital Drive
4	Waukegan, IL 60085
5	Attorney for Plaintiff
6	
7	

8   COUNTY OF YORK

9   STATE OF ILLINOIS

10

11   JOHN A. GALLWAY,   )

12   )

13   Plaintiff,   )   COMPLAINT FOR

14   )

15   V.   )   DAMAGES

16   )

17   JAMES E. SMITH,   )   CASE NO. PI–24452

18   )

19   Defendant.   )

20   _____

21

22

23

24

25

26

27

28

KEY TERMS

Advance fees   20

Attorney fees   18

Billable hours   20

Calendaring   15

Contingency fees   20

Fax machines   28

Legal cap   38

LEXIS   34

Mail log   15

Modem   31

Network   29

Nonbillable hours   22

Project fees   20

Retainer fees   20

WESTLAW   34

SELF-TEST

A.   Indicate whether the following statements are true (T) or false (F):

_____ 1. Contingency fees are charged in divorce cases.

_____ 2. A modem is required to send material from your computer.

_____ 3. Billable hours represent the total hours to be billed to an individual client.

_____ 4. Most attorneys do not bill clients for telephone calls.

_____ 5. Attorney fees in probate are hourly only.

B.   Circle the correct answer for the following questions:

1. Contingency fees represent

   a. an hourly amount.

   b. a percentage of the award received from the adverse party.

   c. a percentage of the client's estate.

   d. a percentage of the client's monthly salary.

2. Fees utilized for billing clients include

   a. contingency fees.

   b. hourly fees.

   c. project fees.

   d. all of the above.

3. The following individuals generally bill hours to the client:

   a. attorney

   b. paralegal

   c. law clerk

   d. a and b

   e. all of the above

4. Machines for destroying confidential paperwork are called

   a. modems.

   b. shredders.

    c. wastebaskets.

    d. incinerators.

5. Incoming mail is recorded on the

    a. calendar.

    b. diary.

    c. mail log.

    d. No recording is necessary.

C. Fill in the blanks:

1. The number of hours billed to the client by the attorney is called

    _____ _____.

2. The paper used for the preparation of legal documents and pleadings is

    known as _____ _____.

3. Who keeps the attorney's calendar? _____.

4. Hours are recorded on timesheets in the following time increments:

    _____.

5. A set fee charged to a client based on the job to be undertaken is called a

    _____ _____.

PROJECTS

oct 28,

1. James Roberts is suing Sally Lopez for damages for personal injuries. Prepare a caption for use on a complaint in your state. If you don't know the format for captions in your state, use the format on page 39. The case number is PI-24422.

2. How would you (as the legal secretary or paralegal) handle each of the following telephone callers to your firm?

a. Mrs. Debolt is calling for the fifth time today. The attorney, Ms. Alter, has told you that she does not want to talk to Mrs. Debolt if she calls again.

b. The attorney has taken the afternoon off to play golf. His client, Mr. Roberts, calls and wants to know the whereabouts of his attorney.

c. Ms. Sanchez, the attorney for whom you work, has left the office without telling you where she went. Her client, Mr. Ross, is calling and wishes to speak to her.

d. Mr. Allen, a client, wants to make an appointment with you, the paralegal who is handling his case.

3. Using the form in Exhibit 2.13, prepare a timesheet for the following activities. Use today's date.

You came into the office at 9:00 a.m. and immediately began working on a deposition summary for James Sanchez's case. The deposition had been taken of Dr. Ramirez. After spending one hour on the summary, you received a telephone call from another client, Mr. George Crocker, about a probate question. You spent 30 minutes on the telephone with Mr. Crocker. After that you went back to your deposition summary of Dr. Ramirez.

EXHIBIT 2.13 Timesheet for Use with Projects

Time Record

Name: _____   Date:_____

Client Number	Client/Case	File Number	Description of Services	Time Hours	Tenths

Upon completing the summary, you went to lunch at 12:15 P.M. You returned to the office at 1:30 P.M. to review the file on Mrs. Ann Rossi's divorce case in preparation for an interview with Mrs. Rossi at 1:45 P.M. Mrs. Rossi arrived promptly at 1:45 P.M. The interview lasted until 2:30 P.M. You then took a coffee break until 2:45 P.M., when you began to prepare written interrogatories for another client, Mr. William Jerries, who had been injured in an automobile accident. The interrogatories were being served on the defendant, Mr. Scott Lybeline. You spent one hour working on the interrogatories when a telephone call interrupted you. Another client, Ms. Kim Fitzman, had some questions about an upcoming court date. You spent 15 minutes on the telephone with her. You then made telephone calls to the following witnesses to give them information about the upcoming court date in Ms. Fitzman's case: Kathryn Down, Robert Rivera, and Caroline Benson. You spent 15 minutes with each telephone call. The remainder of the afternoon was spent summarizing a deposition in another case involving client Larry Simpson. You left the office at 5:15 P.M.

4. Prepare your own timesheet for one day this week. List all activities in which you are engaged and the amount of time spent on each.

Court Structure

CHAPTER OBJECTIVES

As a result of studying this chapter, you will learn the following material:

1. **Court Structure**   The court systems on both the state and federal level will be presented. You will learn the differences between trial and appellate courts and the hierarchy of courts in both systems.
2. **Legal Concepts**   The concepts of jurisdiction, venue, and Statutes of Limitation will be explained. You will learn their importance to the judicial system.
3. **Court Offices**   The method of operation of the courts and various offices in the courts will be presented. You will become familiar with the operation of the Court Clerk's Office and will learn how to interact with this vital administrative organization.
4. **Administrative Agencies**   The role of administrative agencies will be discussed. You will learn the kinds of issues that come before these agencies.

THE COURT SYSTEMS

There are fifty-one court systems in the United States—one for each state and the federal system. Within each state, each court has its own local rules and procedures that must be followed. Law office personnel must be familiar with the federal, state, and local rules that are applicable in each location as well as the statutes that indicate the time limits within which materials must be filed with the courts. Time constraints are critical when filing documents with the proper court. If a deadline is missed, the client may be precluded from filing the case later. Missed deadlines are a major reason for malpractice suits against attorneys. Therefore, a good office calendaring system is essential in dealing with court deadlines.

One of the best ways to gain knowledge of a particular court's procedures is to attend a trial. Most courtrooms are open to the public. You can go to the courtroom and observe the trial while studying the procedures. Before attending a trial, it is beneficial to study the state and federal codes and practice manuals on the local court's rules. This chapter will provide an overview of a "typical" state court system and the federal court system, as well as the people who work in these courts.

Jurisdiction and Venue

Before looking at the court systems themselves, it is necessary to understand two important concepts related to the judicial system: jurisdiction and venue.

jurisdiction
The power of a particular court to hear a case brought before it.

court of original jurisdiction
The trial court where an action is initiated.

statutes
Laws enacted by the legislature.

court of appellate jurisdiction
The court to which a case is appealed from a lower trial court.

appellate court
A higher court to which a case can be appealed from a lower court.

venue
The proper geographic area where a case should be tried.

defendant
The person or entity being sued by the plaintiff.

Motion for a Change of Venue
A request that a trial be moved to a location other than the one where it should be held.

civil actions
Lawsuits in which the plaintiff sues the defendant for money damages.

plaintiff
The person or entity that brings a suit against the defendant.

lawsuit
Litigation; a civil action; occurs when a plaintiff sues a defendant.

equity suit
A suit to force the defendant to do an act or stop doing an act; includes suits for restitution, injunctions, and restraining orders.

statutory law
Law contained in statutes.

case law
Decisions of appellate and supreme courts that establish precedents for other courts to follow.

stare decisis
The principle that holds that courts should follow the precedents set in earlier cases.

Jurisdiction.   **Jurisdiction** is the power of a particular court to hear a case brought before it. **Courts of original jurisdiction** are the trial courts where an action is initiated. Jurisdictions vary from state to state; therefore, you should check the **statutes** (laws) of your own state to learn the jurisdiction of its various courts.

   Courts of appellate jurisdiction are those to which a case is appealed from the trial court. Some **appellate courts** are required to hear all cases appealed. Others have the option of hearing a case or refusing it. You should check your state's statutes for the applicable appellate procedures.

Venue.   Not to be confused with the concept of jurisdiction is the proper venue for the specific court. **Venue** refers to the appropriate geographic area in which a case should be heard, usually where the **defendant** resides or where the incident occurred (the defendant is the person or entity against whom the case is brought). Sometimes an attorney will file a **Motion for a Change of Venue,** listing reasons why the location of the trial should be moved to another district. The most common reason for requesting a change of venue is pretrial publicity about the case that may prevent the defendant from getting a fair trial because potential jurors may have been influenced by reports they have heard. The judge will consider the defendant's ability to get a fair trial in that particular location in deciding whether to change the venue.

Courts of Law and Equity

Under the English legal system, on which our system is based, two separate courts existed; one set of courts heard common law (legal) cases, while the other heard equitable issues. In the United States, these courts have been merged into one system. **Civil actions** where the **plaintiff** (the person bringing the suit) is asking for money damages are known as actions "at law." For example, an automobile accident that results in personal injuries and damage to the car may lead to a civil **lawsuit** for money damages for injuries and repairs. In an **equity suit,** the plaintiff is asking for restitution or attempting to force the defendant to do or stop doing an act. Typical examples are a suit for an injunction to stop a chemical plant from dumping pollutants into a stream and a suit for a restraining order to prevent an abusive spouse from approaching the victim. Some cases involve both legal and equitable issues and are held at the same time. For example, your client may wish to sue for damages as a result of being beaten and may request a restraining order against the defendant at the same time.

STATE LAWS

Each state has its own constitution that establishes the court system for that particular state. The constitution also sets forth the power of the state legislature and governor. State laws are enacted by the legislature and are set forth in codes, which are an alphabetic compilation of the statutes by subject. This type of law is known as **statutory law.** As in the English common law system, the decisions of appellate and supreme courts establish precedents that are to be followed in future cases by courts in that jurisdiction. These precedent-setting cases are known as **case law.** The principle by which earlier cases set precedents for later cases is known as **stare decisis.** Thus, each state has two types of laws—statutory and case law. The state constitution takes precedence over both statutory and case law in that particular state.

A STATE COURT SYSTEM

The following discussion explains the structure of a typical state court system. However, each state has its own court structure, and law office personnel must be familiar with the system in their state. The court structure in your own state may be found in the Court Clerk's Office or the local law library.

State Trial Courts

Trial courts constitute the lowest level of courts in the state's structure. Hence, they are called "courts of original jurisdiction." Most states have two levels of trial courts—**Municipal** and **Superior.** Civil cases involving lower dollar amounts are heard in Municipal Courts, while cases involving larger amounts are heard in Superior Courts. For instance, in California, a Municipal Court can hear civil cases up to $25,000, while a Superior Court would hear cases involving more than $25,000 (see Exhibit 3.1). The levels of courts may have different names, depending on the state. For example, New York calls its highest level trial courts "Supreme Courts"; they are the equivalent of Superior Courts in other states.

In some states, the Municipal Court system includes **Small Claims Courts** where litigants can settle simple civil cases without the expense of an attorney. These courts generally have an upper limit of about $5,000.

In the criminal area, a Superior Court hears cases involving the more serious crimes—felonies—while a Municipal Court hears misdemeanors, which are lesser crimes. Generally, cases heard on the trial level in Municipal Court may be appealed to the Appellate Department of the Superior Court.

Obtain a chart similar to Exhibit 3.1 showing the court structure in your own state and include it in the State Specific Information box.

Municipal Court
A lower-level trial court that hears minor civil and criminal matters.

Superior Court
A state trial court that hears major civil and criminal actions.

Small Claims Court
A low-level court where litigants can pursue simple civil cases without an attorney; limited to matters involving small amounts of money.

State Appellate Courts

When a case is appealed from the trial court, the state Appellate Court must decide whether errors were made at the trial level, whether the lower court's decision should be overruled or upheld, or whether a new trial should be ordered. In reaching its decision, the Appellate Court considers the record of the trial in the lower court and the arguments of the attorneys on both sides. No actual trials take place at the appellate level, and no witnesses are called, although the attorneys do present oral arguments before the court.

At the beginning of the appellate process, the trial court transcripts and all of the pleadings from the original case are forwarded to the Appellate Court. No new facts may be introduced at this level. Each attorney prepares an Appellate Brief that attempts to persuade the court to rule in the client's favor. Briefs include all the case precedents and statutes that support the client, as well as the attorney's most compelling arguments. After the justices have had an opportunity to review the case, it is set for oral argument. Usually, three justices hear the arguments. Both attorneys appear before the justices and present their cases. The justices ask questions and may make a ruling at that time or may issue a written ruling later. Although clients do not participate in the proceedings, some attorneys invite them to attend the oral argument.

Paralegals are often assigned to perform legal research for the preparation of the Appellate Court Brief. The paralegal may also be asked to update ("Shepardize") cases, find code sections, or actually draft portions of the brief.

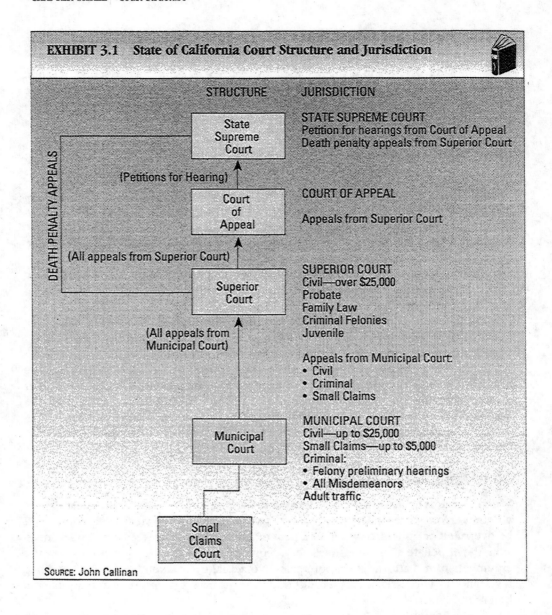

EXHIBIT 3.1   State of California Court Structure and Jurisdiction

STRUCTURE   JURISDICTION

STATE SUPREME COURT
Petition for hearings from Court of Appeal
Death penalty appeals from Superior Court

State Supreme Court

(Petitions for Hearing)

COURT OF APPEAL

Appeals from Superior Court

Court of Appeal

(All appeals from Superior Court)

SUPERIOR COURT
Civil—over $25,000
Probate
Family Law
Criminal Felonies
Juvenile

Superior Court

Appeals from Municipal Court:
• Civil
• Criminal
• Small Claims

(All appeals from Municipal Court)

MUNICIPAL COURT
Civil—up to $25,000
Small Claims—up to $5,000
Criminal:
• Felony preliminary hearings
• All Misdemeanors
Adult traffic

Municipal Court

DEATH PENALTY APPEALS

Small Claims Court

SOURCE: John Callinan

State Supreme Courts

Supreme Court
A name that is often used for the highest court in a state judicial system, also the highest federal court (U.S. Supreme Court).

The highest court in each state is usually called the **Supreme Court,** although some states use other names for their highest court. In New York and Maryland, the highest court is called the Court of Appeals. A few states have more than one Supreme Court. In Texas and Oklahoma, for example, the Supreme Court is the highest court for civil cases, whereas the Court of Criminal Appeals is the highest court for criminal cases.

Hearings in a Supreme Court are conducted similarly to those in the Appellate Court. Attorneys have a specified period of time to present their oral arguments, after which the justices may ask questions. The justices then consider these arguments and render a decision at a later date.

STATE OF _____ COURT STRUCTURE AND JURISDICTION

**STATE
SPECIFIC
INFORMATION**

Not all cases can be appealed to the state Supreme Court. Generally, only death penalty cases are automatically reviewed. In all other instances, the state Supreme Court will hear appeals from the Court of Appeals on a discretionary basis.

THE FEDERAL COURT SYSTEM

The only court actually established in the U.S. Constitution (Article III) is the U.S. Supreme Court. Under Article III of the Constitution, however, Congress was given the power to establish inferior federal courts as it sees fit:

> The judicial power of the United States shall be vested in one supreme court, and in such inferior courts as the Congress may from time to time establish.

Like state courts, the federal courts are structured in three tiers—trial courts, appellate courts, and the Supreme Court (see Exhibit 3.2).

Federal District Courts

The U.S. District Courts are the trial courts on the federal level. There are ninety-four federal judicial districts, with at least one district located in each state. Larger and heavily populated states, such as New York and California, have several districts. Most cases heard in a District Court involve questions of federal law, such as federal statutes, treaties, or the Constitution. Cases against the U.S. government, cases involving diversity of citizenship (where the plaintiff and defendant reside in different states and the amount in controversy is over $50,000), and cases in specialized areas such as customs and admiralty also come under the original jurisdiction of the District Courts. Federal crimes are also prosecuted in the District Courts. These crimes include racketeering, security fraud, bank robbery, mail fraud, certain drug-related crimes, and kidnapping.

The larger District Courts have several judges. Trials are conducted in a manner similar to those on the state level. Either party may request a jury trial in civil actions if money damages are sought.

Circuit Courts of Appeal

Cases appealed from the U.S. District Courts are heard in the thirteen federal Circuit Courts of Appeal. Each circuit includes several states. The number of justices in each circuit depends on the size of the court and the number of cases being heard. Each individual case is heard before a panel of three justices, however.

The United States Supreme Court

The highest federal court is the U.S. Supreme Court, which is located in Washington, D.C., and hears cases from the first Monday in October until some time in June. Nine justices sit on the Court, one of whom is the Chief Justice, who presides over the Court. All decisions of the Federal Circuit Courts of Appeal may be appealed to the Supreme Court. The Supreme Court may also hear cases where the highest state court has issued a decision that challenges the validity of a federal law.

Appeals to the Supreme Court usually begin with the **appellant** (the person bringing the appeal) petitioning the Court for a **writ of certiorari.** This writ asks the Supreme Court to hear the case; if four of the justices agree, the Court will hear the

appellant
A litigant who appeals a case from a lower court.

writ of certiorari
The writ used to ask the U.S. Supreme Court to hear an appeal.

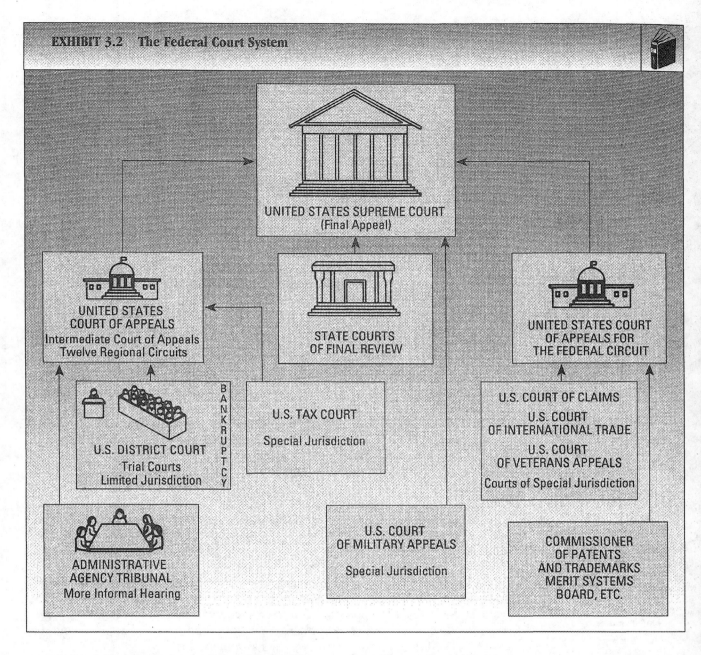

EXHIBIT 3.2   The Federal Court System

UNITED STATES SUPREME COURT
(Final Appeal)

UNITED STATES
COURT OF APPEALS
Intermediate Court of Appeals
Twelve Regional Circuits

STATE COURTS
OF FINAL REVIEW

UNITED STATES COURT
OF APPEALS FOR
THE FEDERAL CIRCUIT

U.S. DISTRICT COURT
Trial Courts
Limited Jurisdiction

BANKRUPTCY

U.S. TAX COURT
Special Jurisdiction

U.S. COURT OF CLAIMS
U.S. COURT
OF INTERNATIONAL TRADE
U.S. COURT
OF VETERANS APPEALS
Courts of Special Jurisdiction

ADMINISTRATIVE
AGENCY TRIBUNAL
More Informal Hearing

U.S. COURT
OF MILITARY APPEALS
Special Jurisdiction

COMMISSIONER
OF PATENTS
AND TRADEMARKS
MERIT SYSTEMS
BOARD, ETC.

case. Generally, the Court only hears cases that raise significant issues. The Court declines to hear the majority of cases referred to it.

Once the Court agrees to hear the appeal, the clerk schedules the case for a hearing. Each side must then submit briefs to the Court. Like other appellate briefs, these are persuasive documents that attempt to convince the Court to rule in the client's favor.

During the hearing before the full Supreme Court, the attorneys present their oral arguments to convince the Court to rule in their favor. The justices have the opportunity to question the attorneys at this time. The Court hands down a written decision at a later date, usually within three to six months.

Specialized Federal Courts

Certain actions are heard only in specialized federal courts. For instance, each district has a Bankruptcy Court that hears all bankruptcy cases for that district.

The following are examples of other specialized federal courts:

1. *U.S. Tax Court.*   Cases involving federal income taxes are heard in the Tax Court. In most cases, the Internal Revenue Service is either the plaintiff or the defendant.

2. *U.S. Court of Claims.*   Lawsuits against the United States that relate to a federal law or a contract where the United States was one of the parties are heard in the Court of Claims.

3. *U.S. Court of Military Appeal.*   Courts-martial are held by the U.S. military, but they may be appealed to the Court of Military Appeals. As the "court of last resort," this is the highest court that may hear military appeals.

4. *U.S. Court of International Trade (Customs Court).*   This specialized court hears cases involving duties on imported goods and collection of revenues.

COURT PERSONNEL

As we have seen, the state and federal courts are organized in much the same way. Not surprisingly, then, the two court systems employ many of the same kinds of personnel, who perform similar functions.

Paralegals and legal secretaries who work with the court system will be in contact with many of these individuals on a daily basis. The following sections will describe the various personnel employed in the court systems.

Judges

judge
The individual who presides over a trial.

A **judge** presides over a trial court. Appellate and Supreme Court judges are known as **justices.** It is important to address these individuals properly. Thus, Justice Warner presides over an Appellate or Supreme Court, while Judge Kwan presides over a trial court.

justices
Judges on the Appellate or Supreme Court level.

In most states, judges are political appointees. In order to be a judge in most states, however, an individual must be an attorney who has practiced law for at least five years. Some states also appoint **commissioners** who may be elevated to a judge's position when one becomes available. Commissioners must also be attorneys but may have practiced law for fewer than five years in some states.

commissioner
A minor judicial position. In some states, commissioners are eligible to fill vacancies among the judges.

Court Clerk

court clerk
A courtroom official who assists the judge, stores evidence introduced at trial, and administers oaths to witnesses; also, the official who runs the Clerk's Office where documents are filed.

There are two different types of **court clerks,** and their functions should not be confused. One court clerk works in the courtroom and assists the judge. The clerk's duties include keeping a record of the day's proceedings, administering oaths to witnesses, and recording and storing exhibits to be introduced at trial. When evidence is presented, the clerk is responsible for preserving it. The clerk is also responsible for noting exhibit numbers as the exhibits are introduced into evidence. Unless paralegals or legal secretaries attend a trial, they will have very little contact with this clerk.

The other type of clerk works in the Clerk's Office, which is located in the courthouse. Here one can purchase court forms, file documents, or obtain information about cases that have been filed in that court. Paralegals and legal secretaries often have contact with clerks in the Clerk's Office. Each courthouse will have one or more clerks available. It is important to remember that clerks are not attorneys and may not give legal advice.

Filing in the Clerk's Office. All cases must be filed in the appropriate Clerk's Office—that is, the Clerk's Office of the court having jurisdiction in the case. When documents are filed, it is imperative that all exhibits and filing fees be attached. Specific filing fee schedules are available from the Clerk's Office. Filing procedures can be found in the Court Rules and/or the Codes or statutes in your state.

Some courts allow documents to be sent by fax machine to the Clerk's Office for filing purposes. When a fax filing is made, an original, signed copy must also be filed within a period of time determined by the individual court.

Bailiff

The **bailiff,** who is generally a sheriff or a marshal, is responsible for assisting the judge, taking care of the jury's needs, and maintaining order in the courtroom. The bailiff also escorts the jury and guards defendants in criminal trials.

Training for bailiffs is usually conducted at a police training facility. Their instruction includes both physical training and legal education. Some bailiffs started as police officers and transferred to the courts.

bailiff
Sheriff or marshal who keeps order in the courtroom.

Court Stenographer (or Reporter)

Court stenographers (also called court reporters) record all testimony presented at the trial. Once the testimony is recorded, the stenographer manually transcribes it into a "transcript." Sometimes, the attorneys request daily transcripts. In that case, two stenographers alternate in recording the testimony. One will record for a time; then the other will record while the first stenographer transcribes the recorded portion; then they switch places. Whenever you attend a trial and notice that the stenographers keep switching, it is probably because an attorney has requested a daily transcript. Some courts are experimenting with the use of tape recorders in addition to court reporters.

court stenographer
The person who records the testimony at a trial.

Juries

Among the most crucial persons at a trial are the jurors. The right to a trial by jury is inherent in the U.S. Constitution, although defendants in criminal cases may waive this right and choose to be tried by a judge alone. In civil cases where money damages are sought, either party may request a trial by jury; the case will be tried by a judge only if both parties agree and do not insist on their right to a jury trial. In cases in equity, however, such as those where a restraining order or injunction is sought, there is no right to a jury trial, and the case will be heard by a judge.

The process of jury selection, which is known as **voir dire,** can be long and cumbersome. Prospective jurors are usually drawn from voter registration rolls or from lists of individuals who hold a driver's license in that state. During the voir dire, a group of

voir dire
The process by which the judge and attorneys select a jury.

prospective jurors come to the courthouse where they are questioned by the attorneys for both sides and by the judge. An unlimited number of prospective jurors may be excused "for cause," generally bias or prejudice. In addition, each attorney has several **peremptory challenges** that can be used to excuse prospective jurors without cause; that is, the attorney can excuse a juror whom he thinks may be likely to vote against his client without having to demonstrate that the juror is actually prejudiced against the client. The number of peremptory challenges available varies depending on the nature of the case.

Most juries consist of twelve individuals, although a few states allow as few as five jurors in certain cases. In Virginia, for instance, civil cases involving $5,000 or less are heard by five-person juries, and cases where the amount in controversy is more than $5,000 are heard by seven persons.

The jury's responsibility is to decide issues of fact in the case. The judge will instruct them on the applicable law. The decision of the jury is called a **verdict,** whereas a decision by a judge is called a **judgment.** If the judge feels that the jury has not properly applied the law to the facts of the case, then she may set aside the verdict and render a judgment in the case. This is known as **judgment n.o.v. (judgment notwithstanding the verdict).** Such judgments are very rare, however.

In civil actions in most states, three-fourths of the jury must find for the plaintiff if the plaintiff is to prevail. In other words, if nine jurors on a twelve-person jury vote for the plaintiff, then the plaintiff will win the suit against the defendant.

In most states, the jury verdict must be unanimous in a criminal case; that is, all members of the jury must be in favor of a guilty verdict for the defendant to be found guilty. If all the jurors cannot agree, a "hung jury" results. The prosecutor must then decide whether to try the case again with a new jury. Note, though, that in recent years some states have enabled nine or ten of the twelve jurors to establish the defendants' guilt.

If the jury finds the defendant guilty, then the **sentence,** or penalty, is imposed on the defendant. Usually, the sentence is imposed at a later time during what is called the "sentencing phase" of the trial. Generally, the judge does the sentencing, but in a few states, including Virginia and Kentucky, the jury may do the sentencing.

Check the rules for juries in your own state and add the information in the State Specific Information box.

---

peremptory challenges
During voir dire, attorneys may challenge a limited number of prospective jurors without cause to excuse them from hearing the case.

verdict
The decision of the jury; must be unanimous in most states in criminal cases but only three-fourths in civil cases.

judgment
A decision made by a judge without a jury.

judgment notwithstanding the verdict (n.o.v.)
A judgment in which the judge overrules the jury's decision.

sentence
Punishment given by the judge to one who is convicted of a crime; usually consists of a set time of incarceration in a jail or state prison.

STATE SPECIFIC INFORMATION

Rules for juries in the state of _____ :

1. Civil: _____-person juries

   _____ must vote for plaintiff to prevail.

2. Criminal: _____-person juries

   _____ must vote for guilt

Special state rules: _____

_____

ADMINISTRATIVE AGENCIES

As our government has become more complex, administrative agencies have prolifer-ated at all levels of government—federal, state, county, and local. Although agencies are not courts of law, they do hold hearings and reach decisions that can have important repercussions for clients.

The following are some examples of federal administrative agencies:

1. *Social Security Administration (SSA).*   Oversees the Social Security sys-tem and makes decisions on such matters as eligibility for benefits.

2. *Federal Communications Commission (FCC).*   Regulates the communi-cations media.

3. *Federal Aviation Administration (FAA).*   Regulates and oversees the nation's airlines.

4. *Environmental Protection Agency (EPA).*   Issues regulations to protect the environment.

At the state level, one of the most important agencies in every state is the Worker's Compensation Board. On the county and local level, consumer protection agencies, planning commissions, and zoning boards are among the most significant agencies.

At all levels, each agency has its own rules for filing documents and conducting hearings. You should consult the rules of the particular agency before filing a case. The rules and regulations will be available in the law office if the attorneys regularly prac-tice before that agency. If the law office does not have the rules, they can be obtained from the agency itself or from a legal publisher.

Although paralegals cannot represent a client in a court of law, they may appear on behalf of a client before some administrative agencies on the state and/or federal level. Often paralegals employed by Legal Aid or Legal Service organizations represent clients before administrative agencies, such as the Social Security Administration or the state Worker's Compensation Board. Many paralegals specialize in worker's compen-sation and represent clients before the state board. Worker's compensation law is a growing and lucrative area for paralegals who wish to do free-lance work. However, some states have changed their rules recently for appearances by paralegals. Check your own state's rules and complete the State Specific Information box.

In the state of _____, paralegals may represent clients before _____ but not before

STATE SPECIFIC INFORMATION

STATUTE OF LIMITATIONS

Every case filed has a **statute of limitations** that indicates the time limit within which the action must be filed with the appropriate court or administrative agency. For exam-ple, if the statute of limitations for filing a personal injury tort action in your state is one year, the action may not be filed thirteen months after the injuries occurred. There is no way to file an action after the time limit has expired (after the statute has run).

statute of limitations
A statute establishing the time limit within which a particular type of case must be filed.

TABLE 3.1 Common Statutes of Limitations	
Tort actions	One year after injury
Oral contracts	Two years after breach
Written contracts	Four years after breach
Criminal acts	Varies by crime
Murder	No statute of limitations

Therefore, your client will be "out of court" and may have the option of suing the attorney for malpractice.

Some examples of statutes of limitations are listed in Table 3.1; state's codes should be consulted to determine the specific statutes of limitations for your state.

In some cases, the statutes may be "tolled" (suspended or stopped temporarily), such as during the defendant's absence from the jurisdiction and during the plaintiff's minority (that is, before the plaintiff reaches the age of majority).

SUMMARY

The state and federal court systems have similar structures; the courts are arranged in a hierarchy with trial courts at the bottom and Appellate and Supreme Courts at the top. Although the various state systems differ slightly, they share several general features. Generally, a state has two levels of trial courts, one for the lesser crimes and minor civil cases, and a higher-level court for major crimes and major civil cases. Above the trial courts are the Appellate Courts, which review decisions reached by the trial courts.

The federal system has only one level of trial court, the Federal District Courts. Cases may be appealed to the Circuit Courts of Appeal and then to the U.S. Supreme Court. Specialized courts on the federal level hear cases such as claims against the U.S. government, tax cases, and cases involving customs duties.

Similar personnel are found in both court systems. A court will ordinarily have a judge, a court clerk, a bailiff, a court stenographer, and, in trial courts, a jury.

At all levels of government, administrative agencies are becoming more important. The Social Security Administration, state Worker's Compensation Boards, and planning commissions are examples of administrative agencies.

All types of cases have statutes of limitations that set time limits after which a case may no longer be filed. Therefore, it is imperative that the paralegal and legal secretary keep track of the statute so that the client will be able to file a suit in a timely fashion.

KEY TERMS

Appellant 50	Case law 46
Appellate court 46	Civil actions 46
Bailiff 53	Commissioner 52

SELF-TEST

A.   Indicate whether the following statements are true (T) or false (F):

___F___ 1. The United States has fifty different court systems.

___T___ 2. You may never file a document late with a court.

___F___ 3. Jurisdiction refers to the proper geographical area in which a case
      should be heard.

___T___ 4. Most state trial courts are Municipal and Superior Courts.

___T___ 5. Small Claims Court is part of the Municipal Court.

B.   Circle the correct answer for the following questions:

1. A major reason for malpractice suits against attorneys is
   a. missed deadlines.
   b. failure to sign documents.
   c. failure to return phone calls.
   d. failure to show up for interviews.

2. The best method of keeping track of court deadlines is
   a. reminder slips.
   b. message forms.
   c. an office calendaring system.
   d. none of the above.

3. Under the English common law system, two different courts heard cases
   related to
   a. law.
   b. legal and equitable issues.

    c. statutes.

    d. civil cases.

4. Civil actions where the plaintiff is asking for money damages are actions

    a. at law.

    b. in equity.

    c. for compensation.

    d. by statutes.

5. Small Claims Courts allow litigants to appear

    a. with an attorney.

    b. with a paralegal.

    c. without an attorney.

    d. all of the above.

C. Fill in the blanks:

1. The United States has _51_ different court systems.

2. _Venue_ refers to the proper geographical area in which a case should be heard.

3. The power of a court to hear a case is called _jurisdiction_

4. State trial courts are called _Municipal_ and _Superior_ courts.

5. Small Claims Court is part of the _munic_ court.

REVIEW QUESTIONS

1. Describe the functions the following individuals perform in the courtroom:

judge

bailiff

juror

court clerk

2. The highest court in the state is the _Sup_____ court. How are cases appealed to this court?

3. Define the following:

Federal District Court

Circuit Court of Appeal

U.S. Supreme Court

PROJECTS

1. Describe how the state and federal courts are organized, including the number of judges/justices on each. Discuss the types of cases that are heard by each of these courts.

2. Prepare a diagram of your state's court system.

3. Find your state's statute of limitations for the following actions, and write them in the spaces provided.

Tort actions: _____6 yrs._____

Oral contracts: _____4 yrs._____

Personal injury: _6 yr._____

Written contracts: ____4yrs_____

express or implied 6yr

Personal injury 6yr.

Breach of contract + sale 4yrs.

Civil Law Practice

CHAPTER OBJECTIVES

As a result of studying this chapter, you will learn the following material:

1. **Torts**   The basic characteristics of a tort will be presented. You will learn what a tort is, be introduced to the basic elements of a negligence action, and learn what strict liability is.
2. **Civil Lawsuit**   The sequence of steps in a civil lawsuit will be discussed. You will follow a case from the initial interview to the pretrial stage.
3. **Interview**   The procedures required for interviewing a client in civil litigation are presented. You will learn how to use a client interview form and how to elicit information from a client.
4. **Initiating a Lawsuit**   The procedures for filing a lawsuit and serving the required documents are discussed. You will learn how to prepare a complaint and summons and how to serve the documents on the defendant.
5. **Pleadings**   Various pleadings are presented. You will learn how to prepare an answer and cross-complaint as well as a complaint.
6. **Discovery**   The various tools and techniques used in discovery are presented. You will learn how to prepare a deposition summary, written interrogatories, and a series of requests and motions.
7. **Duties and Responsibilities**   The duties and responsibilities of the paralegal and legal secretary in a civil law office will be presented. You will learn the functions the paralegal and legal secretary perform at each stage of the lawsuit.

TORTS IN THE CIVIL LAW PRACTICE

Most paralegals and legal secretaries are employed in civil law offices. Their major responsibilities include interviewing clients and witnesses, preparing documents, conducting investigations, doing research, and engaging in case management. Since most civil lawsuits involve tort law, this section provides a brief introduction to torts. Bear in mind, however, that the law of torts is taught as a separate course in most paralegal programs.

A **tort** is a civil wrong or injury that results in damages to another's person or property. The most common torts are negligence cases, such as automobile accidents and personal injuries; such cases account for the majority of tort actions filed. These suits range in complexity from simple "fender bender" accidents that are settled with an insurance company to complex medical malpractice actions that go to trial.

In tort law, the **plaintiff** initiates the lawsuit against the **defendant.** The individual who is accused of causing the injury (the defendant) is known as the **tortfeasor.**

The law of **negligence** has been defined as a requirement that all individuals have a duty to conduct themselves so as not to create an unreasonable risk of harm to oth-

tort
A civil wrong or injury.

plaintiff
The individual or entity that files a lawsuit.

defendant
The individual against whom a lawsuit is filed.

tortfeasor
The individual who commits a tort.

negligence
Failure to exercise the degree of care that an ordinarily prudent person would exercise under the same or similar circumstances; must include the elements of duty, breach, causation, and damage.

ers. In other words, we must conduct our activities with reasonable care so as not to injure another's person or property. If we breach that duty, we may be held liable in a negligence action. To prevail in a negligence action, the plaintiff must prove all of the following elements:

1. *Duty.*   The defendant owed a duty of due care to the plaintiff.

2. *Breach.*   The defendant breached that duty.

3. *Causation.*   The breach actually caused the plaintiff's injuries.

4. *Damages.*   The plaintiff suffered measurable damages.

For example, assume that Ms. Fitzgerald drove through a red light and hit Mr. Langford's car, causing damages to the automobile and injuries to Langford. Here, Fitzgerald had the *duty* to drive her automobile in a careful manner so as not to cause an unreasonable risk of harm to Langford. She *breached* this duty by driving through the red light. By so doing, she *caused* injures to Langford and damages to his car. The measurable *damages* can be proved by the bills from the body shop for fixing Langford's automobile and by the doctor and hospital bills he incurred.

Products Liability Actions

Products liability actions are a special kind of tort action. In these actions, a lawsuit is brought against a merchant or manufacturer because of a defective product. The defect may be in the product itself, in the product's design, in the product's packaging, or in the manner in which it was manufactured. In most cases, the lawsuit is instituted against the seller, the manufacturer, or both. For example, if a new automobile tire blows up, causing an accident in which the plaintiff is injured, he may be able to sue the manufacturer of the tire if he can prove that the tire blew up because of a defect in its manufacture. In another example, if a person opening a bottle of juice is injured when the bottle explodes as it is being opened, the person may initiate a lawsuit for a defect in the product's packaging.

Strict Liability

strict liability
Liability that is imposed without proof of negligence because the defendant was engaging in an activity that is inherently dangerous.

The theory of **strict liability** is that when injuries are caused by certain activities the defendant will be held liable despite any excuses or justifications. The courts have consistently held that some activities are so inherently dangerous that they are forbidden under any circumstances. If the defendant commits one of the strict liability torts, he may be found liable for damages without any proof of intent or negligence. Strict (or absolute) liability is imposed for the following activities:

1. *Keeping Wild Animals as Pets.*   Any damages caused by these animals are charged to the defendant-owner. If you have a pet tiger in a locked cage and the tiger escapes and injures someone, you may not claim that you are not liable because the animal was in a locked cage. Just keeping the tiger as a pet makes you liable for any injuries it causes.

2. *Ultrahazardous Activities.*   Any activity that involves a substantial risk of harm to others or their property is forbidden. This includes the use, sale, and manufacture of explosive devices. To be considered ultrahazardous, an activity must be one that cannot be performed safely and that is not commonly performed in the community. If you are using dynamite to demolish a building and someone is injured from flying debris, you cannot claim that you were using the utmost care and caution in the blasting activity. Just using the dynamite makes you liable for any injuries it causes.

THE CIVIL LAWSUIT

Many paralegals and legal secretaries are employed in law offices that engage in civil litigation (civil lawsuits). In addition to the responsibilities mentioned earlier, they may be asked to prepare memoranda, pleadings, court documents, and forms. Some paralegals also interview clients and witnesses.

We will begin our study of the civil lawsuit with the initial client interview and follow the suit to the trial and judgment phase. In some states, the period from the initial client interview to the judgment may be quite lengthy—often it takes years.

Initial Interview by the Attorney

The first stage in the lawsuit is the initial interview of the prospective client by the attorney. The attorney must discuss the fee arrangements with the client prior to conducting the initial interview, however. Usually, the client will want to know the fees to be paid before deciding whether or not to retain the attorney's services.

In many states, the attorney is required to prepare a written **retainer agreement** that is signed by both the client and the attorney. The document must set forth exactly what fees the client will be required to pay, such as whether the client pays for filing fees in addition to the hourly or contingency fees. A sample retainer agreement is shown in Exhibit 4.1.

After the attorney discusses fees with the client, the paralegal will often conduct the initial interview of the client.

retainer agreement
A fee agreement between a client and an attorney.

EXHIBIT 4.1   A Retainer Agreement

This agreement is made this 20th day of October, 1996, by and between JOSEPH PACHECO, hereinafter referred to as Client, and JEFFREY M. WILLIAMS, hereinafter referred to as Attorney.

Client agrees to pay Attorney the sum of $300 per hour for time expended for the preparation of his dissolution documents. Client agrees to pay paralegal fees of $80 per hour for any time expended by the Attorney's paralegal in this matter. Client agrees to pay Attorney $350 per hour for any time spent by the Attorney on Client's behalf in court.

Client further agrees to pay for any out-of-pocket expenses incurred by the Attorney involved in the dissolution, including court filing fees, copying expenses, mailing, service fees, toll telephone charges, expert testimony, witness fees, and any other administrative costs.

By entering their signatures below, both parties agree to the terms of this agreement. Client understands that Attorney does not guarantee any specific settlement in this case.

_____
JOSEPH PACHECO

_____
JEFFREY M. WILLIAMS

The Paralegal's Role in the Initial Interview.   The purpose of the initial interview is to gather facts from the client about the case. Once the client has decided to retain this particular law firm and the attorney has explained the fee arrangements, the paralegal may conduct the fact-gathering portion of the interview. The legal secretary may sit in on the interview or may assist in the preparations for the interview by gathering any forms or documents that are needed.

Your role in the client interview begins when the receptionist calls to say that the client is waiting. You should go to the reception area to greet the client. Introduce yourself and shake hands. Escort the client back to your office or other interview site.

At the start of the interview, you should introduce yourself to the client and explain your function. If you are a paralegal, discuss what *paralegal* means and what you can and cannot do for the client. Many lay people are not aware of the functions and responsibilities of a paralegal, and some may think that you are a lawyer.

Most law offices have client interview forms, such as that shown in Exhibit 4.2. Before asking questions from the form, however, you should establish rapport with the client. Some clients will be upset about their problems; you should let them tell their story before asking specific questions. It is also important to remember that the relationship between the paralegal and the client must be based on trust. The client must have the utmost trust in you before you begin asking personal questions about the case.

You may have to ask the client to sign various forms or authorizations so that records, such as medical, hospital, or police reports, can be obtained. All of the necessary forms should be handy so that the interview does not have to be interrupted while you search for the proper forms. A checklist should be prepared for the client specifying items that must be provided.

Interruptions.   Have you ever been in someone's office where the telephone kept ringing? For most people, a ringing telephone can be a very stressful and disturbing interruption. In addition, if the client is explaining a point to you and you stop to answer your telephone, you may have difficulty remembering what you were discussing before you received the call.

Allowing yourself to be interrupted during a client interview sends a message to the client that she is not very important. The interruptions will also make the interview longer than necessary.

Ask the secretary or receptionist to answer your telephone and take messages whenever you conduct a client interview. If your telephone always rings in your office, either unplug it or turn the volume down. At the same time, ask your secretary to make sure other people in the office do not interrupt you during the interview. It may be advisable to keep your office door closed to prevent interruptions, as well as noise from the outer office.

Instruct your secretary that you should be interrupted only in an emergency. If an urgent call comes in, your secretary should take the call, put the caller on "hold," and give you a note with the caller's name and a brief message. Then you can decide whether the situation really is an emergency.

Conducting the Interview.   Each interviewer has her own individual way of establishing rapport with the client and conducting the interview, but some general suggestions can be made. Be professional but not too formal. Be friendly but not personal. The key to a good interview is listening carefully. While listening to the client's words,

EXHIBIT 4.2   Client Interview Form

AUTOMOBILE ACCIDENT INTAKE FORM

Date: _____

CLIENT:
Name: _____

Telephone   Home: _____ Work: _____

Address: _____

Date of Birth: _____ Age: _____

Social Security Number: _____

Driver's License Number: _____

Spouse: _____

Children: _____

Employer: _____ Telephone: _____

Insurance Company and Agent: _____

Policy Number: _____

Referred by: _____ Telephone: _____

STATUTE OF LIMITATIONS—CLAIM FILING:

Date of Accident: _____

Automobile Negligence SOL: _____

Governmental Entity Tort Claims Notice by (date): _____

DEFENDANTS:
Driver:
1.   Name: _____

         Address: _____

         Telephone   Home: _____ Work: _____

         Insurance Company and Agent: _____

         Driver's License Number: _____

EXHIBIT 4.2   Client Interview Form *Continued*

2.   Name: _____

        Address: _____

        Telephone   Home: _____ Work: _____

        Insurance Company and Agent: _____

        Driver's License Number: _____

Owner of car operated by Defendant:

1.   Name: _____

        Address: _____

        Telephone   Home: _____ Work: _____

        Insurance Company and Agent: _____

2.   Name: _____

        Address: _____

        Telephone   Home: _____ Work: _____

        Insurance Company and Agent: _____

FACTS:
Place of Accident: _____

Facts: _____

_____

_____

NEGLIGENCE CLAIMED:

_____

_____

_____

INJURIES:
Injuries sustained: _____

_____

EXHIBIT 4.2   Client Interview Form *Continued*

_____

_____

Current condition: _____

_____

_____

TREATMENT:
Current Treating Doctor

Name: _____ Specialty: _____

Address: _____

When consulted: _____

Other Doctors Consulted/Treating:

1.   Name: _____ Specialty: _____

      Address: _____

      When consulted: _____

2.   Name: _____ Specialty: _____

      Address: _____

      When consulted: _____

3.   Name: _____ Specialty: _____

      Address: _____

      When consulted: _____

Hospital Client Taken to After Accident:

Name: _____

Address: _____

EXHIBIT 4.2   Client Interview Form *Continued*

OTHER POSSIBLE WITNESSES (LIABILITY AND DAMAGES):

1.   Name: _____

      Address: _____

      Telephone   Home: _____ Work: _____

      Nature of testimony: _____

2.   Name: _____

      Address: _____

      Telephone   Home: _____ Work: _____

      Nature of testimony: _____

3.   Name: _____

      Address: _____

      Telephone   Home: _____ Work: _____

      Nature of testimony: _____

4.   Name: _____

      Address: _____

      Telephone   Home: _____ Work: _____

      Nature of testimony: _____

5.   Name: _____

      Address: _____

      Telephone   Home: _____ Work: _____

      Nature of testimony: _____

REMARKS:

_____

_____

_____

EXHIBIT 4.2   Client Interview Form *Concluded*

SETTLEMENT OFFERS:

Settlement offers before referral: $ _____

How given (in writing, orally, etc.)   _____

Settlement demand before referral: $ _____

STATEMENTS MADE BY CLIENT:
If client made any statements about accident or injuries

To whom made: _____

When made: _____

How made (tape-recorded, written, etc.): _____

---

watch his body language. If the client appears uncomfortable when asked a certain question, come back to that question later in the interview to determine whether there may be a problem with the answer. Try to decide not only if the client is being truthful, but if he is credible. Credibility relates to believability. The client may be telling the truth but may appear to be lying. Many attorneys will settle cases out of court if the client will not make a credible witness at trial.

Ethical Considerations.   Under the attorney-client privilege, all information obtained during the interview must be kept confidential. Explain this concept to the client to encourage her to speak freely.

To assure the client that the information she provides is confidential, other clients' cases should not be discussed during the interview. Do not leave open files or documents on your desk so that the client can read another client's case materials. If your desk is cluttered with material from another case, the client should be interviewed in a conference room or another available office. If this is not possible, the material on the desk should be placed in file folders before the client arrives. Allow about fifteen to thirty minutes to straighten the office and reread any information about the client's case before the interview.

Closing the Interview.   When all necessary information has been obtained, it is time to end the interview. Ask the client if he has any questions, thank him for coming, and tell him to call the office if he has any subsequent questions. Stand up, conclude the interview, and escort the client to the reception area.

Don't be too abrupt with the client. At the same time, do not prolong the interview beyond the time required. Most interviews can be completed in thirty minutes to an hour. Give the client a checklist of all items that must be provided along with a pre-addressed stamped envelope.

A follow-up letter should be sent to the client to reinforce information discussed at the interview. In the letter, thank the client for choosing the law firm and indicate any additional items or information required. A sample letter is shown in Exhibit 4.3.

Report to the Attorney.   After the interview has been conducted, the paralegal should prepare a report for the attorney. The purpose of the report is to provide the attorney with information about the case and to help the attorney decide what subsequent action to take on the client's behalf.

Most law firms require a certain format for the interview report. The following information should be included:

1. A brief description of the facts of the case

2. Your evaluation of the client

3. What the client wants the firm to do for her

4. Your evaluation of the case and what should be done

5. Your plans for follow-up

Attach the completed interview form to the report so the attorney can review all of the pertinent facts. At the same time, the date of the client's injury should be noted in the tickler file, along with a notation regarding the statute of limitations, which varies by state and the type of action.

Settling with Insurance Companies

In an action for property damages or personal injury, you should always determine whether the parties have insurance and the monetary limits of the policy. In most states, the insurance company of the person at fault pays the damages. Many states utilize the system of **comparative negligence,** where damages are assessed based on the percentage of fault of each individual. For instance, if the defendant is determined to be 80 percent at fault and the plaintiff is 20 percent at fault, then the defendant must pay 80 percent of the plaintiff's damages, and the plaintiff must pay 20 percent of his own damages. A few states use a system of **contributory negligence,** where the defendant may be found not at fault if the plaintiff contributed at all to his injuries. In these states, even if only 10 percent of the injuries can be attributed to the plaintiff, the defendant may be found not liable.

In most firms, the plaintiff's attorney will attempt to settle the case with the attorney for the defendant's insurance company before filing a lawsuit. During the negotiations, the attorney must keep the client informed of any settlement offers by the defendant. Ultimately, the client must decide whether to accept an offer of settlement from the defendant or the insurance company. Attorneys may not accept offers for settlement on behalf of the client unless the client approves of the settlement offer.

Settling a case with the insurance company is often easier and less costly than filing a lawsuit against the defendant. It is important not to settle the case too quickly, however, because sometimes several months may elapse before the client's injuries are fully established.

Filing Suit

If an adequate settlement cannot be reached, a lawsuit will be filed. The plaintiff must file a **pleading** to commence the lawsuit. A pleading is a document in which the par-

comparative negligence
A system in which damages are assessed based on the degree (or percentage) of fault of each party.

contributory negligence
A system in which a defendant may be found to be not at fault if the plaintiff contributed at all to the injuries.

pleading
A document setting forth the formal allegations made by a party to a suit.

EXHIBIT 4.3 A Sample Thank You Letter

Michaels & Williams
1122 Main Street
Your Town, Your State 40000
(500) 633-3333

June 27, 1996

Ms. Kimberley Fitzgerald
1441 Makaha Lane
Your Town, Your State

RE: <u>Fitzgerald v. Longfellow</u>

Dear Ms. Fitzgerald:
Thank you for the opportunity of serving your legal needs in your upcoming civil litigation case. We appreciate your hiring our firm, and we will do our best to meet your requirements in this action.

As requested at your interview, please provide this office with the following documents within the next week:

1. Police report of the accident of May 1, 1996.

2. All medical bills to date. (This will be an ongoing process, so please send us a copy of all your medical bills as they are received.)

3. Bills from the body shop that fixed your car.

Be sure to keep an ongoing diary of any pain you might experience as a result of your injuries from this accident. In addition, note any time lost from work and additional expenses incurred as a result of the accident (such as automobile rental while yours was being repaired).

Please call me if you have any questions about your case. The best time to reach me is between 3:00 and 5:00 p.m.

Very truly yours,

Your Name
Your Title

ties set forth the formal allegations of their claims and defenses. Two of the most important pleadings are the complaint and the answer, which will be discussed in this section.

In most states, all pleadings and documents prepared for the court are typed on **"legal cap,"** which is lined and numbered paper. Some states use 8 1/2-by-11-inch paper, while others use 8 1/2-by-13-inch or 8 1/2-by-14-inch paper. Be sure to check local court rules to learn the proper size to use in your state. Exhibit 4.4 shows an example of legal cap.

legal cap
Lined and numbered paper used for legal pleadings and documents.

The Complaint.   The first pleading filed by the plaintiff is the **complaint,** which sets forth any causes of action that the plaintiff has against the defendant. You may be asked to prepare a draft of the complaint. Computer packages that provide an outline of a complaint are available. The paralegal or legal secretary simply fills in the information that is unique to the particular case. The complaint should contain the facts and allegations upon which the plaintiff is basing the lawsuit, along with a **prayer for damages,** which indicates the damages the plaintiff is seeking. Exhibit 4.4 shows an example of a complaint. The numbers in the exhibit correspond to the numbers in the following discussion:

complaint
The first pleading filed in a lawsuit by the plaintiff.

prayer for damages
The section of a complaint that indicates the damages the plaintiff is seeking.

1. In many states, the name, address, and telephone number of the attorney appear at the top of the complaint. Most attorneys have legal cap with this information already printed, as on a letterhead. Next comes the attorney's position in the case—"Attorney for Plaintiff" or "Attorney for Defendant."

2. The court identification is centered on the page below the attorney's designation. The proper court heading varies from state to state, so check your office files to find a sample of a pleading before proceeding. For this example, we will use the California court heading.

3. Next the complaint indicates the names of the parties and identifies them as plaintiff or defendant. The "Does" clause in the example is a temporary name used as a place holder so that the names of other defendants may be added as they become known. For instance, if your client was involved in an automobile accident caused by the defendant, you may learn later that the defendant was delivering goods for his employer at the time of the accident. In that case, the employer's name would be added as a defendant. In most states, if the complaint does not include a "Does" clause, another lawsuit may have to be filed later to sue any defendants not named in the complaint. Some states allow the plaintiff to amend the complaint by adding additional names at a later date.

4. To the right of the parties are the case number (or index number) and the title of the document. The court clerk stamps the case number on the documents when the complaint is filed. You must make note of this number because it will be used on all subsequent documents in the case.

5. After the preliminary information, the actual allegations of the plaintiff are listed. Each allegation must be included.

6. The prayer for damages begins with the "WHEREFORE" clause and lists the damages the plaintiff hopes to receive. Three types of damages may be requested:

    a. *Special (or compensatory) damages.*   These damages cover actual out-of-pocket expenses such as doctor bills, car repairs, and hospital bills.

EXHIBIT 4.4   A Sample Complaint

1   JEFFREY M. WILLIAMS

(1) 2   Michaels & Williams

3   1122 Main Street

4   Seal Beach, CA 90740

5   (310) 123-5555

6   Attorney for Plaintiff

7

8   (2) SUPERIOR COURT OF ORANGE COUNTY

9   STATE OF CALIFORNIA

10   _____

11   STEVEN P. LUCAS,   )   CASE NO. 24442

12   )   (4)

13   Plaintiff,   )   COMPLAINT FOR PERSONAL

14   v.   (3))   INJURIES AND MONEY

15   )   DAMAGES

16   CLARK W. MORGAN, and)

17   DOES 1–4   )

18   )

19   Defendant.   )

20   _____

21   JURISDICTION

22   1. That Plaintiff, STEVEN P. LUCAS (hereinafter referred to as Plaintiff),

23   resides in the City of Seal Beach, County of Orange, State of California.

(5) 24   2. That Defendant, CLARK W. MORGAN (hereinafter referred to as

25   Defendant), resides in the City of Capistrano Beach, County of Orange, State of

26   California.

27   3. That the cause of action arose in the City of Seal Beach, Orange County,

28   State of California.

EXHIBIT 4.4   A Sample Complaint *Continued*

GENERAL ALLEGATIONS

4.   That on October 20, 1996, at approximately 8:30 a.m., the Plaintiff was exercising reasonable care in driving his automobile in a southerly direction on Pacific Coast Highway when a vehicle driven by the Defendant collided with Plaintiff's vehicle. The collision occurred as Defendant attempted to drive his vehicle across Pacific Coast Highway at Electric Avenue.

5.   That the Defendant owed the Plaintiff the following duties of due care:

   A. Duty to stop at the stop sign on Electric Avenue before crossing Pacific Coast Highway.

   B. Duty to make reasonable observations of vehicles in plain view before crossing Pacific Coast Highway.

   C. Duty not to drive his motor vehicle in a reckless, careless, or heedless manner with willful and wanton disregard for the safety and rights of others, within the meaning of Vehicle Code Section 2224.3(b) of the California State Codes.

6.   That the Defendant breached each of the above duties and violated the following statutes of the State of California:

   A. Duty to stop at the stop sign on Electric Avenue before crossing Pacific Coast Highway.

   B. Duty to make reasonable observations of vehicles in plain view before crossing Pacific Coast Highway.

   C. Duty not to drive his motor vehicle in a reckless, careless, or heedless manner with wanton and willful disregard for the safety and the rights of others, within the meaning of Section 2224.1 of the State of California Vehicle Code.

7.   That at the time of the collision, Plaintiff was a generally healthy male, forty-five years of age.

8.   That as a result of the collision, the Plaintiff suffered several physical injuries, which prevented him from working for three months, and property damage to

⑤

EXHIBIT 4.4   A Sample Complaint *Concluded*

1   his vehicle. The costs that Plaintiff incurred as a result of the collision included $55,000 in

2   medical bills, $18,000 in lost wages, and $20,000 in automobile repair costs.

3   　　　9.　　That the injuries sustained by the Plaintiff as a result of the collision were

4   solely and proximately caused by the Defendant.

5

6

7   WHEREFORE, the Plaintiff prays for the following relief:

8   　　　1.　　Compensatory damages in an amount according to proof,

9   　　　2.　　Damages deemed fair and just to compensate Plaintiff for damage sus-

10 tained as presented by the evidence according to proof,

11 　　　3.　　Attorneys' fees, court costs, and other costs as provided by law,

12 　　　4.　　Such other further relief as the court deems just and proper.

13 　　　　　　　　　　　　Respectfully submitted

14

15 　　　　　　　　　　　　JEFFREY M. WILLIAMS

16 　　　　　　　　　　　　Attorney for Plaintiff

17

18 DATE: November 5, 1996

19

20 Steven P. Lucas declares as follows:

21 　　　That I am the plaintiff in the above-entitled action; that I have read the forego-

22 ing Complaint for Damages and know the contents therein; that the same is true of my

23 own knowledge, except for those matters stated on my information and belief, and as to

24 those matters, I believe them to be true.

25 　　　I declare under penalty of perjury that the foregoing is true and correct.

26 Executed on this _____ day of November, 1996.

27

28 　　　　　　　　　　　　_____

　　　　　　　　　　　　STEVEN P. LUCAS

     b. *General damages*.   These damages are to compensate the plaintiff for pain and suffering and actual permanent injuries that result from the accident or incident. General damages do not reflect actual dollar amounts expended by the plaintiff but are intended to "make him whole" again.

     c. *Punitive damages.*   These damages are intended to punish the defendant for his wrongful acts and are only awarded if the defendant's actions were grossly negligent or purposeful.

7. The last item on the complaint is the attorney's signature, which follows the prayer for damages and is placed flush with the right margin. Exhibit 4.5 shows examples of typical attorney signature lines.

8. Sometimes the complaint includes a **verification** stating that the plaintiff knows or believes the facts in the complaint are true. The plaintiff's signature appears after the verification. If the complaint is verified, then all subsequent pleadings must be verified. At the end of Exhibit 4.4 a sample verification is shown.

verification
An addition to a complaint stating that the plaintiff knows or believes the allegations in the complaint are true.

summons
A form accompanying the complaint that informs the defendant of the lawsuit and orders the defendant to respond within a specified time.

Summons.   The complaint must be accompanied by a **summons** (see Exhibits 4.6 and 4.7). This is a typed form that is attached to the complaint for filing with the court. The summons orders the defendant to respond to the complaint in a specific period of time, usually thirty days, although in New York the time period is twenty days. It is important to check your own state's requirements for a response. Enter the time period in the State Specific Information Box.

In the state of _____ , the defendant has _____ days to answer the complaint.

STATE SPECIFIC INFORMATION

The time period starts to run the day after the defendant is served, that is, after the defendant receives the summons. Five additional days are allowed if the complaint is

---

EXHIBIT 4.5   Sample Attorney Signature Lines

Sole-practice attorney   _____

                                JEFFREY M. WILLIAMS

                                Attorney for Plaintiff

Law firm   MICHAELS & WILLIAMS

                                By: _____

                                JEFFREY M. WILLIAMS
                                Attorney for Plaintiff

EXHIBIT 4.6   An Example of a Summons from New York

B 106—Summons with notice, blank court.
personal or substituted service. 12 pt. type, 4-94

© 1993 JULIUS BLUMBERG, INC.,
PUBLISHER, NYC 10013

Index No.

Date purchased

Plaintiff(s) designate(s)

County as the place of trial.

The basis of the venue is

_____

Plaintiff(s)

against

Summons
with Notice

Plaintiff(s) reside(s) at

Defendant(s)   County of

To the above named Defendant(s)

You are hereby summoned to answer the complaint in this action and to serve a copy of your answer, or, if the complaint is not served with this summons, to serve a notice of appearance, on the Plaintiff's Attorney(s) within   days after the service of this summons, exclusive of the day of service (or within 30 days after the service is complete if this summons is not personally delivered to you within the State of New York); and in case of your failure to appear or answer, judgment will be taken against you by default for the relief demanded in the complaint.

Dated,   Attorney(s) for Plaintiff

Defendant's address: Office and Post Office Address

Notice: The nature of this action is

The relief sought is

Upon your failure to appear, judgment will be taken against you by default for the sum of $
with interest from   19   and the costs of this action.

EXHIBIT 4.6   An Example of a Summons from New York *Concluded*

AFFIDAVIT OF SERVICE

STATE OF NEW YORK, COUNTY OF   SS: The undersigned, being duly sworn, deposes and says; deponent is not a
party herein, is over 18 years of age and resides at
That on   at   M., at
deponent served the within summons,   *on*   defendant,

INDIVIDUAL   by delivering a true copy *of each* to said defendant personally; deponent knew the person so served to be the person described as
1. ☐   said defendant therein.

CORPORATION   a   corporation, by delivering thereat a true copy *of each* to
2. ☐   personally, deponent knew said corporation so served to be the corporation described in said summons as said defendant and
                   knew said individual to be   thereof.

SUITABLE AGE PERSON   by delivering thereat a true copy *of each* to   a person of suitable age
3. ☐   and discretion. Said premises is defendant's—actual place of business—dwelling place—usual place of abode—within the state.

AFFIXING TO DOOR, ETC.   by affixing a true copy *of each* to the door of said premises, which is defendant's—actual place of business—dwelling place—
4. ☐   usual place of abode—within the state. Deponent was unable, with due diligence to find defendant or a person of suitable age
                   and discretion thereat, having called there

MAILING TO   Within 20 days of such delivery or affixing, deponent enclosed a copy of same in a postpaid envelope properly addressed to
RESIDENCE   defendant at defendant's last known residence, at   and deposited
USE WITH 3 OR 4   said envelope in an official depository under the exclusive care and custody of the U.S. Postal Service within New York State.
5A. ☐
MAILING TO   Within 20 days of such delivery or affixing, deponent enclosed a copy of same in a first class postpaid envelope properly
BUSINESS   addressed to defendant at defendant's actual place of business, at
USE WITH 3 OR 4
5B. ☐   in an official depository under the exclusive care and custody of the U.S. Postal Service within New York State.
                   The envelope bore the legend "Personal and Confidential" and did not indicate on the outside thereof, by return address
                   or otherwise, that the communication was from an attorney or concerned an action against the defendant.

DESCRIPTION   ☐ Male   ☐ White Skin   ☐ Black Hair   ☐ White Hair   ☐ 14-20 Yrs.   ☐ Under 5'   ☐ Under 100 Lbs.
USE WITH   ☐ Female   ☐ Black Skin   ☐ Brown Hair   ☐ Balding   ☐ 21-35 Yrs.   ☐ 5'0"-5'3"   ☐ 100-130 Lbs.
1, 2, OR 3   ☐ Yellow Skin   ☐ Blonde Hair   ☐ Mustache   ☐ 36-50 Yrs.   ☐ 5'4"-5'8"   ☐ 131-160 Lbs.
☐   ☐ Brown Skin   ☐ Gray Hair   ☐ Beard   ☐ 51-65 Yrs.   ☐ 5'9"-6'0"   ☐ 161-200 Lbs.
                              ☐ Red Skin   ☐ Red Hair   ☐ Glasses   ☐ Over 65 Yrs. ☐ Over 6'   ☐ Over 200 Lbs.
                   Other identifying features:

Sworn to before me on

Print name beneath signature. ....

LICENSE NO. ....

Index No.

Plaintiff(s)

against

Defendant(s)

𝔖𝔲𝔪𝔪𝔬𝔫𝔰 𝔴𝔦𝔱𝔥 𝔑𝔬𝔱𝔦𝔠𝔢
ACTION NOT BASED UPON A
CONSUMER CREDIT TRANSACTION

Attorney(s) for Plaintiff(s)

Office, Post Office Address and Tel. No.

EXHIBIT 4.7   A Sample Summons from Indiana

STATE OF INDIANA
FOUNTAIN CIRCUIT COURT

Plaintiff

   v.   NO._____

Defendant

SUMMONS

THE STATE OF INDIANA TO DEFENDANT_____

   ADDRESS: _____

You have been sued by the person(s) named "plaintiff", in the court stated above.

The nature of the suit against you is stated in the complaint which is attached to this summons. It also states the demand which the plaintiff has made against you.

You must answer the complaint in writing, by you or your attorney, within twenty (20) days, commencing the day after you receive this summons, (you have twenty-three (23) days to answer if this summons was received by mail), or judgment will be entered against you for what the plaintiff has demanded.

If you have a claim for relief against the plaintiff arising from the same transaction or occurrence, you must assert it in your written answer.

The following manner of service of summons is hereby designated:

_____

Date _____ , 19_____ .

_____
           Attorney for Plaintiff

_____

_____

Telephone: _____   _____
                                      Clerk of the Fountain Circuit Court

RETURN ON SERVICE OF SUMMONS

I hereby certify that I have served the within summons:

(1) By delivering a copy of the Summons and a copy of the complaint to the defendant, _____

_____ on the _____ day of _____ , 19_____ .

(2) By leaving a copy of the summons and a copy of the complaint at _____

_____ , the dwelling place or usual place of abode of the

defendant _____ with a person of suitable age and discretion residing

therein, namely _____ and by mailing a copy of the summons to the

defendant _____ by first class mail, to _____ ,

_____ , the last known address of the defendant.

Sheriff's Fees: _____

Additional _____   _____
                                      Sheriff of Fountain County, Indiana

          By _____

EXHIBIT 4.7   A Sample Summons from Indiana *Concluded*

CLERK'S CERTIFICATE OF MAILING

I hereby certify that on the _____ day of _____ , 19 ____ , I mailed a copy of this

summons and a copy of the complaint to the defendant, _____ ,

by _____ mail, requesting a return receipt, at the address furnished by the plaintiff.

_____
Clerk of the Fountain Circuit Court

Dated _____ , 19____ .

RETURN ON SERVICE OF SUMMONS BY MAIL

I hereby certify that the attached return receipt was received by me showing that the summons and a copy

of the complaint mailed to defendant _____ was accepted by the defendant

on the _____ day of _____ , 19 ____ .

I hereby certify that the attached return receipt was received by me showing that the summons and a copy

of the complaint was returned not accepted on the _____ day of _____ , 19 ____ .

I hereby certify that the attached return receipt was received by me showing that the summons and a copy

of the complaint mailed to defendant _____ was

accepted by _____ on behalf

of said defendant on the _____ day of _____ , 19 ____ .

_____
Clerk of the Fountain Circuit Court

ACKNOWLEDGEMENT OF SERVICE

I hereby acknowledge receipt of a copy of the summons and a copy of the complaint in the above-entitled

cause at _____ on

the _____ day of _____ , 19 ____ .

_____
Signature of Defendant

mailed to the defendant. Be sure to note on your calendar the date the answer is due. If the defendant does not respond within the required time period, the plaintiff may be able to file a default against the defendant and win the case.

For example, assume your state allows thirty days for responses and you serve the complaint on the defendant by personal service on May 1 (the different types of service are explained later in this section). Since the period begins to run the day after service, add 31 days to May 1; the response is due on June 1. If the complaint is served by mail, then the response is due on June 6.

The legal secretary should type the summons form and attach it to the complaint for filing with the court. Many legal software package companies sell computer packages that enable you to prepare the court forms on your laser printer. You merely key in the information as the program prompts you, and the form is prepared automatically. Otherwise, you must prepare the form on a typewriter, being careful to put all information in the proper boxes.

Filing the Complaint.   In some states, the complaint and summons may be filed with the court by mail. It is advisable to use certified mail with a return receipt requested. The filing fee must be included, along with a self-addressed stamped envelope so that the copies of the complaint and the original summons can be returned to you.

In the interest of expediency, however, the complaint will usually be filed in person. Many law firms employ attorney services to file and serve their documents. If your firm uses a service, be sure that you use an up-to-date fee schedule from the proper court and the latest forms, which may be obtained from the Court Clerk's Office. Include a check for the filing fee when you deliver the documents to the service.

No matter how the complaint and summons are filed, you must make sure they are prepared properly. If the documents are not prepared correctly, the court clerk will not accept them for filing. Since some courts require a "blue back," call the branch court clerk where you are filing to determine whether or not the backing is required. Blue backs are blue covers placed on the back of legal documents. They are made of a heavy blue paper and are stapled to the last page of pleadings in some states with the top edge overlapping and stapled to the document. The summons, complaint, and any exhibits are attached in that order. The clerk will stamp the case number on the summons and complaint.

The number of copies you must prepare is determined by the number of defendants in the case. At a minimum, you will need three copies—one for the court, one for service on the defendant, and one for your files. Some courts require an original plus one copy for filing purposes. Be sure to check the local court rules in your own community. For every additional defendant, add another copy. Sometimes an additional copy is provided to the plaintiff.

Since some states may have different methods for filing, you should check with your instructor or call your local Court Clerk's Office to determine filing requirements in your state. Note any differences between the requirements described here and those of your own state in the State Specific Information box.

The requirements for filing a complaint in the state of _____ include the following:

_____

STATE SPECIFIC INFORMATION

Serving the Defendant. One of the copies of the complaint and the original summons, which will be returned to you by the court clerk, must now be served on the defendant. In most cases, the defendant will be served personally with the summons and complaint. Although some states require service to be accomplished by a constable or deputy, most states allow service by an individual over the age of majority who is not a party to the action. Some law firms use an attorney service, and some ask the paralegal or legal secretary to serve the documents. Some states also require that the defendant be provided with an affidavit of service. Again, it is important to ascertain your own state's requirements. Note them in the State Specific Information box.

The state of _____ requires the plaintiff to serve the following items on the defendant along with the complaint.

_____

STATE SPECIFIC INFORMATION

Personal Service. The most common method for serving the defendant is by personal service. The service is accomplished by handing the complaint and summons to the defendant and telling her what they are. If the defendant refuses to accept the documents, you may drop them at her feet. The documents must be given to the defendant personally, however, and not left in her mailbox, on her front porch, or on her desk. The time and date served must be noted on the proof of service.

Service by Mail. Service by mail is accomplished by sending the documents to the defendant by certified mail with return receipt requested. The date received must be noted since the response will be due thirty days from the date the receipt is signed. Be sure to check to make sure the receipt is signed and the date of the signature.

Some states automatically add five days to the thirty allowed for personal service. If this is the case in your state, then the response is due thirty-five days from the date of mailing.

Substituted Service. If the defendant cannot be served personally (for example, he is out of the country or cannot be found), some states allow another individual to be substituted. Thus, if the defendant cannot be served where he works, the individual who is in charge of the workplace at the time may be served in place of the defendant. If the defendant cannot be found at home, an adult member of the family may be served. However, a copy must then be sent to the defendant at the address served.

Most states require that personal or mail service must be attempted before using substituted service. Some jurisdictions require the court's permission to use substituted service.

Service by Publication. As a last resort, the defendant may be served by publication in a newspaper of general circulation. However, most states require that the plaintiff prove that the defendant could not be served by any other means. The attorney must make a motion to the court with accompanying affidavits stating how she had attempted to find the defendant. The court will then issue a ruling on the motion affirming or denying service by publication. Publication must be in a newspaper in the town or county of the defendant's last residence.

Agents for Process.   If a corporation is a defendant, the authorized agent for the organization must be served. Corporations are required to designate agents for process in each state in which they operate. If you do not know the agent, contact the Secretary of State's Office in your state to learn the name and address of the agent.

Proof of Service (or Affidavit of Service).   To prove that the summons and complaint have been served on the defendant, a proof of service by the individual who actually serves the documents must prepare a proof of service. The date, place, and time served must be indicated, along with the method of service. Some states also require a description of the defendant. Exhibit 4.8 shows another example of a summons and a proof of service.

Date of Service.   Be sure to note on the calendar the due date for the defendant to answer the complaint. Remember that in most states, the time period is thirty days, starting with the day after service. In many states, however, extensions of time may be granted, usually with the agreement of both attorneys.

Review the requirements for service described here and note any differences in your state in the State Specific Information box.

Service requirements for the state of _____ include the following:

_____

_____

STATE SPECIFIC INFORMATION

Responses by the Defendant

In most states, the defendant has thirty days from the date after service to respond to the complaint. If there is no response, the plaintiff may be able to file a **default judgment** against the defendant and win the case. Some states utilize a form for this purpose; in other states, a separate pleading called a **request to enter default** is required.

The most common responses from the defendant include the following:

1. Answer
2. Answer and cross-complaint (or counterclaim)
3. Demurrer
4. Demurrer and motion to strike
5. Motion to strike

All will be described in this section.

Answer.   The most common response by the defendant is the **answer.** Generally, the defendant will deny the allegations in the complaint and issue a "general denial." In that case the plaintiff must prove each and every allegation set forth in the complaint. A sample answer with general denial is shown in Exhibit 4.9.

In some cases, the defendant will admit some allegations in the complaint and deny others. To win the lawsuit, the plaintiff must prove the allegations the defendant denies.

default judgment
A judgment issued by the court in favor of the plaintiff when the defendant does not answer the complaint in the allotted time.

request to enter default
A document filed by the plaintiff after the defendant does not answer the complaint in the allotted time, usually 30 days. The plaintiff asks the court to rule in his favor.

answer
The defendant's response to the plaintiff's complaint.

EXHIBIT 4.8   A Sample Summons and Proof of Service

SUMMONS
(CITACION JUDICIAL)

982(a)(9)

NOTICE TO DEFENDANT: *(Aviso a Acusado)*

  JOSEPH PAUL MARINO

FOR COURT USE ONLY *(SOLO PARA USO DE LA CORTE)*

YOU ARE BEING SUED BY PLAINTIFF:
(A Ud. le está demandando)

  MARIA ANN ALTERIO

You have *30 CALENDAR DAYS* after this summons is served on you to file a typewritten response at this court. A letter or phone call will not protect you; your typewritten response must be in proper legal form if you want the court to hear your case. If you do not file your response on time, you may lose the case, and your wages, money and property may be taken without further warning from the court. There are other legal requirements. You may want to call an attorney right away. If you do not know an attorney, you may call an attorney referral service or a legal aid office (listed in the phone book).	*Después de que le entreguen esta citación judicial usted tiene un plazo de 30 DIAS CALENDARIOS para presentar una respuesta escrita a máquina en esta corte.* *Una carta o una llamada telefónica no le ofrecerá protección; su respuesta escrita a máquina tiene que cumplir con las formalidades legales apropiadas si usted quiere que la corte escuche su caso.* *Si usted no presenta su respuesta a tiempo, puede perder el caso, y le pueden quitar su salario, su dinero y otras cosas de su propiedad sin aviso adicional por parte de la corte.* *Existen otros requisitos legales. Puede que usted quiera llamar a un abogado inmediatamente. Si no conoce a un abogado, puede llamar a un servicio de referencia de abogados o a una oficina de ayuda legal (vea el directorio telefónico).*

The name and address of the court is: *(El nombre y dirección de la corte es)*

CASE NUMBER: *(Número del Caso)*
12345

  Superior Court of Orange County
  222 Civic Center, Seal Beach, California

The name, address, and telephone number of plaintiff's attorney, or plaintiff without an attorney, is:
(El nombre, la dirección y el número de teléfono del abogado del demandante, o del demandante que no tiene abogado, es)

  Jeffrey M. Williams
  MICHAELS & WILLIAMS
  1122 Main Street, Seal Beach, California

DATE: Clerk, by _____, Deputy
(Fecha)   *(Actuario)*   *(Delegado)*

[SEAL]	**NOTICE TO THE PERSON SERVED:** You are served
	1. [X] as an individual defendant.
	2. [ ] as the person sued under the fictitious name of *(specify):*
	3. [X] on behalf of *(specify):*
	under: [ ] CCP 416.10 (corporation) [ ] CCP 416.60 (minor)
	[ ] CCP 416.20 (defunct corporation) [ ] CCP 416.70 (conservatee)
	[ ] CCP 416.40 (association or partnership) [X] CCP 416.90 (individual)
	[ ] other:
	4. [X] by personal delivery on *(date):* April 1, 1996

Form Adopted by Rule 982   *(See reverse for Proof of Service)*
Judicial Council of California   **SUMMONS**
982(a)(9) [Rev. January 1, 1984]   CCP 412.20

SOURCE: Reprinted from California Judicial Council Forms, published by West Publishing Company.

EXHIBIT 4.8   A Sample Summons and Proof of Service *Concluded*

PROOF OF SERVICE — SUMMONS
(Use separate proof of service for each person served)

1. I served the
   a. [X] summons [X] complaint [ ] amended summons [ ] amended complaint
      [ ] completed and blank Case Questionnaires [ ] Other *(specify)*:
   b. on defendant *(name)*:
      Joseph Paul Marino
   c. by serving [X] defendant [ ] other *(name and title or relationship to person served)*:

   d. [X] by delivery [X] at home [ ] at business
      (1) date: April 1, 1996
      (2) time: 10:25 a.m.
      (3) address: 411 Sunell Drive, Seal Beach, California

   e. [ ] by mailing
      (1) date:
      (2) place:

2. Manner of service *(check proper box)*:
   a. [X] **Personal service.** By personally delivering copies. (CCP 415.10)
   b. [ ] **Substituted service on corporation, unincorporated association (including partnership), or public entity.** By leaving, during usual office hours, copies in the office of the person served with the person who apparently was in charge and thereafter mailing (by first-class mail, postage prepaid) copies to the person served at the place where the copies were left. (CCP 415.20(a))
   c. [ ] **Substituted service on natural person, minor, conservatee, or candidate.** By leaving copies at the dwelling house, usual place of abode, or usual place of business of the person served in the presence of a competent member of the household or a person apparently in charge of the office or place of business, at least 18 years of age, who was informed of the general nature of the papers, and thereafter mailing (by first-class mail, postage prepaid) copies to the person served at the place where the copies were left. (CCP 415.20(b)) *(Attach separate declaration or affidavit stating acts relied on to establish reasonable diligence in first attempting personal service.)*
   d. [ ] **Mail and acknowledgment service.** By mailing (by first-class mail or airmail, postage prepaid) copies to the person served, together with two copies of the form of notice and acknowledgment and a return envelope, postage prepaid, addressed to the sender. (CCP 415.30) *(Attach completed acknowledgment of receipt.)*
   e. [ ] **Certified or registered mail service.** By mailing to an address outside California (by first-class mail, postage prepaid, requiring a return receipt) copies to the person served. (CCP 415.40) *(Attach signed return receipt or other evidence of actual delivery to the person served.)*
   f. [ ] Other *(specify code section)*:
      [ ] additional page is attached.

3. The "Notice to the Person Served" (on the summons) was completed as follows (CCP 412.30, 415.10, and 474):
   a. [X] as an individual defendant.
   b. [ ] as the person sued under the fictitious name of *(specify)*:
   c. [ ] on behalf of *(specify)*:
      under: [ ] CCP 416.10 (corporation)   [ ] CCP 416.60 (minor)   [ ] other:
              [ ] CCP 416.20 (defunct corporation)   [ ] CCP 416.70 (conservatee)
              [ ] CCP 416.40 (association or partnership) [ ] CCP 416.90 (individual)
   d. [X] by personal delivery on *(date)*: April 1, 1996
4. At the time of service I was at least 18 years of age and not a party to this action.
5. Fee for service: $ 25.00
6. Person serving: Jane Adams
   a. [ ] California sheriff, marshal, or constable.
   b. [X] Registered California process server.
   c. [ ] Employee or independent contractor of a registered California process server.
   d. [ ] Not a registered California process server.
   e. [ ] Exempt from registration under Bus. & Prof. Code 22350(b).

   f. Name, address and telephone number and, if applicable, county of registration and number:

      45 Marin Road
      Seal Beach, California
      (500) 123-5555

I declare under penalty of perjury under the laws of the State of California that the foregoing is true and correct.

(For California sheriff, marshal, or constable use only)
I certify that the foregoing is true and correct.

Date:

Date:

▶ _____
        (SIGNATURE)

▶ _____
        (SIGNATURE)

982(a)(9) [Rev. January 1, 1984]

EXHIBIT 4.9   A Sample Answer

1 Jeffrey M. Williams
2 Michaels & Williams
   1122 Main Street
3 Your Town, Your State
   Telephone: (500) 633-3333
4
5 Attorneys for Defendant

6   SUPERIOR COURT OF COUNTY OF YOURS
7   STATE OF YOURS

8

9 STEVEN P. STANDMAN   )   CASE NO. 15940

10   Plaintiff   )

11   v.   )   ANSWER

12 REVA C. BECKMAN, d/b/a   )

13 BECKMAN SKATES COMPANY   )

14   Defendant   )

15 _____)

16

17   COMES NOW the defendant, REVA C. BECKMAN, and in answer to the

18 complaint in the above-entitled action, states that:

19   At all times mentioned in the complaint, she was doing business as

20 BECKMAN SKATES COMPANY; all skates manufactured at her place of business

21 are inspected prior to being packaged and shipped. Any defects in the skates were

22 caused by the plaintiff, STEVEN P. STANDMAN, due to his negligent use thereof,

23 and the said defendant is not liable therefor.

24   WHEREFORE, defendant demands judgment on the complaint or dismissal of

25 all liability along with the costs of suit herein.

26 DATED: September 6, 1996

27   _____
                                      JEFFREY M. WILLIAMS
28   Attorney for Defendant

The defendant may also bring up any appropriate **affirmative defenses** in the answer. When an affirmative defense is asserted, the defendant does not deny the allegations in the complaint, but sets forth a justification for his actions.

affirmative defense
A defense that sets forth a justification for the defendant's actions rather than denying the allegations.

Cross-Complaint or Counterclaim.

A cross-complaint, or counterclaim as it is called in some states, may be filed with the answer when the defendant has a claim against the plaintiff arising from the same or another related transaction. The cross-complaint sets forth the allegations that the defendant is claiming against the plaintiff. The defendant must file the cross-complaint with the answer, or he may be barred from doing so later. If the cross-complaint (or counterclaim) relates to a different transaction, however, then it may be filed later as a separate action. In that case, the defendant would probably file a complaint against the plaintiff and not a counterclaim or cross-complaint.

Some states use the term *cross-complaint* to refer to a complaint filed by one defendant against another defendant in a case where the plaintiff is suing more than one party. In those states, the defendant uses a countercomplaint or counterclaim to file a countersuit against the plaintiff.

A cross-complaint (or counterclaim) has the same format as a complaint, except that the defendant is called the cross-complainant and the plaintiff is the cross-defendant. This change in terminology can be extremely confusing, especially when several defendants are filing cross-claims against the plaintiff and other defendants. In those situations, it is extremely important to maintain good indexing systems for tracking documents and parties.

Demurrer.

In some cases, the plaintiff will file a complaint that has no legal grounds. Perhaps the defendant committed an act, but there is no statute forbidding the action. Or perhaps the plaintiff's attorney has misstated the cause of action or has made other legal errors. In those cases, the defendant's attorney will file a **demurrer,** a pleading that maintains that the plaintiff's complaint has no legal basis. Points and Authorities (commonly known as P&As) that support the defendant's contentions must accompany the demurrer. These will include a statement of the issue or argument along with the citation of the case or statute from which it was obtained. For instance, if the defendant is objecting on the ground that the plaintiff does not have the legal capacity to sue, the Points and Authorities must include the number of the statute or code section that states what constitutes "legal capacity to sue."

demurrer
A defendant's pleading stating that there are no legal grounds for the plaintiff's complaint.

After the plaintiff is served and the documents are filed with the court, a hearing is held where both attorneys present their oral arguments to the judge, who rules on the demurrer. If the court rules that the "demurrer is sustained without leave to amend," the defendant wins the lawsuit. In some cases, the court will allow the plaintiff to amend the complaint. If the court "overrules the demurrer," the defendant must file an answer within the allotted time period.

Motion to Strike.

In some cases, the complaint may be legally sufficient, but some of its allegations may be legally objectionable. In that event, the defendant will file a **Motion to Strike,** asking that the objectionable allegations be removed. The motion must set forth the objectionable wording along with points and authorities to support the defendant's contentions. The exact page and line number of the objectionable words must be noted in the Motion to Strike. The court will hold a hearing on the motion similar to the hearing held for demurrers.

Motion to Strike
A motion filed by the defendant to strike legally objectionable language from the complaint.

**Motion for Summary
Judgment**
The plaintiff files a Motion for
Summary Judgment if there is
no defense that the defendant
can claim. The defendant files a
Motion for Summary Judgment
if the action has no merit.

Motion for Summary Judgment.   Either party may file a **Motion for Summary Judgment.** The plaintiff files the motion to assert that there is no defense that the defendant can claim in the action. The defendant files the motion to claim that the action has no merit. In either case, affidavits of witnesses or parties to the action must be filed along with the motion.

The judge will hold a hearing on the motion where the attorneys will present their oral arguments. The court will then issue an order setting forth its decision. If the judge grants the motion, the lawsuit is over and the party that made the motion prevails, but if the judge denies the motion, the lawsuit continues.

Discovery

discovery
The formal investigation stage of
the lawsuit. Both parties share
information using discovery
documents.

The most paper-intensive part of the lawsuit is the **discovery** phase, which is the pretrial phase during which each party obtains information about the lawsuit from the other side to use in preparing for trial. Paralegals and legal secretaries perform several important functions during discovery: preparing documents, keeping track of pleadings and due dates, investigating, doing research, summarizing and cataloging documents, and maintaining document control. The most common discovery devices include the following:

1. Depositions

2. Written Interrogatories

3. Requests for Admission

4. Requests for Production

5. Requests for Physical or Mental Examinations

deposition
A pretrial examination of parties
or witnesses to a lawsuit.

deponent
The person whose testimony is
taken at a deposition.

transcript
A typed record of a deposition
or court proceeding; a writing
made from the original. Usually
prepared from a court
reporter's notes of the
proceeding.

Depositions.   In a **deposition,** the attorney who requested the deposition asks questions of the party or witness, known as the **deponent,** who may be cross-examined by the other attorney. If the individual answers a question differently at the deposition from his later testimony at trial, the attorney may cross-examine him about the discrepancy for purposes of destroying his credibility.

Depositions may be taken of either parties or witnesses to an action. Both attorneys are present. A certified reporter is also present at the deposition and prepares a verbatim **transcript** of the proceedings.

Depositions are paid for by the requesting party, who is provided with a copy of the transcript by the reporter. If the attorney knows the deponent will be unavailable for testifying at the trial, some states allow a videotaped deposition to be substituted for testimony at trial. A videotaped deposition is generally more effective than a transcript at trial because it allows the judge and jury to observe the witness's expressions and body language as well as to hear the answers. Otherwise the deposition may be read by the attorneys at the trial if the deponent is unavailable to testify.

In some states, the attorney requesting the deposition must file a Notice to Take Deposition with the court and serve it on the individual whose deposition is being requested. Exhibit 4.10 is a Notice to Take Deposition Upon Oral Examination from New York. When preparing this form, the paralegal or legal secretary fills in the appropriate information as follows (the numbers in the exhibit correspond to the numbers in the list):

1. *Caption.*   This section includes the names of the parties to the action and the case number or index number.

EXHIBIT 4.10   A Notice to Take Deposition Upon Oral Examination From New York

B 438—Notice To Take Deposition Upon Oral Examination
Blank Court 6-85

Blumbergs Law Products

COPYRIGHT 1973 BY JULIUS BLUMBERG, INC., LAW BLANK PUBLISHERS

Index No.

MARIA ANN ALTERIO

①   *against*   Plaintiff(s)

**NOTICE
TO TAKE DEPOSITION
UPON ORAL
EXAMINATION**

JOSEPH PAUL MARINO

Defendant(s)

Sir   **PLEASE TAKE NOTICE,** *that pursuant to Article 31 of the Civil Practice Law and Rules the testimony, upon oral examination, of* Roberto Carrillo
whose address is   411 Sunell Drive, Staten Island, New York 10308

② *as a* witness *will be taken before*   Hon. J. R. Hoover
who is not an attorney, or employee of an attorney, for any party or prospective party herein and is not a person who would be disqualified to act as a juror because of interest or because of consanguinity or affinity to any party herein, at
222 Civic Center, Staten Island, New York
on the 3d *day of* April 19 96 *at* 10 *o'clock in the* morning *noon of that day with respect to evidence material and necessary in the—prosecution-defense—of this action:*

That the said person to be examined is required to produce at such examination the following:

③ Payroll records for Joseph Paul Marino from the period May 1, 1995 to May 15, 1996

The circumstances or reasons such notice is sought or required are as follows: ¹

④ *Dated,*

To

Attorney(s) for

⑤ _____
MELISSA CHAN
Attorney(s) for Plaintiff
Office and Post Office Address
1122 Main Street
Staten Island, New York

1.   If to a non-party and CPl.R §3101(a)(4) applies.

SOURCE: Reprinted with permission. Forms may be purchased from Julius Blumberg, Inc. NYC 10013, or any of its dealers. Reproduction prohibited.

EXHIBIT 4.10   A Notice to Take Deposition Upon Oral Examination From New York
Concluded

State of New York, County of   ss.:

being duly sworn, deposes and says; that deponent is not
a party to the action, is over 18 years of age and resides
at
That on the   day of   19
deponent served the within notice to take deposition on

attorney(s) for
herein, at his office at

during his absence from said office
strike out either (a) or (b)
(a) by then and there leaving a true copy of the same
with

his clerk; partner; person having charge of said office.
(b) and said office being closed, by depositing a true copy
of same, enclosed in a sealed wrapper directed to said
attorney(s), in the office letter drop or box.

Sworn to before me this
day of   19

State of New York, County of   ss.:

being duly sworn, deposes and says; that deponent is not
a party to the action, is over 18 years of age and resides
at
That on the   day of   19
deponent served the within notice to take deposition on

attorney(s) for
at

the address designated by said attorney(s) for that purpose
by depositing a true copy of same enclosed in a postpaid
properly addressed wrapper, in — a post office — official depository under the exclusive care and custody of the United
States Postal Service within New York State.

Sworn to before me, this
day of   19

Index No.

                                                                Plaintiff
                              against

                                                                Defendant

Notice to take Deposition
upon Oral Examination

Attorney(s) for
    Office and Post Office Address

Service of a notice, etc., of which the within
is a copy is admitted this
day of   19

Attorney(s) for

2. ***Body.***   This portion includes the name and address of the individual whose deposition is being taken, his status, and the individual hearing the deposition. In your state, this notice may not include a judge's name since many states hear depositions with both attorneys present. The location and the date and time of the deposition are also included here.

3. ***What to Bring.***   In this section, the paralegal or legal secretary lists the items the witness is required to bring to the deposition.

4. ***Date and Attorneys.***   The date of the notice should be typed in along with the names and addresses of the attorneys.

Deposition Summaries.   Many depositions fill hundreds of pages of transcripts, but the attorney will be primarily interested in reading only the pertinent portions. Therefore, the paralegal or legal secretary may be asked to prepare a summary of the deposition. The summary should include any discrepancies in the witness's testimony as well as a summary of the testimony itself. The most common types of summaries are a topical deposition summary, a page/line deposition summary, an issue deposition summary, and an index to a video deposition. The following instructions will help you prepare each type of summary (in each case, the numbers in the exhibit correspond to the numbers in the list).

Exhibit 4.11 shows a topical deposition summary, and the following instructions will help in preparing one:

EXHIBIT 4.11   Topical Deposition Summary

①

FEELEY V. RIVERA

Case No. 42196

Deponent Name: Lucelly Osorio

Date of Deposition: May 1, 1996

Deposition Volume: No. 1

Topic/Subject	Transcript Page/Line	Summary Page
Personal	2/15	1
Employment history	3/5	1
Medical history	8/2	1
Psychiatric treatment	10/4	1
Psychiatric treatment	14/5	2
Educational history	17/19	2

②   **③**   **④**

1. **Heading.**   Type the name of the case, the case number, the name of the individual being deposed, the date of the deposition, and the volume number being summarized.

2. **Topic/subject.**   Separate the deposition by subject matter and indicate each topic covered.

3. **Transcript Page/line.**   Indicate the page and the line number of each individual topic in the deposition. This shows the attorney where the material appears in the deposition transcript.

4. **Summary Page.**   Indicate the page number on which each individual topic appears in the deposition summary.

Use the following instructions to prepare a page/line deposition summary (see Exhibit 4.12 for an example):

1. **Heading.**   This includes the case name and number, the deponent's name, the date of the deposition, and the volume number.

2. **Page/line.**   This shows at what page and line number in the transcript the material under "subject" and "summary" appear.

3. **Subject.**   What is the general subject area?

4. **Summary.**   This provides a brief summary of the information contained on that line and page and about that general subject. This summary should necessarily be brief but should indicate any discrepancies in the testimony. For example, see the summary of psychiatric information in Exhibit 4.12.

Use the following instructions in preparing an issue deposition summary (see Exhibit 4.13 for an example):

1. **Heading.**   This includes the title of the summary, the case name and number, the name of the individual whose deposition is being taken, and the date and volume number.

2. **Headings.**   List here each individual subject or issue discussed in the deposition.

3. **Page.**   Indicate here the page number on which the discussion of each individual subject or issue appears in the deposition transcript.

These instructions will help in preparing an index to a video deposition (see Exhibit 4.14 for an example):

1. **Heading.**   This includes the type of index, the case name, the client's name, the name of the person whose deposition is being taken, the date of the deposition, and the volume number.

2. **Time/date.**   Since this is a videotaped deposition, it is advisable to indicate the numbers that appear on the video display at the point where this portion of the testimony appears. It is necessary to have a VCR player with a display for time and date.

3. **Page/line.**   Here you will list the page number and line number at which this portion of the testimony appears in the transcript.

4. **Summary.**   This provides a summary of what appears in the deponent's testimony at this point in the transcript and videotape.

EXHIBIT 4.12   Page/Line Deposition Summary

Monugian v. Castillo

Case No. 33333

Deponent Name: Linda Madsen-Stone
Date of Deposition: March 6, 1996
Deposition Volume No. 1

② Page/Line	③ Subject	①	④ Summary
2/15	Personal		Resides at 222 Western Avenue, Akron, Ohio, phone: (999) 222-1111
3/5	Procedures		Explanation of deposition procedures
6/4	Employment		Currently employed by Ross Enterprises, 435 Irvine Boulevard, Akron, Ohio, as accountant for 6 months. Prior to that, accountant for Attorney Deanna Caudillo, 123 Broad Street, Akron, Ohio, 8 months
8/2	Medical		No present medication. Treated for back pain and psychiatric problems last three years.
10/4	Psychiatric		Saw Dr. Danielli for one year in Akron.
14/5	Psychiatric		Denies seeing psychiatrist for emotional or psychiatric problems.
16/9	Psychiatric		Dr. Danielli's office located on Madison Street but can't remember address. Deponent's attorney will provide.
17/19	Education		Completed Whittier School in Whittier, Ohio, 1992. Completed paralegal classes in 1994. CPA 1995.

Written Interrogatories.   **Written interrogatories** are questions asked of the opposing side (the adverse party) that must be answered in a specified period of time, usually thirty days. The questions may be asked of parties to the action only.

You may assist the attorney in drafting the questions, and you may also assist the client in preparing the answers to interrogatories that have been served by the adverse party. In California, the courts have instituted a set of form interrogatories that may be

written interrogatories
Written questions propounded to the adverse party in the lawsuit which must usually be answered within 30 days.

EXHIBIT 4.13   Issue Deposition Summary

<u>Morales v. Guerrero</u>

Case No. 55555

Deponent Name: Susan Dawoodi

Date: May 1, 1996

Deposition Volume No. 1

①

Subject/Issue	Page(s)
Personal/background	
Personal information	2
Employment history	6
Educational history	9
Medical history	
Current status	8
Psychiatric history	11, 16

②   ③

---

utilized, along with thirty-five additional questions prepared by the requesting party (see Exhibit 4.15).

In states that do not limit the number of interrogatories that may be asked, it is not unusual to find several pages of questions that a party must answer. Serving a voluminous set of interrogatories on a party may provide an incentive for that party to settle the case quickly.

The same heading and captions are required for written interrogatories as are used for other court documents in the case. Exhibit 4.16 shows sample written interrogatories from the state of Illinois.

Requests for Admission.   A Request for Admission is served on a party to the action only. The request asks the opposing party to agree to admit any points that are not in dispute and do not have to be litigated. In some cases, the plaintiff may serve a set of requests asking the defendant to admit each and every allegation in the complaint. Most states require that requests be answered in thirty days. In some states, every request that is not answered in time is deemed to have been admitted. It can

---

EXHIBIT 4.14   Index to a Video Deposition

Daniels v. Kennelly—Case No. 11111

Deponent: William Minot

Date: December 26, 1996

Volume No. 1

①

Time/Date No.*	Page/Line	Summary
00:40:08	5/9	Identification of parties and attorneys
01:38:00	7/14	Witness William Minot sworn in
01:55:20	8/25	Attorney Melissa Chan begins direct examination
02:22:07	9/20	Exhibit 1 identified and authenticated by deponent (contract between Minot and Daniels dated 7/17/92)
02:50:03	10/25	Personal background of witness
03:30:02	12/5	Educational history of witness

* Times and dates are indicated as they appear on the video display.

②   ③   ④

---

readily be seen that in those cases the plaintiff may win the case based just on the unanswered requests of the defendant. Some states require further action before the requests are deemed admitted, however.

Requests for Production.   In some cases, one party may have documents, reports, or other items of evidence that are relevant to the lawsuit and that the other party wishes to examine. A Request for Production is served on the adverse party asking her to produce certain items of interest. The party served may either provide the items to the other side or, if the material is voluminous and not easily transported, may allow the other party to examine the material at its location during the ordinary course of business.

For instance, if the plaintiff is claiming that a machine is defective, a Request for Production may ask for the reports or videotapes that include the testing conducted on the machine.

Requests for Physical or Mental Examination.   If the plaintiff is claiming physical and/or mental injuries as a result of the incident, the defendant may request that

EXHIBIT 4.15   Form Interrogatories from California

ATTORNEY OR PARTY WITHOUT ATTORNEY *(Name and Address):*	TELEPHONE NO.:

ATTORNEY FOR *(Name)*

NAME OF COURT AND JUDICIAL DISTRICT AND BRANCH COURT, IF ANY:

SHORT TITLE OF CASE:

FORM INTERROGATORIES	CASE NUMBER:
Asking Party:	
Answering Party:	
Set No.:	

Sec. 1. Instructions to All Parties

(a) These are general instructions. *For time limitations, requirements for service on other parties, and other details, see Code of Civil Procedure section 2030 and the cases construing it.*

(b) These interrogatories do not change existing law relating to interrogatories nor do they affect an answering party's right to assert any privilege or objection.

Sec. 2. Instructions to the Asking Party

(a) These interrogatories are designed for optional use in the superior courts only. A separate set of interrogatories, Form Interrogatories—Economic Litigation, which have no subparts, are designed for optional use in municipal and justice courts. However, they also may be used in superior courts. See Code of Civil Procedure section 94.

(b) Check the box next to each interrogatory that you want the answering party to answer. Use care in choosing those interrogatories that are applicable to the case.

(c) The interrogatories in section 16.0, Defendant's Contentions—Personal Injury, should not be used until the defendant has had a reasonable opportunity to conduct an investigation or discovery of plaintiff's injuries and damages.

(d) Additional interrogatories may be attached.

Sec. 3. Instructions to the Answering Party

(a) In superior court actions, an answer or other appropriate response must be given to each interrogatory checked by the asking party.

(b) As a general rule, within 30 days after you are served with these interrogatories, you must serve your responses on the asking party and serve copies of your responses on all other parties to the action who have appeared. See Code of Civil Procedure section 2030 for details.

(c) Each answer must be as complete and straightforward as the information reasonably available to you per-

mits. If an interrogatory cannot be answered completely, answer it to the extent possible.

(d) If you do not have enough personal knowledge to fully answer an interrogatory, say so, but make a reasonable and good faith effort to get the information by asking other persons or organizations, unless the information is equally available to the asking party.

(e) Whenever an interrogatory may be answered by referring to a document, the document may be attached as an exhibit to the response and referred to in the response. If the document has more than one page, refer to the page and section where the answer to the interrogatory can be found.

(f) Whenever an address and telephone number for the same person are requested in more than one interrogatory, you are required to furnish them in answering only the first interrogatory asking for that information.

(g) Your answers to these interrogatories must be verified, dated, and signed. You may wish to use the following form *at the end of your answers:*

"I declare under penalty of perjury under the laws of the State of California that the foregoing answers are true and correct.

_____   _____   "
(DATE)   (SIGNATURE)

Sec. 4. Definitions

Words in **BOLDFACE CAPITALS** in these interrogatories are defined as follows:

(a) **INCIDENT** includes the circumstances and events surrounding the alleged accident, injury, or other occurrence or breach of contract giving rise to this action or proceeding.

(b) **YOU OR ANYONE ACTING ON YOUR BEHALF** includes you, your agents, your employees, your insurance companies, their agents, their employees, your attorneys, your accountants, your investigators, and anyone else acting on your behalf.

(Continued)   Page 1 of 8

SOURCE: Reprinted from California Judicial Council Forms, published by West Publishing Company.

EXHIBIT 4.15   Form Interrogatories from California *Continued*

FI–120

(c) **PERSON** includes a natural person, firm, association, organization, partnership, business, trust, corporation, or public entity.

(d) **DOCUMENT** means a writing, as defined in Evidence Code section 250, and includes the original or a copy of handwriting, typewriting, printing, photostating, photographing, and every other means of recording upon any tangible thing and form of communicating or representation, including letters, words, pictures, sounds, or symbols, or combinations of them.

(e) **HEALTH CARE PROVIDER** includes any **PERSON** referred to in Code of Civil Procedure section 667.7(e)(3).

(f) **ADDRESS** means the street address, including the city, state, and zip code.

Sec. 5. Interrogatories

The following interrogatories have been approved by the Judicial Council under section 2033.5 of the Code of Civil Procedure:

CONTENTS

1.0 Identity of Persons Answering These Interrogatories

☐ 1.1 State the name, **ADDRESS**, telephone number, and relationship to you of each **PERSON** who prepared or assisted in the preparation of the responses to these interrogatories. (Do not identify anyone who simply typed or reproduced the responses.)

2.0 General Background Information — Individual

☐ 2.1 State:
(a) your name;
(b) every name you have used in the past;
(c) the dates you used each name.

☐ 2.2 State the date and place of your birth.

☐ 2.3 At the time of the **INCIDENT**, did you have a driver's license? If so, state:
(a) the state or other issuing entity;
(b) the license number and type;
(c) the date of issuance;
(d) all restrictions.

☐ 2.4 At the time of the **INCIDENT**, did you have any other permit or license for the operation of a motor vehicle? If so, state:
(a) the state or other issuing entity;
(b) the license number and type;
(c) the date of issuance;
(d) all restrictions.

☐ 2.5 State:
(a) your present residence **ADDRESS**;
(b) your residence **ADDRESSES** for the last five years;
(c) the dates you lived at each **ADDRESS**.

☐ 2.6 State:
(a) the name, **ADDRESS**, and telephone number of your present employer or place of self-employment;
(b) the name, **ADDRESS**, dates of employment, job title, and nature of work for each employer or self-employment you have had from five years before the **INCIDENT** until today.

☐ 2.7 State:
(a) the name and **ADDRESS** of each school or other academic or vocational institution you have attended beginning with high school;
(b) the dates you attended;
(c) the highest grade level you have completed;
(d) the degrees received.

☐ 2.8 Have you ever been convicted of a felony? If so, for each conviction state:
(a) the city and state where you were convicted;
(b) the date of conviction;
(c) the offense;
(d) the court and case number.

☐ 2.9 Can you speak English with ease? If not, what language and dialect do you normally use?

☐ 2.10 Can you read and write English with ease? If not, what language and dialect do you normally use?

☐ 2.11 At the time of the **INCIDENT** were you acting as an agent or employee for any **PERSON**? If so, state:
(a) the name, **ADDRESS**, and telephone number of that **PERSON**;
(b) a description of your duties.

☐ 2.12 At the time of the **INCIDENT** did you or any other person have any physical, emotional, or mental disability or condition that may have contributed to the occurrence of the **INCIDENT**? If so, for each person state:
(a) the name, **ADDRESS**, and telephone number;

EXHIBIT 4.15   Form Interrogatories from California *Continued*

FI–120

(b) the nature of the disability or condition;

(c) the manner in which the disability or condition contributed to the occurrence of the **INCIDENT**.

☐ 2.13 Within 24 hours before the **INCIDENT** did you or
any person involved in the **INCIDENT** use or take any
of the following substances: alcoholic beverage, mari-
juana, or other drug or medication of any kind (prescrip-
tion or not)? If so, for each person state:
(a) the name, **ADDRESS**, and telephone number;
(b) the nature or description of each substance;
(c) the quantity of each substance used or taken;
(d) the date and time of day when each substance was
used or taken;
(e) the **ADDRESS** where each substance was used or
taken;
(f) the name, **ADDRESS**, and telephone number of
each person who was present when each
substance was used or taken;
(g) the name, **ADDRESS**, and telephone number of any
HEALTH CARE PROVIDER that prescribed or furnished the substance and the condition for which
it was prescribed or furnished.

**3.0 General Background Information —
Business Entity**

☐ 3.1 Are you a corporation? If so, state:
(a) the name stated in the current articles of incorporation;
(b) all other names used by the corporation during the
past ten years and the dates each was used;
(c) the date and place of incorporation;
(d) the **ADDRESS** of the principal place of business;
(e) whether you are qualified to do business in
California.

☐ 3.2 Are you a partnership? If so, state:
(a) the current partnership name;
(b) all other names used by the partnership during the
past ten years and the dates each was used;
(c) whether you are a limited partnership and, if so,
under the laws of what jurisdiction;
(d) the name and **ADDRESS** of each general partner;
(e) the **ADDRESS** of the principal place of business.

☐ 3.3 Are you a joint venture? If so, state:
(a) the current joint venture name;
(b) all other names used by the joint venture during the
past ten years and the dates each was used;
(c) the name and **ADDRESS** of each joint·venturer;
(d) the **ADDRESS** of the principal place of business.

☐ 3.4 Are you an unincorporated association?
If so, state:
(a) the current unincorporated association name;
(b) all other names used by the unincorporated association during the past ten years and the dates each
was used;
(c) the **ADDRESS** of the principal place of business.

☐ 3.5 Have you done business under a fictitious name
during the past ten years? If so, for each fictitious name
state:
(a) the name;

(b) the dates each was used;

(c) the state and county of each fictitious name filing;

(d) the **ADDRESS** of the principal place of business.

☐ 3.6 Within the past five years has any public entity
registered or licensed your businesses? If so, for each
license or registration:
(a) identify the license or registration;
(b) state the name of the public entity;
(c) state the dates of issuance and expiration.

4.0 Insurance

☐ 4.1 At the time of the **INCIDENT**, was there in effect
any policy of insurance through which you were or
might be insured in any manner (for example, primary,
pro-rata, or excess liability coverage or medical expense
coverage) for the damages, claims, or actions that have
arisen out of the **INCIDENT**? If so, for each policy state:
(a) the kind of coverage;
(b) the name and **ADDRESS** of the insurance company;
(c) the name, **ADDRESS**, and telephone number of
each named insured;
(d) the policy number;
(e) the limits of coverage for each type of coverage
contained in the policy;
(f) whether any reservation of rights or controversy or
coverage dispute exists between you and the insurance company;
(g) the name, **ADDRESS**, and telephone number of the
custodian of the policy.

☐ 4.2 Are you self-insured under any statute for the
damages, claims, or actions that have arisen out of the
INCIDENT? If so, specify the statute.

5.0 *[Reserved]*

6.0 Physical, Mental, or Emotional Injuries

☐ 6.1 Do you attribute any physical, mental, or emotional
injuries to the **INCIDENT**? If your answer is ''no,'' do not
answer interrogatories 6.2 through 6.7.

☐ 6.2 Identify each injury you attribute to the **INCIDENT**
and the area of your body affected.

☐ 6.3 Do you still have any complaints that you attribute
to the **INCIDENT**? If so, for each complaint state:
(a) a description;
(b) whether the complaint is subsiding, remaining the
same, or becoming worse;
(c) the frequency and duration.

☐ 6.4 Did you receive any consultation or examination
(except from expert witnesses covered by Code of Civil
Procedure, § 2034) or treatment from a **HEALTH CARE
PROVIDER** for any injury you attribute to the **INCIDENT**?
If so, for each **HEALTH CARE PROVIDER** state:
(a) the name, **ADDRESS**, and telephone number;
(b) the type of consultation, examination, or treatment
provided;

EXHIBIT 4.15   Form Interrogatories from California *Continued*

FI–120

(c) the dates you received consultation, examination, or treatment;

(d) the charges to date.

☐ 6.5 Have you taken any medication, prescribed or not, as a result of injuries that you attribute to the **INCIDENT**? If so, for each medication state:
(a) the name;
(b) the **PERSON** who prescribed or furnished it;
(c) the date prescribed or furnished;
(d) the dates you began and stopped taking it;
(e) the cost to date.

☐ 6.6 Are there any other medical services not previously listed (for example, ambulance, nursing, prosthetics)? If so, for each service state:
(a) the nature;
(b) the date;
(c) the cost;
(d) the name, **ADDRESS**, and telephone number of each provider.

☐ 6.7 Has any **HEALTH CARE PROVIDER** advised that you may require future or additional treatment for any injuries that you attribute to the **INCIDENT**? If so, for each injury state:
(a) the name and **ADDRESS** of each **HEALTH CARE PROVIDER**;
(b) the complaints for which the treatment was advised;
(c) the nature, duration, and estimated cost of the treatment.

7.0 Property Damage

☐ 7.1 Do you attribute any loss of or damage to a vehicle or other property to the **INCIDENT**? If so, for each item of property:
(a) describe the property;
(b) describe the nature and location of the damage to the property;
(c) state the amount of damage you are claiming for each item of property and how the amount was calculated;
(d) if the property was sold, state the name, **ADDRESS**, and telephone number of the seller, the date of sale, and the sale price.

☐ 7.2 Has a written estimate or evaluation been made for any item of property referred to in your answer to the preceeding interrogatory? If so, for each estimate or evaluation state:
(a) the name, **ADDRESS**, and telephone number of the **PERSON** who prepared it and the date prepared;
(b) the name, **ADDRESS**, and telephone number of each **PERSON** who has a copy;
(c) the amount of damage stated.

☐ 7.3 Has any item of property referred to in your answer to interrogatory 7.1 been repaired? If so, for each item state:
(a) the date repaired;
(b) a description of the repair;
(c) the repair cost;

(d) the name, **ADDRESS**, and telephone number of the **PERSON** who repaired it;
(e) the name, **ADDRESS**, and telephone number of the **PERSON** who paid for the repair.

8.0 Loss of Income or Earning Capacity

☐ 8.1 Do you attribute any loss of income or earning capacity to the **INCIDENT**? If your answer is ''no,'' do not answer interrogatories 8.2 through 8.8.

☐ 8.2 State:
(a) the nature of your work;
(b) your job title at the time of the **INCIDENT**;
(c) the date your employment began.

☐ 8.3 State the last date before the **INCIDENT** that you worked for compensation.

☐ 8.4 State your monthly income at the time of the **INCIDENT** and how the amount was calculated.

☐ 8.5 State the date you returned to work at each place of employment following the **INCIDENT**.

☐ 8.6 State the dates you did not work and for which you lost income.

☐ 8.7 State the total income you have lost to date as a result of the **INCIDENT** and how the amount was calculated.

☐ 8.8 Will you lose income in the future as a result of the **INCIDENT**? If so, state:
(a) the facts upon which you base this contention;
(b) an estimate of the amount;
(c) an estimate of how long you will be unable to work;
(d) how the claim for future income is calculated.

9.0 Other Damages

☐ 9.1 Are there any other damages that you attribute to the **INCIDENT**? If so, for each item of damage state:
(a) the nature;
(b) the date it occurred;
(c) the amount;
(d) the name, **ADDRESS**, and telephone number of each **PERSON** to whom an obligation was incurred.

☐ 9.2 Do any **DOCUMENTS** support the existence or amount of any item of damages claimed in interrogatory 9.1? If so, state the name, **ADDRESS**, and telephone number of the **PERSON** who has each **DOCUMENT**.

10.0 Medical History

☐ 10.1 At any time before the **INCIDENT** did you have complaints or injuries that involved the same part of your body claimed to have been injured in the **INCIDENT**? If so, for each state:
(a) a description;
(b) the dates it began and ended;
(c) the name, **ADDRESS**, and telephone number of each **HEALTH CARE PROVIDER** whom you consulted or who examined or treated you.

FI-120 [Rev. July 1, 1987]   (Continued)   Page 4 of 8

EXHIBIT 4.15   Form Interrogatories from California *Continued*

FI-120

10.2 List all physical, mental, and emotional disabilities you had immediately before the **INCIDENT.** (You may omit mental or emotional disabilities unless you attribute any mental or emotional injury to the **INCIDENT.**)

10.3 At any time after the **INCIDENT,** did you sustain injuries of the kind for which you are now claiming damages. If so, for each incident state:
(a) the date and the place it occurred;
(b) the name, **ADDRESS,** and telephone number of any other **PERSON** involved;
(c) the nature of any injuries you sustained;
(d) the name, **ADDRESS,** and telephone number of each **HEALTH CARE PROVIDER** that you consulted or who examined or treated you;
(e) the nature of the treatment and its duration.

11.0 Other Claims and Previous Claims

11.1 Except for this action, in the last ten years have you filed an action or made a written claim or demand for compensation for your personal injuries? If so, for each action, claim, or demand state:
(a) the date, time, and place and location of the **INCIDENT** (closest street **ADDRESS** or intersection);
(b) the name, **ADDRESS,** and telephone number of each **PERSON** against whom the claim was made or action filed;
(c) the court, names of the parties, and case number of any action filed;
(d) the name, **ADDRESS,** and telephone number of any attorney representing you;
(e) whether the claim or action has been resolved or is pending.

11.2 In the last ten years have you made a written claim or demand for worker's compensation benefits? If so, for each claim or demand state:
(a) the date, time, and place of the **INCIDENT** giving rise to the claim;
(b) the name, **ADDRESS,** and telephone number of your employer at the time of the injury;
(c) the name, **ADDRESS,** and telephone number of the worker's compensation insurer and the claim number;
(d) the period of time during which you received worker's compenstation benefits;
(e) a description of the injury;
(f) the name, **ADDRESS,** and telephone number of any **HEALTH CARE PROVIDER** that provided services;
(g) the case number at the Worker's Compensation Appeals Board.

12.0 Investigation — General

12.1 State the name, **ADDRESS,** and telephone number of each individual:
(a) who witnessed the **INCIDENT** or the events occurring immediately before or after the **INCIDENT;**
(b) who made any statement at the scene of the **INCIDENT;**
(c) who heard any statements made about the **INCIDENT** by any individual at the scene;

(d) who **YOU OR ANYONE ACTING ON YOUR BEHALF** claim has knowledge of the **INCIDENT** (except for expert witnesses covered by Code of Civil Procedure, § 2034).

12.2 Have **YOU OR ANYONE ACTING ON YOUR BEHALF** interviewed any individual concerning the **INCIDENT?** If so, for each individual state:
(a) the name, **ADDRESS,** and telephone number of the individual interviewed;
(b) the date of the interview;
(c) the name, **ADDRESS,** and telephone number of the **PERSON** who conducted the interview.

12.3 Have **YOU OR ANYONE ACTING ON YOUR BEHALF** obtained a written or recorded statement from any individual concerning the **INCIDENT?** If so, for each statement state:
(a) the name, **ADDRESS,** and telephone number of the individual from whom the statement was obtained;
(b) the name, **ADDRESS,** and telephone number of the individual who obtained the statement;
(c) the date the statement was obtained;
(d) the name, **ADDRESS,** and telephone number of each **PERSON** who has the original statement or a copy.

12.4 Do **YOU OR ANYONE ACTING ON YOUR BEHALF** know of any photographs, films, or videotapes depicting any place, object, or individual concerning the **INCIDENT** or plaintiff's injuries? If so, state:
(a) the number of photographs or feet of film or videotape;
(b) the places, objects, or persons photographed, filmed, or videotaped;
(c) the date the photographs, films, or videotapes were taken;
(d) the name, **ADDRESS,** and telephone number of the individual taking the photographs, films, or videotapes;
(e) the name, **ADDRESS,** and telephone number of each **PERSON** who has the original or a copy.

12.5 Do **YOU OR ANYONE ACTING ON YOUR BEHALF** know of any diagram, reproduction, or model of any place or thing (except for items developed by expert witnesses covered by Code of Civil Procedure, § 2034) concerning the **INCIDENT?** If so, for each item state:
(a) the type (i.e., diagram, reproduction, or model);
(b) the subject matter;
(c) the name, **ADDRESS,** and telephone number of each **PERSON** who has it.

12.6 Was a report made by any **PERSON** concerning the **INCIDENT?** If so, state:
(a) the name, title, identification number, and employer of the **PERSON** who made the report;
(b) the date and type of report made;
(c) the name, **ADDRESS,** and telephone number of the **PERSON** for whom the report was made.

12.7 Have **YOU OR ANYONE ACTING ON YOUR BEHALF** inspected the scene of the **INCIDENT?** If so, for each inspection state:

EXHIBIT 4.15   Form Interrogatories from California *Continued*

FI–120

(a) the name, **ADDRESS**, and telephone number of the individual making the inspection (except for expert witnesses covered by Code of Civil Procedure, § 2034);

(b) the date of the inspection.

13.0 Investigation — Surveillance

☐ **13.1** Have **YOU OR ANYONE ACTING ON YOUR BEHALF** conducted surveillance of any individual involved in the **INCIDENT** or any party to this action? If so, for each surveillance state:

(a) the name, **ADDRESS**, and telephone number of the individual or party;

(b) the time, date, and place of the surveillance;

(c) the name, **ADDRESS**, and telephone number of the individual who conducted the surveillance.

☐ **13.2** Has a written report been prepared on the surveillance? If so, for each written report state:

(a) the title;

(b) the date;

(c) the name, **ADDRESS**, and telephone number of the individual who prepared the report;

(d) the name, **ADDRESS**, and telephone number of each **PERSON** who has the original or a copy.

14.0 Statutory or Regulatory Violations

☐ **14.1** Do **YOU OR ANYONE ACTING ON YOUR BEHALF** contend that any **PERSON** involved in the **INCIDENT** violated any statute, ordinance, or regulation and that the violation was a legal (proximate) cause of the **INCIDENT**? If so, identify each **PERSON** and the statute, ordinance, or regulation.

☐ **14.2** Was any **PERSON** cited or charged with a violation of any statute, ordinance, or regulation as a result of this **INCIDENT**? If so, for each **PERSON** state:

(a) the name, **ADDRESS**, and telephone number of the **PERSON**;

(b) the statute, ordinance, or regulation allegedly violated;

(c) whether the **PERSON** entered a plea in response to the citation or charge and, if so, the plea entered;

(d) the name and **ADDRESS** of the court or administrative agency, names of the parties, and case number.

15.0 Special or Affirmative Defenses

☐ **15.1** Identify each denial of a material allegation and each special or affirmative defense in your pleadings and for each:

(a) state all facts upon which you base the denial or special or affirmative defense;

(b) state the names, **ADDRESSES**, and telephone numbers of all **PERSONS** who have knowledge of those facts;

(c) identify all **DOCUMENTS** and other tangible things which support your denial or special or affirmative defense, and state the name, **ADDRESS**, and telephone number of the **PERSON** who has each **DOCUMENT**.

16.0 Defendant's Contentions — Personal Injury

[See Instruction 2(c)]

☐ **16.1** Do you contend that any **PERSON**, other than you or plaintiff, contributed to the occurrence of the **INCIDENT** or the injuries or damages claimed by plaintiff? If so, for each **PERSON**:

(a) state the name, **ADDRESS**, and telephone number of the **PERSON**;

(b) state all facts upon which you base your contention;

(c) state the names, **ADDRESSES**, and telephone numbers of all **PERSONS** who have knowledge of the facts;

(d) identify all **DOCUMENTS** and other tangible things that support your contention and state the name, **ADDRESS**, and telephone number of the **PERSON** who has each **DOCUMENT** or thing.

☐ **16.2** Do you contend that plaintiff was not injured in the **INCIDENT**? If so:

(a) state all facts upon which you base your contention;

(b) state the names, **ADDRESSES**, and telephone numbers of all **PERSONS** who have knowledge of the facts;

(c) identify all **DOCUMENTS** and other tangible things that support your contention and state the name, **ADDRESS**, and telephone number of the **PERSON** who has each **DOCUMENT** or thing.

☐ **16.3** Do you contend that the injuries or the extent of the injuries claimed by plaintiff as disclosed in discovery proceedings thus far in this case were not caused by the **INCIDENT**? If so, for each injury:

(a) identify it;

(b) state all facts upon which you base your contention;

(c) state the names, **ADDRESSES**, and telephone numbers of all **PERSONS** who have knowledge of the facts;

(d) identify all **DOCUMENTS** and other tangible things that support your contention and state the name, **ADDRESS**, and telephone number of the **PERSON** who has each **DOCUMENT** or thing.

☐ **16.4** Do you contend that any of the services furnished by any **HEALTH CARE PROVIDER** claimed by plaintiff in discovery proceedings thus far in this case were not due to the **INCIDENT**? If so:

(a) identify each service;

(b) state all facts upon which you base your contention;

(c) state the names, **ADDRESSES**, and telephone numbers of all **PERSONS** who have knowledge of the facts;

(d) identify all **DOCUMENTS** and other tangible things that support your contention and state the name, **ADDRESS**, and telephone number of the **PERSON** who has each **DOCUMENT** or thing.

☐ **16.5** Do you contend that any of the costs of services furnished by any **HEALTH CARE PROVIDER** claimed as damages by plaintiff in discovery proceedings thus far in this case were unreasonable? If so:

(a) identify each cost;

EXHIBIT 4.15   Form Interrogatories from California *Continued*

FI–120

(b) state all facts upon which you base your contention;
(c) state the names, **ADDRESSES**, and telephone numbers of all **PERSONS** who have knowledge of the facts;
(d) identify all **DOCUMENTS** and other tangible things that support your contention and state the name, **ADDRESS**, and telephone number of the **PERSON** who has each **DOCUMENT** or thing.

16.6 Do you contend that any part of the loss of earnings or income claimed by plaintiff in discovery proceedings thus far in this case was unreasonable or was not caused by the **INCIDENT**? If so:
(a) identify each part of the loss;
(b) state all facts upon which you base your contention;
(c) state the names, **ADDRESSES**, and telephone numbers of all **PERSONS** who have knowledge of the facts;
(d) identify all **DOCUMENTS** and other tangible things that support your contention and state the name, **ADDRESS**, and telephone number of the **PERSON** who has each **DOCUMENT** or thing.

16.7 Do you contend that any of the property damage claimed by plaintiff in discovery proceedings thus far in this case was not caused by the **INCIDENT**? If so:
(a) identify each item of property damage;
(b) state all facts upon which you base your contention;
(c) state the names, **ADDRESSES**, and telephone numbers of all **PERSONS** who have knowledge of the facts;
(d) identify all **DOCUMENTS** and other tangible things that support your contention and state the name, **ADDRESS**, and telephone number of the **PERSON** who has each **DOCUMENT** or thing.

16.8 Do you contend that any of the costs of repairing the property damage claimed by plaintiff in discovery proccedings thus far in this case were unreasonable? If so:
(a) identify each cost item;
(b) state all facts upon which you base your contention;
(c) state the names, **ADDRESSES**, and telephone numbers of all **PERSONS** who have knowledge of the facts;
(d) identify all **DOCUMENTS** and other tangible things that support your contention and state the name, **ADDRESS**, and telephone number of the **PERSON** who has each **DOCUMENT** or thing.

16.9 Do **YOU OR ANYONE ACTING ON YOUR BEHALF** have any **DOCUMENT** (for example, insurance bureau index reports) concerning claims for personal injuries made before or after the **INCIDENT** by a plaintiff in this case? If so, for each plaintiff state:
(a) the source of each **DOCUMENT**;
(b) the date each claim arose;
(c) the nature of each claim;
(d) the name, **ADDRESS**, and telephone number of the **PERSON** who has each **DOCUMENT**.

16.10 Do **YOU OR ANYONE ACTING ON YOUR BEHALF** have any **DOCUMENT** concerning the past or present physical, mental, or emotional condition of any plaintiff in this case from a **HEALTH CARE PROVIDER** not previously identified (except for expert witnesses covered by Code of Civil Procedure, § 2034)? If so, for each plaintiff state:
(a) the name, **ADDRESS**, and telephone number of each **HEALTH CARE PROVIDER**;
(b) a description of each **DOCUMENT**;
(c) the name, **ADDRESS**, and telephone number of the **PERSON** who has each **DOCUMENT**.

17.0 Responses to Request for Admissions

17.1 Is your response to each request for admission served with these interrogatories an unqualified admission? If not, for each response that is not an unqualified admission:
(a) state the number of the request;
(b) state all facts upon which you base your response;
(c) state the names, **ADDRESSES**, and telephone numbers of all **PERSONS** who have knowledge of those facts;
(d) identify all **DOCUMENTS** and other tangible things that support your response and state the name, **ADDRESS**, and telephone number of the **PERSON** who has each **DOCUMENT** or thing.

20.0 How the Incident Occurred — Motor Vehicle

20.1 State the date, time, and place of the **INCIDENT** (closest street **ADDRESS** or intersection).

20.2 For each vehicle involved in the **INCIDENT**, state:
(a) the year, make, model, and license number;
(b) the name, **ADDRESS**, and telephone number of the driver;
(c) the name, **ADDRESS**, and telephone number of each occupant other than the driver;
(d) the name, **ADDRESS**, and telephone number of each registered owner;
(e) the name, **ADDRESS**, and telephone number of each lessee;
(f) the name, **ADDRESS**, and telephone number of each owner other than the registered owner or lien holder;
(g) the name of each owner who gave permission or consent to the driver to operate the vehicle.

20.3 State the **ADDRESS** and location where your trip began, and the **ADDRESS** and location of your destination.

20.4 Describe the route that you followed from the beginning of your trip to the location of the **INCIDENT**, and state the location of each stop, other than routine traffic stops, during the trip leading up to the **INCIDENT**.

20.5 State the name of the street or roadway, the lane of travel, and the direction of travel of each vehicle involved in the **INCIDENT** for the 500 feet of travel before the **INCIDENT**.

EXHIBIT 4.15   Form Interrogatories from California *Concluded*

FI–120

☐ 20.6 Did the **INCIDENT** occur at an intersection? If so, describe all traffic control devices, signals, or signs at the intersection.

☐ 20.7 Was there a traffic signal facing you at the time of the **INCIDENT**? If so, state:
(a) your location when you first saw it;
(b) the color;
(c) the number of seconds it had been that color;
(d) whether the color changed between the time you first saw it and the **INCIDENT**.

☐ 20.8 State how the **INCIDENT** occurred, giving the speed, direction, and location of each vehicle involved:
(a) just before the **INCIDENT**;
(b) at the time of the **INCIDENT**;
(c) just after the **INCIDENT**.

☐ 20.9 Do you have information that a malfunction or defect in a vehicle caused the **INCIDENT**? If so:
(a) identify the vehicle;
(b) identify each malfunction or defect;
(c) state the name, **ADDRESS**, and telephone number of each **PERSON** who is a witness to or has information about each malfunction or defect;
(d) state the name, **ADDRESS**, and telephone number of each **PERSON** who has custody of each defective part.

☐ 20.10 Do you have information that any malfunction or defect in a vehicle contributed to the injuries sustained in the **INCIDENT**? If so:
(a) identify the vehicle;
(b) identify each malfunction or defect;
(c) state the name, **ADDRESS**, and telephone number of each **PERSON** who is a witness to or has information about each malfunction or defect;
(d) state the name, **ADDRESS**, and telephone number of each **PERSON** who has custody of each defective part.

☐ 20.11 State the name, **ADDRESS**, and telephone number of each owner and each **PERSON** who has had possession since the **INCIDENT** of each vehicle involved in the **INCIDENT**.

50.0 Contract

☐ 50.1 For each agreement alleged in the pleadings:
(a) identify all **DOCUMENTS** that are part of the agreement and for each state the name, **ADDRESS**, and telephone number of each **PERSON** who has the **DOCUMENT**;
(b) state each part of the agreement not in writing, the name, **ADDRESS**, and telephone number of each **PERSON** agreeing to that provision, and the date that part of the agreement was made;
(c) identify all **DOCUMENTS** that evidence each part of the agreement not in writing and for each state the name, **ADDRESS**, and telephone number of each **PERSON** who has the **DOCUMENT**;
(d) identify all **DOCUMENTS** that are part of each modification to the agreement, and for each state the name, **ADDRESS**, and telephone number of each **PERSON** who has the **DOCUMENT**;
(e) state each modification not in writing, the date, and the name, **ADDRESS**, and telephone number of each **PERSON** agreeing to the modification, and the date the modification was made;
(f) identify all **DOCUMENTS** that evidence each modification of the agreement not in writing and for each state the name, **ADDRESS**, and telephone number of each **PERSON** who has the **DOCUMENT**.

☐ 50.2 Was there a breach of any agreement alleged in the pleadings? If so, for each breach describe and give the date of every act or omission that you claim is the breach of the agreement.

☐ 50.3 Was performance of any agreement alleged in the pleadings excused? If so, identify each agreement excused and state why performance was excused.

☐ 50.4 Was any agreement alleged in the pleadings terminated by mutual agreement, release, accord and satisfaction, or novation? If so, identify each agreement terminated and state why it was terminated including dates.

☐ 50.5 Is any agreement alleged in the pleadings unenforceable? If so, identify each unenforceable agreement and state why it is unenforceable.

☐ 50.6 Is any agreement alleged in the pleadings ambiguous? If so, identify each ambiguous agreement and state why it is ambiguous.

EXHIBIT 4.16   Sample Written Interrogatories

STATE OF ILLINOIS)		IN THE FRANKLIN COUNTY
) SS.		CIRCUIT COURT
COUNTY OF FRANKLIN)		
		CAUSE NO.
DAVID M. KASHEN,)		
)		
Plaintiff,)		
)		
vs.)		
)		
INSURANCE COMPANY,)		
CLAIMS, and J. A.)		
)		
Defendants.)		
)		
_____)		

INTERROGATORIES

Comes now the Plaintiff, David M. Kashen, by Barbara Grasso, and pursuant to the Illinois Rules of Trial Procedure, propounds the following Interrogatories to be answered separately and fully, under oath, by each Defendant, on or before April _____, 1996. The Interrogatories which follow are to be deemed continuing, and you are requested to provide, by way of supplementary answers thereto, such additional information as you or any other person acting on your behalf may hereafter obtain which will augment or modify your answers now given to the Interrogatories below. Such supplementary responses are to be served upon the Plaintiff within thirty (30) days after receipt of such information.

All information is to be divulged which is in Defendants' possession or control, or within the possession and control of Defendants' attorneys, investigators, agents, employees or other representatives of Defendants.

INTERROGATORIES

1.   State the name, address, title, and duties of the person answering these interrogatories and the place where these interrogatories are answered.
ANSWER:

2.   State the name, address, and job title of each person who was contacted in answering these interrogatories or who provided information relevant to the answering of the interrogatories and the proper designation of each book, document, or record which was searched in answering interrogatories.
ANSWER:

3.   Are all Defendants' names correctly stated in the Complaint on file in this cause? If not, state the correct name of each party Defendant at the time of the conduct complained of in the Complaint and at the present time.
ANSWER:

EXHIBIT 4.16   Sample Written Interrogatories *Continued*

---

4.   State the general corporate history of each corporate Defendant from the date of incorporation to the present, including the date and place of incorporation, date first qualified to do business in Illinois and Wisconsin, whether or not you continuously carried on business in Illinois and Wisconsin since that date, and the specific or primary business engaged in by Defendant corporations.
ANSWER:

5.   Please state whether each corporation Defendant is a subsidiary, parent corporation or sister corporation to another corporation. If so, give complete details as to the other corporation's state of incorporation, address of its principal place of business in state or registered office, date of incorporation, and the specific or primary business engaged in by that corporation. Additionally, state whether the corporation is qualified to do business in Illinois, and whether it has continuously carried on business in Illinois since the date of qualification.
ANSWER:

6.   State the name and address of each person who acted as a director of each corporate Defendant, from the dates of incorporation to the date of these interrogatories. Please specify what period of time each director served.
ANSWER:

7.   State the full legal name, address, and job title of the employee of each corporate Defendant who is best qualified to testify as to the type of information relating to each corporate Defendants' insurance and/or adjusting business in Illinois and Wisconsin which is stored in each Defendants' computers, as well as to how easily said information may be retrieved. If you state that no employee in Wisconsin or Illinois is qualified to testify as to said information, please state the full legal name, address, and job title of the person or persons, wherever located, who is or are best qualified to testify as to such information.
ANSWER:

8.   Please state the following:
   a. The date each claim referred to in the Complaint herein was filed with Defendants;
   b. The date said claims became due and payable under the terms of said policy;
   c. The date said claims were acknowledged as being due and payable by Defendants;
   d. The date said claim or claims were actually paid;
   e. The inception and expiration dates of said policy purchased by Joan Kashen as referred to in the Complaint.
ANSWER:

EXHIBIT 4.16   Sample Written Interrogatories *Continued*

9.   State the name of each person who participated in the decision to pay or not pay the claims for benefits of Joan Kashen and Ann Kashen, arising out of the accident referred to in the Complaint.
ANSWER:

10. State the name, address, and job title at the time of issuance of the policy of the person who issued the policy to Joan Kashen. Also state the name, address, and job title of the person who authorized the insurance.
ANSWER:

11. Please state in detail on what grounds Plaintiff's claim for $25,000.00 was denied.
ANSWER:

12. If Defendants assert that Plaintiff's claim for compensation was not "denied," state in detail why Defendants did not pay Plaintiff's uninsured motorist claim commensurate with his injuries, and also state in detail why Defendants paid the uninsured claims of Joan Kashen and Ann Kashen rather than the Plaintiff's.
ANSWER:

13. If Defendant stated to Barbara Grasso, counsel for Joan Kashen, that D. would pay the Plaintiff $5,000.00 of uninsured motorist coverage and $25,000.00 of liability coverage of Joan Kashen's policy, which statements were untrue, please state in detail why such statements were made.
ANSWER:

14. State whether or not there have been, or are now, lawsuits pending against any and all Defendants herein or any agents of Defendants herein, claiming injury or damage due to breach of contract, breach of fiduciary duty, fraudulent, wanton or intentional misrepresentation, fraud in the inducement, unethical business practices, and any other negligent or wanton conduct involving the settlement of claims by Defendants. If so, for each such lawsuit state:
a. The date of the filing of each lawsuit.
b. The court in which such lawsuit was filed.
c. The action or court number of each such lawsuit.
d. The name and addresses of all parties, including plaintiff and defendant to each such lawsuit.
e. The jurisdiction in which each such action was filed.
f. The jurisdiction in which each such action came or will come to trial if different from answer in (e).
g. The disposition of each such lawsuit.
h. The name and address of each person or entity having possession, control, or custody of any and all records relating to such legal action against Defendants involving such a claim or sim-

EXHIBIT 4.16   Sample Written Interrogatories *Continued*

ilar claim.
ANSWER:

15. State whether Defendants or any agent of Defendants, employees, independent contractors or other representatives of Defendants had any knowledge whatsoever prior to the occasion made the basis of this suit, of any alleged, reckless, or intentional misrepresentation of the type or similar to the type made the basis of this lawsuit. If so, for each person or entity, state:
    a. The date on which such person or entity first had such knowledge.
    b. The substance and extent of such knowledge.
    c. The name and address of such person or entity.
    d. Whether any notes, correspondence, memorandum, or other documents created or helped to create such knowledge.
    e. Whether any notes, correspondence, memorandum, or other documents which were made by such person or entity reflect or depict such knowledge.
ANSWER:

16. Please attach a copy of each document referred to in the immediate preceding interrogatory.
17. State the name and address of each person or persons known by Defendants to have any knowledge whatsoever of matters pertinent to the occurrence made the basis of Plaintiff's Complaint.
ANSWER:

18. List each and every defense known to Defendants at this time which Defendants presently intend to assert.
ANSWER:

19. State whether or not any representative of Defendants has obtained a statement from any person or persons in connection with this matter which is the subject of Plaintiff's lawsuit, and the automobile accident which gave rise to Plaintiff's claim herein. If the answer is yes, state the following:
    a. The name and address of each individual from whom such a statement was taken.
    b. The date said statements were taken.
    c. The identity of the person or entity who has present possession of said statements.
ANSWER:

20. State whether any communications, notes, correspondence, memorandum, or other documents were ever made by Defendant or any agent of Defendants regarding the alleged misrepresentations made by Defendant, as set forth in Plaintiff's Complaint. If so, please attach a copy of each document or the contents of any such communication referred to in the immediately preceding interrogatory.
ANSWER:

EXHIBIT 4.16   Sample Written Interrogatories *Continued*

21. State whether any communications, notes, correspondence, memorandum, or other documents of any kind were made by Defendant regarding conversations between Defendant and Joan Kashen and conversations between Defendant and the Plaintiff. If so, please attach a copy of each document or the content of any such communication referred to in the immediately preceding interrogatory.
ANSWER:

22. Please state the substance of the facts and opinions to which each and every expert is expected to testify and set forth a summary of the grounds of each such opinion held by each and every said expert.
ANSWER:

23. Please state the conclusions or opinions of each and every expert witness you have retained, hired, or consulted in the preparation of the above-captioned case.
ANSWER:

24. Please state the names and addresses of each and every expert witness with whom Defendants have consulted in and about the handling and preparation of this case.
ANSWER:

25. Please set for the educational background of each and every expert witness that you expect to testify in the trial of this case with whom you have consulted in the preparation and handling of this case.
ANSWER:

_____

Barbara Grasso
Supreme Court #15624-79
1480 Penn Avenue
Chicago, Illinois
(500) 471-2601

EXHIBIT 4.16   Sample Written Interrogatories *Concluded*

CERTIFICATE OF SERVICE

. I hereby certify that a copy of the foregoing has been served upon Defendants by United States mail, first class, postage prepaid, this _____ day of April, 1995.

_____
Barbara Grasso

Barbara Grasso
Grasso & Deitz
1480 Penn Avenue
Chicago, Illinois

ATTORNEY FOR PLAINTIFF

the plaintiff undergo a physical or mental examination by the defendant's own doctor. This request is particularly common when the plaintiff's doctor is diagnosing injuries that are extreme or excessive. If the doctors' reports are substantially different, the court may order a third doctor to examine the plaintiff.

Investigations.   Throughout the course of the discovery process, both parties' attorneys will be conducting investigations. The attorney who is better prepared and more thorough will have an advantage in negotiating a settlement. You may assist in this process by conducting a thorough investigation of all of the facts of the case in addition to drafting the pleadings and cataloging and controlling documents. Be fastidious in looking at each and every fact and every piece of evidence in the case. Read medical records thoroughly. It is imperative that the attorney be kept apprised of all that you find.

For instance, if the plaintiff is claiming an injury to a certain part of the body, check the X-rays to be sure the injury is the same as the plaintiff claims. Recently, adverse parties, particularly in cases where extensive injuries are claimed, have been having plaintiffs videotaped without their knowledge as they go about their daily activities. In some cases, the evidence may prove that the plaintiff is not suffering from the injuries claimed.

Plaintiffs should be informed that they may be investigated by the adverse party. You should always report any discrepancies in the evidence to the attorney.

Observe the reactions of witnesses during interviews. Compare the statements of different witnesses to the same event to be sure that there are only slight discrepancies in their accounts of the incident.

Other Documents That May Be Needed

Subpoenas.   To force a party or witness to appear at a deposition or other proceeding, you may issue a **subpoena,** which is signed by the judge and orders the person to appear at the designated time and place. Since a subpoena is a court-issued ⌐ment, a person may be held in contempt of court for failure to appear and may ⌐ired to pay damages. In most states, the witness should be paid witness ⌐e subpoena must be served in person and proof of service filed ⌐is required to bring something to the proceeding, a ⌐request may include documents, letters, pay- ⌐bit 4.17 shows a subpoena duces tecum for ⌐paralegal or legal secretary would fill in the ⌐e exhibit correspond to the numbers in the

⌐se includes the name of the court and the ⌐index number (or case number), and the ⌐w York also requires a calendar number, ⌐l states.

⌐e party whose deposition is being taken

⌐paralegal or legal secretary fills in the loca- ⌐ion. The form in Exhibit 4.17 indicates that ⌐court of law with a judge present. In most

EXHIBIT 4.17   A Subpoena Duces Tecum from New York

Blumbergs Law Products   B 69—Subpoena duces tecum, blank court, with witness' stipulation to remain subject to attorney's call, 9-91

© 1973 BY JULIUS BLUMBERG, INC., PUBLISHER, NYC 10013

COURT SUPERIOR COURT

COUNTY OF RICHMOND

Index No. 12345

①   MARIA ANN ALTERIO

                                                Plaintiff

                against

    JOSEPH PAUL MARINO   *Defendant*

Calendar No.

JUDICIAL SUBPOENA

DUCES TECUM

𝔗𝔥𝔢 𝔓𝔢𝔬𝔭𝔩𝔢 𝔬𝔣 𝔱𝔥𝔢 𝔖𝔱𝔞𝔱𝔢 𝔬𝔣 𝔑𝔢𝔴 𝔜𝔬𝔯𝔨

②   *TO*   ROBERTO CARRILLO

                                                            GREETING:

      WE COMMAND YOU, *That all business and excuses being laid aside, you and each of you appear and attend before* JUDGE ROBERT HAYWORTH

at   Dept. 5

③   *on the* 2nd   *day of* May   *19* 96 *at* 10   *o'clock, in the*   morning *noon,*

and at any recessed or adjourned date to give testimony in this action on the part of the

                              Plaintiff

and that you bring with you, and produce at the time and place aforesaid, a certain

④   Payroll records for JOSEPH PAUL MARINO from the period May 1, 1995 to December 1, 1995

now in your custody, and all other deeds, evidences and writings, which you have in your custody or power, concerning the premises.

      Failure to comply with this subpoena is punishable as a contempt of Court and shall make you liable to the person on whose behalf this subpoena was issued for a penalty not to exceed fifty dollars and all damages sustained by reason of your failure to comply.

      WITNESS, *Honorable*   *one of the*

of said Court, at   *the*   *day of*   *19*

⑤   Melissa Chan

    Attorney(s) for   Plaintiff

Office and Post Office Address

1122 West Street

Staten Island, New York

EXHIBIT 4.17   A Subpoena Duces Tecum from New York *Concluded*

AFFIDAVIT OF SERVICE

STATE OF NEW YORK, COUNTY OF   **SS:**   The undersigned, being duly sworn, deposes and says; deponent

is not a party herein, is over 18 years of age and resides at

That on   19   at   M., at

deponent served the within subpoena on   defendant therein named,

INDIVIDUAL
1. ☐   by delivering a true copy to said witness personally; deponent knew the person so served to be the person described as said witness therein.

CORPORATION
2. ☐   a   corporation, by delivering thereat a true copy to
personally, deponent knew said corporation so served to be the corporation described in said subpoena and knew said individual to be   thereof.

SUITABLE AGE PERSON
3. ☐   by delivering thereat a true copy to   a person of suitable age and discretion. Said premises is witness'—actual place of business—dwelling place—usual place of abode—within the state.

AFFIXING TO DOOR, ETC.
4. ☐   by affixing a true copy to the door of said premises, which is witness'—actual place of business—dwelling place—usual place of abode—within the state. Deponent was unable, with due diligence to find witness or a person of suitable age and discretion thereat, having called there

MAILING TO RESIDENCE USE WITH 3 OR 4
5A. ☐   Within 20 days of such delivery or affixing, deponent enclosed a copy of same in a postpaid envelope properly addressed to witness at witness' last known residence, at
and deposited said envelope in an official depository under the exclusive care and custody of the U.S. Postal Service within New York State.

MAILING TO BUSINESS USE WITH 3 OR 4
5B. ☐   Within 20 days of such delivery or affixing, deponent enclosed a copy of same in a first class postpaid envelope properly addressed to witness at witness' actual place of business, at
in an official depository under the exclusive care and custody of the U.S. Postal Service within New York State. The envelope bore the legend "Personal and Confidential" and did not indicate on the outside thereof, by return address or otherwise, that the communication was from an attorney or concerned an action against the witness.

DESCRIPTION USE WITH 1, 2, or 3
☐

☐ Male	☐ White Skin	☐ Black Hair	☐ White Hair	☐ 14-20 Yrs.	☐ Under 5'	☐ Under 100 Lbs.
☐ Female	☐ Black Skin	☐ Brown Hair	☐ Balding	☐ 21-35 Yrs.	☐ 5'0"-5'3"	☐ 100-130 Lbs.
	☐ Yellow Skin	☐ Blonde Hair	☐ Mustache	☐ 36-50 Yrs.	☐ 5'4"-5'8"	☐ 131-160 Lbs.
	☐ Brown Skin	☐ Gray Hair	☐ Beard	☐ 51-65 Yrs.	☐ 5'9"-6'0"	☐ 161-200 Lbs.
	☐ Red Skin	☐ Red Hair	☐ Glasses	☐ Over 65 Yrs.	☐ Over 6'	☐ Over 200 Lbs.

Other identifying features:

At the time of said service, deponent paid (tendered) in advance $ the authorized traveling expenses and one day's witness fee.

Sworn to before me on   19

....
Print name beneath signature

LICENSE NO. ....

Index No.   **COURT**
COUNTY OF

Plaintiff

against

Defendant

Judicial Subpoena
DUCES TECUM

Office; Post Office Address; Telephone No.

Attorney(s) for

It is stipulated that the undersigned witness is excused from attending at the time herein provided or at any adjourned date but agrees to remain subject to, and attend upon, the call of the undersigned attorney.
Dated:

Witness

Attorney(s) for

cases, however, the deposition is taken in a law office with both attorneys present.

4. *What the Witness Must Bring.*   Since this is a subpoena duces tecum, the witness is required to bring certain items with him. In Exhibit 4.17, payroll records are being requested.

5. *Attorney's Name and Address.*   This section contains the name, address, and signature of the attorney who is requesting the material.

Motions.   Motions may be filed for a number of reasons throughout the lawsuit. Whenever an attorney wishes to have the judge rule on an issue, a motion will be filed. The motion is prepared on legal cap and includes points and authorities in support of the request. A copy is served on the adverse party's counsel of record. A hearing is held where the attorneys present their arguments in support of and against the motion. The court issues an order stating whether the motion is granted or denied.

In some situations, as in motions for restraining orders for domestic violence, immediate results must be obtained. In those cases, only one party may be present at the hearing because of the immediacy of the situation or because the party is physically afraid to have the adverse party served. Any motion made where the hearing is attended by only one side is known as an "ex parte motion" (ex parte means "one side only").

The following are examples of some common motions:

1. Motion for Change of Venue

2. Motion for Extension of Time

3. Motion for Dismissal

4. Motion to Compel Answers to Discovery

Stipulations.   **Stipulations** are agreements that are made between the attorneys but are binding on the parties to the action. A stipulation may be in the form of a written document or may be made in open court. The most common stipulations relate to extensions of time or amending pleadings. A sample Stipulation for Extension of Time is shown in Exhibit 4.18.

stipulation
An agreement made between attorneys that is binding on the parties.

SETTLING THE CASE

Both attorneys will be discussing the case during the course of the investigation and discovery phase. The better the investigation you conduct, the better prepared the attorney will be to obtain a favorable settlement for the client. If you are working for the defense attorney and conduct a thorough investigation, the client may not have to pay as large a settlement as was originally demanded.

Usually, the attorneys conduct settlement negotiations. Sometimes, however, paralegals assist in this phase, particularly when the paralegal has conducted most of the investigation and has prepared and studied the documents carefully. Most cases are settled at this point, and the lawsuit ends.

If the case reaches a final settlement, it will be dismissed "with prejudice," meaning that the plaintiff may not file a suit in the same action at a later date. If the case is dismissed "without prejudice," the plaintiff may file the suit again later within the statute of limitations.

EXHIBIT 4.18   A Sample Stipulation for Extension of Time

1	Jeffrey M. Williams
2	Michaels & Williams
	1122 Main Street
3	Your Town, Your State
	Telephone: (555) 111-2222
4	
	Attorneys for Defendant
5	
6	
7	SUPERIOR COURT OF THE COUNTY OF YOURS
	STATE OF YOURS
8	
9	STEVEN P. STANDMAN) CASE NO. XXY111
10	Plaintiff)
11	)
12	v.) STIPULATION
13	JUDITH ANN ALTER)
14	Defendant)
15	_____)
16	Attorneys for Plaintiff and Defendant hereby stipulate to an extension of time
17	for Defendant to plead to the Complaint in the above-entitled action to an additional
18	fifteen (15) days, with the due date extended to October 20, 1996.
19	
20	
21	Dated:_____ JEFFREY M. WILLIAMS
22	Attorney for Defendant
23	Dated:_____ MICHAEL G. EVENS
24	233 Marshall Parkway
	Your Town, Your State
25	
26	Attorney for Plaintiff
27	
28	

Settlement Conference

In some states, a mandatory settlement conference (or pretrial conference) is held with the judge and the attorneys prior to the trial. At that time, the judge attempts to have the parties settle any disputed facts or issues so that they will not have to be litigated at trial. In many cases, the lawsuit is settled during the settlement conference.

In other states, the settlement conference is not mandatory. The parties must agree to the conference, which is attended by both attorneys and the judge.

If no settlement can be reached after all of the discovery and settlement conferences have been held, the matter will be set for trial. Trial procedures will be discussed in Chapter 7.

Arbitration

Another way of settling a dispute is to submit the case to **arbitration** where a disinterested third party (the arbitrator) hears the evidence and issues a decision based on the merits of the case. Both parties must agree to the choice of arbitrator. In some states, arbitrators are retired judges or attorneys. The arbitration proceeding itself is similar to a settlement conference.

If the case is submitted to **binding arbitration,** the arbitrator's decision is final. If the parties agree only to nonbinding arbitration, however, then either party may appeal the arbitrator's decision to the courts. Although the rules vary among the states, it is unusual to have binding arbitration because our system of government allows all individuals to have their "day in court." If the parties have agreed to **mandatory arbitration** prior to the institution of the lawsuit, they must try to resolve their dispute through the arbitration process before they will be granted a trial date. If no prior agreement on mandatory arbitration has been reached, the parties may agree to **voluntary arbitration.** Some states have both **private arbitration,** which is administered by a private organization, and **court arbitration,** which is governed by local court rules. Ascertain the rules for your own state and write them in the State Specific Information box.

arbitration
The settlement of a case by a disinterested third party; may be binding or not depending on the parties' agreement.

binding arbitration
Arbitration in which the arbitrator's decision is final and cannot be appealed to the courts.

mandatory arbitration
Arbitration that is compulsory under a prior agreement of the parties.

voluntary arbitration
arbitration that the parties accept without compulsion (e.g., no prior agreement requiring mandatory arbitration).

private arbitration
Arbitration that is administered by a private organization.

court arbitration
Arbitration that is governed by local court rules.

Arbitration procedures in the state of _____ are as follows:

_____

_____

STATE SPECIFIC INFORMATION

ROLE OF THE PARALEGAL

Paralegals are valuable members of the litigation team. Generally, they are required to perform numerous tasks beginning with the client's initial visit to the law firm. The following list presents the paralegal's responsibilities in the civil law practice in chronological order:

1. ***Initial Client Interview.*** Gather all the facts from the client at the initial interview. Get releases from the client for any confidential information required. Discuss procedures with the client while being careful not to give any legal advice. Write a letter after the interview confirming additional items the client must send or bring into the office.

2. ***Memorandum to Attorney.***   Prepare a memorandum of facts gathered at the interview for the attorney. Evaluate the client's veracity, appearance, and credibility. Meet with the attorney to determine the next step.

3. ***Investigation.***   Some firms hire private investigators to conduct the factual investigation of the case; in other firms paralegals perform this function. Some duties and responsibilities during the fact-gathering phase might include getting a copy of the police report, obtaining medical records, returning to the scene of the incident to find witnesses, interviewing prospective witnesses, and preparing written memoranda for the attorney.

4. ***Formal Discovery.***   Unlike the investigation phase of the case, all items gathered during the formal discovery phase are discoverable by the adverse party. The paralegal may be engaged in the following tasks: gathering evidence, obtaining formal witness statements, preparing written interrogatories, assisting clients in answering interrogatories propounded to them, summarizing interrogatory answers for the attorney, summarizing depositions for the attorney, and preparing other formal discovery documents. Paralegals may also be involved in cataloging all of the pleadings and documents on both sides of the case.

5. ***Settlement Negotiations.***   Some law firms allow paralegals to negotiate settlements for clients with insurance companies. In other firms, the attorney conducts the negotiations. The paralegal gathers all of the client's bills together, presents the total to the attorney, and summarizes any additional information required for the negotiations. Paralegals may be asked to prepare settlement documents.

6. ***Pretrial Activities.***   Paralegals prepare all materials to include in the Trial Book, discussed in Chapter 7. All documents, witness statements, depositions, and pleadings necessary for the trial are catalogued and placed in the Trial Book.

ROLE OF THE LEGAL SECRETARY

Legal secretaries employed in civil law are very busy and often work long hours. Since deadlines are crucial in this field of law, the legal secretary must be very well organized and keep an up-to-date and accurate calendar. The legal secretary is a very important part of the litigation team and generally has a considerable amount of responsibility. The following are the main duties of the legal secretary:

1. ***Initial Interview.***   The legal secretary makes the appointment with the client and writes a confirming letter stating the date and time agreed upon. When the client arrives for the interview, the legal secretary greets the client and perhaps offers a cup of coffee or tea. If the paralegal or attorney is delayed, the legal secretary may engage the client in conversation to make the time pass more quickly. Some attorneys ask legal secretaries to gather preliminary information from the client.

     The legal secretary prepares the client file in the manner prescribed by the particular firm. Some firms put the pleadings on the left side of the folder and the correspondence on the right. A summary sheet of documents in the file is prepared and attached to the file. Some firms require that an action sheet be put on the front of the folder with any actions taken on the case noted, such as interviews and meetings. If in doubt as to how the file should be organized, look at an earlier file in the firm's records.

After the interview, the legal secretary may draft a form letter to be signed by the attorney thanking the client for hiring the law firm. Other letters may be written requesting medical records, police reports, or other required records. Again, if in doubt about the format for the letter, look at letters in the firm's files. If any of these letters are prepared in many cases, prepare a form letter on the computer and modify it for each individual client.

2. ***Memorandum to Attorney.***   The paralegal may write a memorandum summarizing the initial client interview and ask the legal secretary to type it. Be sure to check the spelling of the client's name and other pertinent information from the interview form. Usually, the client file is prepared at this point in the manner discussed above.

3. ***Investigation.***   Although the attorney or paralegal usually conducts the actual case investigation, the legal secretary may be asked to prepare various witness statements and documents. The legal secretary will set up appointments with witnesses and confirm the meeting in a letter. The secretary will begin to gather material for the file and make sure all deadlines are met. If witnesses are traveling from another city or state, travel arrangements must be made. A determination must be made as to whether the law firm will pay the witness's expenses and the manner in which this will be accomplished. Often the law firm will already have established a relationship with a travel agency, which will complete this task. Sometimes the legal secretary may have to pick the witnesses up at the airport.

4. ***Discovery.***   This phase of the lawsuit may be the most challenging and time-consuming for the legal secretary. All documents must be carefully catalogued and due dates noted on the calendar. The secretary must ensure that all documents are prepared in a timely fashion. Keeping track of all discovery tools prepared by both sides of the lawsuit is imperative. Case numbers, citations, and all materials must be proofread carefully.

5. ***Settlement and Pretrial Activities.***   Although the secretary may not be involved in the actual settlement negotiations, the secretary must set up all meetings and interviews during this time. Often many individuals must be contacted to determine the best time and date for all to meet. Coordination of activities during this period is critical. The secretary may also be asked to summarize the client's expenses for the attorney to utilize during the actual negotiations. Settlement documents must be prepared, and pretrial conferences with the court must be scheduled.

Table 4.1 summarizes the duties and responsibilities of the paralegal and legal secretary in the civil litigation practice. As can readily be seen, their duties often overlap depending on the size of the law office. Additionally, paralegals and legal secretaries often work as teams to assist the attorney in the litigation process.

SUMMARY

Lawsuits are filed by individuals or entities against other individuals or entities. This chapter has taken the student through a civil lawsuit from the initial interview of the client to the pretrial stage. Most suits involve torts, or civil wrongs, committed by the

TABLE 4.1   Duties and Responsibilities of the Paralegal and the Legal Secretary

PARALEGAL DUTIES	LEGAL SECRETARY DUTIES
Initial client interview	Initial client interview
Gather facts	Make appointments
Discuss procedures	Gather facts
Write letters	Write letters
Prepare interview report	Type interview report
	Prepare client file
Investigation	Investigation
Gather facts	Gather facts
Obtain records and information	Obtain records and information
Find and interview witnesses	Prepare witness reports
	Make witness appointments
	Gather file material
Formal discovery	Formal discovery
Catalog documents	Catalog documents
Gather evidence	Prepare witness statements
Obtain witness statements	Draft interrogatories
Draft interrogatories	Assist in deposition summaries
Summarize depositions	Set up client meetings
Assist client in answering interrogatories	Draft answers
Settlement and pretrial	Settlement and pretrial
Assist in negotiations	Arrange negotiations meetings
Gather client's bills	Gather client's bills
Summarize materials	Coordinate activities
Summarize client's expenses	Summarize client's expenses
Prepare settlement documents	Prepare settlement documents
	Schedule pretrial conferences

defendant against the plaintiff. Negligence and products liability are important concepts in torts law.

Paralegals assist the attorney in conducting the preliminary investigation by interviewing the client and witnesses. After these interviews, the attorney determines whether or not a formal lawsuit should be filed. If a lawsuit is filed, a complaint and summons must be filed with the court and served on the defendant. Formal discovery is conducted by both sides, utilizing written interrogatories, depositions, requests for admission, and requests for production. Settlement negotiations with insurance companies are utilized to negotiate a fair settlement for the client without having to go to trial. In some cases, however, the two sides cannot reach an agreement, and the case goes to trial. Legal secretaries play an important role in the litigation process and perform many tasks.

KEY TERMS

Affirmative defense 87	Motion for Summary Judgment 88
Answer 83	Motion to Strike 87
Arbitration 115	Negligence 61–62
Binding arbitration 115	Plaintiff 61–62
Breach 62	Pleading 70
Causation 62	Prayer for damages 72
Comparative negligence 70	Private arbitration 115
Complaint 72	Request to enter default 83
Contributory negligence 70	Retainer agreement 63
Court arbitration 115	Stipulation 113
Damages 62	Strict liability 62
Default judgment 83	Subpoena 110
Defendant 61–62	Subpoena duces tecum 110
Demurrer 87	Summons 76
Deponent 88	Tort 61–62
Deposition 88	Tortfeasor 61–62
Discovery 88	Transcript 88
Duty 62	Verification 76
Legal cap 72	Voluntary arbitration 115
Mandatory arbitration 115	Written interrogatories 93

SELF-TEST

A.   Match the following terms with their definitions:

_____ 1. Plaintiff   a. First pleading filed in a lawsuit

_____ 2. Defendant   b. Litigation

_____ 3. Lawsuit   c. Individual instituting a lawsuit

_____ 4. Tort   d. Civil wrong or injury

_____ 5. Complaint   e. Person or entity being sued

B.   Indicate whether the following statements are true (T) or false (F):

_____ 1. The most common type of tort action is defamation.

_____ 2. The defendant responds to the plaintiff's complaint with a deposition.

_____ 3. The deposition may be used for parties and witnesses.

_____ 4. During the client interview, legal advice is given freely by the paralegal or legal secretary.

C.   Fill in the blanks:

1. Written questions sent by one party to the other party in a lawsuit are called

   _____.

2. If the questions in (1) are sent to the defendant, answers must usually be provided to the plaintiff in _____ days.

3. The lawsuit is commenced by the filing of a _____.

4. The most common response to the defendant is called a(n)

   _____.

5. If a party wishes the other party to provide documents during the discovery

   process, the proper document to prepare is the _____.

REVIEW QUESTIONS

1. List the different parts of the complaint.

2. Describe each part of the complaint you listed in Question 1 and explain its purpose.

3. List the various discovery documents and tools available to each party in a lawsuit.

4. Describe each of the discovery documents you listed in Question 3.

5. Which discovery documents may be used on witnesses, and which are used only for parties to the action?

PROJECTS

1.   Proofread the draft of a complaint in Exhibit 4.19. The complaint may include errors in spelling, sentence structure, or format. Then correct the errors and retype the complaint.

2.   Make a caption for a complaint in your state for a personal injury action by John Sanchez against Kevan Feeley for personal injuries of $50,000.

3. 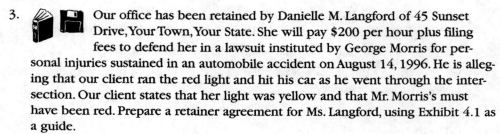 Our office has been retained by Danielle M. Langford of 45 Sunset Drive, Your Town, Your State. She will pay $200 per hour plus filing fees to defend her in a lawsuit instituted by George Morris for personal injuries sustained in an automobile accident on August 14, 1996. He is alleging that our client ran the red light and hit his car as he went through the intersection. Our client states that her light was yellow and that Mr. Morris's must have been red. Prepare a retainer agreement for Ms. Langford, using Exhibit 4.1 as a guide.

EXHIBIT 4.19   Sample Complaint for Project 1

Caption: Superior Court—Los Angeles County, Frederick Allen and Rose Alan v. Oliver Hall.

Plaintiffs by their attorney, Jeffrey Wiliams, file this Complaint and complaining of the defendant above named allege as follows:

I   The plaintiffs at all times herein mentioned were and are residents of that portion of the City of Los Angeles, County of Los Angeles, State of California.

II   That plaintiffs are informed and believe and on such information an belief allege that defendant is a resident of the City of Las Angels, County of Las Angeles, State of California.

III   Plaintiffs are informed and blieve and on such information and belief allege that all times herein mentioned defendant, Olivier Hale was owner of a certain 1989 Doge Coranet automobile, 1989 California license #643 BBB.

IV   At all times herein mentioned 19th Street and Barrett Street were and are intersecting public streets in the City of Los Angeles, County of Los Angeles, State of California, and running in a north-south direction and an east-west direction, respectively.

VI   On July 14, 1995, at or about the hour of 2:00 p.m. plaintiff, Frederick Allen was operating said 1983 Ford Mustang automobile along and on said Barrett Street in a general westerly direction at the intersection of 10th and Barrett Street

VII   At said time and place defendant so negligently, carelessly, recklessly and unlawfully drove and operated his said 1989 Dodge Coronet automobile along on said Barrett Street in a general westerly direct so as to proximately cause the injuries and damages hereinafter described.

VIII   As a direct and proximate result of the negligence, carelessness, and unlawfulness of defendant and the resulting collision, are herein alleged, plaintiff Rose Allen received and sustained great bodily injury and became, and still continues to be, sick, sore, lame and disabled, and sustained serious personal and badily injuries and wound consisting of, among other things, but not limited to, severe injuries, bruises, contusions and strain to all the muscles of her body and particularly of the shoulders, arms, neck, back, chest and legs' lacerations, breaking, rupsure and other injuries to the

EXHIBIT 4.19   Sample Complaint for Project 1 *Continued*

muscles, tendons, and ligaments of, and bruises, contusions and injeries to and upon, her face arms,

shoulder, trunk, back, spine, hips, legs, feet and body' severe shock to her whole body, head, lims,

spine and nervous system; injury to her kidneys, heart, lungs an other inturnal organs and portions of

her body; as well as other injuries both external and internal, and to many different portions of her

body, many of which are of so severe and serious a nature that they probably will, and a reasonable

certain to be, permanent, and by reason of which plaintiff became, ever since has been, and will be,

permanently sick, sore, lame and disableed, all to her damage in the sum of $125,000.00

IX   As a further direct and praximate result of the negligense of defendent, as herein alleged,

plaintiffs were required to and did employ physicians and surgeons for meducal examination, treat-

ment and care of said injuries, and did incur medical and incidental expenses, among other, in the fol-

lowing amounts to date:

(1)	Services of physicians and surgeons	$8,350.00
(2)	Hospital services	10,312.50
(3)	X-rays	865.00
(4)	Inhalation therapy	3,096.50
(5)	Ambulance	25.00
(6)	Drugs and medicenes	1,380.00

Total to date 24,029.00

24014.00

PLaintiffs are informed and blieve and on such information and belief allege that by reason

of said negligence of defendant plaintiffs have incurred other and will incur further medical and inci-

dental expenses for the care and treatment of said injuries, the exact amount of which is for the care

and treatment of said injuries, the exact amount of which is unknown at the present time. Plaintiffs

EXHIBIT 4.19   Sample Complaint for Project 1 *Concluded*

will ask leave to amend this complaint to set forth the exact amount thereof when fully and finally ascertained.

X   Immediately prior to and at the time of said collision plaintiff's 1973 Ford Mustang automobile was in good mechanical condition. As further direct and proximate result of defendant's negligence, as herein alleged, plaintiffs' said automobile was damaged and depreciated to the extent of $2,000, which sum is a reasonable amount for the necessary repairs to said automobile.

XI   As a further direct and proximate result of the negligence of defendant, as herein alleged, plaintiffs have lost the use of their 1973 Ford Mustng automobile for a period of 20 days, to their damage in the sum of $237.

WHEREFORE, plaintiffs pray for judgment against the defendant for:

(1)   General damages in the sume of $125,000

(2)   All medical and incidental expenses according to proof

(3)   All loss of use of plaintiffs' automobile in the sum of $2370.00

(4)   Repairs to plaintiffs' automobile in the sum of $2,000

(5)   Such other and further relief as to this Court may seem proper

_____

Jeffrey Williams

Attorney for the Plaintiffs

4. Our office has been retained by Michael W. Daniels, 225 Sky Lane, Your Town, Your State, in his case against Jonathan Alters. Prepare a retainer agreement for Mr. Daniels, using Exhibit 4.1 as a guide. The payment terms are as follows: 30 percent contingency fee arrangement; the client will also pay for filing fees for documents to be filed with the court. If the case goes to trial, the contingency fee is 40 percent for any time the attorney spends at trial.

5. Using the format for your state, prepare a complaint in the following action. If you do not have access to the forms of your state, use Exhibit 4.4 as a guide.

     Joseph Pacheco is suing Daniel Murray for injuries sustained in an automobile accident on March 6, 1996, at the corner of Broad and Division Streets in Your Town. Mr. Pacheco was stopped at a red light in his 1987 Audi 500CS (license VVV 123), when Mr. Murray failed to stop and his 1993 Ferrari coupe (license XXX 222) hit the rear of Mr. Pacheco's car. The plaintiff requests $10,000 for damage to his car and $20,000 for personal injuries.

6. Prepare Mr. Murray's answer to the complaint you drafted in Project 5 in the form of a general denial. Use the format for your state, or use Exhibit 4.9 as a guide.

7. Using the forms for your state, prepare a summons, proof of service, and request to enter default for the lawsuit described in Project 5.

8. Attorney Williams has asked you to draft questions to ask the plaintiff in the scenario described in Project 3 for possible inclusion in a set of written interrogatories. Draft what you consider to be the ten most relevant questions to ask George Morris.

9. Our firm's client is Jonathan Livingston of 486 Wilderness Lane, Your Town, Your State. Mr. Livingston is suing the defendant and relates the following information: He was driving south on the 605 freeway on the morning of March 6, 1996. At 8:00 A.M. as he was approaching Firestone Boulevard, the cars in front of him stopped; he also stopped. The car behind him hit the rear of his car. The car was driven by Robert L. Harmon, who the client had observed drinking a can of beer while driving. The plaintiff (our client) was driving a black 1987 Honda CRX; the defendant was driving a red Toyota pickup truck. The plaintiff was not able to exit his vehicle because the door was jammed. Paramedics were called, and the client lost consciousness and woke up in the hospital. He got the name and address of the defendant from a witness at the scene. The defendant's address is 245 Newton Street, Your Town, Your State. The client did not get the witness's name and doesn't know if a police report was taken. The plaintiff sustained a broken leg, three broken ribs, a fractured skull, herniated disks in his back, and numerous facial injuries for which plastic surgery will be required. There were no passengers in either car. Up to the present, the plaintiff has medical bills of $65,000; damage to his automobile is $7,500. The case number is 12345.

     Prepare the appropriate form interrogatories using the forms for your state. If you do not have access to the forms for your state, use the California form interrogatories in Exhibit 4.15. If you feel additional questions should be asked of the defendant that are not covered in the form, then write them up. Follow the instructions on the form.

10.   Our firm's client, Jessica Hull, was injured in an automobile accident that occurred on the corner of Lampson Avenue and Seal Beach Boulevard in Your Town on September 6, 1994. Our client was driving north on Seal Beach Boulevard when the defendant, Linda Jorgensen, was driving west on Lampson Avenue and ran a red light, colliding with our client's automobile. The accident occurred at 11:00 P.M. The weather was clear. Our client was severely injured; her damages so far amount to $100,000.

Assume that the case will be heard in the closest superior court in your county. Jessica Hull's address is 505 Foxglove Drive, Your Town, Your State; Linda Jorgensen's address is 333 Lynley Court, Your Town, Your State. The case number is C-12398.

Draft written interrogatories to the defendant, Linda Jorgensen, using the format for your state. If you do not have access to the form for your state's interrogatories, use the written interrogatories in Exhibit 4.16 as a guide.

In addition to writing the written interrogatories, write a memorandum to Attorney Williams indicating how you will proceed with a further investigation of this case. Bear in mind that the only facts you have are those indicated above, and this is the first set of written interrogatories being prepared in the case.

Criminal Law

CHAPTER OBJECTIVES

As a result of studying this chapter, you will learn the following material:

1. ***Crimes and Criminal Law***   The differences between civil law and criminal law will be presented. You will also learn what felonies, misdemeanors, and infractions are.

2. ***Elements and Categories of Crimes***   The elements and basic categories of crimes will be introduced. You will learn the characteristics of crimes against the person, crimes against the public, and crimes against property.

3. ***Definitions of Crimes***   The most common crimes will be defined. You will become familiar with crimes in each of the basic categories.

4. ***Criminal Procedures***   The basic procedures from arrest through trial and sentencing will be presented. You will learn how to prepare a subpoena and a Motion to Suppress Evidence, as well as the other responsibilities of a paralegal working for both the prosecution and the defense.

CRIMINAL AND CIVIL LAW

Thus far we have discussed civil law, which deals with the rights and responsibilities of individuals. As we have seen, in a civil lawsuit, a private individual or entity brings a suit against another individual or entity; private attorneys represent both the plaintiff and the defendant. In contrast, criminal law deals with wrongful acts against society. In a criminal action, the plaintiff is the state or society as a whole, not the individual victim of the criminal act. Criminal offenders are prosecuted by attorneys who represent the government of the prosecuting state. Private attorneys or public defenders represent the defendant.

ELEMENTS AND CATEGORIES OF CRIMES

The states and the federal government pass criminal laws to punish individuals who commit acts that are objectionable in a civilized society. When individuals are found guilty of crimes, they may be sent to prison to deter them from committing further crimes and to set an example in the hope that others will also be deterred from committing crimes. Sometimes, prisons attempt to rehabilitate the inmates as well as incarcerate them by providing educational facilities and work opportunities. In this section, we will examine the nature of the criminal acts for which people may be sent to prison and will also discuss the various categories of crime.

Criminal Acts and Their Elements

felony
A serious crime punishable by incarceration in a state prison for more than one year.

Criminal acts can be divided into felonies and misdemeanors based on how serious they are. A **felony** is a serious crime that exposes the defendant to imprisonment for more than one year. Most persons convicted of felonies are incarcerated in state prisons, but some offenses such as drug trafficking violate federal laws and can lead to incarceration in federal prison. Murder, manslaughter, kidnapping, robbery, arson, rape, and burglary are all felonies. A **misdemeanor** is a less serious crime that is punishable by incarceration in the county jail for up to one year. Petty theft, drunk driving, malicious mischief, and simple assault are examples of misdemeanors.

misdemeanor
A minor crime punishable by incarceration in a county jail.

Most crimes have two elements—the criminal intent and the committing of the criminal act. For instance, you may have the desire to kill someone, but if you never commit the act, there is no murder. On the other hand, if you kill someone accidentally and do not have the intent to kill, as in an automobile accident, no murder has been committed. In some crimes, such as the rape of a minor **(statutory rape),** simply carrying out the act implies intent. Other crimes that do not require specific intent include strict liability crimes.

statutory rape
The rape of a minor.

infraction
A minor offense, such as a traffic violation, that is punishable by fine.

Not all offenses are crimes. An **infraction** is an offense that does not constitute a crime and is punishable by a fine. Many traffic violations are infractions. For instance, if you park your car in a "no parking" zone, you may get a ticket and pay a fine, but you will not go to jail unless you fail to pay the fines to the point that a warrant is issued for your arrest.

Categories of Crime

Based on the person or entity at which they are directed, crimes can be categorized as crimes against the person, crimes against the public, or crimes against property.

homicide
The unlawful killing of another without justification.

Crimes against the Person.   Crimes that are directed against an individual are known as crimes against the person. They include the following:

Felony Murder Rule
A doctrine that holds that if a death occurs during the commission of a serious felony, all defendants who were involved may be convicted of first-degree murder, regardless of which defendant actually caused the death.

1. *Homicide.*   **Homicide** is the unlawful killing of another without justification. It can be broken down further into first-degree murder, second-degree murder, and manslaughter. First-degree murder is an intentional killing or a death under the **Felony Murder Rule** doctrine. Under this rule, if a death occurs during the commission of a serious felony, all defendants involved in the felony may be found guilty of first-degree murder, regardless of which of them caused the death. Premeditated murder, poisoning, and murder by torture are also examples of first-degree murder. Second-degree murder includes any intentional killing not classified as first-degree murder. Manslaughter generally involves killing someone without actual criminal intent, such as during a fight or during the "heat of passion."

Special Circumstances Rule
A rule that holds that if a victim dies during the commission of a serious felony, as specified by statute, the defendant may receive the death penalty if he committed the felony, if he aided or abetted its commission with the intent to kill, or if he aided or abetted with reckless indifference to human life and was a major participant in the crime.

Many states have adopted the Felony Murder Rule, but differ on the enumerated felonies; most include kidnapping, torture, and robbery, however. Some states have also adopted a **Special Circumstances Rule** for capital punishment (the death penalty). Under this rule, if the victim died during the commission of a kidnapping, torture, or other felonies enumerated in the state's statutes, the defendant may receive capital punishment if he committed the crime in question, if he **aided and abetted** with the intent to kill, or if he aided and abetted with reckless indifference to human life and was a major participant in the crime. In other words, if three individuals kidnap a person who subsequently dies, all three defendants may be charged with Felony Murder with Special Circumstances and receive the death penalty. These rules vary considerably by state, and you should check your state's laws to learn whether it has a Felony Murder Rule and whether it imposes capital punishment under a Special Circumstances Rule. Record your findings in the State Specific Information box.

aiding and abetting
Assisting someone in committing a crime; knowledge of unlawful purpose with intent to commit, encourage, or facilitate commission of the crime by act or advice.

STATE SPECIFIC INFORMATION

The state of _____ has the following rules for murder:

- Murder is defined in the statutes as follows: _____
  _____
  _____
  _____

- Felony Murder Rule: _____
  _____
  _____

- Special Circumstances: _____
  _____
  _____
  _____

- Capital Punishment: _____
  _____
  _____
  _____

---

2. ***Mayhem.***   Most states define **mayhem** as the permanent disfigurement of another; it includes the loss of a limb, eye, or other part of the body. The act must be purposeful and not accidental.

3. ***Rape.***   In most states, a forcible sexual attack on a female by a male constitutes **rape.** Some states have expanded this definition to include unnatural sex acts on men as well as women. Rape can be further defined as sexual intercourse with a person without consent. Most state laws consider any sexual activity with a minor to be statutory rape, even if the minor consented to

mayhem
The purposeful and permanent disfigurement of another.

rape
A forcible sexual attack; sexual intercourse without consent.

the act. Under earlier laws, a man could not be guilty of raping his wife, but modern law has overruled this holding in most states, so that today a man may be found guilty of raping his wife.

All states have instituted laws against child molestation. Sexual activity with children is forbidden, even if no rape is involved.

assault
Attempted battery.

battery
Harmful or offensive touching of another without consent.

4. *Assault and Battery.*　In the criminal sense, an **assault** is an attempted battery. Once the battery is successful, then the perpetrator may be charged with both. **Battery** is the harmful or offensive touching of another. Most states consider battery with a weapon to be a more serious crime than battery without a weapon. In addition, if an individual is deliberately attacked with a weapon by another but not killed, the crime may escalate to attempted murder. A defendant who attempts a battery but does not succeed may be charged with assault. In some states, once the battery is completed, the assault merges into the battery, and the defendant is charged only with battery.

kidnapping
The transportation of an individual from one place to another against his will.

5. *Kidnapping.*　The transportation of an individual from one place to another against her will is **kidnapping.** In many states transporting the victim only a few feet may be sufficient to constitute the crime. If an individual is taken across state lines, the kidnapping escalates to a federal crime.

Crimes against the Public.
Crimes against the public can be divided into two groups: crimes against public morality and crimes against public order.

Crimes against Public Morality.
Many crimes against the public are considered to be crimes against public morality. The following are examples of such crimes:

prostitution
The provision of sexual favors in exchange for money.

1. *Prostitution.*　**Prostitution** is the providing of sexual favors in exchange for money. It is illegal in all states except Nevada, where each county may decide whether it is a crime in that county.

indecent exposure
The intentional exposure of private parts of the body in public.

2. *Indecent Exposure.*　**Indecent exposure** is the intentional exposure of private parts of the body in a public place. Nude dancing is an example of indecent exposure. The appellate courts in most states have upheld statutes prohibiting nude dancing and requiring dancers to have certain body parts covered.

Miller v. California
The case in which the U.S. Supreme Court defined obscenity.

obscenity
Any material that appeals to the prurient interest, shows offensive sexual conduct as defined by applicable state law, and lacks serious literary, artistic, political, or scientific value.

3. *Obscenity.*　Although purveyors of pornography use their First Amendment rights to free speech as a defense, the U.S. Supreme Court has consistently held that obscenity is not protected speech. In *Miller v. California,* 413 U.S. 15 (1973), the U.S. Supreme Court defined **obscenity** as any material that:

a. appeals to the prurient interest,
b. shows offensive sexual conduct as defined by the applicable state law, and
c. lacks serious literary, artistic, political, or scientific value.

The laws against child pornography are considerably more stringent, however. All exploitation of children is prohibited.

Crimes against Public Order.
Crimes against public order are offenses that disturb the orderly running of society. They include the following:

1. ***Rioting.***   When a group of individuals behave in a disorderly manner, their actions may constitute a riot. In most states a riot must involve a very large number of "rioters" who refuse to disperse even when told to do so by the police. Those individuals may be subject to arrest and may be charged with rioting. Generally, rioting will also involve the destruction of property or the harassment of others.

2. ***Disorderly Conduct.***   Disorderly conduct is a less serious crime and may include playing loud music late at night, being very loud in a public place, or committing any other act that disturbs the peaceful environment of others.

3. ***Drug Sales.***   The sale and use of illicit drugs are illegal in all states. Drug trafficking has become a very serious problem in today's society. The federal government has enacted drug trafficking statutes in an attempt to stop drug smuggling.

Crimes against Property.   Most crimes against property involve taking the property of another unlawfully by stealing, force, fire, or deceit. The most serious crime against property is **arson,** which is the unlawful and intentional burning of another's property. In some states, the property must be a house or other building. In most states, arson has been extended to include the burning of one's own house or building if the purpose is to defraud an insurance company.

arson
The intentional burning of another's home or building.

Burglary is the unlawful entry of another's building with the intention of committing a felony inside the building. In some states, unlawful entry with the intent to commit a misdemeanor is also a burglary. Only part of the body needs to enter the building; thus, reaching through a window in order to steal money is a burglary.

burglary
The unlawful entry of a building belonging to another with the intent to commit a felony inside the building.

Robbery is the taking of another's property from his person by threat or force. An individual who threatens a storekeeper in order to get the money in the cash register may be guilty of robbery. If someone were to break into the store at night after the storekeeper has left, that individual may be guilty of burglary if he intended to commit a felony.

robbery
Taking another's property from her person by threat or force.

Many different kinds of theft are considered criminal acts. **Larceny** is the taking and carrying away of another's personal property with the intent to steal it. Taking property that is lawfully in your possession with the intent to steal is **embezzlement.** An example is an attorney who uses her client's settlement funds that have been deposited in a trust account for her own purposes.

larceny
Taking and carrying away another's property with the intent to steal.

The crimes described here are among the most common, but many other crimes also exist, and when committed, they can lead to imprisonment in a state or federal prison or county jail. Any student who is interested in learning more about this field of law is encouraged to take a course in Criminal Law.

embezzlement
Taking property that is lawfully in one's possession with the intent to steal.

Defenses

Although the defendant may actually have committed the criminal act with which she is charged, various defenses that create an excuse can be presented at the trial. If the defendant's attorney can prove the defense, the accused will be found "not guilty." The most common defenses are listed in Table 5.1; not all of these defenses may be valid in every state, however. Of course, instead of presenting one of these defenses, the defendant may contend that she did not commit the crime and plead "not guilty."

TABLE 5.1 Valid Defenses to Crimes	
Self-defense	The defendant must prove he was defending himself. A person may not use more force to defend himself than is reasonable or more than was used by the other party. An individual may use deadly force only to defend his person, not his property. Deadly force is only allowed if it is also being used by the other party.
Defense of others	Similar to self-defense. The defendant must prove the individual being defended was not the aggressor. A person may not use more force than was being used by the other party and may not use deadly force unless deadly force was being used against the person being defended. Deadly force may not be used in defense of property.
Insanity	The defendant must prove that when the crime was committed, she was not capable of understanding the nature of the criminal act or that it was wrong. (The insanity defense varies by state.)
Temporary insanity	The defendant must prove that she was "insane" at the time the criminal act was committed even though she later regained her sanity.
Coercion	The defendant must prove that he committed the criminal act under compulsion from another, who used threats or force to make him commit the crime.
Entrapment	The defendant must prove that he was coerced into committing the criminal act by a police officer. For the defense to succeed, the crime must have been initiated by the officer, not the defendant. A person may also be entrapped by someone (i.e., a snitch) who was directed to entrap him by a police officer.

CRIMINAL PROCEDURES

Once an individual commits a crime, certain procedures are followed from the time of arrest to the trial and sentencing. This section will present the steps in the criminal justice process, including a brief overview of what happens at trial. A more detailed discussion of trial procedures will appear in Chapter 6.

Arrest

warrant
An order issued by a magistrate authorizing the police to make an arrest, conduct a search, or carry out other procedures as part of the criminal justice process.

probable cause
A reasonable ground for believing that a person has committed a crime.

The ideal situation arises when a police officer actually sees a crime being committed and arrests the perpetrator at the scene. No **warrant,** or order authorizing an arrest, is required in this case because **probable cause** exists; that is, the police officer has cause to reasonably believe the perpetrator committed the criminal act because he personally saw it being committed.

CHAPTER FIVE   Criminal Law

Such situations are rare, however, and the police usually must investigate the evidence in the case before arresting a suspect. Often police detectives spend a considerable amount of time and effort conducting an investigation prior to making an arrest. Once an arrest warrant is issued for an individual, the police may seek her out and arrest her. After the police take the suspect into custody, she is transported to the police station, fingerprinted, photographed, and booked (charged) with the crime.

Interview and Investigation

Most individuals who have been charged with a crime call their lawyers at this time. As a paralegal employed by a criminal defense attorney, you may be asked to interview the client in jail. If you are working for the prosecuting attorney, you may be asked to begin investigating the defendant's background, prior crimes, and alibi. Among other things, you may have to search out any witnesses to the crime. If you visit the neighborhood where the crime was committed, you should go on the same day of the week at approximately the same time that the crime was committed.

Individuals who are arrested may not be interrogated unless they have been read their *Miranda* rights, which were first set out in the famous case *Miranda v. Arizona.* Confessions obtained without reading the *Miranda* rights may not be admissible into evidence, but can be used for impeachment purposes in some states (that is, used to challenge the credibility of the defendant if she tells a different story at trial). If the accused wishes to speak to her attorney at any time, the interrogation must stop. If the accused knowingly discusses the crime with the police at this point, anything she says may be used against her in court. Often, the defendant's attorney will file a Motion to Suppress Evidence arguing that the confession should be suppressed because the accused did not knowingly give up her rights and that the interrogation consequently violated her Fifth Amendment right against self-incrimination. More commonly, Motions to Suppress Evidence argue that evidence should be suppressed because it was seized illegally in violation of the Fourth Amendment to the Constitution.

Miranda v. Arizona
The case in which the U.S. Supreme Court set out the rights of the accused during interrogation by the police. The rights are known as the *Miranda* rights.

Arraignment

At the **arraignment,** the accused and his attorney appear before the judge to hear the charges and enter a plea. If the defendant cannot afford an attorney, the court will appoint one, usually a public defender. The judge may allow the accused to post bail to get out of jail, or if the accused has ties to the community and is not likely to flee or commit another crime, the judge may release him on his "own recognizance" (known as an OR release). The judge will also ask the defendant whether he pleads guilty, not guilty, or **nolo contendere.** Literally translated from the Latin, nolo contendere means "I will not contest it." Although this plea is treated as an admission of guilt, the defendant is not actually admitting guilt or innocence. An accused may plead "nolo" (nolo contendere) to prevent a guilty plea from being used against him in a subsequent proceeding. For instance, if the accused is charged with battery in the criminal proceeding and his victim wishes to bring a civil suit against him for her personal injuries, a nolo contendere plea may not be used against the defendant at the civil trial. If he had pleaded guilty, however, the plaintiff could use that plea against him at the civil trial.

arraignment
The step in the criminal justice process when the defendant is brought before a judge to hear the charges and enter a plea.

nolo contendere
Latin for "I will not contest it." A plea by which the defendant does not admit guilt, but also does not contest the charges.

Preliminary Hearing or Pretrial Settlement

Some states have **preliminary hearings** to determine whether enough evidence exists against the defendant to hold a trial. Other states have settlement conferences where the defendant may plead to a lesser offense or plead guilty. Once the defendant pleads guilty, the judge renders the sentence and the case ends.

Plea Bargaining

Since many states' prisons are very crowded, a defendant may be given an opportunity to plead guilty to a lesser offense and have the charges reduced from a serious felony to a less serious one or from a felony to a misdemeanor. This process is known as **plea bargaining.** For example, after discussions between the prosecutor and the defense attorney, the defendant who is charged with rape (a felony) may agree to plead guilty to a related misdemeanor, such as sexual battery. The defendant then receives a less stringent sentence such as incarceration in the county jail for several months, instead of several years in the state prison. As another example, the defendant may be charged with a more serious felony (e.g., murder) and plead guilty to a lesser felony (e.g., manslaughter) to receive a shorter sentence in the state prison.

Plea bargaining has been the subject of considerable debate. Proponents say it saves money and helps alleviate the court's workload by reducing the number of cases that must go to trial. It also makes it possible for a defendant to be found guilty without the prosecution having to prove his guilt at trial. In addition, in some cases the defendant may implicate others in exchange for a plea bargain. Then the prosecution can bring charges against the other perpetrators.

Opponents of plea bargaining say that it allows repeat offenders to be freed quickly and, in some cases, to commit the same crimes again. Whatever its advantages and disadvantages, plea bargaining is used in most states, especially those with high crime rates and very crowded prisons.

To plea bargain effectively, both the prosecution and the defense must be well prepared for the discussions. The more evidence the prosecution has amassed, the better the prosecutor can argue that the defendant should plead guilty to a serious charge. Similarly, the more thoroughly the defense attorney has prepared his case, the better the plea bargain he can get for his client. In most cases, plea bargains are utilized with guilty defendants.

Grand Jury

In some states a grand jury hears testimony to determine if the prosecution has sufficient evidence to go to trial. The prosecutor presents evidence to the grand jury, but the defendant is not present and is not given an opportunity to present a defense. The prosecutor can call witnesses who usually must appear before the grand jury without an attorney. After hearing the evidence, the grand jury decides whether to hand down an indictment; if it does so, the defendant is held over for trial. As described earlier, some states use a preliminary hearing instead of a grand jury. Some states call a grand jury only in cases of major crimes that have been well publicized.

Trial and Sentencing

In most states, the defendant chooses whether or not to have the case heard by a judge or a jury. A few states, however, allow the prosecuting attorney to request a jury trial.

In order to find the defendant guilty, the judge or jury must find that the evidence shows guilt beyond a reasonable doubt, which is a very high standard. In most states all twelve jurors must agree on the defendant's guilt. However, Oregon allows a guilty verdict if ten out of twelve jurors agree, while Louisiana allows a guilty verdict if only nine of the twelve agree.

The prosecution presents its witnesses first, followed by the defense. To ensure that a witness will appear at the trial or other court proceeding, a subpoena may be used. Exhibit 5.1 shows a sample subpoena prepared by a prosecuting attorney.

After all of the evidence is presented, the verdict is rendered. If the jury reaches a guilty verdict, the judge imposes the sentence on the defendant. Some states, such as Virginia and Kentucky, allow the jury to impose the sentence. The *sentencing phase* is a separate proceeding in most states. The defendant may present character witnesses in an attempt to persuade the judge to impose a lighter sentence. A report indicating whether the defendant might successfully be released on probation may also be submitted as part of the sentencing recommendations.

Hung Jury.   If the jury is divided and cannot agree on a verdict (or, in states that allow nonunanimous verdicts, less than the required number agree), a "hung jury" results. In this case, the defendant is found neither guilty nor not guilty. States use various procedures when a hung jury results, but usually the district attorney has the option of retrying the defendant. In that case, a new trial is conducted with a new jury.

Double Jeopardy.   When an individual is tried for the same crime twice, he may claim **double jeopardy** as a defense at the second trial. Note that if the first trial results in a hung jury, a second trial does not constitute double jeopardy. For a second trial to constitute double jeopardy, the first trial must have been completed to the point where the judge or jury rendered a verdict. A defendant who has been found "not guilty," may not be retried for the same crime.

double jeopardy
Being tried for the same crime twice.

Appeals

Only death penalty cases are automatically appealable to the state's highest court, usually called the State Supreme Court. Other cases may be appealed if legal errors were made at the trial or if the defense attorney can prove that the judge or jurors were biased or prejudiced against the defendant.

Defendant's Right to Be Present

With the exception of a grand jury, the defendant has the right to be present at all stages of the proceedings described in this section, including oral arguments on any motions that the attorney may make before the court.

The defendant must always be present at felony proceedings, but may sign a waiver relinquishing the right to be present at hearings on motions in misdemeanor proceedings in Municipal Court. The waiver may apply to any or all of the following hearings:

1. When the case is set for trial

2. When a continuance is ordered

3. When a motion to set aside the indictment is heard

EXHIBIT 5.1   A Sample Subpoena

IN THE MUNICIPAL COURT OF SOUTH BAY JUDICIAL DISTRICT
COUNTY OF LOS ANGELES, STATE OF CALIFORNIA

THE PEOPLE OF THE STATE OF CALIFORNIA,

	Plaintiff,	No. **94M00**
v.		
	Defendant	

THE PEOPLE OF THE STATE OF CALIFORNIA TO: **94-000**

OFFICER CLARK   #11XXX

You are hereby commanded to appear in the above entitled court in THE COURT HOUSE, 222 CIVIC CENTER, SEAL BEACH, CA 99999 **Division 7 on October 1, 1996, at 8:30 AM** to testify as a witness on the part of the People of the State of California in the above entitled criminal action against the above named defendant.

Dated: 9-25-96   SV#0000

Robert Lopez, City Prosecutor
Seal Beach

NOTE: <u>DISOBEDIENCE TO THIS SUBPOENA MAY BE PUNISHABLE AS CONTEMPT OF COURT (PENAL CODE SECTION 1331). IF PLACED ON CALL FAILURE TO RESPOND AS AGREED MAY RESULT IN CONTEMPT OF COURT (PENAL CODE SECTION 1331.5).</u>

<u>PROOF OF SERVICE</u>

I declare under the penalty of perjury that I served this subpoena as follows:

Date of service: _____   Time of service: _____

Address of service: _____

Person served: _____   Name of server: _____

Signature of server: _____

NOTE: <u>PLEASE DRESS APPROPRIATELY (NO SHORTS, TANK TOPS, BARE FEET).</u>

4. When a motion for bail is heard

5. When questions of law are presented to the court

Paralegals may be asked to draft these waivers and/or have them signed by the defendant during the initial interview. A sample Waiver of Personal Appearance is shown in Exhibit 5.2.

PRETRIAL PREPARATIONS BY THE PROSECUTION

A paralegal who is employed by the prosecution will be very busy finding witnesses and additional evidence during the pretrial stage of the case. He may work with the investigating officer who initiated the case, check computer records to determine if the defendant has been found guilty of other crimes, and do research in the law library or on the computer. Other tasks include interviewing defense witnesses and preparing subpoenas for prosecution witnesses (see Exhibit 5.1).

Paralegals may also conduct discovery on the defense to determine what evidence they will present and what witnesses they will call to testify. A paralegal may be asked to read over any statements made by the defendant to compare them to statements made at the preliminary hearing or statements made by other witnesses. Other assignments may include preparing exhibits for the trial and completing preliminary research on motions to be filed with the court.

Paralegals on the prosecution side should conduct as thorough an investigation as possible so that the district attorney can prove the defendant is guilty beyond a reasonable doubt.

PRETRIAL PREPARATIONS BY THE DEFENSE

The prosecution's evidence and the circumstances under which it was obtained must be examined to determine its value and whether it was obtained legally. If not, a Motion to Suppress Evidence must be prepared. Most Motions to Suppress Evidence challenge the evidence as the product of an illegal search and seizure and/or a warrantless search. The motion may also challenge the admissibility of confessions or other statements made by the defendant. Any time a search of a building is conducted without a warrant, the search presents an opportunity for the defendant to challenge the admissibility of any evidence seized on the basis of an illegal search and seizure. Research must be conducted for the preparation of the motion and the Points and Authorities to accompany the motion. Evidence and witnesses obtained by the prosecution must be examined. Exhibit 5.3 shows an example of a Motion to Suppress Evidence.

Any information that the prosecution will introduce into evidence at the trial may be obtained in advance by the defense attorney. A paralegal working for the defense must examine the evidence and witnesses' statements carefully to determine any discrepancies. The paralegal's investigation may involve examining the manner in which all of the evidence was obtained against the client to determine whether any of her constitutional rights were violated. If violations occurred, the attorney may file a Motion to Suppress Evidence, and the judge will rule on whether the evidence will be disallowed.

EXHIBIT 5.2   A Defendant's Waiver of Personal Appearance

1 Jeffrey M. Williams
   MICHAELS & WILLIAMS
2 1122 Main Street
   Seal Beach, California
3 (310) 123-5555

4

5 Attorney for Defendant

6

7

8   MUNICIPAL COURT OF THE STATE OF CALIFORNIA

9

10   COUNTY OF MARIN

11

12

13

14

15 PEOPLE OF THE STATE OF
    CALIFORNIA.   )
16   )
              Plaintiff   )
17   )   Case No.
    vs.   )
18   )   DEFENDANT'S WAIVER
)   OF PERSONAL APPEARANCE
19   )
)
20   Defendant.   )
    _____
21

22

23

24

25

26   I, _____, have been advised of my right to be present at all stages

27 of the proceedings, including but not limited to presentation of and arguments on

28 questions of law, and to be confronted by and to cross-examine all witnesses.

EXHIBIT 5.2   Defendant's Waiver of Personal Appearance *Concluded*

1   I hereby waive the right to be present at the hearing of any motion or order

2   proceeding in this cause, including when the case is set for trial, when a continu-

3   ance is ordered, when a motion to set aside the indictment or information under

4   the provisions of Penal Code section 995 is heard, when a motion for reduction of

5   bail or for a personal recognizance release is heard, when a motion to reduce

6   sentence is heard, and when questions of law are presented to or considered by

7   the Court.

8

9   I hereby ask the court to proceed when I am absent pursuant to this waiver

10   with the court's permission, and agree that my interest is deemed represented at

11   all times by the presence of my attorney, the same as if I myself were personally

12   present in court.

13

14   I further agree that notice to my attorney that my presence in court on a

15   particular day at a particular time is required will be deemed notice to me.

16   DATED: _____   _____.

17   APPROVED:

18   DATED: _____   _____.

19   Jeffrey M. Williams

20   Attorney At Law

21

22

23

24

25

26

27

28

EXHIBIT 5.3   A Motion in Limine Pursuant to Evidence Code Section 402 to Exclude Any Statements in Violation of Miranda or the Privilege against Self-Incrimination

1 JEFFREY M. WILLIAMS
2 MICHAELS & WILLIAMS
   1122 Main Street
3 Seal Beach, California
   (310) 123-5555
4

5

6 Attorney for Defendant

7

8   IN THE SUPERIOR COURT OF THE STATE OF CALIFORNIA
9   IN AND FOR THE COUNTY OF MARIN

10

11

12 THE PEOPLE OF THE STATE OF   )
    CALIFORNIA,   )   Case No. SC0120
13   )
14   Plaintiff   )   MOTION IN LIMINE
)   PURSUANT TO
15 v.   )   EVIDENCE CODE
)   SECTION 402 TO
16   )   EXCLUDE
17 DEFENDANT,   )   ANY STATEMENTS
)   IN VIOLATION
18   )   OF MIRANDA
19   Defendant.   )   OR THE PRIVILEGE
)   AGAINST
20 _____)   SELF-INCRIMINATION
21

22

23

24 By this motion, Defendant seeks to suppress certain statements or utterances

25 obtained in violation of his Fifth Amendment rights.

26 This motion is based upon the attached Memorandum of Points and Authorities, the

27 files and records of this case, and such further evidence and arguments as may be

28 received at the hearing of this motion.

EXHIBIT 5.3	**A Motion in Limine Pursuant to Evidence Code Section 402 to Exclude Any Statements in Violation of Miranda or the Privilege against Self-Incrimination** *Continued*

1

I.

2

INTRODUCTION

3 Defendant, DEFENDANT X, stands charged with violating Penal Code §§ 209 and

4 211. By this motion, Defendant seeks to exclude any statements attributed to him as

5 obtained in violation of his Fifth Amendment rights.

6

II.

7

Memorandum of Points and Authorities and Argument

8 By this motion, Defendant specifically requests an evidentiary hearing to determine

9 if any police witnesses or agents will claim that Defendant made any statements or

10 utterances following Defendant's detention and arrest in the above matter.

11 California Evidence Code Section 402. If the prosecution intends to offer statements

12 of Defendant, Defendant seeks a hearing to determine if any of the purported

13 statements were obtained in violation of his Fifth Amendment rights and the express

14 mandate of *Miranda v. Arizona* (1966) 440 U.S. 934.

15

16 In *Miranda v. Arizona, supra,* 440 U.S. 934, the Supreme Court held that in the

17 context of "custodial interrogation," certain procedural safeguards are necessary

18 to protect a defendant's Fifth and Fourteenth Amendment privilege against

19 compulsory self-incrimination. More specifically, the court held that "the

20 prosecution may not use statements, whether exculpatory or inculpatory, stemming

21 from custodial interrogation of the defendant unless it demonstrates the use of

22 procedural safeguards effective to secure the privilege against self-incrimination."

23 Id. at 444.

24

25 Those safeguards included the now familiar Miranda warnings namely, that the

26 defendant be informed "that he has the right to remain silent, that anything he says

27 can be used against him in a court of law, that he has the right to the presence of

28 an attorney, and that if he cannot afford an attorney, one will be appointed for him

**EXHIBIT 5.3   A Motion in Limine Pursuant to Evidence Code Section 402
to Exclude Any Statements in Violation of Miranda or the
Privilege against Self-Incrimination** *Continued*

1   prior to any question, if he so desires" or their equivalent. Id. at 479; see *People v.*

2   *Jennings* (1988) 46 Cal.3d 963, 976 [for a recent restatement of Miranda rule].

3

4   The court defined custodial interrogation as "questioning initiated by law

5   enforcement officers after a person has been taken into custody or otherwise

6   deprived of his freedom of action in any significant way." *Miranda,* supra, 440 U.S.

7   at 444; *Rhode Island v. Innis* (1984) 446 U.S. 291, 297; *In re Corey L.* (1988) 203

8   Cal.App.3d 1020, 1024. It is clear that custody in the *Miranda* sense does not

9   necessitate a formal arrest, nor does it require physical restraint in a police station,

10 nor the application of handcuffs, and may occur in a suspect's home or a public

11 place other than a police station. *Orozco v. Texas* (1969) 394 U.S. 324, 326; *Oregon v.*

12 *Mathiason* (1976) 429 U.S. 492, 494; *People v. Boyer* (1989) 48 Cal.3d 247, 272; see

13 also *People v. Hatt* (1988) 205 Cal.App.3d 1178.

14

15 The Supreme Court has defined interrogation as police conduct that reflects "a

16 measure of compulsion above and beyond that inherent in custody itself." *Rhode*

17 *Island v. Innis, supra,* 446 U.S. at 300. That court has held that interrogation may be

18 police conduct that is the "functional equivalent" of express questioning, including

19 "any words or actions on the part of the police (other than those normally attendant

20 to arrest and custody) likely to elicit an incriminating response from the suspect."

21 Id. at p. 301. The California Supreme Court has further held that interrogation

22 includes any "process of inquiry that lends itself, even if not so designed, to eliciting

23 damaging statements." *People v. Pettingill* (1978) 21 Cal.3d 231, 244; *People v.*

24 *Dominick* (1986) 182 Cal.App.3d 1174, 1190–1191; *People v. Pompa* (1989) 212

25 Cal.App.3d 1308, 1312–1313.

26

27 In addition to overcoming the *Miranda* hurdle, the prosecution also has the burden

28 to prove that any statement made by the defendant was made voluntarily, under the

EXHIBIT 5.3   A Motion in Limine Pursuant to Evidence Code Section 402 to Exclude Any Statements in Violation of Miranda or the Privilege against Self-Incrimination *Concluded*

1 totality of the circumstances. *People v. Hernandez* (1988) 204 Cal.App.3d 639; *In re*

2 *Juma P.* (1988) 204 Cal.App.3d 1228; *People v. Barker* (1988) 182 Cal.App.3d 921.

3   III.

4   **CONCLUSION**

5 Based on the foregoing, Defendant respectfully requests that, if the prosecution

6 seeks to introduce any statements or utterances attributed to Defendant at trial, that

7 a hearing be held to determine whether that statement is in violation of Defendant's

8 Fifth Amendment rights.

9 Dated: 7/20/96

10

11   Respectfully submitted,

12

13

14

15   JEFFREY M. WILLAMS

16   Attorney for Defendant

17

18

19

20

21

22

23

24

25

26

27

28

SUMMARY

This chapter has presented an introduction to criminal law and the criminal justice system. Criminal law deals with wrongful acts against society. In contrast to civil law where suits are brought by an individual or an entity, in criminal law the plaintiff is the state or society, represented by the prosecuting attorney.

More serious crimes such as murder and rape are felonies, while less serious crimes such as petty theft and malicious mischief are misdemeanors. Minor offenses such as traffic violations are infractions; they are punishable by a fine and are not considered crimes. Most crimes have two elements: criminal intent and the commission of the criminal act. Crimes can be further classified into three categories: crimes against the person, crimes against the public, and crimes against property. The chapter presented representative examples in each category.

The criminal justice process begins with the arrest of a suspect. The chapter traced the process through all of its steps: arrest, interview, investigation, arraignment, preliminary hearing, grand jury, trial, sentencing, and the appeals process. Some possible defenses that a defendant might use were also presented. The chapter concluded by describing typical duties of a paralegal in both a criminal prosecution and a defense.

KEY TERMS

Aiding and abetting   129

Arraignment   133

Arson   131

Assault   130

Battery   130

Burglary   131

Double jeopardy   135

Embezzlement   131

Felony   128

Felony Murder Rule   128

Homicide   128

Indecent exposure   130

Infraction   128

Kidnapping   130

Larceny   131

Mayhem   129

Miller v. California   130

Miranda v. Arizona   133

Misdemeanor   128

Nolo contendere   133

Obscenity   130

Plea bargaining   134

Preliminary hearing   134

Probable cause   132

Prostitution   130

Rape   129

Robbery   131

Special Circumstances Rule   128

Statutory rape   128

Warrant   132

SELF-TEST

A. Indicate whether the following statements are true (T) or false (F):

_____ 1. Felonies include murder and robbery.

_____ 2. Misdemeanors include kidnapping and arson.

_____ 3. Robbery involves entering a residence at night to steal.

_____ 4. Burglary involves taking another's property from his person.

_____ 5. The preliminary hearing is held to determine whether enough evidence
       exists to hold the defendant over for trial.

B.   Circle the correct answer for the following questions:

1. The proceeding where the accused is brought before a judge to hear the
   charges against him is called

   a. a preliminary hearing

   b. an arraignment.

   c. a trial.

   d. bail.

2. When the defendant's attorney wants evidence excluded from the trial
   because the police conducted an illegal search of the premises, she files a

   a. Motion to Exclude Evidence.

   b. Motion to Stop Evidence.

   c. Motion for Waiver.

   d. Motion to Suppress Evidence.

3. The elements of most crimes are

   a. intent and planning.

   b. act and planning.

   c. planning and motive.

   d. intent and act.

   e. motive and act.

4. Plea bargaining involves

   a. a not guilty plea.

   b. pleading guilty to a lesser offense.

   c. having a trial.

   d. none of the above.

5. Crimes punishable by incarceration in the county jail are called

   a. felonies.

   b. infractions.

   c. misdemeanors.

   d. homicides.

C.   Fill in the blanks:

1. To ensure the presence of a witness at the trial, a _____ is

   prepared and served.

2. The document signed by the defendant so that he does not have to be at a

   hearing to reduce sentence is called a _____ .

3. In order to exclude evidence from the trial, a _____ must be filed.

4. The process whereby the defendant pleads guilty to a lesser charge and receives a shorter sentence is known as _____ .

5. If an individual helps the defendant commit a murder, she is said to be _____ and _____ .

REVIEW QUESTIONS

1. Describe the procedures followed after the accused is arrested.

2. What are the paralegal's responsibilities when employed by the prosecutor?

3. What are the paralegal's responsibilities when employed by the defense?

4. What is the difference between assault and battery? May a defendant be charged with both? If so, under what circumstances?

5. Define the terms *felony* and *misdemeanor* and explain the differences between them.

PROJECTS

1. Proofread the Memorandum of Points and Authorities in Exhibit 5.4 and correct any errors. Then revise it for our office with the following information:

- Defendant: Robert M. Cook
- Wife's name: Jane Cook
- Date: June 23, 1996
- Time: 10:00 A.M.
- Place: Department 50
- Defendant's residence: 421 Sand Street
  Your town, Your state
- Victim's name: Steven Roberts
- Date of occurrence: October 22, 1995
- Date of document: Use today's date

2. Proofread the partial document in Exhibit 5.5. Correct any errors and revise the document for our office. When you revise the document, include the caption using the proper format for our state. The plaintiff should be the People of Your State; the defendant is Robert M. Cook. The case

EXHIBIT 5.4   A Memorandum of Points and Authorities

1   JEFFREY M. WILLIAMS

2   MICHAELS & WILLIAMS

3   1122 MAIN STREET

4   SEAL BEACH, CA 99999

5   (310) 123-5555

6

7   Attorney for Defendant

8

9

10   **IN THE SUPEROIR COURT OF THE STATE, OF CALFORNIA**

11   **IN AND FOR THE CAUNTY OF MARIN**

12

13   THE PEPLE OF THE STaTEOF)

14   CALIFORNIA,   )   Case No.

15   )

16   Plaintiff   )   **MEMURANDUM OF POINTS AND**

17   v.   )   **AND AUTHORITIES IN SUPPORT OF**

18   )   **MOTION FOR RELEAS**

19   )   **ONOWN RECOGNIZANCE**

20   Defendant.   )

21   )

22   )

23   )

24   )   DATE: 12/1/96

25   )   TIME: 1:30 P.M.

26   PALCE: DEPT. B

27   **Introducton**

28   By this motion, Deferdant, Richard Fallon, seeks to bee released on his own

EXHIBIT 5.4   A Memorandum of Points and Authorities *Continued*

1   recognzance so that he can put fourth his best efforts to completely make the victim

2   whole in this case and be home with his family for christmas.

3   Should the court grant this motion, teh defendant would be stayingh with his

4   wife, Sharon Fallon, at there residence at 644 Hancock Drive in Brookdale.

5   Althuogh at one time the defendant had Extensive real proporty holdings, at at

6   this time all properties in the defendants' name have been turned over to the victim,

7   Jorge Santos, in satisfaction of civil judgements arising from the same opperative

8   facts as this matter before the court. The remainder of Mr. Fallon's interests are

9   contingent upon Mr. Fallon's liquidation for the victim's benefit. The victim has tactily

10 agred too reconvey Mr. Fallon's properties in exchange for clash. Mr. Follon believes

11 that between the date of his preliminary hearing and the sentencing in this matter

12 he would be able to liqudate enough contingency interests to pays the full restitution.

13   The facts underlying this offense occurred in May 1995. Since then, Mr. Falen

14 has had plenty of oportunity to flee yet has reamained in the area. His ties to

15 Northern california are solid: all of his family is here. He has longstanding friends

16 and ties tot the community as shown by the several letters attached hereto. Mr.

17 Fallon has noe record of violence nor is their any indication that that he poses a

18 danger to the community.

19   The interest of justice will served if Mr. Fallen can be released on O.R.

20 because the high incentive in making the victim whole as it relates to his sentenc-

21 ing.

22   Based on the attacked letters and points and authorities, Mr. Fallon respect-

23 fully requests a releaze on her own recognzance.

24 **1. information Considered At Hearing**

25   The soul issue at the O.R. hearing is whether the detainee will appear for sub-

26 sequent court proceedings of released on his or her own recognizance. [*Van Atta v.*

27

28

EXHIBIT 5.4   A Memorandum of Points and Authorities *Continued*

1   *Scott* (1980) 27 Cal.3d 424, 438, 166 Cal.Rptr. 149, 613 P.2d 210). To answer this this

2   question the trial court must consideer the following factors (*supra; cf.* Penal Code

3   section 1272.1, bail pending appeal):

4   1. The detaine's ties to the community, including his or her employment or

5   other sources of income (e.g.,contracts), the daration and location of his resident,

6   family attachments, property holdings, and any indpendent reasons for wanting to

7   leave or remain in the community;

8   3. The detainee's record of appearance at past court hearings, or of flight to

9   Avoid prosecution; and

10   3. The severity of the sentence hte detainee faces.

11 However, if the defendant has bean arrested for a violent felony, [see Penal Code

12 section 667.5(c)], the magistrate or judge must also determine whether or not it

13 appears by clearand convincing evidence that the defendant has previously been

14 charged with a felony offense and has willfully and without excuse from the court

15 failed to appear in court as required while that chage was pennding. If it soe

16 appears, O.R. release will not be ordered [Penal Code section 1319(b)].

17   Mr. Falen has substanstial ties to the community, no wrap sheet or record of

18 avoiding prosecution and no history of violence.?

19

20 **2. Burdens of production and Prooif**

21   In the case if *Van Atta v. Scott (supra,* at 438–444), the California supreme

22 Court considered the barden of producing evidence and proof at an O.R. hearing.

23 The conclusions the Court reached were highly favorable to defendents seeking

24 O.K. release, and should result in increased use of the, procedure.

25

26 The Court first considered the burdan of producing evidence at the O.R. hearing

27 (see Evidence Code section 110, definition off burden of producing evidence). It con-

28 cluded that the detianee is obligatied to come forward with evidence of his or her

EXHIBIT 5.4   A Memorandum of Points and Authorities *Concluded*

1   Ties to the community, since the defendant has much greater acess to such infor-

2   mation then the prosecution, and would have a great incentive to produce it (*Van*

3   *Atta w. Scott, supra,* at 438). Howver, the burden of production is on the prosecution

4   (*supra,* at 438–439) concerning the other issueds considered at the hearing, includ-

5   ing the detainee's record for making appearances and the severity of the passible

6   sentence (Evidence COde section 110).

7   in considering the proper placment of the burden of proof (see Evidence Code

8   section 115), the court focussed on the individual's great interest in feredom, and

9   the distortions that result from the difficulties a detainee in costody has in marshal-

10 ing evidence. It concluded that the prosecution must baer the burden of proving that

11 the defendant would not appear us required if given an O.R. release (*Van Atta v.*

12 *Scot, supra,* at 444). The court did nt make a statement indicating the degree of

13 proof by which the burden must be carried.

14   It would seem to follow from *Van atta,* then, than in the case of a person

15 arrested for a vilent felony [see Penal Code section 667.5(c)] the prosecution has the

16 burden of produceing evidence that the deferdent has previously been charged with

17 a felony offense and has willfully and without oxcuse from the court failed to to

18 appear as required while that charge was penting. in that instance, the standard of

19 prooof is that off clear and convincing evidence [see Penal Code section 1319(b)].

20

21   Respectfuly submitted,

22

23

24

25 Dated: November 5, 1996

26

27   Jeffrey M. Williams

28   attorney for Defendant

EXHIBIT 5.5   A Memorandum of Points and Authorities

1   PROPER CAPTION HERE

2   IN THE SUPEEROR COURT OF THE STATE OF XYZ

3   IN AND FOR THE COUNWY OF LATZ

4

5   PEOPLE OF XYZ,

6

7   Plaintiff,   Cas Nos.

8

9   v.   Memorandum of Points & Authorities

10

11   ROBERT M. COOOK,

12

13   Defendant.

14

15

16   INTRDUCTION

17

18   The perpos of this motion is to dismis Count 1 (berglary, Criminal Code Section

19   222) and COunt 2 (recieving stoln propty, Crimnl Code 224.)

20   The motn to dismis Coun 1 is basd on the fact that their is no evidenc of an

21   entrie. The defendent had permishun to be in the residense and their is no evidense

22   that the defendent posesed stoln propty or had the intent to steal or commit a felon

23   therin.

24   The defendent movs to dismis Count 2 becauz the Peopl did not and could not

25   prove the corpes delectie of the crime of recieving soln property (specificly that the

26   propertie was stoln) independant of the defendand's extrajudishal statments.

27

28   STATMENT OF THE CASE

EXHIBIT 5.5   A Memorandum of Points and Authorities *Concluded*

1   By way iof felonie complaynt, defendent was charjed with violating Criminal

2   Code Section 455, Possesshun of Stolen Propertie, a 9mm Luger handgun. The pre-

3   liminary hearing was condukted befor the Honorabl James Pattison on Septembr 22,

4   1995, the Informashun was filed alledging in Count 1, a violashun of Crimnl 455, (resi-

5   denshal burglery) and in Coun 2, a violashun of Crimnl 333 (recieveing stoln proper-

6   tie.) The defendent pleadeeed not guiltie and a jurie trail was set.

7

8   STATMENT OF FACS

9

10   The only witnesss who testifeed at the preliminarie hearing was Deputie

11 Samuel Adams of the Local County Sherrriff's Department for the COunty of

12

13

14

15

16

17

18

19

20

21

22

23

24

25

26

27

28

number is CR-22225. The Criminal Code sections cited in the introductory paragraph are the correct sections.

3. Assume you work for a criminal defense attorney. The client, Jody Klossen, has just been arrested for drunk driving. The attorney asks you to interview Ms. Klossen at county jail. What questions would you ask Ms. Klossen about the charge?

4. Assume you are investigating the case in Project 3. You have found a witness who Jody Klossen says was with her when she was arrested. Ms. Klossen says that the witness, Mark Hauser, will testify that she was not drinking alcohol on the evening in question. Make a list of questions to ask Mr. Hauser.

5. Our client is Scott Marshall, whose address is 222 Gilltee Lane, Your Town, Your State. He has been accused of killing Yusef Ray with a .38 pistol. You have been asked by the attorney to research the following question and prepare a memo to the attorney on your findings: Our client and his wife, Ashley, were separated, but he had some items in her apartment that he had not yet picked up. The police went to Ashley's apartment and asked to search it. She said they could. In the closet among our client's belongings, the police found the .38 pistol used in the killing. We are seeking to suppress the evidence (the gun) because the wife did not have a right to give permission to search items belonging to her husband. The question you must answer is: Did the police have the right to search the closet containing the husband's possessions if the husband and wife are separated and only the wife gave permission for the search? Cite appropriate cases because the next step will be to prepare a motion to suppress the gun.

6. Prepare a Motion to Suppress Evidence for the situation in Project 5. Use the format and headings appropriate for your state, or use Exhibit 5.3 as a guide.

The Trial Process

CHAPTER OBJECTIVES

As a result of studying this chapter, you will learn the following material:

1. ***Trial Book***   The preparation of the Trial Book will be discussed. You will learn what to include in the Trial Book and will also learn how to prepare a chart for the jury selection process.

2. ***Evidence***   The preparation of evidence for trial will be discussed. You will learn how to obtain and prepare evidence, including how to comply with authentication requirements and the Best Evidence Rule.

3. ***Sequence of Trial***   The sequence of events at a trial will be presented. You will learn what happens at each point and what role you are likely to play.

4. ***Enforcing Judgments***   Various ways of enforcing judgments will be presented. You will learn the forms and documents required to enforce a civil judgment.

5. ***Appeals***   Basic appellate procedures will be presented. You will learn how to prepare an appellate court brief.

PREPARING FOR TRIAL

Trials occur in both the criminal and the civil arenas. The paralegal and the legal secretary play important roles in the pretrial process, in the trial itself, and in posttrial procedures such as appeals. The preparations for the trial include preparing the Trial Book, helping witnesses get ready to testify, and gathering evidence.

Preparation of the Trial Book

At the beginning of the case, the paralegal and legal secretary initiate the preparation of the Trial Book. The Trial Book is a notebook that organizes everything that the attorney needs at trial so items can be retrieved quickly when needed. Usually, the Trial Book is a three-ring binder with a series of tab dividers that help to index and organize the various documents included in the notebook. Exhibit 6.1 shows a typical Trial Book for a civil lawsuit.

The content and organization of the Trial Book will be determined by the supervising attorney and may vary depending on the case. The following are some typical items that may be included in a Trial Book:

*   Copies of the complaints and answers of the parties.
*   Copies of all motions and pleadings filed in the case.

EXHIBIT 6.1   Typical Trial Notebook for a Civil Case

LawFiles Civil Trial Notebook™

— *Contents* —

Section 1: Trial Preparation

- White tabs for research, briefs, orders, trial administration and strategies

- Green tabs for pleadings, discovery and damages

Section 2: Trial

- Purple tabs for motions in limine, jury selection and opening statement

- Yellow tabs for testimony; includes witness and exhibits lists, plaintiff's and defense witnesses

- Pink tabs for trial motions, closing argument, jury instructions and verdict

10 Write-on Tabs are provided for witness names or to add supplemental categories of information.
Use ball point pen, pencil or Sharpie marker.

6 Trial Forms are to assist in preparation and through trial:

- Deadlines/To Do
- Witness Address and Phone List
- Deposition Summary
- Juror Profile
- Jury Selection Chart
- Exhibits List

These forms are to be kept as masters. Photocopy as needed.

Tabs (right side of notebook):

- Plaintiff's Witnesses
- Motions in Limine
- Trial Plan/Order of Proof
- Contact List
- Defense Witnesses
- Voir Dire/Jury Selection
- Pleadings
- Trial Deadlines/To Do
- Trial Motions and Orders
- Opening Statement
- Interrogatories
- Case Chronology/Timeline
- Closing Argument
- Master Witness List/Trial Subpoenas
- Admissions/Stipulations
- Research/Points of Law
- Jury Instructions
- Documents Produced
- Trial Briefs/Memoranda of Law
- Verdict Forms
- Master Exhibits List
- Damages
- Pre-Trial Orders

Bindertek®   800-456-3453   Item #IND-T   © Bindertek 1993, 1995

SOURCE: Reprinted with permission. LawFiles Trial Notebook, Courtesy of Bindertek, Sausalito, California.

- Answers to written interrogatories.

- Deposition transcripts and/or summaries.

- Notes on any discrepancies between the interrogatories and depositions in a particular witness's testimony. These notes are usually arranged in the order in which the witnesses will appear at trial.

- An outline of the issues to be raised in the case.

- Copies of exhibits to be introduced at trial.

- An index of the exhibits.

- A chronological list of events in the lawsuit.

- A copy of the Trial Brief, which most attorneys prepare to describe the issues being decided in the case.

- Copies of jury instructions.

- A schedule of witnesses. This schedule should include the names of the witnesses and the approximate dates when they will appear at the trial, as well as notes on any discrepancies in previous statements made by each witness. In most states, the parties exchange witness lists so that there will be no surprises at the trial. The paralegal is often responsible for investigating the statements made by the adverse party's witnesses to learn the substance of their testimony and identify any discrepancies in their previous statements.

- A possible list of questions for each witness or perhaps an outline of information that should be explored.

Another item that might be included in the Trial Book is a chart of the jury box for the jury selection process. The chart would include a seating chart with the names of prospective jurors and where they are seated. Post-It™ Notes are excellent for this chart because they are easy to remove. One Post-It™ Note is prepared for each prospective juror; the note includes the person's name and any comments by the attorney or paralegal. If an individual is challenged and removed, then the note with that juror's name is replaced with a note for a new prospective juror. This method is used until all twelve jurors are chosen. Exhibit 6.2 shows an example of a jury selection chart.

Witness Preparation

Before the trial, the paralegal may be responsible for helping the witnesses prepare to testify. Although the paralegal may not tell a witness what to say, it is appropriate to describe the general types of questions that will be asked. Preparing the witness for **cross-examination** by the adverse party's attorney may also be the responsibility of the paralegal. The witness should be provided with a copy of any previous statements, such as depositions or other sworn statements. Discrepancies should be noted and discussed with the witness so that she will be prepared to explain the discrepancies if asked about them at trial. If the attorney plans to introduce any exhibits into evidence when the witness testifies, the paralegal should familiarize the witness with the exhibits.

Ask the witness if she would like to talk further about the appearance. If the witness is nervous about testifying, you might suggest that she visit a trial in progress before testifying. Make sure the witness understands courtroom etiquette, including proper dress. The witness should dress conservatively and professionally.

cross-examination
The questioning of a witness by the opposing attorney.

EXHIBIT 6.2   Sample Jury Chart (Police Brutality Case)

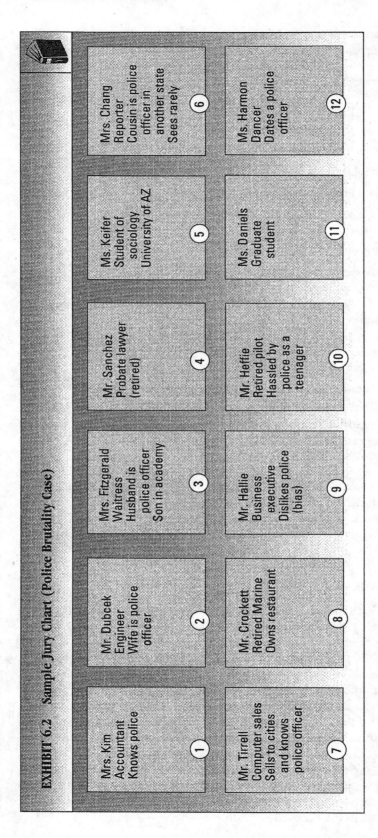

Mrs. Kim Accountant Knows police ①	**Mr. Dubcek** Engineer Wife is police officer ②	**Mrs. Fitzgerald** Waitress Husband is police officer Son in academy ③
Mr. Sanchez Probate lawyer (retired) ④	**Ms. Keifer** Student of sociology University of AZ ⑤	**Mrs. Chang** Reporter Cousin is police officer in another state Sees rarely ⑥
Mr. Tirrell Computer sales Sells to cities and knows police officer ⑦	**Mr. Crockett** Retired Marine Owns restaurant ⑧	**Mr. Hallie** Business executive Dislikes police (bias) ⑨
Mr. Heffie Retired pilot Hassled by police as a teenager ⑩	**Ms. Daniels** Graduate student ⑪	**Ms. Harmon** Dancer Dates a police officer ⑫

It may be necessary to serve some witnesses with a subpoena to ensure their appearance at the trial. Try to call or write to the witness before issuing the subpoena to let her know it will be coming. Explain why her testimony is important and stress that you will try to minimize the time she must spend in the courtroom.

When the trial begins, you should have the original subpoenas along with the proof of service with you in the courtroom so that you will have proof that the individual witnesses were actually served. If a witness who has been served with a subpoena fails to appear at the scheduled time, she may be held in contempt of court for violating a court order.

A copy of the witness schedule should be retained by the legal secretary. It should include each witness's name and telephone number. If a particular witness's testimony will be postponed, the paralegal should call the witness or the legal secretary from the court. If the court adjourns early one day, all subsequent witnesses may have to be contacted and told to appear on a later date. In addition to the copy of the witness list in the Trial Book, the paralegal should also keep a copy.

During the trial, the paralegal and/or legal secretary should keep in touch with the witnesses. Those who are nervous about testifying may need more reassurance.

Evidence

The paralegal and/or legal secretary may be asked to gather and/or prepare evidence for the trial. This may include taking pictures, drawing charts, or preparing other demonstrative evidence. The paralegal or legal secretary may be asked to gather evidence from other sources as well. Whenever evidence comes from outside the firm, its source should be noted.

All evidence that will be introduced at the trial must be authenticated; that is, the custodian, writer, or preparer must state that the evidence is what it purports to be. This **authentication** may be accomplished by a sworn statement or testimony at trial or by a certified copy of the document. When gathering the evidence, the paralegal or legal secretary must check to be sure all documents have been authenticated and all other evidence has been preserved properly. Under the **Best Evidence Rule,** an attorney introducing records, letters, or reports into evidence must either use the original or show why it was not available for introduction. The paralegal should therefore check to make sure that originals are on hand or, if that is impossible, that their absence can be explained.

All evidence should be logged in the Trial Book. A chronological record should be maintained showing the time the evidence will be introduced at the trial. To ensure that the evidence will be safe until the trial, all items should be kept in a locked file drawer. Papers should be placed in sealed envelopes with their authentication. Lists should be kept with notations on the location and authentication of all evidence.

authentication
A formal act that certifies that a document is correct so that it may be admitted into evidence; evidence proving a document is what it purports to be.

Best Evidence Rule
A rule that requires that when a document is admitted into evidence at trial, either the original must be used or the attorney must show why it is not available.

THE TRIAL

We have already discussed one of the main differences between civil and criminal trials. As Chapter 5 explained, civil suits are generally brought by private persons or entities against other private persons or entities, although the government or one of its agencies can also be the plaintiff or defendant. In contrast, in a criminal case, the plaintiff is always the people or the state (not the individual victim), represented by the prosecuting attorney.

preponderance of the evidence
The burden of proof in civil suits. It means that the event in question is more likely than not to have happened in that manner.

beyond a reasonable doubt
The standard of proof in criminal cases; a higher standard than the preponderance of the evidence standard used in civil cases.

The other major difference between civil and criminal trials is the burden of proof required for the jury to reach its decision. Juries in civil trials must reach a decision by the **preponderance of the evidence,** which means that the event is more likely than not to have happened in that manner. In many states only three-fourths of the jurors must find for the plaintiff for the plaintiff to prevail.

In a criminal trial, the standard for finding the defendant guilty is **beyond a reasonable doubt,** which is a very high standard. Many articles and books have been written about the meaning of this standard. Although "beyond a reasonable doubt" does not mean that the jury has no doubt that the defendant is guilty, it does mean that the jury has no *reasonable* doubt, bearing in mind that there will always be a slight doubt even with considerable evidence.

Aside from these differences in the parties and the burden of proof, civil and criminal trials are very similar. Both proceed through the same steps and follow similar procedures.

The Paralegal at Trial

Today, more than ever, paralegals are attending trials to assist their attorney employers. Paralegals may help in picking the jury, gathering evidence, and preparing witnesses. They may watch the witnesses testifying to assess their credibility based on their body language and nonverbal communication, as well as on their answers to the attorney's questions. Paralegals also keep the Trial Book and prompt the attorney on events as they occur.

Conducting the Trial

A trial generally proceeds through the following sequence:

1. Voir dire (picking the jury)
2. Opening statements
3. Direct examination of witnesses
4. Cross-examination of witnesses
5. Closing arguments
6. Jury instructions
7. Jury deliberations
8. Judgment or verdict

Each will be discussed in this section.

voir dire
The process in which the judge and attorneys select a jury.

Voir Dire.   During the **voir dire** (literally "to speak the truth") the attorneys and the judge conduct the preliminary examination of the prospective jurors. The paralegal should observe the proceedings carefully so he can help the attorney select the best possible jury. You should watch the facial expressions, gestures, and body language of the jurors as well as listen to their answers to questions. Watch for signs that a juror may have negative feelings toward the client or the attorney.

Keep a chart as shown in Exhibit 6.2 for the attorney and make notes on each person as appropriate. When a juror is excused, remove that note from the chart and replace it with a new one with the new name. The attorney may ask your opinion on individual jurors. Be honest about whether you think the juror should be kept or rejected. Give the attorney your reasons. Your contributions can help the attorney select the best jury for the client.

Attorneys have an unlimited number of **challenges for cause.** A challenge for cause allows an attorney to dismiss a juror if the attorney can show bias or prejudice by the prospective juror. Each attorney also has a limited number of **peremptory challenges;** the number varies depending on the nature of the case. No reason is required to dismiss a juror with a peremptory challenge. However, peremptory challenges cannot be used to exclude potential jurors based solely on race or ethnic background. The attorney should be careful not to use up his peremptory challenges too soon, or he may be unable to dismiss a later juror whom he does not want.

Opening Statements.

Once the jury is selected, the attorneys present their **opening statements.** The plaintiff's attorney speaks first, followed by the defendant's attorney. These statements provide a brief introduction to the facts of the case from the perspective of the respective parties. This is the first opportunity that the attorneys have to make a good impression on the jury. Each attorney instructs the jury on what they should note in the evidence and stresses the facts in his client's favor. The attorneys may not use the opening statement to present an argument; this is reserved for closing arguments.

During the opening statements, the paralegal should watch the jury carefully to determine how they are reacting to the attorney. Does their body language show belief or disbelief? Are they listening to the attorney? The attorney should be made aware of any potential problems.

Examination of Witnesses.

After the opening statements, the attorneys present their cases by calling witnesses to the stand to answer questions. Evidence is also introduced and marked as exhibits. The plaintiff's attorney begins the process with the **direct examination** of the witnesses for his party. After the plaintiff's attorney questions each of his witnesses, the defense may cross-examine that witness. The defense attorney may only cross-examine the witness about information brought out during direct examination, however. Then the plaintiff's attorney may institute redirect examination (questioning the witness again), but only on information brought out on cross-examination. Occasionally, the defense may institute re-cross-examination (questioning the witness a second time), but only on information brought out during redirect examination. Thinking of the examination process as a series of boxes within boxes as in Exhibit 6.3 will help make this concept clearer. Notice that the boxes become smaller, reflecting the scope of the questioning, as the examination process continues. The testimony of the plaintiff's witnesses represents the plaintiff's case in chief. At the end of all testimony by the witnesses, the plaintiff's attorney rests his case.

At this point, the defense attorney presents her case in the same manner as the plaintiff's attorney did. Witnesses are called and examined and evidence introduced. The plaintiff cross-examines the witnesses; the defense redirects; the plaintiff may re-cross-examine. Then the defense attorney rests her case.

During witness examination, the paralegal should watch the jury as well as the witnesses. Determine if the jury is paying attention. If a juror is sleeping, a pencil discreetly dropped on the floor may awaken him. Watch the impression each witness is making on the jury by observing their body language. Watch the reaction of the jury members to each attorney's presentation.

---

challenges for cause
Dismissal of prospective jurors where bias or prejudice can be shown.

peremptory challenges
Dismissal of prospective jurors without having to give a reason; may not be used to exclude jurors solely on the basis of race or ethnic background.

opening statement
The introduction to the facts of the case each attorney presents to the jury at the beginning of the trial.

direct examination
The questioning of a witness by the attorney who called that witness.

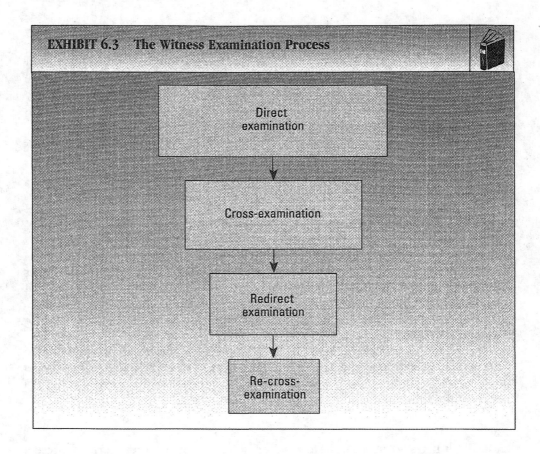

EXHIBIT 6.3   The Witness Examination Process

Direct
examination

↓

Cross-examination

↓

Redirect
examination

↓

Re-cross-
examination

You may also be asked to gather your side's witnesses. Be sure they are in court at the scheduled time. You may have to sit with them in the corridor while they are waiting to testify. In this event, you obviously will not be able to observe the witnesses' testimony or the impression the attorney is making on the jury.

Closing Arguments.   Once both sides have presented their respective cases, the attorneys present their **closing arguments.** Again, the plaintiff's attorney goes first. He presents a summary of the evidence and the witnesses' testimony from the plaintiff's perspective. Then the defense attorney presents her closing arguments. In many states, the plaintiff's attorney is allowed to make a rebuttal argument.

The closing arguments are the last opportunity the attorneys have to talk to the jury. They want to present the best possible summation of the case from their own client's perspective. Some attorneys believe the closing argument is the most critical phase of the trial because it is the last statement the jury will hear from the attorneys before deliberations begin.

The paralegal should watch the jury carefully during closing arguments to determine their reactions to the attorney. Their body language may suggest belief or disbelief. It may also show their favorable or unfavorable impression of the attorney.

Jury Instructions.   Paralegals may assist in the preparation of **jury instructions,** which are typed by the legal secretary. Books in the law library will provide sample

closing argument
The summary of the case each attorney presents to the jury at the end of the trial.

jury instructions
The instructions the judge gives to the jury before deliberations to explain the law the jury should apply.

instructions for different legal issues. Both attorneys may submit jury instructions to the judge to be read to the jury. The judge also has her own instructions for the jury. If there is no jury, the attorneys present their instructions to the judge. After the judge reads the instructions to the jury, they go into the jury room to deliberate. The deliberations may take a few hours or several days.

Jury Deliberations. When the jury enters the jury room, they elect a foreman or forewoman, who becomes the spokesperson for the group. After discussing the case and the evidence, the jury votes on the guilt or liability of the defendant. The foreman or forewoman then collects the votes and reads the verdict to the court.

Judgment or Verdict. Civil juries render a **judgment.** If the plaintiff is suing for money damages, the judgment includes the amount of the damages awarded.

Criminal juries render a **verdict**—guilty or not guilty. If the verdict is guilty, the judge sentences the defendant. In Virginia and Kentucky, the jury is allowed to sentence the defendant. In some states the sentence is imposed in a separate proceeding, called the sentencing phase of the trial.

judgment
The decision in a civil case; may include money damages.

verdict
The decision reached by a jury in a criminal case as to whether the defendant is guilty or not guilty; must be unanimous in most states.

AFTER THE TRIAL

Contacting the Jurors

Once the jury reaches its decision and is dismissed by the judge, most jurisdictions allow attorneys to contact individual jurors. They are an excellent source of information about the impression the attorney and the witnesses made. The jurors' impressions of various evidence introduced at the trial may also be useful. For instance, they may point out that a chart you made to show the sequence of events was unclear. Information of this type may be extremely valuable for subsequent trials.

The attorney may ask the paralegal to contact the jurors, who may or may not be eager to speak with you. An informal telephone call explaining your function and the reason for the call may be a first step to a later interview. Always ask if this is a good time to call or whether another time might be more convenient. Explain the reason for your call. Try to arrange a private interview with the juror at his convenience. If coming to your office would be inconvenient, arrange to meet at the juror's home.

Contact the jurors as soon after the trial ends as possible. Information will be fresh in their minds and therefore more valuable to you.

Enforcing Civil Judgments

Sometimes the jury in a civil case awards the plaintiff a substantial judgment against the defendant, but the defendant fails to pay the amount due. In that case, the attorney will have to institute further proceedings to force payment.

The first step in this process is a supplementary proceeding known as an **Examination of Judgment Debtor.** This proceeding is a court hearing where the defendant appears and testifies about her assets. The format for this procedure varies from state to state, so you should check the local court rules on the proper documents to prepare.

After the hearing, you may file a **writ of execution** against the defendant's assets. This document tells the defendant that unless she pays the judgment within a certain

Examination of Judgment Debtor
A formal court hearing where the defendant appears to answer questions about her assets.

writ of execution
A writ filed against assets of the debtor to enable a creditor to satisfy a judgment. The assets may be sold to pay the debt.

time, the sheriff or marshal will take possession of the property and sell it at a public sale. The proceeds from the sale will be used to pay the judgment. Any money left over will be returned to the defendant. A writ of execution may be filed against either real or personal property (real property is land and other real estate; personal property is all other property). Forms are available in the Court Clerk's Office for this purpose. Some states refer to these documents as **writs of attachment** (see Exhibit 6.4).

If the defendant has no property, or the property is insufficient to pay the judgment, the plaintiff may file a **garnishment** against the defendant's wages. A certain percentage of the wages will be paid to the plaintiff each pay period until the judgment has been satisfied.

Judgments are usually valid for eight to ten years. Therefore, if the defendant has insufficient assets to satisfy the judgment today, you may still collect on the judgment for the next eight to ten years. At the end of that time period, some states allow the plaintiff to file an order to renew the judgment.

Appeals

The losing party in a civil suit may decide to appeal the decision to a higher court, as may a defendant who has been found guilty in a criminal case. If a defendant is found not guilty, the prosecution may not appeal the verdict. The party who appeals the case is known as the **appellant**. The opposing party is called the **appellee**. Appeals may be taken based on an error made at the trial that deprived the appellant of a fair trial. The error must have been so critical that it could affect the outcome of the case. Errors that do not affect the outcome are known as "harmless errors" and do not provide grounds for an appeal.

The time to appeal a case varies among the states but is usually between thirty and sixty days from the date of the final judgment. The Notice of Appeal must be filed in the trial court that heard the case initially. A copy must be served on the adverse party. In the federal courts, the appeal must be filed with the original trial court within thirty days from the entry of judgment. A sample Notice of Appeal is shown in Exhibit 6.5.

Appellate Court Briefs.   Although the format for the appellate court brief varies from state to state, many states follow the federal rules. A federal appellant's brief should include the following:

1. A table of contents, which includes a table of cases, authorities, and statutes.

2. A statement of the subject matter and appellate jurisdiction.

3. A statement of the issues that are being reviewed.

4. A statement of the nature of the case and its disposition in the lower court. This should include a statement of the relevant facts with reference to the trial court record.

5. The argument of the issues presented along with the reason the appellate court should reverse the trial court. This section must include citations to the authorities used.

6. A conclusion that includes the relief sought.

The appellee is allowed an opportunity to respond to the appellant's brief; the appellee's brief should include the same sections as the appellant's brief except that the statement of jurisdiction and the statement of the issues of the case are not

---

writ of attachment
A writ of execution.

garnishment
A procedure that enables a creditor to obtain a percentage of the defendant's wages for payment of a debt owed.

appellant
The individual or entity that appeals a case.

appellee
The individual or entity against whom the appellant appeals; the opposing party.

EXHIBIT 6.4   A Sample Writ of Execution

ATTORNEY OR PARTY WITHOUT ATTORNEY *(Name and Address)*:   TELEPHONE NO.:   FOR RECORDER'S USE ONLY

[XX] Recording requested by and return to:
> Jeffrey M. Williams
> Michaels & Williams
> 1122 Main Street, Seal Beach, California 99999

[X] ATTORNEY FOR   [X] JUDGMENT CREDITOR   [ ] ASSIGNEE OF RECORD

NAME OF COURT: **County Superior Court**
STREET ADDRESS: **224 Civic Center Drive**
MAILING ADDRESS: **PO Box 11122**
CITY AND ZIP CODE: **Seal Beach, California 99999**
BRANCH NAME:

PLAINTIFF: Richard L. Danielson

DEFENDANT: Joanne V. Peterson

WRIT OF	[X] **EXECUTION (Money Judgment)** [ ] **POSSESSION OF** [ ] **Personal Property** [ ] **Real Property** [ ] **SALE**	CASE NUMBER: **C-444555** FOR COURT USE ONLY

1. **To the Sheriff or any Marshal or Constable of the County of:**
   Orange
   You are directed to enforce the judgment described below with daily interest and your costs as provided by law.

2. **To any registered process server:** You are authorized to serve this writ only in accord with CCP 699.080 or CCP 715.040.

3. *(Name)*: Richard L. Danielson
   is the [X] judgment creditor [ ] assignee of record
   whose address is shown on this form above the court's name.

4. **Judgment debtor** *(name and last known address)*:

   > Joanne V. Peterson
   > 529 Beach Drive
   > Newtown, California

   [ ] additional judgment debtors on reverse

5. **Judgment entered on** *(date)*: May 9, 1995
6. [ ] **Judgment renewed on** *(dates)*:

7. **Notice of sale** under this writ
   a. [ ] has not been requested.
   b. [X] has been requested *(see reverse)*.
8. [ ] Joint debtor information on reverse.

[SEAL]

9. [ ] See reverse for information on real or personal property to be delivered under a writ of possession or sold under a writ of sale.
10. [ ] This writ is issued on a sister-state judgment.
11. Total judgment . . . . $ 55,499
12. Costs after judgment (per filed order or memo CCP 685.090) . $ 200
13. Subtotal *(add 11 and 12)* . . . . . $ 55,699
14. Credits . . . . $
15. Subtotal *(subtract 14 from 13)* . $ 55,699
16. Interest after judgment (per filed affidavit CCP 685.050) . . . . . . $ 101
17. Fee for issuance of writ . . . . . . $ 50
18. **Total** *(add 15, 16, and 17)* . . . . $ 55,850
19. Levying officer: Add daily interest from date of writ *(at the legal rate on 15)* of . . . . $ 22.00
20. [ ] The amounts called for in items 11–19 are different for each debtor. These amounts are stated for each debtor on Attachment 20.

Issued on *(date)*: May 15, 1996

Clerk, by _____ , Deputy

— NOTICE TO PERSON SERVED: SEE REVERSE FOR IMPORTANT INFORMATION —

(Continued on reverse)

Form Approved by the
Judicial Council of California   **WRIT OF EXECUTION**   Code of Civil Procedure, §§ 699.520, 712.010, 715.010

EXHIBIT 6.4   A Sample Writ of Execution *Concluded*

SHORT TITLE:	CASE NUMBER:
Danielson v. Peterson	C—444555

Items continued from the first page:

4. ☐ **Additional judgment debtor** *(name and last known address)*:

7. ☐ **Notice of sale** has been requested by *(name and address)*:

8. ☐ **Joint debtor** was declared bound by the judgment (CCP 989–994)
    a. on *(date)*:   a. on *(date)*:
    b. name and address of joint debtor: b. name and address of joint debtor:

    c. ☐ additional costs against certain joint debtors *(itemize)*:

9. ☒ *(Writ of Possession or Writ of Sale)* **Judgment** was entered for the following:
    a. ☐ Possession of real property: The complaint was filed on *(date)*:   *(Check (1) or (2))*:
          (1) ☐ The Prejudgment Claim of Right to Possession was served in compliance with CCP 415.46.
                The judgment includes all tenants, subtenants, named claimants, and other occupants of the premises.
          (2) ☐ The Prejudgment Claim of Right to Possession was NOT served in compliance with CCP 415.46.
                (a) $ was the daily rental value on the date the complaint was filed.
                (b) The court will hear objections to enforcement of the judgment under CCP 1174.3 on the following
                     dates *(specify)*:
    b. ☒ Possession of personal property
         ☒ If delivery cannot be had, then for the value *(itemize in 9e)* specified in the judgment or supplemental order.
    c. ☒ Sale of personal property
    d. ☐ Sale of real property
    e. Description of property:
    1995 Porsche Carrera automobile, estimated value $65,000.00

— NOTICE TO PERSON SERVED —

WRIT OF EXECUTION OR SALE.   Your rights and duties are indicated on the accompanying Notice of Levy.
WRIT OF POSSESSION OF PERSONAL PROPERTY.   If the levying officer is not able to take custody of the property, the levying officer will make a demand upon you for the property. If custody is not obtained following demand, the judgment may be enforced as a money judgment for the value of the property specified in the judgment or in a supplemental order.
WRIT OF POSSESSION OF REAL PROPERTY.   If the premises are not vacated within five days after the date of service on the occupant or, if service is by posting, within five days after service on you, the levying officer will remove the occupants from the real property and place the judgment creditor in possession of the property. Personal property remaining on the premises will be sold or otherwise disposed of in accordance with CCP 1174 unless you or the owner of the property pays the judgment creditor the reasonable cost of storage and takes possession of the personal property not later than 15 days after the time the judgment creditor takes possession of the premises.
► *A Claim of Right to Possession form accompanies this writ (unless the Summons was served in compliance with CCP 415.46).*

---

* *NOTE:* Continued use of form EJ-130 (Rev. Jan. 1, 1989) is authorized until June 30, 1992, *except* if used as a Writ of Possession of Real Property.

EJ-130 [Rev. September 30, 1991*]   **WRIT OF EXECUTION**   Page two

EXHIBIT 6.5   A Sample Notice of Appeal

1	Patricia Barragan
2	Attorney at Law
3	12222 Ocean Avenue
4	Long Beach, CA 90008
5	
6	Attorney for Defendant
7	

NOTICE OF APPEAL TO A COURT OF APPEALS FROM

A JUDGMENT OF A FEDERAL DISTRICT COURT

UNITED STATES DISTRICT COURT FOR THE

SOUTHERN DISTRICT OF CALIFORNIA

DANIELSON DELIVERY SERVICE,   )

              Plaintiff,   )

      v.   )   Notice of Appeal

PETERSON PLUMBING COMPANY,   )   Case No. WP-22233

            Defendant.   )

    Notice is hereby given that PETERSON PLUMBING COMPANY, defendant above named, hereby appeals to the United States Court of Appeals for the Ninth Circuit from the final judgment entered in this action on the 20th day of October, 1996.

                                    _____

                                      PATRICIA BARRAGAN
Attorney for PETERSON PLUMBING
COMPANY
12222 Ocean Avenue
Long Beach, CA 90008

Line numbers: 8, 9, 10, 11, 12, 13, 14, 15, 16, 17, 18, 19, 20, 21, 22, 23, 24, 25, 26, 27, 28

required unless the appellee is dissatisfied with those presented by the appellant. The appellant then has the opportunity to present a reply brief.

Technical Requirements. The federal appellant's and appellee's briefs must also satisfy certain technical requirements. The briefs must be no more than fifty pages in length, and the reply brief is limited to twenty-five pages. The appellant's brief must be filed within forty days after the record is filed. The appellee's brief is due within thirty days of the date the appellant's brief is served.

The federal court requires that twenty-five copies of the brief be filed and that two copies be served on each party. If the appellant fails to file the brief within the allotted time, the appellee may move for dismissal of the appeal. If the appellee fails to file within the time allotted, he will not be allowed to present oral arguments unless special permission is obtained from the court.

Under Rule 32 of the Federal Rules of Civil Procedure, federal briefs must also meet the following requirements:

1. The briefs must be typed or printed.

2. At least 11 point type must be used.

3. The briefs should be on opaque unglazed paper.

4. If typed, the briefs should be bound in volumes. The pages should be 6⅛ by 9¼ inches with the typing occupying an area 4⅙ by 7⅙ inches.

5. If another process, such as printing, is used, the bound pages must not exceed 8½ by 11 inches, and the typing must not exceed 6½ by 9½ inches.

6. The text must be double-spaced.

7. The cover should be blue for the appellant's brief and red for the appellee's brief.

The paralegal and legal secretary should be extremely careful to follow all of the requirements of the court. Check with your own state court to determine their technical and formatting requirements. Since most briefs are printed, you should proofread the galleys very carefully. Once the brief is returned from the printer, **"Shepardize"** all of the cases cited to be sure they are still "good law." Shepardizing means looking up all citations included in the brief in Shepard's Case Citations to be sure none of the cases have been overruled. If so, the attorney should be informed.

During a field trip to the Supreme Court of California with a paralegal class, the author observed an attorney citing a case in support of his position. One of the justices asked if he had Shepardized the case and said that if he had, he would have known that the case had been overruled by a subsequent decision of the same court. This experience taught the students a valuable lesson on the importance of Shepardizing.

Shepardize
Looking up a citation in Shepard's Case Citations to make sure the case has not been overruled; updating research by finding the latest cases and statutes.

SUMMARY

This chapter takes the student through the complete trial process. In preparation for trial, a Trial Book is compiled to assist the attorney during the court proceeding. The trial begins with the selection of the jury (voir dire) by the attorneys. Once the jury is selected, the attorneys for both sides make their opening statements. Next each side, beginning with the plaintiff, presents its case by calling witnesses and presenting evidence. Direct examination of each witness by the plaintiff's attorney is followed by cross-examination by the defendant's attorney. After the plaintiff's case is presented, the defense begins. The defense attorney questions each witness (direct examination); the plaintiff's attorney then cross-examines the witness. When the cases have been presented, closing arguments are given by both attorneys, after which the judge gives the jury instructions indicating the law they should follow during their deliberations.

If the plaintiff receives a favorable decision in a civil trial, the defendant may be required to pay money damages to the plaintiff. Various methods of collection are available if the defendant does not pay voluntarily.

Either party in a civil case may appeal an adverse judgment to the next higher court, as may a defendant who is found guilty in a criminal case. Appellate court briefs must be prepared carefully to meet the requirements of the particular court.

KEY TERMS

Appellant   164

Appellee   164

Authentication   159

Best Evidence Rule   159

Beyond a reasonable doubt   160

Challenges for cause   161

Closing argument   162

Cross-examination   157

Direct examination   161

Examination of Judgment Debtor   163

Garnishment   164

Judgment   163

Jury instructions   162

Opening statement   161

Peremptory challenges   161

Preponderance of the evidence   160

Shepardize   168

Verdict   163

Voir dire   160

Writ of attachment   164

Writ of execution   163

SELF-TEST

A.   Indicate whether the following statements are true (T) or false (F):

_____ 1. A chronological list of the events in the suit is included in the Trial Book.

_____ 2. Witness schedules include only the witnesses' names and the dates they will appear in court.

_____ 3. Only the attorney may prepare the witnesses to testify at the trial.

_____ 4. Witnesses should dress conservatively for the trial.

_____ 5. To ensure that a witness will appear at the trial, a complaint may be served on the witness.

B.   Circle the correct answer for the following questions:

1. Before evidence is introduced at the trial, it must be

   a. demonstrated.

   b. published.

    c. authenticated.

    d. shown to the jury.

2. The rule that requires an attorney to introduce the original of any records, letters, or reports into evidence or show why the original was not available is called the

    a. Best Evidence Rule.

    b. Records Evidence Rule.

    c. Authentic Records Rule.

    d. Trial Book Rule.

3. The burden of proof required for the jury to reach a verdict in a criminal trial is

    a. a preponderance of the evidence.

    b. beyond a doubt.

    c. beyond any doubt.

    d. beyond a reasonable doubt.

4. Voir dire refers to the

    a. opening statements.

    b. cross-examination of witnesses.

    c. jury selection process.

    d. jury instructions.

    e. closing arguments.

5. Which of the following occur during a trial?

    a. voir dire.

    b. opening statements.

    c. jury instructions.

    d. (a) and (b) only.

    e. (a), (b), and (c).

C.   Fill in the blanks:

1. The preliminary examination of the prospective jurors is called

    _____ .

2. The _____ attorney is the first to give an opening statement.

3. After the defense presents its closing arguments, the plaintiff is allowed to

    make a _____ argument.

4. Civil juries render a _____ while criminal juries render a

    _____ .

5. In most states, a jury in a criminal case must return a guilty verdict unani-

mously, but generally a plaintiff in a civil case can prevail if

_____ of the jury members vote for the defendant's liability.

REVIEW QUESTIONS

1. Discuss the stages of the trial and how the paralegal or legal secretary assists at each stage.

2. Explain the differences between a trial in a civil case and a trial in a criminal case.

3. What does "beyond a reasonable doubt" mean?

4. Explain the difference between "beyond a reasonable doubt" and a "preponderance of the evidence."

5. What is the purpose of a Trial Book? List five items that would be included in the Trial Book.

PROJECTS

1. Review the discussion of the Trial Book at the beginning of the chapter. Prepare a list of items you would include in a Trial Book for the following cases:

   a.   Client Paul Stevens is suing defendant Robert Beckman for injuries sustained in an automobile accident.

   b.   Client Susan Beck is suing the Local Groceries Company for injuries sustained when she slipped on a banana peel in the produce department.

2. Prepare a blank chart for jury selection.

3. Prepare a Notice of Appeal from an adverse judgment received on December 26, 1995. Use Exhibit 6.5 as a model. Our client is Ms. Emily Azpeitia, the plaintiff; her address is 128 Alabaster Court, Your Town, Your State. The defendant is Jonathan Rasmussen; his address is 999 Winding Brook Lane, Your Town, Your State.

4. Our client, Mrs. Betty Jo Maldonado, was involved in an automobile accident on May 5, 1996, at 3:00 P.M. at the corner of Main and Broad Streets in Your Town. She alleges that the defendant, Joseph Pacheco, ran the red light and hit her car on the driver's side. She was driving a 1995 Lexus four-door LS400. The defendant was driving a 1994 Chevrolet pickup truck. Attorney Williams has asked you to draft some questions to ask the following witnesses:

   • Witness 1: Ms. Joan Maldonado was a passenger in her mother's automobile at the time of the accident and was injured. She is our witness.

   • Witness 2: Joanne Pacheco, the defendant's wife, was a passenger in his truck at the time of the collision. She is a witness for the defense. Mr. Williams has asked you to draft questions to ask Mrs. Pacheco on cross-examination. She is expected to say that the light was green and that our client ran the red light.

5. Attorney Jeffrey Williams has asked you to meet with a client, Ms. Kitzman, to discuss her appearance at an upcoming trial. She is suing the defendant for personal injuries sustained in an automobile accident. Prepare a list of items that should be addressed during your discussion with her, including how she should dress for the trial, the types of questions she may be asked, and any other information you feel is appropriate.

6. Assume the client in Project 5 is not able to visit the office. Draft a letter to her from Mr. Williams addressing the key points that should be discussed and explained to her about her testimony at the upcoming trial.

Probate and Estate Planning

CHAPTER OBJECTIVES

As a result of studying this chapter, you will learn the following material:

1. **Wills** An introduction to the law of wills will be presented. You will learn the terminology used in wills, the different types of wills, methods of preparing a will, and the basic clauses likely to appear in a will.

2. **Trusts** The law of trusts will be introduced. You will learn the advantages of trusts, some of the different types of trusts and when they are appropriate, and the basic format of various trust instruments.

3. **Probate** The probate process will be presented. You will learn how to probate an estate from the initial filing of the petition to the final distribution.

WILLS

People write wills to indicate how they want their property to be distributed after they die. Often people say they do not need a will because they have very little property. But having a will ensures that whatever you have will go to the person you want to have it. Furthermore, if an individual has minor children and wants to specify who will care for them after the parents' deaths, a will is essential. For these reasons, everyone needs a will.

Some terminology is unique to wills, as well as to the related fields of probate and estate planning; therefore, the appropriate terms are defined here:

Decedent.	The deceased person.
Testator.	The person who makes a will.
Testate.	Dying with a will.
Intestate.	Dying without a will.
Legacy.	A gift of personal property left in a will.
Legatee.	A person who is left personal property by will.
Devise.	A gift of real property by will.
Devisee.	A person who is left real property by will.
Probate.	The court procedure used to validate a will, appoint a personal representative, and distribute property.
Executor.	An individual named in the will who is responsible for handling the decedent's affairs, including paying bills of the estate and distributing the property.

Estate.   The property a decedent owned at death.

Administrator.   An individual appointed to administer an estate when the decedent did not have a will or did not name an executor in the will.

Types of Wills

Most wills are formal, typed documents, but holographic, or handwritten, wills can also be valid. A few states still recognize nuncupative, or oral, wills in certain circumstances.

Formal Wills.   To avoid potential disputes after the testator's death, a will should conform to certain formal standards. A **formal will** should be typed, and the testator must sign it in the presence of at least two witnesses, who also sign at the same time. It is advisable to choose witnesses younger than the testator so that they will be available to "prove up" the will upon the testator's death. In some states, the attorney and the legal secretary may witness the wills, but many states do not allow attorneys to witness the wills of their clients.

Individuals who have large and/or complicated estates should usually seek the advice of an attorney in making a will, as should persons who wish to leave their property to nonrelatives. Some states require that all estates acquire the services of an attorney for probate purposes.

Holographic Wills.   A will created entirely in the handwriting of the testator is called a **holographic will.** It must be signed and dated in the testator's handwriting and does not require witnesses. Proving the validity of a holographic will may be difficult, however, unless someone can testify that the handwriting is indeed the testator's. Consequently, the will may be challenged in a will contest. For this reason, clients should be advised that formal wills are preferable to holographic wills.

Nuncupative Wills.   A **nuncupative will** is an oral will. Such wills were originally used in wartime when soldiers dying on the battlefield would give instructions on the disposal of their property. Most states no longer recognize nuncupative wills, although a few states still allow them in cases where an individual with very little property gives deathbed instructions on its disposition.

Requirements for Making a Will

To make a valid will, one must have testamentary capacity and testamentary intent.

Testamentary Capacity.   To make a valid will, the maker must have **testamentary capacity,** or the mental capacity to understand the meaning of the material in the will. In other words, the testator must be capable of knowing that the document is a will and that it is disposing of his property. The testator must also meet the state's requirement for legal age, which is usually the age of majority. A will is void if the maker lacked testamentary capacity at the time the will was made.

Testamentary Intent.   A testator must also have the intent to make a will disposing of her property at the time the will is made. There can be no mistake or undue influ-

---

formal will
A typed will signed by the testator in the presence of at least two witnesses, who must sign the will at the same time.

holographic will
A will entirely in the handwriting of the testator.

nuncupative will
An oral will.

testamentary capacity
The mental capacity to understand the meaning of the material in the will.

ence on the testator when the will is signed. **Mistake** is an unintentional omission or error. For instance, if the testator does not sign the will in the presence of the witnesses, the will may be considered invalid. **Undue influence** is taking advantage of the testator's weakness, age, or distress to affect the will. It includes any act that overpowers the intent of another. In cases of mistake and undue influence, testamentary intent is lacking because the will does not truly reflect the testator's intentions.

In some cases, when a testator leaves her property to nonrelatives, the relatives may challenge the validity of the will in a will contest, claiming that the **beneficiaries** (the persons who inherited the property) used undue influence. A court must then decide whether undue influence was indeed exerted on the testator or whether she truly intended to leave her property to the beneficiaries—perhaps because they had been kind to her while her relatives ignored her. Since the testator cannot testify, will contests are difficult to prove and can become very emotional, particularly when large amounts of money or property are involved. Witnesses must be obtained to prove or disprove the will. The paralegal should attempt to find individuals who knew the testator at the time she was making her will and to whom she might have expressed her intentions. If there are no witnesses, then both parties will testify, and the court will decide the issue based on their credibility.

The Format of a Formal Will

Although formal wills do not have to adhere to a rigid format, they generally follow certain conventions. Formal wills are typed double-spaced. The paragraphs are generally numbered consecutively, either with words (e.g., FIRST, SECOND, THIRD) or numbers (e.g., 1, 2, 3). Individual pages must be numbered. Some law firms use legal cap (lined and numbered paper; see Chapter 2) for wills while others use bond paper. Some law firms have special paper with **"Last Will and Testament"** printed at the top. Most lawyers also ask the legal secretary to put a backing on the will, similar to the blue back discussed in earlier chapters. Exhibit 7.1 shows an example of a formal will, and the following discussion describes the clauses that commonly are included in wills.

Statement of Intent/Introduction.
This clause states the testator's intent to make this will and revokes earlier wills. A sample clause follows:

> I, KARA LOUISE KELSO, residing in the City of Seal Beach, County of Orange, State of California, being of lawful age and sound and disposing mind and memory, do hereby make, publish and declare this to be my last will and testament. I hereby revoke all prior wills or codicils made by me.

Payment of Debts.
All debts of the estate must be paid before the assets are distributed. The first bills paid are those of the testator's last illness, funeral expenses, and estate administration. After the debts are paid, the estate assets are distributed to the heirs. This paragraph is the first of the numbered paragraphs in the will:

> FIRST: I hereby direct that all of my just debts, estate expenses, expenses of last illness, and funeral expenses be paid as soon after my death as is practicable.

Statement of Family Relationships.
This paragraph is a relatively simple clause that lists all of the testator's children and the spouse, if living. It should include the names and dates of birth of all children, as in the following example:

mistake
An unintentional omission or error in making a will.

undue influence
Taking advantage of a testator's weakness, age, or distress to influence the asset distribution in the will.

beneficiary
One who inherits from an estate.

Last Will and Testament
A heading that is often preprinted on the paper used for formal wills because it is the formal name for a will.

EXHIBIT 7.1   A Sample Formal Will

LAST WILL AND TESTAMENT

OF

STEVEN STENMAN

I, STEVEN STENMAN, of 984 Longfellow Drive, Worcester, Massachusetts, being of lawful age and of sound and disposing mind and memory and not acting under fraud, duress, menace of the undue influence of any person or thing, do hereby make, publish and declare this instrument to be my Last Will and Testament, and I do hereby revoke all other Wills and Codicils to Wills heretofore made by me as follows:

FIRST: I direct that all my just debts and expenses of last illness and funeral expenses be paid from my estate as soon after my demise as can lawfully and conveniently be done.

SECOND: I declare that at the time of the execution of this Will, I am married to JANET ANN STENMAN and have three children as follows:

> JONATHAN MICHAEL STENMAN, date of birth: June 20, 1975
>
> VIRGINIA MARIE STENMAN, date of birth: April 29, 1978
>
> JEFFREY MICHAEL STENMAN, date of birth: September 1, 1980

THIRD: I hereby nominate and appoint as Executor of my Last Will and Testament, JAMES ALAN STENMAN, of Dover, Delaware, to serve without bond. In the event JAMES ALAN STENMAN cannot or will not serve for any reason whatsoever, I then appoint MARC WILLIAM ROBERTS, of Chicago, Illinois, to serve without bond.

FOURTH: I declare that all of my property is community property and from my share thereof, I bequeath all of my property to my wife, JANET ANN STENMAN. In the event JANET ANN STENMAN shall predecease me or shall not be alive at the time of the distribution of my estate, I then direct that my estate be divided equally among my children JONATHAN MICHAEL STENMAN, VIRGINIA MARIE STENMAN, and JEFFREY MICHAEL STENMAN, in equal shares.

FIFTH: In the event JONATHAN MICHAEL STENMAN, VIRGINIA MARIE STENMAN, and JEF-FREY MICHAEL STENMAN, shall predecease me or shall not be alive at the time of the distribution of

EXHIBIT 7.1   A Sample Formal Will *Continued*

my estate, I then direct that his or her share shall lapse and shall be distributed in toto to the survivor.

SIXTH: In the event my wife, JANET ANN STENMAN, shall predecease me or shall not be alive at the time of the distribution of my estate, and if any of my children, or all of them, are minors under the law at that time, I hereby appoint MARY ELIZABETH MARTIN, my sister, to serve as their guardian, with full authority to support them from the proceeds of my estate, until they reach the age of majority. If MARY ELIZABETH MARTIN shall be unable or unwilling to serve, then I appoint my brother, JAMES ALAN STENMAN, to serve as their guardian, with full authority to support them from the proceeds of my estate, until they reach the age of majority.

SEVENTH: I have intentionally and with full knowledge failed to provide for any other persons living at the time of my demise except as otherwise provided herein. If any person, whether a beneficiary under this Will or not, shall contest this Will or object to any of the provisions hereof, I give to such person so contesting or objecting the Sum of One Dollar ($1.00) and no more in lieu of the provisions which I have made herein or which I might have made herein to such person or persons so contesting or objecting.

EIGHTH: I give, devise, and bequeath the rest, residue, and remainder of my estate to my above-named spouse, JANET ANN STENMAN.

IN WITNESS WHEREOF, I have hereunto set my hand this 9th day of October, 1996, at Worcester, Massachusetts.

_____

The foregoing instrument, consisting of three (3) pages, was at the date hereof, by STEVEN STENMAN signed as and declared to be his Will, in the presence of us who, at his request and in his presence, and in the presence of each other, have subscribed our names as witnesses thereto. Each of us observed the signing of this Will by STEVEN STENMAN and by each other subscribing witnesses and knows that each signature is the true signature of the person whose name was signed.

EXHIBIT 7.1   A Sample Formal Will *Concluded*

Each of us is now more than twenty-one (21) years of age and a competent witness and resides at the address set forth after his or her name. We are acquainted with STEVEN STENMAN. At this time, he is over the age of eighteen (18) years, and to the best of our knowledge, he is of sound mind and is not acting under duress, menace, fraud, misrepresentation, or undue influence.

Name _____   Address _____

_____

Name _____   Address _____

_____

SECOND: I declare that I am married to DANIEL KELSO and have three children as follows:

1. My daughter, MARIE ELIZABETH KELSO, date of birth: September 10, 1990;
2. My son, MICHAEL WILLIAM KELSO, date of birth: March 1, 1991;
3. My son, JASON DANIEL KELSO, date of birth: July 9, 1993.

All references to "my spouse" or "my children" shall refer to those individuals above named.

pretermitted heir statute
A statute that provides that if a child of the testator is not mentioned in the will, the omission is presumed to be unintentional, and the child receives the share he would have received if the testator had died intestate.

Pretermitted Heir Statute.   Each state has a **pretermitted heir statute** that allows any child not included in this list to receive the amount of the estate that he would have received if there had been no will (this is called "taking against the will"). Pretermitted means "omitted," and these statutes presume that if a child's name is left out of the will, the omission was unintentional and occurred simply because the testator forgot to mention that child. Therefore, if a testator wishes to disown a child and leave him no property, the attorney will advise her that the child must still be mentioned in this clause; otherwise the child may take against the will.

Divorce or Dissolution.   The attorney should advise a client at the time of a divorce that her will should be changed to avoid leaving the estate to her ex-spouse. Other provisions of the will may also need to be changed.

Appointment of Guardian for Minor Children.   This clause nominates the individual or individuals whom you wish to be guardian of your child upon your death. If an individual with children dies, the other parent will likely become their guardian. The will should also appoint an alternate guardian, however, in the event that both parents die at the same time. The testator should discuss the appointment with the prospective guardian before naming that person in the will. The testator may also wish to name a second guardian in case the first is unable or unwilling to serve. Great care should be taken in choosing the guardian, who should be someone with whom the children have a good relationship and who can be trusted to take care of the children with the proceeds from the estate. The following is an example of a clause appointing a guardian:

> THIRD: In the event my spouse shall predecease me, or we should die together, then I nominate ALICIA SANCHEZ, of Los Angeles, California, to be guardian of the person and property of my minor children who survive me. If ALICIA SANCHEZ is unable or unwilling to serve, then I appoint MARIA GARCIA, of Whittier, California, as guardian.

Appointment of Executor.   The **Executor** is the individual who handles the affairs of the estate, including payment of debts and distribution of assets. Some older wills use the term *Executrix* to refer to a female Executor. Many married individuals choose their spouse for this position. If the estate is large and/or complicated, however, some attorneys may advise that an accountant, an attorney, an expert in financial or property management, or an organization such as a bank be named as Executor. In that case, the Executor will charge the estate for services provided. State statutes establish fees for Executors; however, an Executor who is an heir will often waive the fee.

Clients should discuss their affairs and estate with the Executor during their lifetime. If possible, an inventory of all assets should be made and given to the Executor. If not, the Executor should be told where all of the important documents are kept.

The Executor is in charge of paying the bills of the estate from the estate assets, administering and supervising the probate of the estate (usually through an attorney), and distributing the estate assets. The Executor may serve **with bond** or **without bond.** Generally, if the testator trusts the Executor to handle all of the estate assets, the will would not require that a bond be posted. If a bond is required, its cost will be taken from the estate assets. The following is an example of a clause naming an Executor:

> FOURTH: I hereby nominate my spouse, DANIEL KELSO, to serve as Executor of my estate, without bond. If my said spouse should predecease me or be unable to serve, then I nominate my sister, KIMBERLY FITZGERALD, to serve, without bond.

Distribution of Assets.   The most important part of the will is the distribution of assets. This clause may be a general clause, leaving all property to a spouse and, if the spouse does not survive by a specified period (e.g., 180 days), then leaving it to the children in equal shares. It may also list various items, such as family heirlooms, that the testator wishes to go to certain individuals. Usually, attorneys will use several clauses for the distribution of assets, particularly if a number of items are to go to specified individuals. Each item must be listed and described in the will.

If an individual is married, both spouses should discuss the disposal of their property after death before the will is made. Generally, married couples leave the property to each other and to their children equally if one spouse **predeceases** (dies before) the other. In some states, a surviving spouse automatically inherits the other's property; in other states, the survivor gets a certain percentage of the property. In community property states, the distribution differs depending on whether the property is separate or community property. Separate property includes property obtained before marriage or by personal gift or inheritance after marriage. Community property, in states using this

---

Executor
An individual named in the will who is responsible for handling the decedent's affairs, including paying bills of the estate and distributing the property.

with bond
Refers to an Executor having to post a bond before administering an estate.

without bond
Refers to an Executor being allowed to administer an estate without having to post bond.

predecease
To die before another; often used in regard to spouses.

system, is property acquired during marriage that is not a personal gift or inheritance. See Chapter 8 on Family Law for further discussion.

The testator will also have to decide whether the children will receive the assets by right of representation (per stirpes) or per capita (see Exhibit 7.2). Under the **per stirpes** method, if a child predeceases his parents but leaves children, those children will inherit the share of the estate their deceased parent would have received if he had not died. To illustrate, suppose the testator had three children (A, B, and C) who have two children each. Child A predeceases the testator. His children will each receive one-sixth of the estate because child A would have received one-third of the estate if he had lived ($\frac{1}{3} \div 2 = \frac{1}{6}$).

Under the **per capita** method of distribution, each surviving child and grandchild receives an equal percentage of the estate. For instance, if the decedent is survived by one child and three grandchildren, each heir receives one-fourth of the estate.

Sometimes individuals prefer a method that is neither per stirpes nor per capita. For example, a testator who is closer to her grandchildren than to her children might want to leave a larger portion of her estate to the grandchildren, as well as leaving a portion to her great-grandchildren in equal proportions for all. Or perhaps the grandchildren whose parents are deceased are in need of funds, while the testator's other children and grandchildren are well off. In that case, the testator might want to leave

per stirpes
A method of distribution in which the children of a deceased parent receive the share of their grandparent's estate that their parent would have received if he were alive.

per capita
A method of distribution in which each surviving child and grandchild receives an equal share of the estate.

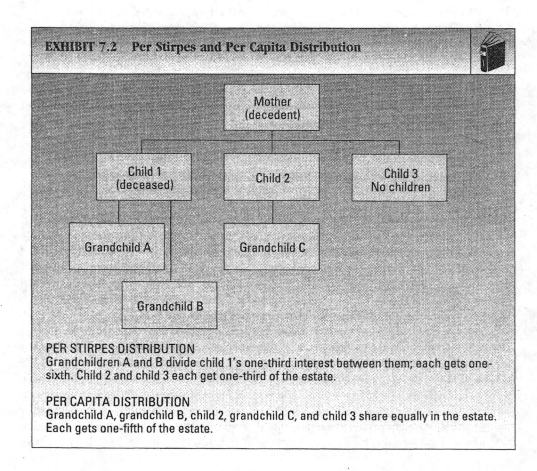

EXHIBIT 7.2   Per Stirpes and Per Capita Distribution

PER STIRPES DISTRIBUTION
Grandchildren A and B divide child 1's one-third interest between them; each gets one-sixth. Child 2 and child 3 each get one-third of the estate.

PER CAPITA DISTRIBUTION
Grandchild A, grandchild B, child 2, grandchild C, and child 3 share equally in the estate. Each gets one-fifth of the estate.

a disproportionate share to the poorer grandchildren. Whatever the case, all arrangements must be specified in the will.

Usually, though, the testator will agree to share the estate equally among the children and then among the grandchildren by right of representation, as in the following clause:

> FIFTH: I give, devise, and bequeath all of my assets, both real and personal and wheresoever situated, to my spouse, DANIEL KELSO. If my spouse should predecease me or shall not survive me by 180 days, then I give all of my assets to my children in equal shares. If any of my children should predecease me, then I give their share of my assets to their children who survive me, by right of representation. If any predeceased child of mine shall have no surviving child or children, then I give, devise, and bequeath their share of my estate to my other children in equal shares.

If a testator has specific assets that she wishes to go to certain individuals, a clause such as the following may be used:

> FIFTH: I give, devise, and bequeath my ruby and diamond ring and my diamond wedding band to my daughter, MARIE ELIZABETH KELSO. If my said daughter predeceases me or fails to survive me by 180 days, I give these rings to my eldest granddaughter. If no granddaughter survives me, then I give these rings to my son, MICHAEL WILLIAM KELSO.
>
> I give, devise, and bequeath all of my real property to my husband DANIEL KELSO. If my said husband should predecease me, then I give all of my real property to my children in equal shares.
>
> I give, devise, and bequeath all of my personal property in equal shares to my said husband and my children.

Joint Tenancy Property.

Joint tenancy property is property that is owned by two or more persons, called the joint tenants. If one of the joint tenants dies, his interest in the property automatically passes to the other joint tenant(s). Therefore, any property owned in joint tenancy by the decedent and another person passes outside the will and is not affected by it. For instance, if an estate has more outstanding debts than its assets are worth (called a negative estate), joint tenancy property cannot be sold to pay the decedent's bills. Joint tenancy property passes to the other owner without having to go through the probate process. In some states, however, joint tenancy property must be included in the estate tax return for estate tax purposes.

Converting the joint tenancy property to the other owner is usually a simple matter. In the case of a bank account, most states require a copy of the death certificate and other formal probate papers naming the Executor. Some states have forms that must be completed to "break the joint tenancy."

General and Specific Bequests.

General bequests are described only in general terms in the will. "All household furnishings" and "all of my property" are examples of general bequests.

In contrast, specific bequests describe specific property. "My 1987 Nissan Sentra" and "my property located at 211 Main Street in Prescott, Arizona," are examples. If the testator does not own that particular property at the time of her death, the gift lapses and the beneficiary gets nothing. For instance, if the testator sells the Nissan Sentra and buys a 1994 Honda Civic after making her will, the beneficiary does not receive the

Honda. Specific bequests are the last to be disposed of in the case of a negative estate (an estate with more liabilities than assets). Similarly, if estate assets must be sold to pay the decedent's debts, the property is sold in the following order: first, the residuary estate; then, general bequests; and, last, specific bequests (the same order is used for a negative estate).

testamentary trust
A trust established in a will.

Testamentary Trust.   If a trust is set up in the testator's will, it is known as a **testamentary trust.** The trust sets forth how the property will be distributed and nominates a trustee to manage the trust and distribute its proceeds. Although testamentary trusts were popular in the past, now more and more individuals are establishing formal trusts during their lifetime and putting all of their assets in them. This topic will be discussed more fully in the Trusts section later in the chapter. Note that in some states if the deceased leaves minor children, the will must designate a trustee for the children's benefit.

A sample trust clause follows. However, this clause is used only when a separate trust instrument is prepared and made a part of the will.

> SIXTH: I nominate my attorney, LYNDA YAMASHITA, of Laguna Beach, California, as Trustee of the trusts established under this will and request that no bond be required.

The One Dollar Clause.   This clause states that if any heirs should contest the will and lose, they will forfeit their inheritance under the will. Attorneys differ as to the importance of including a one dollar clause in the will. Its purpose is to discourage will contests by disgruntled heirs who have not received as much of the testator's estate as they felt they deserved. Instead of a formal clause, some attorneys merely stipulate in the will that anyone who contests it shall receive nothing under the will. Some attorneys advise the testator to leave one dollar to any disinherited children. Others advise the client merely to mention that a child is being disinherited.

residuary estate
The remainder of an estate after enumerated property.

residuary clause
The clause in a will that distributes the residuary estate.

Residuary Clause.   After all property has been distributed in the will, a clause must be added to distribute any items left out or acquired after the will is written. Such property is known as the **residuary estate.** In essence, then, the **residuary clause** distributes the remaining assets of the testator. In a negative estate, the residuary estate is used first to pay the bills of the estate. The residuary clause is generally included in the last paragraph of the will that disposes of property. The following is an example of a residuary clause:

> SEVENTH: I give, devise, and bequeath the rest, residue, and remainder of my estate to my above-named children in equal shares.

Signature Clause.   After all the assets have been distributed, the signatures of the testator and the witnesses are required. Some states require two witnesses, while others require three. You should always check the rules for your own state before preparing a will.

The signature clause should be on a page that contains at least two lines of the body of the will; the clause should not be on a separate page. The purpose of this requirement is to ensure that no one can substitute a new will later and merely attach the testator's signature page to it. Having the testator initial each page of the will at the bottom is another safeguard. Some attorneys also require that the last word on the page of the will be a hyphenated word. The following is an example of a signature clause:

>   IN WITNESS WHEREOF, I have hereunto subscribed my name this 1st day of July, 1994, at Seal Beach, California.

>   _____
>   KARA LOUISE KELSO

Witness Clause.   Witnesses sign at the same time as the testator and state that they were present when the testator signed and that they knew the testator. Part of the witness (attestation) clause should be included on the same page as the testator's signature. It is advisable for the testator and the witnesses to sign the will on the same page. The witness clause may be single-spaced, although the rest of the will is double-spaced. Some states may require that the will be notarized. Other states require that the attestation clause include a statement by the testator that she is of legal age and is the maker of the will. The following is an example of a witness clause:

>   The foregoing document, consisting of four pages including this page, was on this date signed by KARA LOUISE KELSO and declared to be her will. We are familiar with the testator and know her to be the individual who signed in our presence and in the presence of each of us. We observed the signing of the will by KARA LOUISE KELSO and by each other witness. Each signature is the signature of the person whose name is signed.
>
>   Each of us is now more than eighteen (18) years old, is a competent witness, and resides at the address signed after her name. We are acquainted with the testator and know she is over the age of eighteen. To our knowledge, she is of sound mind and not acting under duress, menace, fraud, or the undue influence of any person.

_____ Address: _____

_____

_____ Address: _____

_____

_____ Address: _____

_____

Storing the Will

Once the will has been signed, the original must be kept in a safe place. Some lawyers choose to keep all clients' original wills in their offices. However, many years may pass between the preparation of the will and the death of the client. Therefore, some lawyers give the original will to their clients with instructions to keep it in a safe place. If the will is burned, torn, or changed or altered in any way, it may be considered void. Some lawyers advise their clients to keep their wills in a fireproof file cabinet.

Someone whom the testator trusts should be made aware of the location of the will. It may not be appropriate to put the will in a safe deposit box because some states seal these boxes upon the individual's death.

Codicils

A **codicil** is a change made to a will after it has been signed. The codicil must be prepared with the same formality as the will itself. In many states, if the will is typed as a formal will, then the codicil must be typed formally as well. Therefore, be sure to prepare the codicil in the same manner as the will. If the will is holographic, the codicil should also be holographic.

Sometimes a testator may attempt to make several changes to the will by way of a codicil. In that event, the codicil may become so cumbersome and difficult to read that it may be advisable to rewrite the will itself. Whenever a codicil is prepared, be sure to read it over to be certain it is understandable. If you cannot understand the changes, then the Probate Court may not understand the changes at the time of death. In that case, a new will that reflects the changes should be prepared.

TRUSTS

In recent years, many attorneys have advised their clients to put their assets into a trust rather than bequeathing their property by will. A trust offers two major advantages over a will. First, no probate procedure is required for a trust. Consequently, the trustee's assets and beneficiaries remain private and are not a matter of public record. In contrast, because a will must go through the probate process, it and all related documents enter the public record. A second advantage is that trusts may enable the maker to avoid estate and inheritance taxes. A trust allows the maker (grantor) to transfer the legal title to assets to a trustee, while the beneficiaries have the equitable title. The grantor may also be the trustee of the trust. During a trustee's lifetime, he has control of the trust assets, which pass to the beneficiaries upon his death. A successor trustee may be identified in the trust in the event the trustee dies or is unable to take care of the assets.

Inter Vivos (living) Trust
A trust established while the grantor (the person making the trust) is alive. All the grantor's property is put into the trust and he may serve as trustee for the beneficiaries, a device that enables him to have the use of the property during his lifetime and have it pass to the beneficiaries at his death. If the trust is revocable, the grantor retains control and can revoke it; if it is irrevocable, he cannot.

An **Inter Vivos Trust** (also known as a living trust) is not considered to be part of the estate assets. Thus, the maker may choose to relinquish ownership of estate assets by using an irrevocable Inter Vivos Trust for the purpose of shifting income tax burdens and reducing the taxable estate at death. By so doing, the grantor (the maker of the trust) relinquishes not only the control of the assets but the right to receive income from them as well. If an individual wishes to retain ownership and control of the assets during his lifetime, the trust may be made revocable; in this case, the trust becomes irrevocable upon the grantor's death. Exhibit 7.3 shows an example of a revocable Inter Vivos Trust.

spendthrift trust
A trust in which the trustee retains control over the property, and the beneficiary receives a monthly income; the purpose of the trust is to prevent the beneficiary from wasting the trust property.

Sometimes the grantor will be concerned about a beneficiary's ability to handle money. In this case, the grantor may create a **spendthrift trust,** which provides the beneficiary with a regular income, but prevents him from controlling the trust property.

Trusts can be very complicated and should only be prepared by an attorney who specializes in this area. They are usually used as a probate avoidance technique since the trust assets pass outside the will and are not probated. Many computer programs are now available that enable a paralegal or legal secretary to prepare a preliminary

EXHIBIT 7.3   A Sample Revocable Inter Vivos Trust

WILLIAM T. BROWN
TRUST AGREEMENT

This trust agreement is made on _____, 19 ___, between William T. Brown of _____ County, State of _____, hereinafter called the "settlor," and William T. Brown of _____ County, State of _____, Charles T. Brown of _____ County, State of _____, and Sarah J. Brown of _____ County, State of _____, hereinafter collectively called the "trustees."

Recitals

I have transferred certain property to the trustees contemporaneously with signing this trust agreement, the receipt of which they acknowledge and which is described on Exhibit "A" attached hereto; and the parties to this agreement acknowledge that all property transferred or devised to the trust now or in the future is to be administered and distributed according to the terms of this trust agreement.

Article I
Reservation of Rights

During my life I reserve the following rights, to be exercised without the consent or participation of any other person:

1. To amend, in whole or in part, or to revoke this agreement by a written declaration.
2. To add any other real or personal property to the trust by transferring such property to the trustees, and to add any other property by my will. The trustees shall administer and distribute such property as though it had been a part of the original trust property.
3. To make payable to the trustees death benefits from insurance on my life, annuities, retirement plans, or other sources. If I do so, I reserve all incidents of ownership, and I shall have the duties of safekeeping all documents, of giving any necessary notices, of obtaining proper beneficiary designations, of paying premiums, contributions, assessments or other charges, and of maintaining any litigation.
4. To receive annual written accounts from all trustees (or the personal representative of any deceased trustee). My approval of these accounts by writings delivered to another trustee shall cover all transactions disclosed in these accounts and shall be binding and conclusive as to all persons.
5. To direct the trustees as to the retention, acquisition, or disposition of any trust assets by a writing delivered to the trustees. Any assets retained or acquired pursuant to such directions shall be retained as a part of the trust assets unless I otherwise direct in writing. The trustees shall not be liable to anyone for any loss resulting from any action taken in accordance with any such direction of mine.
6. To examine at all reasonable times the books and records of the trustees insofar as they relate to the trust.

Article II
Disposition of Trust Assets

Unless I am disabled, the trustees, after paying the proper charges and expenses of the trust, shall pay to me during my lifetime the entire net income from the trust property in monthly installments, and the trustees shall also pay to me and any other person who is a financial dependent of mine, in accordance with my written instructions, such portions of the principal of the trust property as I direct. If I become disabled by reason of illness, accident, or other emergency, or I am adjudicated incompetent, the trustees, other than myself, are authorized and directed to pay to me or for my benefit such portions of the trust income or principal as the trustees deem necessary to provide for my care, comfort, support, and maintenance.

  Upon my death, the trustees, if requested by the personal representative of my estate shall, or in their own discretion may, directly or through the personal representative of my estate, pay the expenses of my last illness and funeral, my valid debts, the expenses of administering my estate, including nonprobate assets; and pay all estate, inheritance, generation-skipping, or other death taxes that become due because of my death, including any interest and penalties.

  Also, upon my death, I give all my tangible personal property to Charles T. Brown, my son, if he survives me, or if he does not survive me, to Sarah J. Brown, my daughter. (I request the recipient of any such tangible personal property to distribute the same as I may have indicated informally by memorandum or otherwise.) The trustees shall distribute all the trust property not effectively disposed of by the preceding provisions of this agreement in equal shares to the persons named below. If any person named below does not survive me, such person's share shall be distributed per stirpes to such person's descendants who survive me.

Charles T. Brown, my son
Sarah J. Brown, my daughter

EXHIBIT 7.3   A Sample Revocable Inter Vivos Trust *Concluded*

Article III
Selection of Trustees

Trustees shall be appointed, removed, and replaced as follows: unless I am disabled, I reserve the right and power to remove any trustee and to appoint successor or additional trustees. If I become disabled, I shall cease to be a trustee. Upon my death or disability, my son, Charles T. Brown, may at any time appoint an individual or corporate trustee and may remove any individual or corporate trustee so appointed.

Article IV
Trustee Powers and Provisions

The powers granted to my trustees may be exercised during the term of this trust and after the termination of the trust as is reasonably necessary to distribute the trust assets. All of the powers are to be distributed without the authorization or approval of any court. I hereby give to my trustees the following powers: (specific administrative powers are listed).

Among the administrative provisions of this trust, I request no bond or other indemnity shall be required of any trustee nominated or appointed in this trust. I expressly waive any requirement that this trust be submitted to the jurisdiction of any court, or that the trustees be appointed or confirmed, that their actions be authorized, or that their accounts be allowed, by any court. This waiver shall not prevent any trustee or beneficiary from requesting any of these procedures.

(General governing provisions may also be added).

The settlor and the trustees have signed this agreement in duplicate on or as of the date appearing in the beginning of this agreement and the trustees accept their appointments as trustees by signing this agreement.

IN THE PRESENCE OF:

_____ Witness	_____
_____ Witness	William T. Brown—Settlor and Trustee
_____ Witness	_____
_____ Witness	Charles T. Brown—Trustee
_____ Witness	_____
_____ Witness	Sarah J. Brown—Trustee

STATE OF _____ }
                        } ss.
COUNTY OF _____ }

On this _____ day of _____ , 19 _____ , before me, a Notary Public within and for said County, personally appeared William T. Brown, a single person, to me known to be the person described in and who executed the foregoing instrument as settlor and trustee, and acknowledged that he executed the same as his free act and deed.

_____
Notary Public

On this _____ day of _____ , 19 _____ , before me, a Notary Public within and for said County, personally appeared Charles T. Brown and Sarah J. Brown, to me personally known, who being by me duly sworn, executed the foregoing instrument as trustees, and acknowledged that they executed the same as their free act and deed.

_____
Notary Public

(Notarial Seal)

SOURCE: Reprinted with permission from *Wills, Trusts, and Estate Administration for the Paralegal,* fourth edition by Dennis Hower. Copyright © 1996 by West Publishing Company. All rights reserved.

draft of a trust instrument using an appropriate software package and adding specific information as needed.

PROBATE

After a death, the family or spouse of the decedent will come to the law office to have the estate administered. This is an emotional time for the family, and they will need empathy and patience from the paralegal and legal secretary. In some cases, they may not be aware of the contents of the decedent's will or even know whether there is a will. They may not know all of the decedent's assets.

If the Decedent Had No Will

Many decedents have no will and no trust instrument. In that case, the individual is said to have died intestate. If the decedent dies without a will, any property held in joint tenancy automatically passes to the other joint tenant(s). The remainder of the decedent's estate passes to his relatives. Their respective portions are determined by state law.

In most states, if an intestate decedent has a surviving spouse, the spouse takes all (or most) of the decedent's estate. If there is no surviving spouse, the estate is divided among the children. Some states give half of the estate to the surviving spouse and the other half to the surviving children. If the decedent has no surviving spouse, children, or grandchildren, the estate would go to his parents or, if they are not alive, to his brothers and sisters and then to more distant relatives.

With the exception of property held in joint tenancy, the estate will likely have to go through the probate process. The Probate Court will appoint an administrator to administer the estate and perform the duties an Executor would perform if the decedent had left a will. The attorney will prepare a Probate Petition to the court to have the administrator appointed (see step 1 under The Probate Process below). Once the administrator has been selected by the court, the legal secretary or paralegal should prepare **letters of administration,** which must be signed by the court. These letters authorize the administrator to carry out his duties (see step 3 under The Probate Process below). The court may also require the administrator to post a bond.

letters of administration
Forms approved by the Probate Court that authorize an administrator to administer an estate.

If the Decedent Had a Will

If the decedent dies testate (with a will), **letters testamentary** (the same as letters of administration except that they are for an Executor) must be prepared for the Executor named in the will. As in the case of intestacy, the Probate Court will sign the letters, authorizing the Executor to administer the estate. Once the administrator or Executor has been authorized, the remainder of the probate process will be much the same, whether the decedent died testate or intestate.

letters testamentary
Forms approved by the Probate Court that authorize an Executor to administer an estate.

THE PROBATE PROCESS

Most law offices have Probate Checklists to ensure that all steps are taken in the proper order. A sample checklist is shown in Exhibit 7.4. As each item is prepared, the legal secretary or paralegal checks it off on the list. Be sure to check the Probate Code for your state to determine the procedures and/or deadlines for your state. Each state's laws are different and must be followed precisely.

EXHIBIT 7.4   A Sample Probate Checklist (Procedures Vary by State)

PROBATE PROCEDURES FOR CALIFORNIA

NAME OF DECEDENT:

_____

DATE OF DEATH: _____

EXECUTOR OR
ADMINISTRATOR:

_____

List of Heirs:

----

1.   Certified copy of death certificate   _____

2.   List of assets and value at date of death   _____

3.   List assets passing outside of will

     Community property _____

     Joint tenancy _____

     Insurance policies _____

     Trusts _____

4.   Probate Petition   Prepared _____   Hearing: _____

5.   Publication   Newspaper? _____   Date: _____

6.   Appointment of Executor or administrator? _____

7.   Letters? _____

8.   Creditors' notices? _____   Dates published? _____

9.   Creditors' claims filed? _____

     Name of Creditor: Claim Amount: Accepted?

10.   Inventory and appraisement filed?

     Fee to appraiser: _____

11.   Is federal estate tax due? ($600,000 value of estate?)

12.   Does property have to be sold?

     a. Notice of proposed action to heirs?

     b. Hearing required?

13.   Have all creditors' claims been satisfied and all property disposed of?

14.   Final accounting and distribution_____   Hearing? _____

15.   Final distribution of: a. Attorney fees

                    b. Executor fees

                    c. Property to heirs

16.   Closed file on: _____

Step 1.   *Prepare the Petition.*   Some states, such as California, have forms for the Probate Petition, which initiates the probate process. Other states require that the petition be prepared on pleading paper (legal cap). In states that require that the petition be drafted, formbooks may be available for your use. The office file may also have petitions that you can use as a model. A petition for New York is shown in Exhibit 7.5.

The petition and other accompanying probate documents should be filed with the court in the county where the decedent lived. Be sure to have a check made out to the court for the filing fees. Some courts require a fee each time a document is filed; others have a single all-inclusive fee that is paid when the petition is filed.

If the decedent had a will, it must be filed with the court at the same time as the petition and other required documents. All codicils must be filed at the same time. If the will is holographic, the legal secretary should prepare a typed copy for the court.

Step 2.   *Notice of Hearing.*   After the petition is filed with the court, the clerk will set the hearing date. All the decedent's creditors and heirs must be notified of the hearing date. Exhibit 7.6 shows an example of a notice from California. Some states require that a notice be published in a local newspaper. The witnesses may either appear at the hearing or sign a form stating that they witnessed the will. Rules vary by state.

Step 3.   *Letters Testamentary or Letters of Administration.*   When the court approves the Executor or Administrator, letters testamentary or letters of administration are prepared. They must be signed by the court and kept in a safe place for future use. A copy of these letters will be needed for many transactions undertaken by the Executor or Administrator, such as closing bank accounts and selling real estate or other assets. Exhibit 7.7 shows an example of letters testamentary from California.

Step 4.   *Notice to Creditors.*   State codes vary as to the notice requirement for creditors. However, most states require that a notice be published in a newspaper where the decedent lived. Many states also require that the Executor or Administrator send notices to known creditors. Most states require that creditors make claims within a specified period of time, such as three to seven months. This time span varies by state. Notice from California appears in Exhibit 7.8.

Step 5.   *Appointment of Inheritance Tax Referee or Probate Referee.*   The Inheritance Tax Referee or Probate Referee is appointed by the court. This individual must provide a written evaluation of certain assets of the estate and determine the taxes owed. This step is not required in all states.

Step 6.   *Estate Checking/Bank Account.*   A separate bank account must be set up for the estate. The Executor or Administrator will have the power to sign checks for payment of estate bills. The account would be in the name of the "Estate of Mary E. Gallo," and the Executor would sign checks as "Daniel Gallo, Executor." This money must not be commingled with the Executor's personal accounts or with those of the law office.

Step 7. *Inventory of Assets.* A separate document or form is prepared listing all assets of the estate and their estimated value or the value placed on them by the Probate or Inheritance Tax Referee. Stocks and bonds should be evaluated as of their value on the date of death. A newspaper with stock quotations for that date would be used for this purpose.

All bank accounts must be found and their balances obtained. Any bank accounts held in joint tenancy pass outright to the joint tenant, however. Most banks require a certified copy of the death certificate for this purpose; others merely allow the other joint tenant(s) to withdraw the money. Bank accounts held in joint tenancy are not included in the inventory of estate assets.

Step 8. *Selling Property to Pay Bills.* In instances where assets must be sold to pay the decedent's bills, the property is sold in the following order: (1) residuary estate, (2) general bequests; and (3) specific bequests. The estate may not be closed until all creditors are paid or their claims are refused by the Executor or Administrator. The time allowed for creditors' claims varies by state. If the personal representative is not given the right to sell estate assets in the will, then he must petition the court for this purpose. If the Executor has paid any bills of the estate from his personal funds, he may file a Creditor's Claim with the court.

Step 9. *Paying Taxes.* In addition to paying taxes owed by the estate, the personal representative should also determine whether the decedent owed federal income tax or state tax for the year in which she died. Each year the estate is open, both state and federal taxes may be due. Paralegals may assist in preparing these tax forms.

Step 10. *Final Accounting and Distribution.* Once the time has expired for the filing of creditors' claims and all bills have been paid, the estate may be ready to close. The courts will require a detailed accounting, called a Petition for Final Distribution, from the personal representative. This must include all assets of the estate, all money taken into the estate, and all bills paid for the estate.

Most states require a court hearing for the final accounting. All heirs must receive a notice of this hearing and may appear if they wish. The heirs also receive a copy of the final accounting. If there are no objections, the judge will sign the Order for Final Distribution. At this point, all assets that have not been sold to pay the estate's bills are distributed to the heirs.

Step 11. *Final Discharge.* After all payments have been made to the attorney and personal representative, all assets have been distributed to the heirs, and the heirs have signed receipts for all assets, the request for final discharge is prepared. All receipts from the heirs must be filed with the court. The final discharge relieves the personal representative of all further responsibility in the estate. Once the final discharge has been approved by the Probate Court, the case is closed.

In some states, the probate process may take as little as six months, in others, particularly where all heirs are not known, the process may take several years.

EXHIBIT 7.5   A Probate Petition for New York

Form P-3
(Probate Petition)

(For Court Use Only)
Date:_____   Fee Paid $_____

SURROGATE'S COURT OF THE STATE OF NEW YORK
COUNTY OF ONEIDA

PROBATE PROCEEDING, Estate of
Decedent:
Residence:

Date of Death:
Representative(s)
    Nominated:
Letters Requested:

}

PROBATE PETITION

File No. _____

TO THE SURROGATE'S COURT, County of Oneida:
It is respectfully alleged:

1. (a). The name(s), domicile(s) (or, in the case of a bank or trust company, its principal office) and interest(s) in this proceeding of the petitioner(s) are as follows:

Name:

Domicile or
Principal Office:
           (Street/Number)   (City, Village/Town)   (State)   (Zip Code)
Citizenship of Petitioner:

Name:

Domicile or
Principal Office:
           (Street/Number)   (City, Village/Town)   (State)   (Zip Code)
Citizenship of Petitioner:

Interest of Petitioner(s) *[check one]:*
    ( ) Executor(s)/Executrix(es) named in decedent's Last Will presented herewith.
    ( ) Other *[specify]*

1. (b). Is the proposed executor/trustee an attorney?   ( ) Yes   ( ) No

2. The name, domicile, date and place of death, and national citizenship of the above named decedent are as follows: [Certified copy of Death Certificate must be filed with this proceeding.]

Name:

Domicile:
           (Street/Number)   (City, Village/Town)   (State)   (Zip Code)

Township of: County of:

Date of Death: Place of Death:

Citizenship:

3. The Last Will, herewith presented, relates to both real and personal property and consists of an instrument or instruments dated as shown below and signed at the end thereof by the decedent and the following subscribing witnesses:

_____   _____
     (Date of Will)   (Witnesses to Will)

_____   _____
     (Date of Codicil)   (Witnesses to Codicil)

4. There is no other will or codicil of the decedent on file in the office of the Surrogate, and upon information and belief, there exists no will, codicil or other testamentary instrument of the decedent later in date to any of the instruments mentioned in paragraph (3) hereof, except:

EXHIBIT 7.5   A Probate Petition for New York *Continued*

5. The decedent left surviving the following persons who would inherit his/her estate pursuant to E.P.T.L. 4-1.1 and 4-1.2 if the decedent had left no will:

  a. [   ] Spouse (husband/wife). If the decedent was divorced, a copy of the divorce decree must be filed with this petition.

  b. [   ] Marital and/or adopted child or children; or descendants of predeceased marital and/or adopted child or children.

  c. [   ] Nonmarital child or children; or descendants of predeceased nonmarital child or children (EPTL 4-1.2).

  d. [   ] Any other issue of the decedent who was the subject of an adoption.

  e. [   ] Father/mother.

  f. [   ] Brothers or sisters, either of the whole or half-blood; or descendants of such predeceased brothers or sisters.

  g. [   ] Grandfather/grandmother.

  h. [   ] Uncles or aunts.

  i. [   ] Descendants of predeceased uncles or aunts.

[Information is required only as to those classes of surviving relatives who would take the property of decedent if there were no will. State number of survivors in each such class. Insert "X" in all subsequent classes. Insert "NO" in all prior classes.]

6. The names, relationships and addresses of all distributees (under EPTL 4-1.1 and 4-1.2), of each person designated in the Last Will herewith presented as primary executor(s)(trixes), of all persons adversely affected by the purported exercise by such Will of any power of appointment, of all persons adversely affected by any codicil and of all persons having an interest under any prior will of the decedent on file in the Surrogate's office, are hereinafter set forth in subdivisions (a) and (b):

  a. All persons and parties so interested <u>who are of full age and sound mind and under no disability</u>, or which are corporations or associations, are as follows:

Name, domicile and post office address	Relationship (If Nonmarital Children So Indicate)	Description of Legacy, Devise or Other Interest, or Nature of Fiduciary Status

EXHIBIT 7.5   A Probate Petition for New York *Continued*

b. All persons so interested who are persons under disability, are as follows:
[Please furnish all information specified in note below]

(NOTE: In the case of each infant, state: (a) name, birth date, age, relationship to decedent, whether marital or nonmarital, domicile and residence address, and the person with whom he/she resides; (b) whether or not he/she has a guardian or testamentary guardian, and whether or not his/her father and mother are living; and (c) the name and residence address of any guardian and any living parent. In the case of each other person under disability, state: (a) name, relationship to decedent and residence address; (b) facts regarding his/her disability, including whether or not a conservator or committee has been appointed and whether or not he/she has been committed to any institution; and (c) the names and addresses of any conservator or committee, any person or institution having care and custody of him/her and any relative or friend having an interest in his/her welfare. In the case of a person confined as a prisoner, state place of incarceration. In the case of unknowns, describe such persons in the same language as will be used in the process. In each case give a brief description of the party's legacy, devise or other interest as in paragraph (6) (a) hereof.)

7. The names and domiciliary addresses of all substitute or successor executor(s)(trixes) and of all trustees, guardians, legatees and devisees, and other beneficiaries named in the Last Will herewith presented, other than those named in paragraph (6), are hereinafter set forth in subdivisions (a) and (b);

a. All such other legatees and devisees who are of full age and sound mind and under no disability, or which are corporations or associations, are as follows:

Name	Address	Description of Legacy, Devise or Other Interest or Nature of Fiduciary Status

b. All such other legatees, devisees and other beneficiaries who are persons under disability, are as follows: *[Please furnish all information specified in note to paragraph (6)(b) hereof]*

8. There are no persons interested in this proceeding other than those hereinabove mentioned.

9. To the best of the knowledge of the undersigned, the approximate total value of all property constituting the decedent's gross testamentary estate is not greater than $ _____ but not less than $ _____ of which $ _____ is Real Property.

(Note: For item 9: Do not include any assets which are jointly held, held in trust for another, or have a named beneficiary.)

10. Upon information and belief, no other petition for the probate of any will of the decedent or for the granting of letters of administration on the decedent's estate heretofore has been filed in any Court.

EXHIBIT 7.5   A Probate Petition for New York *Concluded*

11. In addition to the assets passing by the provisions of the will being offered for probate herein the following right of action exists for the wrongful death of the decedent. Write "none" or state briefly the cause of action and against whom it exists.

WHEREFORE, your petitioner(s) pray(s): (a) that process be issued to all necessary parties to show cause why the Last Will herewith presented should not be admitted to probate; (b) that an order be granted directing the service of process pursuant to the provisions of Article 3 of the SCPA, upon the persons named in paragraph (6) hereof who are non-domiciliaries, or whose names or whereabouts are unknown and cannot be ascertained; and (c) that such Last Will be admitted to probate as a will of real and personal property and that letters issue thereon as follows:

[Check and complete appropriate request]

(   ) Letters Testamentary to:
(   ) Letters of Administration CTA to:
(   ) Letters of Trusteeship to:

Dated:_____

(1) _____   (2) _____
         (Signature of Petitioner)   (Signature of Petitioner)

_____   _____
          (Print Name)   (Print Name)

STATE OF NEW YORK ⎫   COMBINED VERIFICATION, OATH AND DESIGNATION
COUNTY OF   ⎬ SS.:   *[For use when a petitioner to be appointed*
                 ⎭   *executor is not a bank or trust company]*

       I,   the undersigned, being duly sworn, say:

1. VERIFICATION: I have read the foregoing petition subscribed by me and know the contents thereof, and the same is true to my own knowledge, except as to the matters therein stated to be alleged upon information and belief, and as to those matters I believe it to be true.
2. OATH of EXECUTOR(S)TRIX(ES) (TRUSTEE) (ADMINISTRATOR CTA): I am over eighteen (18) years of age and a citizen of the United States. I am the Execut   (Trustee) (Administrator CTA) named in the Last Will described in the foregoing petition and will well, faithfully and honestly discharge the duties of such Execut   (Trustee) (Administrator CTA). I am not ineligible to receive letters and will duly account for all moneys and other property that will come into my hands.
3. DESIGNATION OF CLERK FOR SERVICE OF PROCESS: I do hereby designate the Clerk of the Surrogate's Court of Oneida County, and his/her successor in office, as a person on whom service of any process issuing from such Surrogate's Court may be made, in like manner and with like effect as if it were served personally upon me whenever I cannot be found and served within the State of New York after due diligence used.

(1) My domicile is:_____
                        (Street/Number)   (City, Village/Town)   (State)   (Zip Code)

(2) My domicile is:_____
                        (Street/Number)   (City, Village/Town)   (State)   (Zip Code)

_____   _____
     (1) (Signature of Petitioner)   (2) (Signature of Petitioner)

On _____ , 19____ , before me personally came _____

to me known to be the person(s) described in and who executed the foregoing instrument. Such person(s) duly swore to such instrument before me and duly acknowledged that he/she executed the same.

_____
                                                     Notary Public
                                                     My Commission Expires:

ATTORNEY

Name of Attorney:_____ Tel. No.:_____

Address of Attorney:_____

EXHIBIT 7.6   A Notice of Hearing from California

DE–121

ATTORNEY OR PARTY WITHOUT ATTORNEY *(Name and Address)*:	TELEPHONE NO.:	*FOR COURT USE ONLY*
ATTORNEY FOR *(Name)*:		

SUPERIOR COURT OF CALIFORNIA, COUNTY OF
STREET ADDRESS:
MAILING ADDRESS:
CITY AND ZIP CODE:
BRANCH NAME:

ESTATE OF (NAME):

DECEDENT

NOTICE OF PETITION TO ADMINISTER ESTATE OF *(name)*:	CASE NUMBER:

1. To all heirs, beneficiaries, creditors, contingent creditors, and persons who may otherwise be interested in the will or estate, or both, of *(specify all names by which decedent was known)*:

2. A PETITION has been filed by *(name of petitioner)*:
   in the Superior Court of California, County of *(specify)*:

3. THE PETITION requests that *(name)*:
   be appointed as personal representative to administer the estate of the decedent.

4. ☐ THE PETITION requests the decedent's WILL and codicils, if any, be admitted to probate. The will and any codicils are available for examination in the file kept by the court.

5. ☐ THE PETITION requests authority to administer the estate under the Independent Administration of Estates Act. (This authority will allow the personal representative to take many actions without obtaining court approval. Before taking certain very important actions, however, the personal representative will be required to give notice to interested persons unless they have waived notice or consented to the proposed action.) The independent administration authority will be granted unless an interested person files an objection to the petition and shows good cause why the court should not grant the authority.

6. ☐ A PETITION for determination of or confirmation of property passing to or belonging to a surviving spouse under California Probate Code section 13650 IS JOINED with the petition to administer the estate.

7. A HEARING on the petition will be held

   on *(date)*:   at *(time)*:   in Dept.:   Room:

   located at *(address of court)*:

8. IF YOU OBJECT to the granting of the petition, you should appear at the hearing and state your objections or file written objections with the court before the hearing. Your appearance may be in person or by your attorney.

9. IF YOU ARE A CREDITOR or a contingent creditor of the deceased, you must file your claim with the court and mail a copy to the personal representative appointed by the court within four months from the date of first issuance of letters as provided in section 9100 of the California Probate Code. The time for filing claims will not expire before four months from the hearing date noticed above.

10. YOU MAY EXAMINE the file kept by the court. If you are a person interested in the estate, you may file with the court a formal Request for Special Notice of the filing of an inventory and appraisal of estate assets or of any petition or account as provided in section 1250 of the California Probate Code. A Request for Special Notice form is available from the court clerk.

11. ☐ Petitioner   ☐ Attorney for petitioner *(name)*:

    (address):

    ▶

    (SIGNATURE OF ☐ PETITIONER ☐ ATTORNEY FOR PETITIONER)

12. This notice was mailed on *(date)*:   at *(place)*:
                                                 (Continued on reverse)   California.

NOTE: If this notice is published, print the caption, beginning with the words NOTICE OF PETITION, and do not print the information from the form above the caption. The caption and decedent's name must be printed in at least 8-point type and the text in at least 7-point type. Print the case number as part of the caption. Print items preceded by a box only if the box is checked. Do not print the *italicized* instructions in parentheses, the paragraph numbers, the mailing information, or the material on the reverse.

Form Approved by the
Judicial Council of California
DE-121 [Rev. July 1, 1989]

NOTICE OF PETITION TO ADMINISTER ESTATE
(Probate)

Probate Code, § 8100

EXHIBIT 7.6   A Notice of Hearing from California *Concluded*

ESTATE OF (NAME):	CASE NUMBER:
DECEDENT	

PROOF OF SERVICE BY MAIL

1. I am over the age of 18 and not a party to this cause. I am a resident of or employed in the county where the mailing occurred.
2. My residence or business address is *(specify)*:

3. I served the foregoing **Notice of Petition to Administer Estate** on each person named below by enclosing a copy in an envelope addressed as shown below AND
   a. ☐ **depositing** the sealed envelope with the United States Postal Service with the postage fully prepaid.
   b. ☐ **placing** the envelope for collection and mailing on the date and at the place shown in item 4 following our ordinary business practices. I am readily familiar with this business' practice for collecting and processing correspondence for mailing. On the same day that correspondence is placed for collection and mailing, it is deposited in the ordinary course of business with the United States Postal Service in a sealed envelope with postage fully prepaid.

4. a. Date of deposit: b. Place of deposit *(city and state)*:

5. ☐ I served with the Notice of Petition to Administer Estate a copy of the petition and other documents referred to in the notice.

I declare under penalty of perjury under the laws of the State of California that the foregoing is true and correct.
   Date:

▶

. . . .   _____
          (TYPE OR PRINT NAME)   (SIGNATURE OF DECLARANT)

NAME AND ADDRESS OF EACH PERSON TO WHOM NOTICE WAS MAILED

DE-121 [Rev. July 1, 1989]   **NOTICE OF PETITION TO ADMINISTER ESTATE**   Page two
                                              (Probate)

SOURCE: Reprinted from California Judicial Council Forms, published by West Publishing Company.

EXHIBIT 7.7   Letters Testamentary Judicial Council Form from California

DE–150

ATTORNEY OR PARTY WITHOUT ATTORNEY *(Name and Address)*:	TELEPHONE NO.:	FOR COURT USE ONLY

ATTORNEY FOR *(Name)*:

SUPERIOR COURT OF CALIFORNIA, COUNTY OF

STREET ADDRESS:

MAILING ADDRESS:

CITY AND ZIP CODE:

BRANCH NAME:

ESTATE OF (NAME):

DECEDENT

LETTERS

CASE NUMBER:

☐ TESTAMENTARY	☐ OF ADMINISTRATION
☐ OF ADMINISTRATION WITH WILL ANNEXED	☐ SPECIAL ADMINISTRATION

LETTERS

1. ☐ The last will of the decedent named above having been proved, the court appoints *(name)*:

   a. ☐ Executor
   b. ☐ Administrator with will annexed

2. ☐ The court appoints *(name)*:

   a. ☐ Administrator of the decedent's estate
   b. ☐ Special administrator of decedent's estate
      (1) ☐ with the special powers specified in the Order for Probate
      (2) ☐ with the powers of a general administrator

3. ☐ The personal representative is authorized to administer the estate under the Independent Administration of Estates Act ☐ **with full authority** ☐ **with limited authority** (no authority, without court supervision, to (1) sell or exchange real property or (2) grant an option to purchase real property or (3) borrow money with the loan secured by an encumbrance upon real property).

WITNESS, clerk of the court, with seal of the court affixed.

Date:

Clerk, by _____ , Deputy

(SEAL)

AFFIRMATION

1. ☐ PUBLIC ADMINISTRATOR: No affirmation required (Prob. Code, § 1140(b)).

2. ☐ INDIVIDUAL: **I solemnly affirm** that I will perform the duties of personal representative according to law.

3. ☐ INSTITUTIONAL FIDUCIARY *(name)*:

   I solemnly affirm that the institution will perform the duties of personal representative according to law.
   I make this affirmation for myself as an individual and on behalf of the institution as an officer.
   (Name and title):

4. Executed on *(date)*:
   at *(place)*:   , California.

   ▶ _____
   (SIGNATURE)

CERTIFICATION

I certify that this document is a correct copy of the original on file in my office and the letters issued the personal representative appointed above have not been revoked, annulled, or set aside, and are still in full force and effect.

(SEAL)

Date:
Clerk, by

_____
(DEPUTY)

Form Approved by the
Judicial Council of California
DE-150 [Rev. July 1, 1988]

LETTERS
(Probate)

Probate Code, §§ 463, 465, 501, 502, 540
Code of Civil Procedure, § 2015.6

SOURCE: Reprinted from California Judicial Council Forms, published by West Publishing Company.

EXHIBIT 7.8   A Notice to Creditors From California

DE–157

NOTICE OF ADMINISTRATION*
OF THE ESTATE OF

_____
(NAME)

DECEDENT

NOTICE TO CREDITORS

1.   *(Name)*:
      (Address):

      (Telephone):
      is the **personal representative** of the **ESTATE OF** *(name)*:   , who is deceased.

2.   The personal representative HAS BEGUN ADMINISTRATION of the decedent's estate in the

      a. **SUPERIOR COURT OF CALIFORNIA, COUNTY OF** *(specify)*:
          STREET ADDRESS:
          MAILING ADDRESS:
          CITY AND ZIP CODE:
          BRANCH NAME:

      b. Case number *(specify)*:

3.   You must FILE YOUR CLAIM with the court clerk (address in item 2a) AND mail or deliver a copy to the personal
      representative before the **later** of the following times as provided in section 9100 of the California Probate Code:

      a. **four months** after *(date)*: [_____] , the date letters (authority to act for the estate) were
          first issued to the personal representative, OR

      b. **thirty days** after *(date)*: [_____] , the date this notice was mailed or personally delivered
          to you.

4.   LATE CLAIMS: If you do not file your claim before it is due, you must file a petition with the court for permission
      to file a late claim as provided in section 9103 of the Probate Code.

WHERE TO GET A CREDITOR'S CLAIM FORM: If a creditor's claim form did not accompany this notice, you
may obtain a copy from any superior court clerk or from the person who sent you this notice. *(Creditor's Claim,
Judicial Council form No. DE-172.)* A letter to the court stating your claim is *not* sufficient.
    IF YOU MAIL YOUR CLAIM: If you use the mail to file your claim with the court, for your protection you should
send your claim by certified mail, with return receipt requested. If you mail a copy of your claim to the personal
representative, you should also use certified mail.

NOTE: To assist the creditor and the court, please send a copy of the Creditor's Claim form with this notice.

(Proof of Service on reverse)

---

* Use this form in estates begun on or after July 1, 1988.

Form Approved by the   **NOTICE OF ADMINISTRATION TO CREDITORS**   Probate Code, §§ 9050, 9052
Judicial Council of California   **(Probate)**
DE-157 [Rev. September 30, 1991]

EXHIBIT 7.8   A Notice to Creditors From California *Concluded*

[Optional]
PROOF OF SERVICE BY MAIL

1. I am over the age of 18 and not a party to this cause. I am a resident of or employed in the county where the mailing occurred.

2. My residence or business address is *(specify)*:

3. I served the foregoing **Notice of Administration to Creditors** ☐ and a blank *Creditor's Claim* form* on each person named below by enclosing a copy in an envelope addressed as shown below AND

   a. ☐ **depositing** the sealed envelope with the United States Postal Service with the postage fully prepaid.

   b. ☐ **placing** the envelope for collection and mailing on the date and at the place shown below in item 4 following our ordinary business practices. I am readily familiar with this business' practice for collecting and processing correspondence for mailing. On the same day that correspondence is placed for collection and mailing, it is deposited in the ordinary course of business with the United States Postal Service in a sealed envelope with postage fully prepaid.

4. a. Date of deposit: b. Place of deposit *(city and state)*:

   I declare under penalty of perjury under the laws of the State of California that the foregoing is true and correct.

Date:

....   ▶ _____
       (TYPE OR PRINT NAME)   (SIGNATURE OF DECLARANT)

NAME AND ADDRESS OF EACH PERSON TO WHOM NOTICE WAS MAILED

*NOTE: To assist the creditor and the court, please send a copy of the Creditor's Claim form with the notice.

DE-157 [Rev. September 30, 1991]   **NOTICE OF ADMINISTRATION TO CREDITORS**   Page two
                                                                        (Probate)

SOURCE: Reprinted from California Judicial Council Forms, published by West Publishing Company.

SUMMARY

Individuals make wills to indicate how they want their property distributed upon their death. Generally, a formal will that adheres to all the requirements set by state statutes is preferable to a holographic (handwritten) will. Wills usually include a number of standard clauses such as the following: statement of intent, payment of debts, statement of family relationships, appointment of executor, distribution of assets, signature, and witnesses. Some property may pass outside the will, such as property held in joint tenancy or in trust.

Trusts may be established to avoid probate. Several different types of trusts are available, and one must discuss the situation carefully with the client to determine which trust is most beneficial in any given circumstances. Inter vivos (revocable living) trusts are among the most common trusts established today.

Wills must be probated upon the death of the maker. The Executor administers the estate and sees to it that the testator's wishes are carried out. If the decedent died intestate (without a will), the court will appoint an administrator to administer the estate. After the formal process, the property is distributed to the heirs.

KEY TERMS

Administrator 174	Mistake 175
Beneficiary 175	Nuncupative will 174
Codicil 184	Per capita 180
Decedent 173	Per stirpes 180
Devise 173	Predecease 179
Devisee 173	Pretermitted heir statute 178
Estate 174	Probate 173
Executor 179	Residuary clause 182
Formal will 174	Residuary estate 182
Holographic will 174	Spendthrift trust 184
Inter Vivos (living) Trust 184	Testamentary capacity 174
Intestate 173	Testamentary trust 182
Last Will and Testament 175	Testate 173
Legacy 173	Testator 173
Legatee 173	Undue influence 175
Letters of administration 187	With bond 179
Letters testamentary 187	Without bond 179

SELF-TEST

A. Indicate whether the following statements are true (T) or false (F):

_____ 1. A person who dies with a will dies intestate.

_____ 2. A devise is a gift of real property by will.

_____ 3. The Executor is responsible for handling the decedent's affairs.

_____ 4. A gift of "all of my property" is a specific bequest.

_____ 5. A gift of "my house at 211 Main Street" is a specific bequest.

B.   Circle the correct answer for the following questions:

1. Negative estates have
    a. no specific assets.
    b. no residuary estate.
    c. very few assets.
    d. more outstanding debts than property.

2. The residuary estate is
    a. what is left after all other property is disposed of.
    b. property purchased after the will was made and not mentioned in the will.
    c. both (a) and (b).
    d. none of the above.

3. To have testamentary capacity, an individual must
    a. be capable of knowing that the document is a will.
    b. know that property is being disposed of in the will.
    c. be of legal age to make a will.
    d. have the mental capacity to understand the meaning of a will.
    e. all of the above.

4. Holographic wills
    a. are typed but not witnessed.
    b. are typed and witnessed.
    c. are written in the handwriting of the testator.
    d. none of the above.

5. Nuncupative wills are
    a. formal wills.
    b. handwritten wills.
    c. witnessed wills.
    d. oral wills.

C.   Fill in the blanks:

1. The most common and the most advantageous will is a _____.

2. A child who is left out of the will may take against the will under the

    _____ statute.

3. A change to a will is made after it has been signed is called a

    _____.

4. When the terms of the grandparent's will specify that a child inherits his

   parent's share if the parent predeceases him, the _____

   method of distribution is being used.

5. When the court approves the Executor or Administrator,

   _____ are prepared.

REVIEW QUESTIONS

1. Define the following terms: will, testate, intestate, Executor, Administrator, holographic will, inter vivos (revocable living) trust, beneficiary, codicil, and decedent.

2. How would you prepare for the signing of a will? Who should be there?

3. Discuss the advantages and disadvantages of each of the following:

   a. formal will

   b. holographic will

   c. inter vivos (revocable living) trust

4. List the procedures that must be followed in the probate of an estate.

PROJECTS

1. 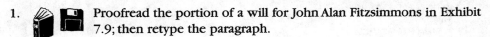 Proofread the portion of a will for John Alan Fitzsimmons in Exhibit
   7.9; then retype the paragraph.

2. 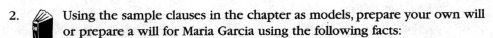 Using the sample clauses in the chapter as models, prepare your own will
   or prepare a will for Maria Garcia using the following facts:

   Maria Garcia wishes to have her will made. She is not married and has three
   children:

   a. Her daughter, Elsa Mary Garcia, was born on October 22, 1990.
   b. Her son, Jonathan Anthony Garcia, was born on May 5, 1992.
   c. Her son, Michael Alonzo Garcia, was born on June 27, 1993.

   Her property consists of a home in Your Town, Your State, two diamond rings, and
   a 1995 Cadillac Eldorado. She wishes to have her property distributed evenly among
   her three children, but she would like one of her diamond rings to go to each of her
   daughters. Her residuary estate should go to her son. Her executor will be her
   brother, Philip Michael Garcia of Your Town, Your State; the alternate executor will be
   her other brother, William Michael Garcia of San Antonio, Texas. The guardian of her
   minor children and her estate will be her sister, Anna Maria Garcia, who also lives in
   Your Town, Your State. Witnesses to the will are the paralegal and the legal secretary
   in your office.

EXHIBIT 7.9   A Portion of a Will

LAST WIL AND TESTAMNT OF

JOHN ALLEN FITZSIMONS

I, JOHN ALAN FITZSIMMNS, of 924 Main Stret, Prescot,

Arizona, being of lawfl age and sond and disposng mind and
memory and not actng undr fraud, dress, menace of the undo
infloence of any person or thing, do hereby make, publish, and
declare this instroment to be my Last Will and Testamnt, and I
do hereby revoce all other Wills and Codisils to Wills
heretoofore made by me as follows:

---

3. How would you prepare for the signing of the will described in Project 2? Who should be there?

4. Assume the client in Project 2, Maria Garcia, would like your office to prepare an inter vivos trust. Using Exhibit 7.3 as a guide, prepare the document for her.

5. Using the information for Maria Garcia in Project 2, prepare the following documents for your state. If you do not have the forms for your state, use the forms in Exhibits 7.5, 7.7, and 7.8. Assume Ms. Garcia's date of death was August 23, 1996.

   a. Petition for Probate

   b. Letters testamentary

   c. Notice to creditors

6. Research the law related to intestate succession in your state. In what order are the assets distributed?

Family Law

CHAPTER OBJECTIVES

As a result of studying this chapter, you will learn the following material:

1. ***Marriage*** Valid, void, voidable, and common-law marriages will be discussed. You will also learn how to prepare a prenuptial agreement.

2. ***Annulment (Nullity) and Legal Separation*** The law related to nullity of marriage and legal separation will be presented. You will learn in what cases these may be used.

3. ***Divorce*** The law relating to divorce will be presented. You will learn how to prepare divorce papers and will become familiar with the issues surrounding child custody, child support, and spousal support.

4. ***Dissolution*** The laws and procedures utilized in states with no-fault divorce and dissolution will be presented. You will learn how to prepare all the required documents and will become acquainted with issues related to custody and support.

5. ***Adoptions*** The law related to adoptions will be discussed. You will learn how to prepare the documents required for adoption.

FAMILY LAW: AN OVERVIEW

Family lawyers specialize in domestic relations issues, such as divorce and adoption. Although family law is a broad area encompassing many aspects, most family law practices rely primarily on divorce (or dissolution) cases, which often raise issues of physical abuse, child custody, alimony and spousal support, child support, and visitation rights.

Family law is changing rapidly as a result of many new developments in recent years. For instance, in the past when a couple divorced, the mother regularly received custody of the children. Now, however, in many states the courts are making joint custody arrangements, where each parent has physical custody of the child for part of the time. Other courts award joint legal custody, where one parent has physical custody of the child and both parents make decisions together on legal issues arising in the child's life.

Family law is an area that requires a great deal of client contact. If you are a "people person" and can listen to other people's problems without becoming emotionally involved, then family law may be the field for you. Generally, divorce clients call the office frequently. Since the attorney may not always be available, the paralegal or legal secretary may have to speak to the client. Divorce and other domestic problems can be very traumatic, so the client may need considerable attention and reassurance.

MARRIAGE

marriage
The legal union of a man and woman as husband and wife.

Marriage is the legal union of a man and woman as husband and wife in a marriage ceremony. The ceremony may be performed by a minister, priest, rabbi, judge, or justice of the peace. A marriage license is issued and becomes a binding agreement between the parties. Each state has different requirements for a valid marriage. For example, many states require the couple to be tested for various diseases and to wait for a certain period before applying for a marriage license.

Most states also have a waiting period between the application for the license and the marriage. Additionally, the parties must be residents of the state in which the marriage occurs for a specified period of time, as determined by state statute. Therefore, you should check the rules of the state where you live. Fill in the State Specific Information Box with the rules of your own state.

STATE SPECIFIC INFORMATION	The following rules for marriage apply in the state of _____: Waiting Period for License: _____ _____ Blood Tests Required: _____ _____ Other Requirements: _____ _____

Common-Law Marriage

common-law marriage
When a man and woman agree to enter a marital relationship and live together as if married but never go through a formal marriage ceremony.

A **common-law marriage** exists when a man and woman agree to enter a marital relationship and subsequently live together, but never go through a formal marriage ceremony. Common-law marriage is recognized in the District of Columbia and in thirteen states, including Alabama, Colorado, Georgia, Idaho, Iowa, Kansas, Montana, Ohio, Oklahoma, Pennsylvania, Rhode Island, South Carolina, and Texas. Most states that do not allow common-law marriages will recognize one that was "celebrated" in another state. In the states where common-law marriage is recognized, its elements are as follows:

1. Both parties must be legally competent to marry.

2. Both parties must agree to enter into a marital relationship.

3. The parties must have an oral or written agreement, preferably written. (In some states the agreement may be implied by the parties' behavior.)

4. The parties must live together as husband and wife (cohabit) and represent themselves to the outside world as being married.

Void and Voidable Marriages

Some marriages are **void** at the outset and can never become valid; others are **voidable** by one of the parties. **Void marriages** include those between close relatives and those where one of the parties is already married to someone else and has not obtained a divorce. State statutes prohibit people from marrying any of the following close relatives:

1. Any ancestor or descendant (e.g., mother, father, grandmother, grandfather, son, daughter, grandchild)

2. A brother or sister

3. An aunt or uncle

4. A first cousin

5. A niece or nephew

Note that an adopted individual becomes a member of the adoptive family. Therefore, a marriage between an adopted child and any of the prohibited relatives would also be void.

A **voidable marriage** has certain defects that make it possible for one of the parties—generally, the innocent party—to have the marriage annulled. The marriage is not automatically void, however, and may become valid if certain events occur. Defects that can lead to a voidable marriage include the following:

1. One of the parties was not of legal age at the time of the marriage and did not have parental consent.

2. At the time of the marriage, one of the parties had a spouse from a former marriage who was still alive, although the party had believed the spouse was dead.

3. An incurable physical incapacity of one of the parties prevents the consummation of the marriage.

4. One of the parties was forced to consent to the marriage.

5. The consent of one of the parties was obtained by fraud.

6. Either party was of unsound mind at the time of the marriage.

With most of these defects, if the parties continue to live together as husband and wife for a specified period of time after the defect ceases to exist, the marriage will be considered valid and may not be voided at a later date. For example, if an individual who was under age at the time of the marriage lives with the spouse for a period of time after reaching legal age, their marriage will be valid. State statutes differ as to the time period involved.

Cohabitation

Cohabitation involves a man and woman living together as husband and wife without the benefit of a marriage contract and without the intent to enter into a common-law marriage. Recent cases have awarded **palimony** where couples part after living together for a long period. Usually, the party who is seeking support must show that

void
Having no legal effect.

voidable
Capable of being adjudged void, but may also be made legal by taking certain steps.

void marriage
A marriage that is not legal; includes marriages between close relatives and bigamous relationships.

voidable marriage
A marriage that may be voided by one of the parties or may be made legal on the occurrence of certain events.

cohabitation
Living together without a marriage contract and without the intent to enter a common-law marriage.

palimony
Support paid to one party after a relationship ends based on an implied contract between the couple while they lived together.

there was an agreement, either oral or written, between the parties that one person would keep house, cook, entertain, and run the household while the other person pursued a career outside the home. In such cases, the working party may have to pay support to the person who stayed home as compensation for services rendered. The courts may not award compensation for sexual services, however, because this would represent an illegal contract based on prostitution.

cohabitation agreement
An agreement made between a couple who live together that sets out how their property is to be divided if the relationship ends.

Disputes about the distribution of property may be avoided if the individuals decide early in their relationship to prepare a **cohabitation agreement** that states clearly which items belong to each person. In this document, the couple set out how the property is to be distributed if they separate. It may also provide for support or a lump-sum payment for one party.

Prenuptial Agreements

prenuptial agreement
An agreement made in contemplation of marriage that delineates the separate property of each party and sets out how property acquired during marriage will be divided if the couple separate.

Many couples who are planning to marry prepare a **prenuptial agreement** that states how their property will be divided if the couple obtains a divorce. The agreement lists the property each party owned before the marriage and sets out the manner in which property acquired during the marriage will be divided. The agreement also stipulates the manner in which debts will be paid and provides for child and/or spousal support. Some clients may feel that a prenuptial agreement is unnecessary because they do not plan to get a divorce. Nevertheless, as divorce becomes more common, more couples are deciding to draw up prenuptial agreements. Such agreements are also popular with divorced individuals who are planning a second marriage and have already experienced the problems that property divisions, support, custody, and other issues can present. Exhibit 8.1 shows an example of a prenuptial agreement.

ENDING A MARRIAGE

A marriage can be ended in three ways: by annulment, by legal separation, or by divorce or dissolution. The first two methods will be examined in this section. Much of your work is likely to involve divorce, however, so this complex topic is treated in a separate section.

Annulment or Nullity

annulment
The act of making a marriage void; also called nullity.

A marriage that is annulled is treated as if it had never existed. Usually, the grounds for **annulment** (or nullity) are the same as those for voidable marriages. Most states will allow only marriages of very short duration to qualify for an annulment. Failure to consummate the marriage is also grounds for an annulment in most states.

Legal Separation

A legal separation is treated in the same manner as a divorce. The couple's property is divided as if they had been divorced. The only difference between a legal separation and a divorce is that if a couple obtain a legal separation, they may not remarry until they obtain a divorce.

EXHIBIT 8.1   A Sample Prenuptial Agreement

This Prenuptial Agreement is entered into this 27th day of June, 1996, by and between JEFFREY WILLIAM ALTERIO and KIMBERLY ANN LONGFELLOW, of Prescott, Arizona, in contemplation of the marriage of the parties. This agreement shall become effective upon the date of the contemplated marriage of the parties.

This Agreement is being made on the basis of the parties' contemplated marriage on December 20, 1996. Neither party has been previously married. Both parties wish to define their rights and responsibilities regarding property and finances.

In consideration of the contemplated marriage between the parties and other consideration enumerated below, the parties agree:

1. REVOCATION

If the parties wish to revoke this Agreement, they must prepare a writing signed by both parties.

2. RELATED INSTRUMENTS

Additional instruments required to accomplish the intent of this Agreement shall be promptly delivered, executed, and acknowledged, at the request of the other party on a timely basis.

3. DISCLOSURES

Each of the parties to this agreement is of lawful age and competent to enter into a contract. Neither party knows of any reasons why he/she may not enter into the contemplated marriage. Both parties enter into this agreement voluntarily and without duress or coercion.

Both parties are fully aware of all terms and provisions of this agreement. Each party has disclosed to the other prior to signing this agreement the extent and value of their individual property interests described herein. Each party has fully divulged to the other party the extent of their financial holdings and the respective value of each holding described herein. All properties described herein represent a full and complete enumeration of their respective property interests as of this date.

4. TAX LIABILITY

No clause in this agreement shall waive the right of either party to report income for federal or state tax purposes in the manner permissible for any other spouses. No rights are hereby waived under the Federal Gift Tax laws or the Federal Estate Tax laws regarding any transfers of property.

5. BINDING CLAUSES

This agreement shall be binding upon and benefit both parties and their heirs, assigns, administrators, executors, and personal representatives.

6. COMPLETE AGREEMENT

This agreement is complete in its entirety with respect to the rights of the individuals herein. All prior agreements and representations regarding the subject matter of this agreement are waived or merged into this agreement.

7. VALIDITY

If any of the clauses of this agreement shall be invalid or unenforceable, then the remaining provisions shall continue to be effective.

8. ASSETS

A. All assets of JEFFREY WILLIAM ALTERIO that shall remain his separate property after the contemplated marriage to KIMBERLY ANN LONGFELLOW are enumerated below:

> 1994 Rolls Royce, Arizona License No. RICH
> Home located at 244 Starlight Lane, in the City of Prescott, State of Arizona.
> 4-carat diamond men's ring with the initial "J" in rubies therein.
> One-acre parcel of land located at 245 Forest Trails Road in the City of Cordova, County of Shelby, State of Tennessee.

B. All assets of KIMBERLY ANN LONGFELLOW that shall remain her separate property after the contemplated marriage to JEFFREY WILLIAM ALTERIO are enumerated below:

> 1995 Lexus ES400 automobile, Arizona License No. KIMMM.
> One-carat emerald-cut diamond solitaire ring.

EXHIBIT 8.1   A Sample Prenuptial Agreement *Concluded*

9. LIABILITIES

All liabilities listed below are considered to be the separate property responsibility of each of the parties and are not to be paid from community funds:

A. JEFFREY WILLIAM ALTERIO shall be responsible for the following debts:
    1. VISA card No. VSA22222 in the amount of $2,500.
    2. DISCOVER card No. DISC55555 in the amount of $5,000.

B. KIMBERLEY ANN LONGFELLOW shall be responsible for the following debts:
    1. CONTEMPO card No. CONTEM3333 in the amount of $5,000.
    2. VISA CARD No. VSA11111 in the amount of $3,000.

Signed this 27th day of June, 1996, in the City of Prescott, County of Prescott, State of Arizona.

_____

JEFFREY WILLIAM ALTERIO

_____

KIMBERLEY ANN LONGFELLOW

DIVORCE ACTIONS

divorce
Formal proceeding to end a marriage.

The laws regarding **divorce** vary considerably from state to state. This section will note the major differences and present the main issues raised by divorce, but you should also become familiar with the laws of your own state.

Some states consider divorce to be an adversary proceeding and treat it similarly to a civil action where one party (the plaintiff) sues the other party (the defendant). In these states, a complaint must be filed to initiate a divorce. Exhibit 8.2 shows a complaint from Tennessee, and Exhibit 8.3 shows a complaint from New York.

Grounds for Divorce

grounds for divorce
Legal cause for divorce; required in some states.

Some states require that a couple must have **grounds for divorce** in order to divorce. The following are the most common grounds for divorce:

1. ***Physical or Mental Cruelty.***   One of the most common grounds for divorce, this includes extreme forms of cruelty administered by one spouse on the other. The injured spouse must prove the abuse by testimony of witnesses, police reports, pictures, or other forms of physical evidence.

2. ***Incurable Insanity.***   In states that allow these grounds, the other party must be able to prove that the spouse is incurably insane. Proof may take the form of medical reports, expert testimony, or other physical evidence. Proving an individual is incurably insane is often difficult, however.

3. ***Adultery.***   If one spouse voluntarily has sexual intercourse with someone other than the other spouse, a divorce action may be filed on the grounds of

EXHIBIT 8.2   A Sample Complaint for Divorce from Tennessee

IN THE CIRCUIT COURT FOR THE COUNTY OF SHELBY, TENNESSEE

MELANIE L. CONLIN,   )
)
          Plaintiff   )
)
vs.   )
)   No. D-42222
JEREMY W. CONLIN,   )
)
          Defendant.   )

COMPLAINT FOR DIVORCE

TO THE HONORABLE CHANCELLORS AND CIRCUIT COURT JUDGES OF SHELBY COUNTY, TENNESSEE:

The Plaintiff would respectfully show the Court the following:

I.

JURISDICTION

Plaintiff or Defendant has resided in Shelby County, Tennessee more than six months preceding the filing of this complaint.

Plaintiff is a bona fide resident of Tennessee and the acts complained of were committed while the Plaintiff was a bona fide resident of Shelby County, Tennessee.

II.

STATISTICAL DATA

	WIFE:	HUSBAND:
NAME:	Melanie L. Conlin	Jeremy W. Conlin
PRESENT ADDRESS:	247 Carrollwood Lane Cordova, Tennessee	299 Germantown Road Germantown, Tennessee
BIRTHPLACE:	Memphis, Tennessee	Biloxi, Mississippi
BIRTHDATE:	October 29, 1960	April 1, 1955
NUMBER OF PREVIOUS MARRIAGES:	0	0
MARRIAGE:	June 6, 1985	

EXHIBIT 8.2   A Sample Complaint for Divorce from Tennessee *Continued*

1 SEPARATION: February 1, 1996

2 MINOR CHILDREN OF THE MARRIAGE
3 AND BIRTHDATES:

4   Jeremy William Conlin, Jr.   March 21, 1988

5   Rebecca Jane Conlin   December 9, 1989

6   Bradley Willis Conlin   September 20, 1993

7   III.

8   GROUNDS

9   Irreconcilable differences have arisen between the parties that will prevent them
10 from living together as husband and wife.

11   IV.

12   AVERMENTS

13 The parties' children live and have lived in Shelby County, Tennessee, for the last six
14 months and specifically at the following places within the last five years:

15   999 Mt. Moriah Road, Memphis, Tennessee   3/21/88–4/1/94

16   247 Carrollwood Lane, Cordova, Tennessee   4/2/94–present

17 Plaintiff has not participated in any other litigation relating to the custody of the sub-
18 ject of this custody litigation. Plaintiff does not have information of any other custody
19 proceeding concerning the subject of this custody litigation in any Court of this or any
20 other state. Plaintiff does not know of any person not a party to this proceeding, who has
21 physical custody of the subject of the custody litigation, or claims to have custody, or
22 visitation rights with respect to the subject of this custody litigation.

23   V.

24

25   PRAYERS

26 WHEREFORE, PREMISES CONSIDERED, Plaintiff prays that:

27   1. Proper process issue and be served upon the Defendant requiring the Defendant
28 to answer this complaint.

EXHIBIT 8.2   A Sample Complaint for Divorce from Tennessee *Concluded*

1   2.   Upon the hearing of this cause the Plaintiff be awarded a Final Decree of

2   Absolute Divorce from the Defendant.

3   3.   The Court adjust and adjudicate the respective rights and interests of the parties

4   in all jointly owned property.

5   4.   The Court approve a Marital Dissolution Agreement if entered into between the

6   parties.

7   5.   Plaintiff be awarded exclusive custody of the parties' minor children, child sup-

8   port both pendente lite and permanent and attorney's fees and suit expenses for defend-

9   ing the interest of said children; that a hearing be held to determine said pendente lite

10 relief and that said child support shall be assigned from the Defendant's income.

11 6.   Plaintiff be awarded such other further and general relief to which Plaintiff may

12 prove entitled.

13

14 _____

15 RICHARD DREY, Attorney for Plaintiff
    4953 Front Street, Suite 555

16 Memphis, Tennessee 38018
    (901) 555-5555

17 Supreme Court No.: 99995

18

19

20

21

22

23

24

25

26

27

28

EXHIBIT 8.3   A Sample Complaint for Divorce from New York

SUPREME COURT OF THE STATE OF NEW YORK
COUNTY OF WESTCHESTER

MARY ANN GUERRERO: Index No.:
:
Plaintiff:
:
-against-:   VERIFIED COMPLAINT
:   ACTION FOR DIVORCE
:
JONATHAN GUERRERO:
:
Defendant.

--- :

The plaintiff, complaining of the defendant, by her attorneys, BURNS & DAILY, alleges:

1. That on or about the 27th day of June, 1979, plaintiff and defendant were married in Peekskill, New York.

2. That for a continuous period of at least two years immediately preceding the commencement of this action, the plaintiff and defendant were and still are residents of the County of Westchester, State of New York.

3. That there are two infant issue of this marriage, to wit: JUDY ANN, born the 25th day of October, 1982; and PHILIP MICHAEL, born the 15th day of September, 1985.

4. After their marriage as aforesaid and until the 20th day of May, 1995, the plaintiff lived with defendant as man and wife, in various places in the State of New York, and during all that period of time, plaintiff was a true and dutiful wife to the defendant and duly performed all of her duties and obligations as such.

5. That during the course of their marriage, plaintiff and defendant encountered irreconcilable differences which led to their separation and subsequent agreement, entered into the 20th day of June, 1995, and that the parties have lived separate and apart pursuant to this written agreement for a period of more than one year.

WHEREFORE, plaintiff asks judgment against the defendant dissolving the bonds of matrimony existing between the plaintiff and defendant herein, for custody of the minor children of this marriage, and child support; and for such other and further relief as this Court may deem just and proper.

DATED: Peekskill, New York

June 30, 1996

Yours, etc.

BURNS & DAILY
Attorneys for Plaintiff
11223 Main Street
Peekskill, New York 19007
(914) 555-2222

By: _____

adultery in states that recognize these grounds. Proof must be obtained in the form of the testimony of witnesses or physical evidence. However, admission by the guilty spouse is generally sufficient to prove adultery.

4. ***Desertion (or Abandonment).***   If one spouse leaves home and remains missing for a period of time, the other spouse may file for divorce based on desertion. State statutes vary as to the amount of time the spouse must be missing. One or two years appear to be the most common, however.

5. ***Felony Imprisonment.***   Some states allow the spouse to file for divorce if the other spouse is serving a prison term for a felony conviction.

Only the most common grounds for divorce have been included here. You should check the state statutes to find the grounds for divorce in your own state. Fill in any other grounds that exist in your state in the State Specific Information box.

Grounds for divorce in the state of _____ : _____

_____

_____

_____

_____

STATE SPECIFIC INFORMATION

Contested Divorces

If one of the parties does not want a divorce, he may contest it by filing an answer. The answer states the reasons why the divorce should not be granted and may also include an affirmative defense. Any of the following affirmative defenses may be claimed:

1. ***Condoning Misconduct.***   If the plaintiff is asking for the divorce based on the defendant's misconduct, the defendant must prove that the plaintiff accepted this misconduct. For example, if Wanda wishes to divorce Harry because he has committed adultery, Harry can contest the divorce by saying that Wanda had been aware of the adultery for some time and accepted it.

2. ***Mental Impairment.***   The defendant must prove that the behavior that provided grounds for the divorce was caused by a mental defect.

3. ***Connivance.***   The defendant must prove that the plaintiff lured her into the misconduct that provided the grounds for divorce.

4. ***Recrimination.***   If the defendant can prove that the plaintiff was also guilty of the misconduct that established grounds for the divorce, the court may deny the divorce. This defense is based on the English common-law theory of "clean hands"; that is, an individual who seeks relief from the court cannot also be at fault in the situation. Both parties must come into the court with "clean hands."

In most cases, the defendant agrees to the divorce but contests the support, property division, custody, or visitation rights offered by the other party. If the parties cannot agree on those issues, the court will decide the most equitable settlement.

condoning misconduct
Defense to divorce; accepting misconduct on the part of the other spouse.

mental impairment
Defense to divorce; proving that behavior providing grounds for divorce was caused by a mental defect.

connivance
Defense for divorce; luring one into misconduct.

recrimination
Defense for divorce; both parties are guilty of misconduct.

TABLE 8.1 Terminology for Divorce and Dissolution	
DIVORCE	**NO-FAULT DIVORCE (DISSOLUTION)**
Divorce	Dissolution
Complaint	Petition
Answer	Response
Plaintiff	Petitioner
Defendant	Respondent
Alimony	Spousal support
Smith v. Smith	*In Re Marriage of Smith*

No-Fault Divorce (Dissolution)

no-fault divorce
A divorce available in many states that requires neither party to prove grounds. Either party desiring a divorce files a petition to commence the action; also called a dissolution.

petition
The form filed to initiate a no-fault divorce or dissolution; also the form filed to initiate an adoption.

dissolution
The term used for no-fault divorce in many states.

An important trend in recent years is the emergence of **"no-fault divorce."** Rather than having to prove grounds for the divorce, one spouse may merely file a document (usually a **petition**) and serve it on the other spouse to commence the action. About half the states allow some form of no-fault divorce, especially where the couple have lived apart under a separation agreement for a specified period. In most of these states, the other party may not contest the divorce, and no grounds are required.

No-fault divorce is known as **dissolution** in many states. Table 8.1 lists the terms used in divorce and the corresponding terms in dissolutions.

Initiating the Dissolution.   Exhibit 8.4 shows the petition that is used in California to initiate an action in dissolution. The petition is accompanied by statements of income, expenses, and property. All pleadings filed in California use forms that may be obtained from the County Clerk's Office. Most other states, however, require office-prepared pleadings.

It is important to learn your own state's rules for filing divorce actions. You should check the files in your office to determine how these actions were filed in the past. Do not hesitate to ask another paralegal or legal secretary if you are unsure.

Residency Requirements

All states require that the petitioner or plaintiff must have lived in that state long enough to establish residency before filing for a divorce. Some state statutes require that the defendant or respondent be a resident of the state for a specified period as well. In California, for instance, the petitioner must have been a resident of the state for six months and of the county for three months to initiate a dissolution proceeding. In contrast, Florida allows immediate residency by the filing of a Declaration of Domicile with the clerk of the court.

Research your own state statutes to find out the residency requirements, and fill in the State Specific Information box.

RESIDENCY REQUIREMENTS
In the state of _____, the plaintiff/petitioner must be a resident of the state for _____ years/months and the county for _____ years/months before filing for a divorce/dissolution. The defendant/respondent must be a resident of the state for _____ years/months and the county for _____ years/months.

STATE SPECIFIC INFORMATION

EXHIBIT 8.4   A Petition for Dissolution from California

1281

ATTORNEY OR PARTY WITHOUT ATTORNEY *(Name and Mailing Address)*:	TELEPHONE NO.:	*FOR COURT USE ONLY*

ATTORNEY FOR *(Name)*:

SUPERIOR COURT OF CALIFORNIA, COUNTY OF

STREET ADDRESS:

MAILING ADDRESS:

CITY AND ZIP CODE:

BRANCH NAME:

MARRIAGE OF

PETITIONER:

RESPONDENT:

PETITION FOR

☐ **Dissolution of Marriage**   ☐ **And Declaration Under Uniform**
☐ **Legal Separation**   **Child Custody Jurisdiction Act**
☐ **Nullity of Marriage**

CASE NUMBER:

1. RESIDENCE (Dissolution only) ☐ Petitioner ☐ Respondent has been a resident of this state for at least six months and of this county for at least three months immediately preceding the filing of this Petition for Dissolution of Marriage.

2. STATISTICAL FACTS
   a. Date of marriage: c. Period between marriage and separation
   b. Date of separation: Years: Months:

3. DECLARATION REGARDING MINOR CHILDREN OF THIS MARRIAGE FOR WHOM SUPPORT MAY BE ORDERED OR WHO MAY BE SUBJECT TO CUSTODY OR VISITATION ORDERS
   a. ☐ There are no minor children.   b. ☐ The minor children are:
      <u>Child's name</u>   <u>Birthdate</u>   <u>Age</u>   <u>Sex</u>

   c. IF THERE ARE MINOR CHILDREN, COMPLETE EITHER (1) OR (2)
      (1) ☐ Each child named in 3b is currently living with ☐ petitioner ☐ respondent
             in the following county *(specify)*:
             During the last five years each child has lived in no state other than California and with no person other than petitioner or respondent or both. Petitioner has not participated in any capacity in any litigation or proceeding in any state concerning custody of any minor child of this marriage. Petitioner has no information of any pending custody proceeding or of any person not a party to this proceeding who has physical custody or claims to have custody or visitation rights concerning any minor child of this marriage.
      (2) ☐ A completed Declaration Under Uniform Child Custody Jurisdiction Act is attached.

4. ☐ **Petitioner requests** confirmation as separate assets and obligations the items listed
      ☐ in Attachment 4   ☐ below:
      <u>Item</u>   <u>Confirm to</u>

NOTICE: Any party required to pay child support must pay interest on overdue amounts at the "legal" rate, which is currently 10 percent. This can be a large added amount.

(Continued on reverse)

Form Adopted by Rule 1281
Judicial Council of California
1281 [Rev. January 1, 1995]

PETITION
(Family Law)

Family Code, §§ 2330, 3409
Calif. Rules of Court, rule 1215

EXHIBIT 8.4   A Petition for Dissolution from California *Concluded*

MARRIAGE OF *(last name, first name of parties)*:

CASE NUMBER:

---

5. DECLARATION REGARDING COMMUNITY AND QUASI-COMMUNITY ASSETS AND OBLIGATIONS AS CURRENTLY KNOWN
   a. ☐ There are no such assets or obligations subject to disposition by the court in this proceeding.
   b. ☐ All such assets and obligations have been disposed of by written agreement.
   c. ☐ All such assets and obligations are listed ☐ in Attachment 5 ☐ below *(specify)*:

6. **Petitioner requests**
   a. ☐ Dissolution of the marriage based on
      (1) ☐ irreconcilable differences. FC 2310(a)
      (2) ☐ incurable insanity. FC 2310(b)
   b. ☐ Legal separation of the parties based on
      (1) ☐ irreconcilable differences. FC 2310(a)
      (2) ☐ incurable insanity. FC 2310(b)
   c. ☐ Nullity of void marriage based on
      (1) ☐ incestuous marriage. FC 2200
      (2) ☐ bigamous marriage. FC 2201

   a. ☐ Nullity of voidable marriage based on
      (1) ☐ petitioner's age at time of marriage. FC 2210(a)
      (2) ☐ prior existing marriage. FC 2210(b)
      (3) ☐ unsound mind. FC 2210(c)
      (4) ☐ fraud. FC 2210(d)
      (5) ☐ force. FC 2210(e)
      (6) ☐ physical incapacity. FC 2210(f)

7. **Petitioner requests** that the court grant the above relief and make injunctive (including restraining) and other orders as follows:

	Petitioner	Respondent	Joint	Other
a. Legal custody of children to	☐	☐	☐	☐
b. Physical custody of children to	☐	☐	☐	☐
c. Child visitation be granted to	☐	☐	☐	☐
☐ supervised as to *(specify)*:				
d. Spousal support payable by (wage assignment will be issued)	☐	☐		
e. Attorney fees and costs payable by	☐	☐		

   f. ☐ Terminate the court's jurisdiction (ability) to award spousal support to respondent.
   g. ☐ Property rights be determined.
   h. ☐ Wife's former name be restored *(specify)*:
   i. ☐ Other *(specify)*:

8. If there are minor children of this marriage, the court will make orders for the support of the children without further notice to either party. A wage assignment will be issued.

9. I have read the restraining orders on the back of the Summons, and I understand that they apply to me when this petition is filed.

I declare under penalty of perjury under the laws of the State of California that the foregoing is true and correct.

Date:

▶ _____
   (SIGNATURE OF PETITIONER)

. . . .
(TYPE OR PRINT NAME OF ATTORNEY)

▶ _____
   (SIGNATURE OF ATTORNEY FOR PETITIONER)

NOTICE: Please review your will, insurance policies, retirement benefit plans, credit cards, other credit accounts and credit reports, and other matters you may want to change in view of the dissolution or annulment of your marriage, or your legal separation. However, some changes may require the agreement of your spouse or a court order (see Family Code sections 231–235).

1281 [Rev. January 1, 1995]

PETITION
(Family Law)

Page two

SOURCE: Reprinted from California Judicial Council Forms, published by West Publishing Company.

Marital Property (or Community Property)

Many states divide property from the marriage based on whether it was acquired during the marriage, before the marriage, or after the separation. In **community property** states, all property acquired during the marriage except individual gifts or inheritances is considered community property and is divided equally upon dissolution of the marriage. **Separate property** includes property acquired before the marriage, property acquired after the separation, and individual gifts and inheritances acquired during the marriage. A gift to the couple, however, would be considered community property and would be divided upon dissolution.

In one case, the wife's parents purchased a house for the couple for a wedding present. When the couple later divorced, the wife sought to keep the house as her separate property. The court held, however, that since the house was given to the couple and not to the wife individually, it was community property and must be divided between the parties.

Other states may make an unequal division of the property acquired during the marriage. However, more states have recognized that since both parties contribute equally to the finances of the marriage, the property acquired should be divided equally as well.

Quasi-community property includes property located in another state that would have been considered community property in the state of the couple's residence. For purposes of the divorce, this property is treated as if it were community property. However, for practical purposes, if the laws related to property ownership are different in the state in which the property is located, the courts will offset that property with other marital property in the settlement agreement. Sometimes, the state where the property is located is not a community property state. In that case, the court would award the property to one party, but would offset that property with other property in the settlement agreement. For instance, Mary and Bob live in a community property state, but also own a piece of land worth $20,000 in a non–community property state. Assume that Mary and Bob divorce, and the court awards the real estate to Bob. In that case, Mary would receive other property worth $10,000 (her half of the interest in the land) to offset the award to Bob.

Pensions and retirement benefits are usually subject to division based on the period of time the individual has been paying into those benefits during the marriage. Therefore, the longer the marriage, often the greater the share of pension benefits the other spouse (the spouse who did not contribute to the benefits) receives.

Preliminary Hearing or Order to Show Cause

Since the whole divorce process often takes considerable time, the courts allow preliminary proceedings where one of the spouses may request a temporary order. Most attorneys advise their clients not to agree to a temporary order, however, if they would not agree to that same order on a permanent basis. Many courts use the temporary order when deciding the issues in the case on a permanent basis.

If one party needs financial support to provide for her needs, then it may be sought in the preliminary or **Order to Show Cause** hearing. Other items that might be requested at this time include attorneys' fees, temporary custody, child support, spousal support, and permission to live in the family home. If there is a problem with physical abuse, then a Temporary Restraining Order (or Stay-Away Order) may be requested against the abusing spouse to keep that spouse away from the abused spouse and the home.

community property
Property acquired during the marriage that is not a gift or inheritance. The concept applies only in community property states.

separate property
Property acquired before marriage or during marriage through gift or inheritance. The concept applies only in community property states.

quasi-community property
Property in another state that would be community property if located in the state where the couple reside.

Order to Show Cause (OSC)
A preliminary hearing in a dissolution action where the court issues temporary orders on such matters as support and child custody.

Child Custody Determination

Under modern statutes, both parents have an equal right to custody of their children. The primary principle used by the court in determining custody is the "best interests of the child." Some questions the court must answer are the following:

1. Which parent wants custody of the child?

2. Which parent does the child want to live with? (This question is more critical with older children. For instance, a judge may be more likely to ask a twelve-year-old which parent he wants to live with than a five-year-old.)

3. How well does the child get along with each parent and with other siblings?

4. How well established is the child in the community in which he lives? Has the family home been in this location for a considerable period of time? Does the child go to school in the neighborhood?

5. What is the mental and physical health of the child and the parents? If the child has physical or mental problems, which parent would be better able to take care of him?

6. What would a change in environment do to the child's stability at this time?

7. Which parent appears to the court to be better able to care for the child's needs?

8. Will changing the custodial arrangements remove the child from this court's jurisdiction?

In most cases where both parents are stable and positive influences on the child, the noncustodial parent will be awarded liberal visitation rights. If there has been a history of abuse by one of the parents, however, the court may order supervised visitation or, in extreme cases, no visitation at all.

From a practical standpoint, custody issues are the most difficult problems in which the family lawyer will be involved. As a paralegal or legal secretary in a family law practice, one must often listen to extremely difficult problems. Being able to leave one's job "at the office" is particularly beneficial in this type of environment.

Child Support

Both spouses are legally required to support their children. Generally, the noncustodial parent pays support for the child to the custodial parent. The amount of support awarded is determined by the best interests of the child. The court looks at the age of the child, the salaries of both parents, the manner in which the child has been living, and the number of children. Child support payments may not be discharged in bankruptcy proceedings. Therefore, a parent who files for bankruptcy must still pay child support.

In addition to food, clothing, and shelter, the parent may be required to provide the following items:

1. Medical, vision, and/or dental insurance

2. Education expenses

3. Medical and hospital expenses

The requirements for child support end when the child reaches the age of majority, usually eighteen.

Some states have instituted criminal penalties against absent parents who do not support their children. For instance, in California, the District Attorney's Office has a special Child Support Division that investigates nonpaying parents and obtains support for the custodial parent through salary garnishments, wage assignments, and tax liens. Sometimes criminal penalties such as incarceration are imposed on a nonpaying parent.

Alimony or Spousal Support

Some spouses are required to pay alimony or support to the other spouse when a divorce is obtained. In deciding whether to award support, the court will consider whether the spouses are both capable of earning a living for themselves or whether one has not worked before and lacks job skills. In the latter case, the court may order a vocational rehabilitation counselor to interview the nonworking spouse to determine the amount of time and training required to make that person a contributing member of the workforce. In such cases, the court may order temporary support for months or years to allow the person to obtain job training.

Other factors that the court may look at in determining alimony include the ages of the parties, the length of the marriage, the couple's standard of living, the ages of the children, and the salary of the paying spouse. Generally, an individual is more likely to get spousal support after a long-term marriage. Some states have defined long-term marriages as those lasting five years or more. Spousal support often lasts until the spouse who is receiving the support dies or remarries.

Marital Settlement Agreement

To expedite the divorce settlement, the attorneys may negotiate an agreement between the parties to divide their assets. If the parties can agree to the division of property, support, visitation rights, custody, and all other issues, then the court will not intervene in the settlement process. The **Marital Settlement Agreement** sets out all of the terms of the settlement and is signed by both parties. If the parties can arrive at an agreement, the court proceedings are less complicated, and the process becomes more tolerable. A sample Marital Settlement Agreement is shown in Exhibit 8.5.

Marital Settlement Agreement
An agreement made by a married couple contemplating divorce that sets forth the manner in which property is to be divided.

Final Decree of Divorce or Dissolution

After a certain period of time has elapsed, usually about six months or a year after the initial complaint or petition was filed with the court, the final decree may be filed. In most states, this is a separate document that is prepared by the attorney. As the paralegal or legal secretary, you should put a note in your "tickler file" to file this document at the appropriate time. There are many horror stories about individuals who thought their divorces were final and remarried, only to find that the final papers were never filed.

California has attempted to address this problem by allowing the parties to file a **Final Decree Nunc Pro Tunc**, which is a final dissolution that is retroactive; that is, it becomes effective as of the time the dissolution would have taken place if the final

Final Decree Nunc Pro Tunc
A final dissolution of a marriage that is filed after the appropriate time for filing a final decree, but is effective as of the time the dissolution would have taken place if the final decree had been filed in a timely manner.

EXHIBIT 8.5   A Sample Marital Settlement Agreement

1
2
3
4
5
6
7
8
9
10
11
12
13
14
15
16
17
18
19
20
21
22
23
24
25
26
27
28

MARITAL SETTLEMENT AGREEMENT
BETWEEN
JAMES R. MARTIN AND
BARBARA S. MARTIN

The parties above named are husband and wife and hereby agree that irreconcil-able differences have caused the irremediable breakdown of their marriage. It is their mutual desire to bring about a final division of their property and a complete settle-ment of their respective property rights to all of their property. To this end, the parties agree to the following:

FIRST: The parties agree that the following items are community property and should be divided equally between them:

1.   House located at 333 Sycamore Lane, Austin, Texas

2.   Lot 264 in the Subdivision Map of Carrollwood Estates, known as 64 Treetop Road, Cordova, Tennessee

These properties shall be sold and the proceeds equally divided between the parties.

SECOND: The parties agree that the following items are separate property and shall remain with the owner.

The separate property of JAMES R. MARTIN consists of the following:

1.   1995 Lexus GS300 sedan, License No. JIMBOW

2.   All of his jewelry as previously agreed upon

The separate property of BARBARA S. MARTIN consists of the following:

1.   1992 Ferrari, License No. FASTTT

2.   All of her jewelry as previously agreed upon.

THIRD: The parties agree that neither party shall receive either support or maintenance and that each party will maintain his/her own medical insurance, life insurance, and retirement plans.

EXHIBIT 8.5   A Sample Marital Settlement Agreement *Concluded*

1   FOURTH: Both parties have read this agreement and accept and understand

2   its terms. No further promises have been made by the parties outside of this Marital

3   Settlement Agreement.

4   FIFTH: Both parties agree to execute all documents required to effectuate

5   the sale and/or transfers of property required by this agreement.

6   SIXTH: Subject to the approval of the Texas Family Law Court, this docu-

7   ment shall be made a part of the decree of divorce of the parties.

8   Executed on the _____ day of _____ , 1996 by:

9

_____

10   JAMES R. MARTIN

11   _____

12   BARBARA S. MARTIN

13

14

15

16

17

18

19

20

21

22

23

24

25

26

27

28

decree had been filed at the appropriate time. This procedure solves the problem of a person who has inadvertently remarried without being divorced.

ADOPTION

The legal procedure whereby an individual or a couple become parents to a child who has not been born to them is known as **adoption.** The child relinquishes all rights and responsibilities that previously existed with the biological parents. The new parents then assume these responsibilities as though the child had been born to them. Clients should be made fully aware of the consequences of the adoption process. The birth parents are no longer considered the legal parents of the child, and their parental rights are terminated, while the adoptive parents assume all rights and responsibilities for that child. The child loses all right to inherit from the birth parents and receives the right to inherit from the adoptive parents. In addition, the child acquires a new set of relatives, including siblings, grandparents, aunts, uncles, and cousins, just as if he had been born into the family.

Independent adoptions have become a new specialty area for some attorneys. Pregnant women contact the attorney, who provides them with resumes of prospective parents for their child. The birth mother can review the resumes of the prospective adoptive parents and interview those that she feels would be appropriate. She thus has the option of actually choosing her child's new parents. In most states, both parents must consent to the adoption in writing.

Agency adoptions are becoming less common because very few babies are given up to agencies for adoption. One or both birth parents must sign a document that relinquishes the child to the agency. The birth parent does not have the opportunity of knowing where the child is placed.

In **stepparent adoptions,** a new spouse adopts the other spouse's child from a previous marriage. The child's other parent must give permission for this adoption to occur. For instance, during Sue and Bob's marriage, they have a son, Michael. Sue and Bob are divorced, and Sue marries Stan. Stan would like to adopt Michael. Bob must sign a form giving permission for the adoption to occur. Stan then becomes Michael's father, and Bob has no rights or responsibilities for Michael.

If one adult adopts another adult, the adopting parent must be at least ten years older than the adopted adult. Although this type of adoption is rare, it offers the advantage of giving the adopted adult the right to inherit from the other adult. The majority of states require the permission of the spouse of the adopting adult before such an adoption may occur.

Procedures for Adoptions

Most states have basic forms or documents that must be filed to accomplish the adoption. These involve a **petition,** a **Consent and Agreement,** and a **decree.** When the client comes into the office to initiate the adoption, the paralegal or legal secretary must complete the petition, which includes the names of the new parents, the name of the child at birth, the date of birth, and the signatures of the adopting parents. A sample Adoption Petition is shown in Exhibit 8.6.

In many states, a Consent and Agreement form must be completed by the adopting parents and by the child if she is over twelve years of age. Permissions must be obtained from the birth parents.

---

adoption
A legal proceeding where adoptive parents become the legal parents of an adopted child. The birth parents give up all legal rights and responsibilities for the child.

independent adoption
An adoption that is not carried out through an agency; usually carried out through an attorney who acts as a middleperson between the biological mother and the adoptive parents.

agency adoption
The adoption of a child through a public or private agency.

stepparent adoption
The adoption by one spouse of the other spouse's children from a former marriage.

petition
The form filed to initiate a no-fault divorce or dissolution; also the form filed to initiate an adoption.

Consent and Agreement
In adoption proceedings, the form in which the adopting parents obtain the approval of the biological parents.

decree
In adoption proceedings, a form issued by the court that states that the child may be adopted and indicates the child's new name.

EXHIBIT 8.6   A Sample Adoption Petition

Michelle M. Tanaka
Attorney at Law
1122 Main Street
Roanoke, VA 99999

(315)999-5555

IN THE CIRCUIT COURT FOR THE CITY OF ROANOKE

STATE OF VIRGINIA

In the Matter of the Adoption Petition of:

JENNIFER LEE and   )
)
ROBERT LEE,   )
)   ADOPTION PETITION
Adoptive Parents and Petitioners.   )   NO. A-48999
_____

Petitioners herein allege as follows:

1.   That at the time of the birth of the minor who is the subject of this petition, her name was MARY MARTINE.

2.   That the petitioners herein are husband and wife and presently reside in the City of Roanoke, State of Virginia, and wish to adopt the minor child, MARY MARTINE, who was born in Marysville County, Virginia, on October 26, 1995. The petitioners are adults and are both more than ten years older than the minor child.

3.   The parents of the minor child will consent to the adoption by said petitioners. The minor child presently resides with the Adoptive Parents.

4.   Both parties agree to the adoption of this child by the other party.

5.   This child is a proper subject for adoption. The home of the Adoptive Parents is a proper home for this child, and they are able to provide suitable care.

6.   All background information required by the Virginia Department of Adoptions will be promptly submitted thereto by the undersigned petitioners.

EXHIBIT 8.6   A Sample Adoption Petition *Concluded*

1   WHEREFORE, petitioners pray that the Court grant this adoption request to

2   enable the parties to maintain a relationship of parent and child. The new name for

3   the child shall be MARY ELIZABETH LEE.

4

5

6   _____
       ROBERT LEE

7

8   _____
9   JENNIFER LEE

10

11

12

13

14

15

16

17

18

19

20

21

22

23

24

25

26

27

28

After the hearing is held before the court, the judge will issue a Decree of Adoption, stating that the child may be adopted and the new name for the child. At this time a copy of the decree may be sent to the state agency where birth records are kept so that a new birth certificate may be issued to the child with her new name and the names of her new parents. Note that single individuals may also adopt children in most states.

SUMMARY

Family law centers around questions related to marriage, divorce, and adoption. States have various requirements for marriage, including such things as blood tests and residency requirements. Thirteen states and the District of Columbia also recognize common-law marriages. Marriages between closely related individuals are never valid and are void from the outset. A voidable marriage has a defect that makes it possible for one of the parties to have the marriage voided; the marriage is not automatically void, however, and may become valid under certain circumstances. A growing trend in family law is the preparation of prenuptial agreements that set out how the couple's property will be divided if they divorce.

Divorce law varies by state. Some states require grounds for divorce, while others have no-fault divorce. In some states, a petition is used to initiate the divorce proceeding, while others require a complaint. Property division, spousal support or alimony, child custody, and child support are all issues that may arise in a divorce. Marital Settlement Agreements are prepared to set out how the property is to be divided upon divorce or dissolution.

Adoptions may be undertaken privately or through an agency. In some cases, stepparents adopt their stepchildren. A petition, consent, and decree are usually required for an adoption.

KEY TERMS

Adoption   224

Agency adoption   224

Annulment   208

Cohabitation   207

Cohabitation agreement   208

Common-law marriage   206

Community property   219

Condoning misconduct   215

Connivance   215

Consent and Agreement   224

Decree   224

Dissolution   216

Divorce   210

Final Decree Nunc Pro Tunc   221

Grounds for divorce   210

Independent adoption   224

Marital Settlement Agreement   221

Marriage   206

Mental impairment   215

No-fault divorce   216

Order to Show Cause (OSC)   219

Palimony   207

Petition   216, 224

Prenuptial agreement   208

Quasi-community property   219

Recrimination   215

Separate property   219

Stepparent adoption   224

Void   207

Voidable   207

Voidable marriage   207

Void marriage   207

SELF-TEST

A. Indicate whether the following statements are true (T) or false (F):

____ 1. All states recognize common-law marriage.

____ 2. Recent cases have awarded "palimony" when couples who have lived together for a long time part company.

____ 3. A cohabitation agreement is prepared by a couple in contemplation of marriage and provides for a subsequent division of property.

____ 4. Void marriages include those between a person and his ancestor and between a person and her descendant.

____ 5. A marriage may be voidable if either party was of unsound mind at the time of the marriage.

B. Circle the correct answer for the following questions:

1. Annulment means

   a. the marriage is treated as if it had never existed.

   b. the same thing as divorce.

   c. a legal separation.

   d. a no-fault divorce.

2. Property acquired during a marriage that is not a gift or an inheritance is known as

   a. separate property.

   b. community property.

   c. communal property.

   d. quasi-community property.

3. A divorce action is initiated by filing a

   a. complaint.

   b. answer.

   c. default.

   d. financial statement.

4. A dissolution action is initiated by filing a

   a. complaint.

   b. petition.

   c. default.

   d. financial statement.

5. The requirement that a person filing for divorce must have lived in that state for a sufficient period of time is called a(n)

   a. domiciled requirement.

   b. residency requirement.

   c. live-in requirement.

   d. address requirement.

C.   Fill in the blanks:

1. Preliminary support may be obtained at the _____ .

2. Which spouse is legally required to support the children?

   _____

3. The court determines the amount of child support based on the

   _____ .

4. The first document filed in a divorce or dissolution action is called the

   _____ in a no-fault divorce state and the

   _____ in a state that has grounds for divorce.

5. Marriages that are void include _____ .

REVIEW QUESTIONS

1. Explain the difference between void and voidable marriages.

2. List the procedures followed for private adoptions.

3. Explain what the court considers in setting the amount of child support a parent must pay.

4. List the issues that are decided at the Order to Show Cause Hearing.

PROJECTS

1. Depending on the law in your state, prepare either a petition for dissolution or a complaint for divorce using the case information provided. If you live in a state that requires grounds for divorce, your instructor will tell you the proper grounds. Prepare the form for your state. If your state forms are not available, use Exhibit 8.2, 8.3, or 8.4. Note: Exhibit 8.4 is not provided on disk.

CASE INFORMATION

- Client's name: Mary E. Gallo
- Address: 245 Sunset Drive, Your Town, Your State
- Court: Use the closest appropriate court in your state.
- Spouse: Michael P. Gallo

- Spouse's address: 459 Academy Street, Your Town, Your State
- Married: June 15, 1985
- Separated: July 4, current year
- Minor children: Anna Gallo, born 9/9/87
                         Paul Gallo, born 4/29/90

The children are currently living with their mother.

The client requests that the following items be designated as her separate property: a three-carat marquise-cut diamond ring, 1995 Chevrolet station wagon, service for 12 Lennox china, service for 12 International sterling silver, and International sterling silver six-piece tea service.

Community (or marital) assets include the following and should be divided between the parties:

- Residence located at 245 Sunset Drive, Your Town, Your State; valued at $250,000 with equity of $200,000.

- Vacation home located at 999 Brentwood Drive, Lake Arrowhead, California; valued at $150,000, which was paid in cash; therefore, total equity is $150,000.

- Furniture and furnishings located at residence: $50,000

- Furniture and furnishings located at California home: $25,000

- Bank account at National Savings Bank, Your Town: $20,000

The client requests dissolution or divorce, full custody of the children, spousal support of $3,000 per month, and child support of $1,000 per month. She also requests that her spouse pay her attorney's fees.

2.   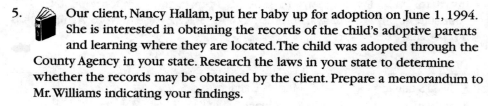 Our clients, John and Norma Ray, wish to adopt a child, Virginia Steadman, whose parents are Steven and Roberta Steadman. Virginia was born on May 30, 1994, in your state. The Steadmans will consent to the adoption, and Virginia's new name will be Virginia Ray. Using the format for your state, prepare a Petition for Adoption. If you do not know the format for your state, use Exhibit 8.6 as a guide.

3.   List the grounds for divorce recognized in your state. If your state is a no-fault state, describe the procedures for filing for divorce or dissolution in your state.

4.   Research and determine the divorce laws in your state as they relate to the following. Prepare a written report on your findings.

   a. Grounds

   b. Filing procedures and fees

   c. Child support

   d. Child custody

   e. Spousal support

5.   Our client, Nancy Hallam, put her baby up for adoption on June 1, 1994. She is interested in obtaining the records of the child's adoptive parents and learning where they are located. The child was adopted through the County Agency in your state. Research the laws in your state to determine whether the records may be obtained by the client. Prepare a memorandum to Mr. Williams indicating your findings.

Types of Business Organizations

CHAPTER OBJECTIVES

As a result of studying this chapter, you will learn the following material:

1. ***Types of Business Organizations***   The characteristics of the different types of business organizations will be presented. You will learn the advantages and disadvantages of sole proprietorships, partnerships, and corporations.

2. ***Methods of Organization***   The manner in which sole proprietorships, partnerships, and corporations are formed will be discussed. You will learn the role the paralegal and legal secretary play in the formation of each type of organization.

3. ***Partnership and Corporate Documents***   The documents required for the formation of a partnership and a corporation will be presented. You will learn how to prepare a partnership agreement, Articles of Incorporation, and Bylaws.

4. ***Dissolution of a Corporation***   The manner in which corporations are dissolved will be discussed. You will learn the differences between voluntary and involuntary dissolutions.

5. ***Consolidations and Mergers***   The basic procedures of consolidations and mergers will be presented. You will learn the effect of consolidation and merger on the corporations involved.

6. ***Bankruptcy***   The basic rules of bankruptcy will be presented. You will learn the difference between Chapter 7 and Chapter 11 bankruptcy.

TYPES OF BUSINESS ORGANIZATIONS

The most common types of business organization are the sole proprietorship, the partnership, and the corporation. Although most businesses are operated as sole proprietorships, one of the other forms of organization may be more advantageous, depending on the client's circumstances.

SOLE PROPRIETORSHIPS

The mainstay of the American economy is the **sole proprietorship,** an unincorporated business that is usually owned by one person. You probably deal with sole pro-

sole proprietorship
An unincorporated business, usually owed by one person, who is subject to unlimited personal liability.

prietorships every day. The dry cleaner's where you take your clothes, the service station where you buy gas, and the local convenience store may be organized in this manner.

Sole proprietorships offer both advantages and disadvantages. One advantage is that sole proprietorships are relatively easy to establish and are not costly to organize. Because they usually are owned by only one individual, the owner does not have to be concerned about disagreements with other owners.

The owner of a sole proprietorship is subject to unlimited personal liability, however, which can be a major disadvantage in today's litigious society. For instance, if someone sues the business and is awarded damages of $100,000 when the assets of the business are worth only $50,000, he would be able to take the owner's personal assets as well as those of the business in settlement of the claim.

Another disadvantage is that a sole proprietorship has less access to capital to undertake new projects than a partnership or corporation has. If the owner wishes to expand the business, she is limited to obtaining personal loans using the business assets or her personal assets as security.

Having only a single owner can also lead to problems. If the owner dies or becomes disabled, there may be no one else who can run the business. The only recourse might be to sell the business, which might result in a loss of profit and revenue.

In some cases, too, other forms of organization may provide certain tax benefits. However, the owner should consult an accountant or tax attorney for advice before changing the form of ownership to save taxes. Sometimes, little or no tax saving may result.

Most states require a sole proprietor to file certain documents. If the business sells items to the public and the state imposes a sales tax, then a sales tax permit must be obtained. In most states, a proprietorship that operates under a name other than the owner's name must file a Fictitious Business Name Certificate (see Exhibit 9.1) in the county where the business is located. Usually, a business license must be obtained in the city where the business is located.

PARTNERSHIPS

partnership
An association of two or more individuals who have joined together to operate a business for profit.

A **partnership** is an association of two or more individuals who have joined together to operate a business for profit. The major reasons for forming a partnership are to share expenses and to increase capital. Although a partnership is a business, the partnership itself is not taxed; instead, partners must declare their share of the partnership profits on their personal income tax returns.

Like sole proprietorships, partnerships offer advantages and disadvantages. Although partnerships may have access to more capital than sole proprietorships, partnerships can involve risks not present in individual proprietorships because each partner is liable for his partner's actions. In fact, partnerships are similar to marriages in that one partner may be held legally responsible for the other partner's actions. For example, if one partner purchases a new car for the business and does not pay for it, his partner may be held liable for the payments. Although one partner may deal honestly and fairly and without fraudulent intent, another partner may engage in illegal activities or dishonest practices for which the honest partner could be held liable.

Consequently, clients should be advised to choose their partners carefully and to select partners whose management practices and beliefs are similar to their own. Knowing an individual's business ethics is only the first step in determining whether

---

EXHIBIT 9.1   A Sample Fictitious Business Name Certificate

FICTITIOUS BUSINESS NAME STATEMENT

File No. 452999292

The following person(s) is (are) doing business as:

FLYING SERVICES, 625 Wilmot Road, Prescott, AZ 85013.

Jeffrey W. Longman, 625 Wilmot Road, Prescott, AZ 85013.

This business is conducted by an individual

_____
JEFFREY W. LONGMAN

This statement was filed with the County Clerk of Prescott County on May 6, 1996.

The registrant(s) commenced to transact business under the fictitious name or names listed above on May 1, 1996.

NOTICE: This Fictitious Business Name Statement expires five years from the date it was filed in the office of the County Clerk. A new Fictitious Business Name Statement must be filed before that time.

The filing of this statement does not of itself authorize the use in this state of a Fictitious Business Name in violation of the rights of another under Federal, State, or common law (See Section 12222 et seq., Business and Professional Code).

---

to choose him for a partner. Partnership agreements should be scrutinized to determine the exact terms of the partnership arrangement, as well as who is responsible for actions of the partnership and whose decisions are final.

General and Limited Partners

Although a partnership may have only two partners, many partnerships have numerous partners and include both general and limited partners. **General partners** are involved in the day-to-day operation of the business. They not only invest money in the partnership but are also responsible for its management. In many partnerships, all partners are general partners.

Sometimes individuals have capital to invest but do not wish to be responsible for the management of the partnership. These partners are **limited partners.** Unlike general partners, limited partners are not personally liable for the other partners' actions. A limited partner may only be held liable for the amount of money he contributed to the partnership.

general partner
A partner who is involved in the management of the partnership and is personally liable for the actions of the other partners.

limited partner
A partner who invests in a partnership but is not involved in its management and is liable only for the amount invested.

A partnership must have at least one general partner who is responsible for the partnership liability; thus, a partnership cannot have only limited partners. Some states have more stringent regulations on limited partners. You should research the statutes in your own state to learn the rules for limited partnerships. List the main requirements in the State Specific Information box.

STATE SPECIFIC INFORMATION

Requirements for limited partnerships in the state of _____ include the following: _____

_____

_____

_____

The Partnership Agreement

Drawing up the partnership agreement is a crucial step in forming a partnership. Although partnership agreements are available in form books and software packages, the paralegal should check a form agreement carefully to be sure that it includes all clauses required by the individual client. The paralegal may also be responsible for discussing the agreement with the client to decide the appropriate clauses to include. The agreement will include the following items:

1. The duration of the partnership
2. Each partner's contribution in money and time
3. How profits will be divided
4. The purpose of the business
5. How partners may transfer their interests
6. How a partner's interest may be "bought out" or purchased by the other partners. (This issue will be particularly critical if your client is the partner whose interest is purchased.)
7. The procedure for voting on issues
8. The duties and responsibilities of each partner
9. The procedures for dissolving the partnership
10. The procedures for adding new partners
11. How policy disagreements will be settled

Exhibit 9.2 shows an example of a partnership agreement. Larger partnerships with more partners may have more complex agreements.

If the partnership includes both limited and general partners, the agreement should delineate the amount of capital the limited partners have invested and their ownership interests in the partnership. Their lack of responsibility for the general partners' actions should also be included.

EXHIBIT 9.2   A Sample Partnership Agreement

This Agreement is made on May 6, 1996 by Gregory Adams and Lisa Harmon, referred to as "Partners" under the following provisions.

1.   The Partners shall associate to form a General Partnership for the purpose of manufacturing candles and any other businesses agreed upon by the Partners.

2.   The Partnership name shall be Adams & Harmon.

3.   The Partnership shall commence on the execution of this Agreement and shall continue until dissolved by agreement of the Partners or terminated under the Agreement.

4.   The Partnership's principal place of business shall be 24 Colonial Road, Salem, Massachusetts.

Initial Capital

5.   The Partnership's initial capital shall be $100,000. Each Partner shall contribute toward the initial capital by depositing the following amounts in the Partnership checking account at the Main Office of the Community Bank in Salem, Massachusetts, May 20, 1996:
Each party shall contribute $50,000.

6.   No Partner shall withdraw any portion of the Partnership capital without the other Partner's express written consent.

7.   The Partners shall share equally in Partnership net profits and shall bear Partnership losses equally.

8.   Partnership books of account shall be accurately kept and shall include records of all Partnership income, expenses, assets, and liabilities. The Partnership books of account shall be maintained on a cash basis. Each Partner shall have the right to inspect the Partnership books at any time.

9.   The Partnership's fiscal year shall end on December 31 each year.

10.   Complete accountings of the Partnership affairs at the close of business on the last days of March, September, and December of each year shall be rendered to each Partner within 10 days after the close of each such month. At the time of such accounting, the net profits of the Partnership shall be distributed to the Partners as provided in this Agreement. Except as to errors brought to the Partners' attention within 10 days after it is rendered, each accounting shall be final and conclusive.

11.   Each Partner shall devote undivided time to and use utmost skill in the Partnership business.

12.   Each Partner shall have an equal right in the management of the Partnership. Each Partner shall have authority to bind the Partnership in making contracts and incurring obligations in the Partnership name or on its credit. No Partner, however, shall incur obligations in the Partnership name or on its credit exceeding $10,000 without the other Partner's express written consent. Any obligation incurred in violation of this provision shall be charged to and collected from the Partner who incurred the obligation.

13.   In compensation for services in the Partnership business, each Partner shall be entitled to a salary of $3,000 per month. The Partnership shall deduct the Partners' salaries as ordinary business expenses prior to computing net profits. A Partner's salary may be increased or reduced at any time by mutual agreement of the Partners.

14.   The term "net profits," as used in this Agreement, shall mean the Partnership net profits as determined by generally accepted accounting principles for each accounting period specified in this Agreement.

15.   Upon 30-days written notice of intent to the other Partner, either Partner may withdraw from the

EXHIBIT 9.2   A Sample Partnership Agreement *Continued*

Partnership at the end of any accounting period specified in this Agreement.

16.   On dissolution of the Partnership by the death, withdrawal, or other act of either Partner, the remaining Partner may continue the Partnership business by purchasing the outgoing Partner's interest in the Partnership assets and goodwill. The remaining Partner shall have the option to purchase the outgoing Partner's interest by paying to the outgoing Partner or the appropriate personal representative the value of the outgoing Partner's interest as determined under Paragraph 17 of this Agreement.

17.   On exercise of the option described in Paragraph 16 of this Agreement, the remaining Partner shall pay to the outgoing Partner or appropriate personal representative the value of the outgoing Partner's Partnership interest as determined by the last regular accounting preceding dissolution plus the full unwithdrawn portion of the outgoing Partner's share in net profits earned between the date of that accounting and the date of dissolution.

18.   If the Partnership is dissolved by the death of either Partner, the remaining Partner shall have 30 days from the date of death in which to purchase the deceased Partner's Partnership interest. The purchase price for the deceased Partner's interest shall be determined under Paragraph 17 of this Agreement. During the 30-day period following either Partner's death, the remaining Partner may continue the Partnership business. The liability of the deceased Partner's estate for Partnership obligations incurred during the period of continuation shall be limited to the amount that the deceased Partner had invested or involved with the Partnership at the time of death and that is includable in the deceased Partner's estate. The deceased Partner's estate shall be entitled, at the election of the personal representative, to either one-half of the Partnership profits earned during the period of continuation or to interest at 10 percent (10%) per annum for the Partnership's use of the deceased Partner's interest as determined under Paragraph 17 of this Agreement during the period of continuation.

19.   On any purchase and sale made pursuant to Paragraphs 16, 17, or 18 of this Agreement, the remaining Partner shall assume all Partnership obligations. The remaining Partner shall hold the withdrawing Partner or the deceased Partner's estate and personal representative, as well as any property belonging to either a withdrawing or deceased Partner, free and harmless from all liability for Partnership obligations. Immediately upon purchase of a withdrawing or deceased Partner's interest, the remaining Partner shall prepare, file, serve, and publish all notices required by law to protect the withdrawing Partner or the deceased Partner's estate and personal representative from liability for future Partnership obligations. All costs incident to the requirements of this Paragraph shall be borne by the remaining Partner.

20.   On dissolution of the Partnership, except as provided in Paragraphs 16, 17, and 18 of this Agreement, the Partnership affairs shall be wound up, the Partnership assets liquidated, its debts paid, and the surplus divided among the Partners according to their then net worths in the Partnership business.

21.   All notices between the Partners shall be in writing and shall be deemed served when personally delivered to a Partner, or when deposited in the United States mail, certified, first-class postage prepaid, addressed to a Partner at the Partnership's principal place of business or to such other place as may be specified in a notice given pursuant to this Paragraph as the address for service of notice on such Partner.

22.   All consents and agreements provided for or permitted by this Agreement shall be in writing. Signed copies of all consents and agreements pertaining to the Partnership shall be kept with the Partnership books.

23.   On all accountings provided for in this Agreement, the goodwill of the Partnership business shall be valued at one dollar ($1) and no more.

24.   This instrument contains the Partner's sole agreement pertaining to their Partnership. It correctly sets out the Partners' rights and obligations. Any prior agreements, promises, negotiations, or representations not expressly set forth in this instrument have no force or effect.

EXHIBIT 9.2   A Sample Partnership Agreement *Concluded*

Executed at Salem, Massachusetts, This _____ day of May, 1996.

_____
GREGORY ADAMS

_____
LISA HARMON

Should the Client Form a Partnership?

The decision of whether to form a partnership or continue as a sole proprietorship can become very complex. When the client comes to discuss the type of organization that is appropriate for her business, the following questions should be asked:

1. Why do you want to change your form of business ownership?

2. Do you need more capital for expansion or other purposes?
   a. If so, would a loan be preferable to forming a partnership?
   b. Are other methods of raising capital available?

3. How well do you know your partner(s)?
   a. Have you had business dealings?
   b. Are you friends?
   c. Do you know anything about the person's business ethics?
   d. Has this individual ever been involved in criminal activity or unethical practices?
   e. Is this person's management style similar to yours?
   f. Have you worked together?

4. Have you considered forming a corporation instead of a partnership? (At this point, the difference between a corporation and a partnership should be explained to the client, who may not be aware of the advantages of a corporation. The ultimate decision, however, rests with the client.)

If the paralegal conducts the discussion with the client, no legal advice may be given. Any questions that require the paralegal to "advise" the client should be referred to the attorney.

CORPORATIONS

A **corporation** is a business entity that exists separately and apart from its owners, who are called **shareholders.** Some corporations have just a few shareholders, while others have thousands. A corporation is said to have "perpetual life" because it is not dissolved upon the death of any of the shareholders. A shareholder's ownership inter-

corporation
A business entity that exists separately and apart from its owners (shareholders) and has perpetual life.

shareholder
An owner of stock in a corporation.

est is represented by shares of stock. The interest can easily be transferred to another by selling the stock.

The primary advantages of the corporate form are the ability to raise considerably larger sums of capital than sole proprietorships or partnerships can raise, the limited liability of the owners of shares, and the corporation's perpetual life. Because many individuals pool their capital to form a corporation, potentially large sums of money can be raised. Unlike sole proprietors and general partners, owners of shares of a corporation's stock will not be liable if a lawsuit is brought against the corporation. If the corporation must pay damages to someone, only corporate assets may be used to satisfy the claim; even if the corporate assets are insufficient, the shareholders' personal assets cannot be used. Finally, having perpetual life means that when a shareholder dies, his shares of stock pass to his heirs, but the corporation itself continues. As we have seen, in other forms of business organization, the death of an owner may mean the dissolution of the business.

In some cases, a corporation enjoys lower tax rates than other forms of business organization. In a small, closely held corporation, the business income may be divided between the business owner and the corporation. By dividing the income, the owner will be in a lower tax bracket and will be assessed less taxes than if he were a sole proprietor and reported all the business income on his personal tax return. For instance, if the owner works in the business and collects a salary, he must report the salary on his personal income tax return; but his salary is deducted from the income of the corporation, which pays no tax on it. If the corporation's income amounts to $150,000 to $200,000 a year or less after deducting all expenses including salaries, this method of dividing the corporate income between the owner and the business will probably result in lower taxes than if the business were run as a partnership or a sole proprietorship. Obviously, this system will only be advantageous in a small corporation with a few owners who collect a salary from the corporation.

A disadvantage of corporations is that they are regulated more stringently than other types of businesses. Creating and maintaining the corporate structure can involve a considerable amount of paperwork. The government may require various documents including Articles of Incorporation, Bylaws, Minutes of Meetings, and Proxy statements. The next sections will explain how a corporation is formed and the role these documents play in creating and maintaining a corporation.

Agent for Process

The first step in forming a corporation is choosing an agent for process. The agent is authorized to act for the corporation and receives service of process and other communications from the office of the state Secretary of State for the benefit of the corporation. The agent should be a trusted employee of the corporation and should be chosen with the utmost care. The paralegal should keep a record of the agent's name and address; the address will generally be the office of the corporation.

Articles of Incorporation

Articles of Incorporation
The first document prepared during the formation of a corporation; include the corporation's name, its purpose, the name and address of the agent for process, and the corporation's stock structure.

The first document prepared for corporate formation is the **Articles of Incorporation,** which include the following:

1. The name of the corporation
2. The purpose of the corporation

3. The name and address of the agent for process

4. The stock structure of the corporation (the number of shares issued and their par value)

5. The duration of the corporation and the names of its initial incorporators and Board of Directors (not required in all states)

Exhibit 9.3 shows an example of Articles of Incorporation. The articles must be filed with the Secretary of State's Office in the state where the corporation is being formed. A name for the corporation must be reserved with that same office.

A corporation may not use the same name as another corporation, nor may it use a name that is so similar to another corporate name that the two organizations could be confused. In the past, a considerable amount of time was spent writing letters back and forth to the Secretary of State's Office to determine the available names for the corporation. Now, however, the paralegal can use software packages to determine if a particular name is available so that the articles may be prepared simultaneously. A name may usually be reserved via computer modem.

After the name has been obtained, the Articles of Incorporation are prepared for mailing to the Secretary of State's Office. If the articles have been prepared properly, a Certificate of Incorporation will be returned to the law office. At that time, the paralegal will usually be asked to order the corporate seal and minutebook from a legal stationery store.

Organizational Meeting

At this point, the new corporation usually holds an initial organizational meeting to elect officers and to draft the **Bylaws,** which are the rules that govern the day-to-day operations of the corporation. Bylaws include such information as the following:

Bylaws
Rules that govern the day-to-day operations of the corporation.

1. The location of the corporation's office.

2. The date and place of the annual shareholders meeting.

3. The powers of the Board of Directors, the date and place of their meetings, and the method by which shareholders may remove individual directors.

4. The types of corporate officers and their terms, duties, and responsibilities.

5. Information about the corporation's stock.

6. Methods of changing the Bylaws.

7. Other general operational information.

Exhibit 9.4 shows an example of corporate Bylaws.

Once all these formalities have been accomplished, the corporation may operate. The corporate paralegal will generally be responsible for keeping track of the time line of the corporate organization to be sure that all matters are handled in a timely fashion.

Annual Report

Once each year the corporation is required to file an **Annual Report,** which is sent to the shareholders and the Secretary of State of the state where the corporation is incorporated. This report describes the actions and business in which the corporation was engaged during the previous year. It also lists the corporation's income and expenses for the year, along with its assets and liabilities. The paralegal and/or legal sec-

Annual Report
A yearly report issued by a corporation describing the past year's activities.

EXHIBIT 9.3   Sample Articles of Incorporation

ARTICLES OF INCORPORATION
OF
ABC CORPORATION

I.

The name of this corporation is: ABC CORPORATION.

II.

The purpose of this corporation is to engage in any lawful act or activity for which a corporation may be organized under the General Corporation Law of California other than the banking business, the trust company business or the practice of a profession permitted to be incorporated by the California Corporations Code.

III.

The name and address in the State of California of this corporation's initial agent for service of process is:

> Dana M. Morrison
> 45 Sunset Boulevard
> Memphis, CA 90555

IV.

This corporation is authorized to issue only one class of shares of common stock; and the total number of shares which this corporation is authorized to issue is two hundred (200).

V.

The liability of the directors of the corporation for monetary damages shall be eliminated to the fullest extent permissible under California law.

VI.

The corporation is authorized to provide indemnification of agents, as that term is defined in Section 317 of the California Corporations Code, for breach of duty to the corporation and its shareholders in excess of that expressly permitted by said Section 317 under any bylaw, agreement, vote of shareholders or disinterested directors or otherwise, to the fullest extent such indemnification may be authorized hereby, subject to the limits on such excess indemnification set forth in Section 204 of the California Corporations Code. The corporation is further authorized to provide insurance for agents as set forth in Section 317 of the California Corporations Code, provided that, in cases where the corporation owns all or a portion of the shares of the company issuing the insurance policy, one of the two sets of conditions set forth in Section 317, as amended, is met.

VII.

Any repeal or modification of the foregoing provisions of Articles V and VI by the shareholders of this corporation shall not adversely affect any right or protection of a director or agent of this corporation existing at the time of such repeal or modification.

DATED: June 27, 1996

_____

WILLIAM M. LANGLEY
Sole Incorporator

EXHIBIT 9.4   Sample Bylaws

BYLAWS
OF
ABC CORPORATION
ARTICLE ONE: SHAREHOLDERS

Section 1. MEETINGS.

(A) TIME. An annual meeting of the shareholders shall be held each year on the first day of April at 2:00 p.m., unless such day should fall on a legal holiday. In such event, the meeting shall be held at the same hour on the next succeeding business day that is not a legal holiday.

(B) PLACE. Annual meetings shall be held at the principal executive office of the corporation or at such other place within the state of California as may be determined by the board of directors and designated in the notice of such meeting.

(C) CALL. Annual meetings may be called by the directors, by the Chairman of the Board, if any, Vice-Chairman of the Board, if any, the President, if any, the Secretary, or by any other officer instructed by the Directors to call the meeting.

(D) SPECIAL MEETINGS. If in any year, the election of directors is not held at the annual meeting of the shareholders or an adjournment of the meeting, the board of directors shall call a special meeting of the shareholders as soon as possible thereafter as is reasonably possible for the purpose of holding the election and transacting such other business as may properly be brought before the meeting.

In the event the board of directors fails to call a special meeting within three months after the date set for the annual meeting, any shareholders may call such a meeting; at such a meeting, the shareholders may elect directors and transact all other business as may be properly brought before the meeting.

(E) NOTICE. Written notice stating the place, day, and hour of each meeting, and, in the case of a special meeting, the general nature of the business to be transacted or, in the case of an Annual Meeting, those matters which the Board of Directors, at the time of mailing of the notice, intends to present for action by the shareholders, shall be given not less than ten days (or not less than any such other minimum period of days as may be prescribed by the General Corporation Law) or more than sixty days (or more than any maximum period of days as may be prescribed by the General Corporation Law).

(F) ACTION BY WRITTEN CONSENT. Any action required by law to be taken at a meeting of the shareholders, except for the election of the directors, and any other action that may be taken at a meeting of shareholders may be taken without a meeting if written consent, setting forth the action so taken, is signed by the holders of outstanding shares having not less than the minimum number of votes that would be necessary to authorize or take such an action at a meeting at which all shares entitled to vote thereon were present and voted, if the consents of all shareholders entitled to vote were solicited in writing. Directors may not be elected by written consent except by unanimous written consent of all shares entitled to vote for the election of directors.

(G) WAIVER OF NOTICE. A shareholder may waive notice of any annual or special meeting by signing a petition notice of waiver either before or after the date of such meeting.

(H) RECORD DATE. For the purpose of determining those shareholders entitled to notice of or to vote at any meeting of shareholders, or to receive payment of any dividend, or in order to make a determination of shareholders for any other proper purpose, the board of directors may fix, in advance, a date as the record date for the determination of shareholders. Such date shall not be more than 60 days, and for a meeting of shareholders, not less than 10 days, or in the case of a meeting where a merger or consolidation will be considered, not less than 20 days, immediately preceding such meeting.

If a record date is not fixed for the determination of shareholders entitled to notice of or to vote at a meeting of shareholders, the record date shall be at the close of business on the business day next preceding the day on which notice is given, or, if notice is waived, at the close of business on the business day next preceding the day on which the

EXHIBIT 9.4   Sample Bylaws *Continued*

meeting is held.

If no record date is fixed, the record date for determining shareholders entitled to give consent to corporate action in writing without a meeting shall be the day on which the first written consent is given, when no prior action by the board of directors is necessary.

If no record date is fixed, the record date for determining shareholders for any other purpose shall be at the close of business on the day on which the board of directors adopts the resolution relating thereto or the 60th day prior to the date of such other action, whichever is later.

When a determination of shareholders entitled to vote at any meeting of shareholders has been made as provided in this section, such determination shall apply to adjournment of such meeting, unless the board of directors fixes a new record date for the adjourned meeting.

(I) QUORUM. The presence, at the shareholders' meeting, in person or by proxy, of persons entitled to vote a majority of the shares of the corporation then outstanding shall constitute a quorum for the transaction of business. In determining whether quorum requirements for a meeting have been met, any share that has been enjoined from voting or that cannot be lawfully voted for any reason shall not be counted.

(J) PROXIES. Every person entitled to vote at a shareholders' meeting of the corporation, or entitled to execute written consent authorizing action in lieu of a meeting, may do so either in person or by proxy executed in writing by the shareholder or by his duly authorized attorney in fact. No proxy shall be valid after 11 months from the date of its execution unless otherwise provided in the proxy.

(K) VOTING. Except in elections of directors, in which each shareholder shall have the right to cumulate his votes, each outstanding share, regardless of class, shall be entitled to one vote on each matter submitted to a vote at a meeting of shareholders. The affirmative vote of the majority of shares represented at a meeting at which a quorum is present shall be the act of the shareholders unless the vote of a greater number or a vote by classes is required by the articles, these bylaws, or the laws of the State of California.

(L) ORDER OF BUSINESS. The order of business at the annual meeting of the shareholders and, insofar as possible, at all other meetings of shareholders, shall be as follows:

1. Call to order.
2. Proof of notice of meeting.
3. Reading and disposing of any unapproved minutes.
4. Reports of officers.
5. Reports of committees.
6. Election of directors.
7. Disposition of unfinished business.
8. Disposition of new business.
9. Adjournment.

ARTICLE TWO: BOARD OF DIRECTORS

Section 1. GENERAL POWERS.

(A) AUTHORITY. Subject to the limitations of the articles of incorporation, these bylaws, and the Corporations Code of the State of California, and the provisions of the Corporations Code concerning corporate action that must be authorized or approved by the shareholders of the corporation, all corporate power shall be exercised by or under the authority of the board of directors, and the business and affairs of the corporation shall be controlled by the board.

(B) NUMBER, TENURE, QUALIFICATIONS, AND ELECTION. The board of directors shall consist of ten persons who shall be shareholders of the corporation. The number of directors may be increased or decreased by approval of the out-

EXHIBIT 9.4   Sample Bylaws *Continued*

standing shares. Directors of the corporation shall be elected at the annual meeting of the shareholders, or at a meeting held in lieu thereof as provided in Article One above, and shall serve until the next succeeding annual meeting and until their successors have been elected and qualified.

Section 2. MEETINGS.

(A) ORGANIZATIONAL MEETING. The board of directors shall hold an organizational meeting immediately following each annual meeting of the shareholders. Additionally, regular meetings of the board of directors shall be held at such times as shall be fixed by resolution of the board. Special meetings of the board may be called at any time by the president or, if the president is absent or refuses to act, any vice-president or any two members of the board.

(B) NOTICE. Notice need not be given of regular meetings of the board of directors, nor is it necessary to give notice of adjourned meetings. Notice of special meetings shall be in writing by mail at least four days prior to the date of the meeting or 48 hours' notice delivered personally or by telephone or telegraph. Neither the business to be transacted at nor the purpose of any such meeting need be specified in the notice. Attendance of a director at a meeting shall constitute a waiver of notice of that meeting except when the director attends for the express purpose of objecting to the transaction of any business in that the meeting is not lawfully called or convened.

(C) QUORUM AND VOTING. A majority of the authorized number of directors shall constitute a quorum for the transaction of business, and the acts of a majority of directors present at a meeting at which a quorum is present shall constitute the acts of the board of directors. At any meeting of the board of directors, if less than a quorum is present, a majority of those present may adjourn the meeting until a quorum is present. If the meeting is adjourned for more than 24 hours, notice of any adjournment to another time or place shall be given prior to the time of the adjourned meeting to the directors who were not present at the time of adjournment.

(D) COMPENSATION. Directors who are not employed as officers of the corporation shall be entitled to receive from the corporation as compensation for their services as directors such reasonable compensation as the board may determine, and shall also be entitled to reimbursement for any reasonable expenses incurred in attending meetings of directors.

(E) INDEMNIFICATION. The corporation shall indemnify all persons who have served or may serve at any time as officers or directors of the corporation, and their heirs, executors, administrators, successors, and assigns, from and against any and all loss and expense, including amounts paid in settlement before or after suit is commenced, and reasonable attorneys' fees, actually and necessarily sustained as a result of any claim, demand, action, proceeding, or judgment that may be asserted against any such persons, or in which any such persons are made parties by reason of their being or having been officers or directors of the corporation. However, this right of indemnification shall not exist in relation to matters where it is adjudged in any action, suit, or proceeding that any such persons are liable for negligence or misconduct in the performance of duty.

(F) COMMITTEES. The board of directors may, by resolution adopted by a majority of the whole board, designate two or more directors to constitute an executive committee. The executive committee, to the extent provided in the resolution, shall have and may exercise all of the authority of the board of directors in the management of the corporation, except that the committee shall have no authority in reference to amending the articles of incorporation, adopting a plan of merger or consolidation, suggesting to shareholders the sale, lease, exchange, mortgage, or other disposition of all or substantially all the property and assets of the corporation other than in the usual course of business, recommending to the shareholders a voluntary dissolution or a revocation thereof, amending, altering, or repealing any provision of these bylaws, electing or removing directors or officers of the corporation, or members of the executive committee, fixing the compensation of any member of the executive committee, declaring dividends, or amending, altering or repealing any resolution of the board of directors which, by its terms, provides that it not be amended, altered, or repealed by the executive committee. The board of directors shall have power at any time to fill vacancies in, to change the size or membership of, and to discharge any such committee.

Any such executive committee shall keep a written record of its proceedings and shall submit such record to the whole board at each regular meeting, and at such other times as may be requested by the board. However, failure to submit

EXHIBIT 9.4   Sample Bylaws *Continued*

such record, or failure of the board to approve any action indicated therein shall not invalidate such action to the extent it has been carried out by the corporation prior to the time the record thereof was or should have been submitted to the board as provided herein.

ARTICLE THREE: OFFICERS

(A) ENUMERATION OF OFFICERS. The corporation shall have as officers a president, vice-president, secretary, and chief financial officer. The board of directors, at its discretion, may appoint such officers as the business of the corporation may require.

(B) ELECTION AND TERM OF OFFICE. The principal officers of the corporation shall be elected by the board of directors at its organizational meeting immediately following the annual meeting of shareholders or as soon thereafter as is reasonably possible. Subordinate officers may be elected as the board may see fit. Each officer shall hold office until his successor is elected and qualified, or until his resignation, death, or removal.

(C) REMOVAL. Any officer may be removed from office at any time, with or without cause, on the affirmative vote of a majority of the board of directors. Removal shall be without prejudice to any contract rights of the officer removed.

(D) VACANCIES. Vacancies in office, however caused, may be filled by election of the board of directors at any time for unexpired terms of such offices.

(E) OFFICERS—POWERS AND DUTIES. The president, vice-president, secretary, chief financial officer, and other officers appointed by the board of directors shall have such powers and duties as prescribed by the board of directors.

(F) ABSENCE OR DISABILITY OF OFFICERS. In the case of the absence or disability of any officer of the corporation and of any person hereby authorized to act in his place during his absence or disability, the board of directors may by resolution delegate the powers and duties of such officer, or to any director, or to any other person whom it may select.

(G) SALARIES. The salaries of all officers of the corporation shall be fixed by the board of directors.

ARTICLE FOUR: STOCK CERTIFICATES

(A) FORM. The shares of the corporation shall be represented by certificates signed by the chairman or a vice-chairman of the board of directors, if any, or the president or a vice-president, and by the chief financial officer or an assistant financial officer, or the secretary or an assistant secretary. Any or all of such signatures may be facsimile. Each such certificate shall also state:

1. The name of the record holder of the shares represented by such certificate;

2. The number of shares represented thereby;

3. A designation of any class or series of which such shares are a part;

4. That the shares are without par value;

5. Any rights of redemption and the redemption price;

6. Any rights of conversion, and the essential terms and periods for conversion;

7. Any liens or restrictions on transfer or on the voting power of such shares;

8. That the shares are assessable, if that is the fact;

9. That assessments to which the shares are subject are collectible by personal action, if that is the fact;

EXHIBIT 9.4   Sample Bylaws *Continued*

10.   When the shares of the corporation are classified or any class has two or more series, the rights, preferences, privileges and restrictions granted to or imposed on the respective classes or series of shares and the holders thereof, as established by the articles or by any certificate of determination of preferences, as well as the number of shares constituting each series and the designation thereof; or a summary of such preferences, privileges and restrictions with reference to the provisions of the articles or certificate or certificates of determination of preferences establishing same; or the office or agency of the corporation from which stockholders may obtain a copy of a statement of such right, preferences, privileges and restrictions or of such summary.

11.   Any right of the board of directors to fix the dividend rights, dividend rate, conversion rights, voting rights, rights in terms of redemption, including sinking fund provisions, the redemption price or prices, or the liquidation preferences of any wholly unissued class or of any wholly unissued series of any class of shares, or the number of shares constituting any unissued series of any class of shares, or designation of such series, or all or any of them; and

12.   For any certificates issued for shares prior to the full payment therefor, the amount remaining unpaid, the terms of payment to become due, and any restrictions on the transfer of such partly paid shares on the books of the corporation.

13.   All certificates for shares of the corporation shall bear the following legend: "These securities have not been registered under the Securities Act of 1933, and may not be offered, offered for sale, or sold in the absence of an effective registration statement under that Act or an opinion of counsel satisfactory to the corporation that registration is not required."

(B) LOST, DESTROYED, AND STOLEN CERTIFICATES. No certificate for shares of stock in the corporation shall be issued in place of any certificate alleged to have been lost, destroyed, stolen, or mutilated except on production of such evidence and provision of such indemnity to the corporation as the board of directors may prescribe.

ARTICLE FIVE: CORPORATE ACTIONS

(A) CONTRACTS. The board of directors may authorize any officer or officers, and any agent or agents of the corporation, to enter into any contract or to execute and deliver any instrument in the name of and on behalf of the corporation, and such authority may be general or confined to specific instances.

(B) LOANS. No loans shall be made by the corporation to its officers or directors, and no loans shall be made by the corporation secured by its shares. No loans shall be made or contracted on behalf of the corporation and no evidence of indebtedness shall be issued in its name unless authorized by resolution of the board of directors. Such authority may be general or confined to specific instances.

(C) CHECKS, DRAFTS OR ORDERS. All checks, drafts, or other orders for the payment of money by or to the corporation and all notes and other evidence of indebtedness issued in the name of the corporation shall be signed by such officer or officers, agent or agents of the corporation, and in such manner as shall be determined by resolution by the board of directors.

(D) BANK DEPOSITS. All funds of the corporation not otherwise employed shall be deposited to the credit of the corporation in such banks, trust companies, or other depositories as the board of directors may select.

ARTICLE SIX: MISCELLANEOUS

(A) INSPECTION OF CORPORATE RECORDS. The corporation shall keep correct and complete books and records of account and shall also keep minutes of all meetings of shareholders and directors. Additionally, a record shall be kept at the principal executive office of the corporation, giving the names and addresses of all shareholders, and the number and class or classes of shares held by each. Any person who is the holder of a voting trust certificate or who is the holder of record of at least ten percent of the outstanding voting shares of the corporation shall have the right to examine and copy, in person or by agent or attorney, at any reasonable time or times, for any proper purpose, the books and records of account of the corporation, the minutes, and the record of shareholders.

(B) INSPECTION OF ARTICLES OF INCORPORATION AND BYLAWS. The original or a copy of the articles of incorporation

---

EXHIBIT 9.4   Sample Bylaws *Concluded*

and bylaws of the corporation, as amended or otherwise altered to date, and certified by the secretary of the corporation, shall at all times be kept at the principal executive office of the corporation. Such articles and bylaws shall be open to inspection to all shareholders of record or holders of voting trust certificates at all reasonable times during the business hours of the corporation.

(C) FISCAL YEAR. The fiscal year of the corporation shall begin on the first day of April of each year and end at 11:59 p.m. on the 31st day of March of the following year.

(D) CORPORATE SEAL. The board of directors shall adopt an official seal for the corporation, which shall be inscribed with the name of the corporation, the state of incorporation, and the words "Corporate Seal."

(E) CONSTRUCTION AND DEFINITION. Unless the context requires otherwise, the general provisions, rules of construction, and definitions in the Corporations Code of the State of California shall govern the construction of these bylaws.

Without limiting the foregoing, the masculine gender includes the feminine and neuter; the singular number includes the plural, and the plural number includes the singular; "shall" is mandatory and "may" is permissive, and "person" includes a corporation as well as a natural person.

ARTICLE SEVEN: AMENDMENTS

These bylaws may be altered, amended, or repealed by approval of the outstanding voting shares or by a majority vote of the board of directors of the corporation.

---

retary should record the date the Annual Report is due in the tickler file and also note an earlier date when preparations should begin to allow the report to be completed by the due date. The Annual Report may be prepared by the attorney or by the corporation itself.

Special Types of Corporations

close corporation
A corporation formed by a small number of people who manage and control the business.

Close Corporations.   A **close corporation** is a corporation formed by a few individuals who also run the corporation. Unlike other corporations, in a close corporation, shareholders actually manage and control the business operations of the corporation. A close corporation may not offer its stock to the public, and the number of shareholders is restricted.

professional corporation
A corporation formed by professionals, such as doctors or lawyers.

Professional Corporations.   In recent years, states have enacted statutes to allow professionals to incorporate. **Professional corporations** are most commonly formed by doctors and lawyers, but may also be formed by many other professionals including accountants, dentists, optometrists, and psychologists. "P.C." after a professional's name shows that the practice is incorporated in this manner. Most states have much more stringent rules and regulations for professional corporations than for ordinary corporations. In addition, many professions have their own rules for incorporation.

Professionals who incorporate may still be held personally liable for their own malpractice, as well as for malpractice committed by persons whom they supervise. A professional cannot be held personally liable, however, for malpractice committed by other professionals in the corporation whom she does not supervise. For example,

Doctors Roth and Wilmot decide to form a professional corporation. Neither supervises the other. If Doctor Roth is sued for malpractice, Doctor Wilmot's personal assets cannot be used to settle the suit; only the assets of the professional corporation and Doctor Roth's personal assets may be used. It should be noted that all professionals are required to carry malpractice insurance.

If a client in a profession wishes to incorporate, you must check your state's rules and regulations for that profession. Contact the licensing board or state agency that oversees that particular profession for the specific regulations. In general, all individuals owning shares in the corporation must be licensed in that particular profession. In addition, they must carry minimum amounts of liability (malpractice) insurance.

Fill in the rules for your own state in the State Specific Information box.

Rules for professional corporations in the state of _____ are as follows: _____

_____

_____

_____

STATE SPECIFIC INFORMATION

Subchapter S Corporations.   A **Subchapter S corporation** is similar in size and structure to a close corporation. A Subchapter S corporation may have no more than twenty-five shareholders, and it is limited to domestic operations. Such a corporation may offer significant tax advantages in the early years of a business when profits are small or nonexistent because the corporate income and losses are reported on the owners' personal tax returns. If a corporation's taxable income is more than $175,000 a year, the owners will pay lower taxes if they organize as a Subchapter S corporation and report the profits on their personal income tax returns than if they organize as a regular corporation and file a corporate tax return. Owners may only deduct losses from their individual tax returns up to the amount of their investment in the corporation.

Subchapter S corporation
A corporation that is limited to twenty-five shareholders and to domestic operations; offers significant tax advantages because the income is reported on the owners' personal income tax returns. In size and structure, it is similar to a close corporation.

Franchises.   In recent years, the franchise market has expanded considerably. A **franchise** is a business that obtains the right to market a company's goods or services in a particular territory; the term also refers to the right itself. Many fast-food restaurants, automobile repair shops, and other businesses are operated as franchises. In this type of operation, the individual owner owns the business itself but leases the facilities from the franchise organization (the parent company that grants the franchise and allows the business to use its name). Usually, the business owner is required to purchase supplies from the franchise organization. Some fast-food establishments are also required to buy their ingredients from certain suppliers to maintain uniform quality.

Franchise organizations employ paralegals and legal secretaries to assist in preparing franchise agreements, property leases, equipment leases, and purchase contracts. Individuals interested in purchasing a franchise often ask an attorney to review the franchise agreement that has been prepared by the franchise organization to be sure that their own rights are protected.

franchise
The right to market a company's goods or services in a particular territory. After purchasing the franchise from a franchise organization, an individual owns the business and leases the equipment and facilities from the parent organization.

Although large franchise organizations are usually corporations, an individual who purchases a franchise may organize it as a sole proprietorship, a partnership, or a corporation.

Nonprofit Corporations.   If a corporation is operated entirely for charitable, religious, scientific, educational, and/or literary purposes, it may qualify as a nonprofit corporation for tax purposes under the Internal Revenue Code. The corporation may not engage in other unrelated activities or benefit the owners economically, although the owners may collect a reasonable salary if they work in the business. All corporate profits must be used to benefit the purpose for which the corporation was formed, such as the individual charity. The corporation may not engage in any political activities, such as supporting political candidates or lobbying for new legislation. Some states may impose additional restrictions on nonprofit corporations; therefore, you should check your own state's statutes for other rules. Add them to the State Specific Information box.

STATE SPECIFIC INFORMATION	Rules for nonprofit corporations in the state of _____ are as follows: _____ _____ _____ _____

Corporate Board of Directors

Board of Directors
The individuals who oversee the running of a corporation.

The **Board of Directors** is a group of individuals who oversee the running of the corporation. The directors have a fiduciary duty to use ethical and sound judgment in managing the corporation's affairs. As fiduciaries of the corporation, the directors owe a duty of loyalty that includes placing the organization's needs before their own personal business interests. A director may not be involved in a conflict of interest such as working as a consultant for a competing company or taking a fee from a competing company. Nor may directors commit any acts that are beyond the scope of their enumerated duties and responsibilities. Directors may not be held personally liable for their mistakes, however, unless it can be proved that they engaged in fraudulent, illegal, or unethical practices, such as entering into agreements for their own personal profit or acting disloyally.

Ultra Vires Acts

ultra vires acts
Acts outside the scope of the corporation's powers as set out in the Articles of Incorporation.

Any actions that are outside the scope of the powers or activities permitted by the Articles of Incorporation are considered **ultra vires acts.** An officer or director who commits an ultra vires act may be held personally liable for the endeavor through a process known as "piercing the corporate veil." If an officer or director commits an ultra vires act, an individual who is injured by it can pierce the corporate veil and sue the officer or director personally. If the action injures the shareholders, they may sue in the same manner.

Shareholder Suits against the Corporation

If a director or officer commits an ultra vires act that injures the shareholders, they may institute a direct action against that director or officer. If the ultra vires act has injured the corporation, the shareholders may file a **derivative suit.** To do so, the shareholders must have held their stock at the time the act occurred ("contemporaneous ownership") and must first have made a demand on the board of directors to take action to protect the corporation's rights in this instance. If the board fails to act, then the shareholders may file a derivative suit. To win the suit, the shareholders must show that the director or officer deliberately mismanaged or committed fraud against the corporation.

derivative suit
A suit by shareholders against a corporation.

Dissolving the Corporation

Corporate **dissolutions** may be either voluntary or involuntary. In a **voluntary dissolution,** the shareholders or directors vote to terminate the corporation. All creditors and shareholders must be notified, and a notice must be filed with the state's Secretary of State, indicating that the corporation is being dissolved. After the creditors are notified and paid and the assets are liquidated, the corporation is dissolved. Any monies left after the creditors are paid are distributed to the shareholders. In some states, a document reporting the dissolution must be filed with the Secretary of State.

In recent years, "corporate raiders" have become increasingly important. They target corporations that have substantial assets, but are making low profits; consequently, the corporation's stock is selling at a low price. The raiders then buy the corporation's stock and when they have purchased enough to gain control of the corporation, they dissolve it and sell off the assets. Large profits can be made when the corporation's assets can be sold for more than is needed to pay its debts.

Only the state may institute **involuntary dissolution** proceedings. In some cases, however, the shareholders may petition the courts for involuntary dissolution. They must be able to prove that the directors are not managing the corporation prudently or that management problems are affecting the operation of the corporation. Some states also allow creditors to apply for an involuntary dissolution of the corporation if they are owed substantial sums and are not being paid.

dissolution
Terminating the existence of a corporation; can be voluntary or involuntary.

voluntary dissolution
The termination of a corporation by the shareholders or the directors who act willingly and are not being forced to terminate by the state or creditors.

involuntary dissolution
The termination of a corporation against the will of the directors; must be initiated by the state, but shareholders or creditors may petition to begin dissolution proceedings.

Consolidations and Mergers

When two or more corporations dissolve and then join together to form a new organization, a **consolidation** has occurred. The shareholders of both original corporations must approve the dissolution of their own corporation and the formation of the new one. In this case, the following occurs:

$$A + B = C$$

In a **merger,** one corporation takes over another corporation. One of the corporations survives and the other disappears, becoming part of the survivor. In this case, the following occurs:

consolidation
The process in which two corporations dissolve and then join together to form a third corporation.

merger
The process in which one corporation takes over another corporation.

$$A \text{ absorbs } B = A$$

The merger must be approved by the shareholders of the corporation that will no longer exist. Shareholders who do not want to have stock in the new corporation can sell their shares back to the corporation. Articles must be filed with the Secretary of State providing notification of the merger.

Paralegals and legal secretaries may be involved in preparing the documentation for dissolutions, mergers, and consolidations. Form books and software packages are available to assist in this endeavor. You should always consult the files to determine if the same task has been performed for another case; if so, you can use the format as a guide.

BANKRUPTCY

Bankruptcy is a federal proceeding handled in the federal courts; therefore, most bankruptcy rules are universal (that is, they are the same in all states). Businesses may file either a Chapter 7 bankruptcy or a Chapter 11 bankruptcy.

This section provides a general description of Chapter 7 and Chapter 11 bankruptcies, but the rules for filing bankruptcy are very complicated, and you should take a separate class in bankruptcy law if you plan to specialize in this area. Bankruptcy is a very busy specialty area of the law, particularly in bad economic times such as the recession of the early 1990s. Bankruptcy law firms were very busy and needed trained paralegals and legal secretaries. Once paralegals learn the various documents to file for different types of bankruptcies, they become very valuable to the firm and may assume a considerable amount of responsibility.

Attorneys in Corporate Bankruptcy Proceedings

The federal courts require each attorney to file a Statement of Compensation with the Bankruptcy Court that reports the fees the attorney is to be paid for the bankruptcy as well as all fees paid to the attorney by the bankruptcy client during the previous year. Usually, the attorney must be a disinterested party in the case. One exception to this rule is that in Chapter 7 bankruptcy, a party with an interest in the case may represent the debtor. Therefore, attorneys employed by a corporation may represent the corporation in a Chapter 7 bankruptcy.

Chapter 7 Bankruptcy

The form of bankruptcy filed most frequently is Chapter 7 bankruptcy, which is used by both businesses and individuals. The debtor has his debts discharged in exchange for giving up certain property that is sold to pay creditors. Many assets are exempt and therefore are not given up to creditors. Some examples of exempt assets would be: part of the value of a home, automobile, household furnishings, and clothing. These exemptions, however, may vary from state to state.

A corporation must enumerate its assets and liabilities, as well as its income and expenses, and must list any exempt property. The Bankruptcy Court appoints a trustee to administer the case. Once the case is completed, the debts that have been discharged in the bankruptcy do not have to be paid. The business ceases its operation, however.

Chapter 11 Bankruptcy (Reorganization)

Businesses may file a Chapter 11 bankruptcy, which provides for the reorganization of the company. This form may be used by very large corporations as well as sole proprietorships. In recent years, many very large corporations have filed Chapter 11.

The major advantage of Chapter 11 bankruptcy is that the company may continue to operate even though it has serious financial problems. During this period, the business theoretically reorganizes to a more economically sound structure. The company must follow stringent rules, and its affairs become public knowledge in that the creditors and the trustee may scrutinize its activities.

Chapter 11 bankruptcy is more expensive and time-consuming than Chapter 7. Nevertheless, for a business that wishes to remain in operation during the reorganization process, Chapter 11 may be the best alternative.

Many documents, including the petition, list of creditors, authorization, schedule of financial affairs, statement of assets and liabilities, and a list of outstanding contracts, must be filed with the Bankruptcy Court in a timely fashion. Deadlines are strict. If you are involved in this type of proceeding, you should consult a bankruptcy manual or contact the U.S. Bankruptcy Court in your area for a copy of its rules and regulations.

Although most bankruptcy rules are governed by federal statutes and are therefore the same in all states, states may have their own rules as well. Check your state's statutes for any special bankruptcy rules and record them in the State Specific Information box.

> In the state of _____, the Bankruptcy Court is located at _____ in the city of _____. The following special rules apply in this state: _____
>
> _____
>
> _____
>
> _____

STATE SPECIFIC INFORMATION

SUMMARY

The different types of business organizations include the sole proprietorship, the partnership, and the corporation. A sole proprietorship is an unincorporated business that is usually owned by a single individual. Sole proprietorships are easy to establish, but they have several disadvantages: the owner is subject to unlimited personal liability; raising capital can be difficult; and the business may have to be dissolved on the death or disability of the owner.

A partnership has access to more capital than a sole proprietorship, and limited partners are liable only for the amount they have invested. General partners, however, are liable not only for their own actions but also for the actions of their partners.

A corporation has access to more capital than a sole proprietorship or a partnership and also offers the advantage of limited liability for shareholders. In addition, a corporation has perpetual life and may offer tax benefits. In addition to the standard stock corporation, several special types of corporations exist, including the professional corporation, Subchapter S corporation, and close corporation.

To form a corporation, the incorporators organize the corporation and file Articles of Incorporation with the Secretary of State of the state where the corporation is located. Once the articles are accepted, an organizational meeting is held to elect a Board of Directors, develop an organization plan for the corporation, and adopt Bylaws. Minutes of the meeting are taken.

The members of the Board of Directors owe a fiduciary duty to the corporation. If they commit ultra vires acts, they may be sued personally by shareholders or others. Shareholders may file a derivative suit.

A corporation may be dissolved voluntarily by the shareholders and board of directors or involuntarily by the state of incorporation. The corporation may also merge with another corporation or be consolidated. In a merger, one corporation absorbs the other; in a consolidation, a third corporation is formed from the combination of the original two. As a last alternative, the corporation may file either a Chapter 7 or a Chapter 11 bankruptcy proceeding in a U.S. Bankruptcy Court.

KEY TERMS

Annual report   239

Articles of Incorporation   238

Board of directors   248

Bylaws   239

Close corporation   246

Consolidation   249

Corporation   237

Derivative suit   249

Dissolution   249

Franchise   247

General partner   233

Involuntary dissolution   249

Limited partner   233

Merger   249

Partnership   232

Professional corporation   246

Shareholder   237

Sole proprietorship   231

Subchapter S corporation   247

Ultra vires acts   248

Voluntary dissolution   249

SELF-TEST

A.   Indicate whether the following statements are true (T) or false (F):

_____ 1.   Partnerships are preferable to corporations because a partner's personal assets are protected from suit in a partnership.

_____ 2.   Articles of Incorporation are prepared to authorize a corporation to operate.

_____ 3.   Ownership in a corporation is represented by shares of stock.

_____ 4.   A corporation and its shareholders share responsibility when suits are brought against the corporation.

_____ 5.   For legal purposes, a corporation exists separate and apart from its shareholders.

B. Circle the correct answer for the following questions:

1. The document that is validated by the state and authorizes the corporation to exist and operate is called
    a. Articles of Incorporation.
    b. common stock.
    c. preferred stock.
    d. Bylaws.

2. The rules of a corporation that govern its operations are called the
    a. Articles of Incorporation.
    b. common stock.
    c. preferred stock.
    d. Bylaws.

3. The officers who are elected by the shareholders to control the operation of the corporation are called the
    a. Board of Trustees.
    b. Board of Directors.
    c. shareholder officers.
    d. corporate officers.

4. Ownership in a corporation may be proved by
    a. a certificate of stock.
    b. a certificate of ownership.
    c. the bylaws.
    d. the articles.

5. Partnerships are
    a. limited corporations.
    b. the same as sole proprietorships.
    c. associations of two or more individuals.
    d. formed to operate a business for profit.
    e. (c) and (d) are correct.

C. Fill in the blanks:

1. The two types of partners are _____ and

    _____ partners.

2. The type of partner who is involved in the day-to-day operations of the business is a _____ .

3. Define a sole proprietorship:_____

    _____

4. Corporate formation begins with the preparation of the

_____ .

5. The individuals who own a corporation are called _____ .

REVIEW QUESTIONS

1. Explain how a name is reserved for a corporation.

2. Explain the differences between a sole proprietorship, a partnership, and a corporation.

3. What are the major advantages and disadvantages of a sole proprietorship? A partnership? A corporation?

4. What information is included in a corporation's Articles of Incorporation?

5. What is a Subchapter S corporation?

PROJECTS

1. Proofread the Certificate of Incorporation in Exhibit 9.5, and retype it using the format for your own state. Change the address of the corporation to your city and your state.

2. Our office has a new client, Scott Lipinski, who would like to form a corporation called SCOTTZ PLANEZ to sell airplanes in your state. Prepare the Articles of Incorporation for this endeavor. Use the format for your state, or use Exhibit 9.3 as a guide.

3. Draft a letter that you would send to the Secretary of State's Office in your state to determine whether the name "SCOTTZ PLANEZ" may be used by the corporation formed in Project 2.

4. Using Exhibit 9.4 as a model, prepare the Bylaws for the corporation formed in Projects 2 and 3 with the following officers' signatures: Scott Lipinski, president; George Crockett, vice-president; Kimberly Fitzgerald, secretary and treasurer; Jeffrey Long, chairman of the board. These individuals comprise the Board of Directors of this corporation. Note: When revising the articles in Exhibit 9.4, Article Three (A) should be changed to indicate the names and titles of the officers. Article Three (E) may also require some changes.

5. Prepare the Articles of Incorporation for your own free-lance paralegal or legal secretary corporation.

6. Research the statutes in your state to determine the rules for limited partnerships. Prepare a memorandum to your instructor listing these rules.

EXHIBIT 9.5   A Certificate of Incorporation

CERTIFICATE OF INCORPORATION
OF
JANE'S BEAUTY SUPPLY, INC.
Under Section 402 of the Business Corporation Law
of the State of New York

The undersigned, for the purpose of forming a corporation pur suant to Section 402 of the Business Corporation Law of the State of New York, certifies:

1. The name of the corporation shall be Jane's Beauty Supply, Inc.

2. The purpose of the Corporation is to engage in any lawful act or activity for which corporations may be organized under the NY business corporation law; provided, however,
that the Corporation is not formed to engage in any act or activity requiring the consent or approval of any State official, department, board, agency or other body without such consent or approval first being obtained.

3. The office of the corporation is to be located at 1001 Kelly Avenue, Utica, NY

4. The aggragate number of shares which the corporation shall have authority to issue is Two Hundred (200) shares all of which are to be of one class of common stock without par value.

?   The Secretary of State is designated as agent of the coproration upon whom process against it may be served. The post office address to which the Secretary of State shall mail a copy of any process against the corporation served upon him is 1001 Kelly Avenue, Utica, New York 13501

6. No shareholder of the corporation shall have any preemptive or preferential right of subscription to any shares of any class of the corporation whether now or here after authorized, or to any obligations con-vertible into shares of any class of the corpora-tion, issued or sold, nor any right of subscription to any thereof other than such right, if any, and at such price as the Board of Directors may in its discretion deter-mine, and the Board of Directors may issue shares of the Corporation or obligations convertible into shares without offering such issue either in whole or in part to the shareholders of the corporation.

IN WITNESS WHEREOF, the undersigned have signed this certificate of incorporation on 1996 and affirms the statements contained herein as true under the penalties of perjury.

_____
Jane S. Smith
1001 Kelly Avenue
Utica, New York 13502

STATE OF New York   )
                          ss.:
County OF OOneida   )

On this   day of   , 1996, before me personality came JANE S. SMITH, to me known and known to me to be the person described in and who executed the forgoing certificate of incorporation and he duly acknowledged to me that he executed the same.

_____
Notary

SOURCE: Courtesy of Vicky Alexandra; Utica, New York.

Real Property

CHAPTER OBJECTIVES

As a result of studying this chapter, you will learn the following material:

1. ***Real and Personal Property***   The characteristics of real and personal property will be discussed. You will learn what real property, personal property, and fixtures are.

2. ***Paralegals and Legal Secretaries***   The responsibilities of the paralegal and legal secretary in a real property law practice will be presented. You will learn about employment opportunities in real property law.

3. ***Property Ownership***   The types of property ownership will be examined.

4. ***Transfer of Real Property***   The steps in transferring real property will be presented. You will become familiar with every aspect of the transfer process from the initial listing with a real estate agent to the closing.

5. ***Deeds***   The various types of deeds will be presented. You will become familiar with warranty deeds, grant deeds, and quitclaim deeds and will also learn how property is described in deeds.

6. ***Leases and Rental Agreements***   The terminology used in leases and rental agreements and their basic format will be presented. You will learn how to prepare leases and rental agreements and will also become familiar with the rights and obligations of tenants and landlords.

REAL AND PERSONAL PROPERTY

This chapter will introduce you to the basic elements of the law of real property. Real estate is an important area of the law and offers many opportunities for both paralegals and legal secretaries. This section will provide some basic definitions and describe the roles of the paralegal and legal secretary. Later sections will discuss types of property ownership, the steps involved in transferring property, and the rights of landlords and tenants.

Personal property includes items that are not attached to land or buildings and are movable or easily transportable from one location to another. For example, a camper and an automobile would be classified as personal property.

Real property includes land and things permanently attached to the land. Homes, garages and other buildings, in-ground swimming pools, minerals in the ground, trees, and fixtures are examples of real property.

personal property
Property that is not attached to the land.

real property
Land and buildings, and items permanently attached to the land.

fixture
An item of personal property that is permanently attached to land or to a building in such a way that it becomes part of the real property.

A **fixture** is an item of personal property that is affixed to land or to a building in such a way that it becomes part of the real property. For example, a light fixture purchased at a store is personal property. Once the light fixture is permanently attached to the ceiling of your home, however, it becomes real property. Other examples of fixtures include furnaces, built-in bookcases, and wall-to-wall carpeting.

Fixtures can also become personal property. For instance, a growing tree is considered to be real property because it is attached to the land. Once that tree is cut down, it becomes personal property.

The Paralegal's Role

Many opportunities are available for paralegals trained in real estate law. In addition to private law offices, possible employers include real estate offices, escrow offices, title companies, mortgage companies, and legal departments of banks. Government offices, such as the Tax Assessor's Office and the Office of the County Recorder, may also be sources of employment.

In a private law firm, paralegals may prepare documents required for a real estate transaction, as well as do research into the ownership of property. They may also prepare documents necessary for closings. If the attorney practices landlord/tenant law, then the paralegal may draft documents for evictions and discuss rights and responsibilities of landlords and tenants with clients.

Paralegals employed in real property law offices should be knowledgeable in the law and should also be attentive to detail.

The Legal Secretary's Role

A legal secretary employed in a property law firm may help prepare documents for real estate transactions. Property descriptions must be proofread carefully to make sure numbers are not transposed. The secretary may also conduct research into property ownership. Tickler files must be maintained for the sequence of events in a real estate transaction to ensure that each step is completed in a timely fashion.

In addition to working for law offices, legal secretaries may also find employment in the offices described for paralegals. Private corporations may also employ legal secretaries trained in real property law.

TYPES OF PROPERTY OWNERSHIP

fee simple
Absolute ownership of property.

Ownership of property in **fee simple** is the absolute ownership of that property. The ownership interest has no limitations and therefore may be passed on to your heirs. Most modern-day property is held in this manner. It should be noted that several individuals may share an interest in the same piece of property in fee simple, as will be discussed later in this chapter.

Tenancy in Common

tenancy in common
Joint ownership of property with no right of survivorship.

When two or more individuals own a piece of property together, with each having a certain proportion, the property is owned as a **tenancy in common.** For example, if three sisters own a farm in tenancy in common, each may have a one-third interest in the property. Each individual may sell her share of the property or leave it to her heirs.

Joint Tenancy

Joint tenancy is a form of ownership in which two or more persons each have an undivided ownership interest in the property with a right of survivorship. Although joint tenancy ownership is not reserved for spouses, many married couples hold their real property in joint tenancy. With joint tenancy, either party may sell or encumber (mortgage the property or use it as security for a loan) the property without the other's permission. The primary advantage of this type of ownership is the right of survivorship; that is, upon the death of one joint tenant, the property passes automatically to the other joint tenant without having to be mentioned in the decedent's will or having to go through probate proceedings. In most states, a simple document is required to transfer full title to the survivor ("break the joint tenancy") upon the death of a joint tenant.

Clients should consult a tax attorney or accountant before taking title to property as joint tenants.

joint tenancy
Ownership of an undivided interest in property by two or more owners with a right of survivorship.

Community Property

In community property states, married couples can hold property acquired during the marriage as **community property.** In this case, the deed would state:

> DAVID CARL HENDRICKS AND JULIANNE ALESSIO-HENDRICKS, a married couple, as community property . . .

Each spouse would then own a one-half interest in the property. In some cases, holding property as community property can offer tax advantages upon the death of one spouse.

community property
In certain states, property acquired by either spouse during marriage, except property acquired by gift or inheritance, is considered to be community property and to belong to both spouses equally.

Tenancy by the Entirety

In a few states, property acquired by a married couple may be owned in **tenancy by the entirety.** Neither party may sell or encumber the property without the express permission of the other party. Upon the death of one spouse, the property passes automatically to the survivor.

tenancy by the entirety
Joint ownership by a husband and wife of property acquired during the marriage; used in a minority of states. Neither party may sell or encumber the property without the express permission of the other party; on the death of one owner, the property automatically passes to the survivor.

Condominiums

In the **condominium** form of ownership, different persons own individual units within a multiple-unit complex. Each unit is owned in fee simple and may be owned by a single individual or by two or more individuals in any of the forms of ownership we have discussed, such as joint tenancy or tenancy in common. The interior of the unit within the building is the bounds of what each owner owns. The owner of a unit may also have the use of a portion of the property not within the bounds of the individual unit, such as a garage, a storage cupboard, or a patio. Any other areas of the complex are known as **common areas** and are owned by all owners of condominiums within the complex as tenants in common. The individual owners may not transfer their ownership of the common areas unless they transfer ownership of their individual unit.

The everyday management of the affairs of the complex is usually handled by a property management company that takes care of the building's maintenance and financial affairs. Each owner may obtain a loan on the individual unit he owns. A master loan is generally obtained for the complex itself.

condominium
Ownership of a unit within a multiple-unit building.

common area
An area in a condominium complex that is owned by all the condominium owners as tenants in common.

Most states require that a master deed for the whole complex be recorded in the County Recorder's Office (this process is similar to the way tract maps are recorded, as described later in the chapter). In addition, each owner of an individual unit will have his own deed that should also be recorded.

The individual owners elect a board of directors from among themselves to establish rules and regulations for the condominium complex. The board may also handle the maintenance and financial affairs of the condominium if a professional management company is not employed.

Cooperatives

cooperative
Similar to a condominium except that the unit is represented by a share of stock.

share of stock represented by a unit
The ownership interest of a cooperative apartment owner.

A **cooperative** apartment is similar to a condominium except that whereas a condominium owner actually owns an individual unit within a large complex, a cooperative owner owns a **share of stock represented by a unit.** Thus, ownership of a cooperative is necessarily more restrictive than ownership of a condominium.

The cooperative complex is governed by a board of directors, who are elected by the individual owners of shares. A cooperative owner may not sell his share without obtaining permission from the board. The board must also approve any prospective purchaser. An owner who wishes to rent his unit must also obtain permission from the board.

One of the major disadvantages of cooperative ownership is the difficulty of obtaining a loan on an individual unit. Therefore, when an owner wishes to sell his apartment, he must either provide a personal loan for the buyer, or as happens more frequently, the buyer must pay cash. Although cooperative apartments may be less expensive than condominiums, they are also more difficult to sell. A client who is considering purchasing a cooperative unit should be advised of these disadvantages. Financing arrangements should be investigated to determine whether a loan may be obtained on the cooperative unit.

TRANSFER OF REAL PROPERTY

Selling real property can be a complex transaction. The following are the steps that usually occur when property is transferred:

1. *Finding a Real Estate Agent.*   Most real estate sales are negotiated through a real estate agent. The seller should talk to recent sellers in the geographical area where the property is located to determine the best agent. An agent can do a computerized analysis of recent sales to recommend the appropriate selling price for the property.

   Agents are paid a percentage of the selling price as their commission, but, the actual percentage is usually negotiable, especially in a competitive market. In a complicated sale of real property, hiring an attorney to negotiate the agreement with the real estate agency may be appropriate.

listing agreement
An agreement made with a real estate agent when property is put up for sale; sets out the agent's commission, the length of the agreement, and the rights and responsibilities of the parties.

2. *Listing Agreement.*   The agreement with the real estate agent is known as a **listing agreement.** It sets out the terms of the agreement, including the agent's commission, the length of the agreement, and the rights and responsibilities of the seller and the agent. As with any other contract, the seller should read the agreement carefully before signing and should also have her attorney examine it.

An important item in the listing agreement is the period of time the agent will have the listing. Three to six months is a typical term, but if the seller has any doubts about the agent's ability to sell the property, a shorter term may be appropriate.

Paralegals may be asked to prepare and/or review listing agreements for the client. They may draft recommendations for changes for the attorney's review.

3. ***The Offer.***   At some point the real estate agent will receive an **offer** from a prospective buyer. At the time the offer is made, the prospective buyer will also give the agent a **deposit,** sometimes called a **binder** or **earnest money deposit.** Basically, this deposit is an indication to the seller that the buyer is genuinely interested in purchasing the property.

4. ***The Counteroffer.***   In some cases, the seller will respond to the buyer's offer with a **counteroffer.** The counteroffer will be higher than the price the buyer offered, but may not be more than the original listing price.

5. ***The Acceptance.***   At some point during the negotiations, the buyer and seller will agree on a mutually acceptable price for the property. Usually, the sale will be conditional upon the buyer obtaining appropriate financing. If the prospective buyer did not make a deposit at the time of the original offer, one must be made at this time.

6. ***Real Estate Sales/Purchase Contract.***   When the buyer and seller have agreed on a price, the agent or the attorney will draw up a **real estate sales contract** setting out the rights and responsibilities of both parties. In some states, standardized contracts prepared by the realtors' associations are available. The California Association of Realtors has drawn up a very detailed agreement (see Exhibit 10.1). The agreement will include standard property information, such as the location and purchase price as well as the following:

   a. Financing—a statement indicating that the sale is conditional upon the buyer obtaining a loan.

   b. Deposit requirements.

   c. The due date for the down payment.

   d. Loan information.

   e. The total purchase price.

   f. Default information.

   g. Escrow information (this may be called "closing" in some states).

   h. The date of possession.

   i. Title report information.

   j. How taxes and other assessments will be prorated between the buyer and the seller.

   k. If the property is a condominium, the cost of association dues and information about parking facilities.

   l. The buyer's right to inspect the property (also known as a "walk through").

   m. The property's condition.

---

offer
A proposal or bid to purchase property at a particular price.

deposit
Money given by a buyer to a seller as a pledge or down payment when an offer to purchase property is made; also called a binder or earnest money deposit.

binder
Money given by a buyer to a seller to seal the bargain when an offer to purchase property is made; also called a deposit.

earnest money deposit
Money given by a buyer to a seller to seal the bargain when an offer to purchase property is made; also called a deposit.

counteroffer
A higher price named by a seller after a would-be buyer has made an offer; may not be higher than the original listing price.

real estate sales contract
An agreement prepared after the buyer and seller have agreed on a price for the property; sets out the rights and responsibilities of both parties.

EXHIBIT 10.1   A Real Estate Purchase Contract from California

REAL ESTATE PURCHASE CONTRACT AND RECEIPT FOR DEPOSIT
THIS IS MORE THAN A RECEIPT FOR MONEY. IT IS INTENDED TO BE A LEGALLY BINDING CONTRACT. READ IT CAREFULLY.
CALIFORNIA ASSOCIATION OF REALTORS® (CAR) STANDARD FORM

DATE: _____, 19_____ AT _____, California,

RECEIVED FROM _____ ("Buyer")

THE SUM OF _____ Dollars $_____

as a deposit to be applied toward the

PURCHASE PRICE OF _____ Dollars $_____

FOR PURCHASE OF PROPERTY SITUATED IN _____, COUNTY OF _____, California,

DESCRIBED AS _____ ("Property").

1. **FINANCING: THE OBTAINING OF THE LOAN(S) BELOW IS A CONTINGENCY OF THIS AGREEMENT.** Buyer shall act diligently and in good faith to obtain all applicable financing.

   A. **FINANCING CONTINGENCY** shall remain in effect until (Check ONLY ONE of the following):

      1. ☐ (If checked). The designated loan(s) is/are funded and/or the assumption of existing financing is approved by Lender.

      OR 2. ☐ (If checked). _____ calendar days after acceptance of the offer. Buyer shall remove the financing contingency in writing within this time. If Buyer fails to do so, then Seller may cancel this agreement by giving written notice of cancellation to Buyer.

   B. **OBTAINING OF DEPOSIT AND DOWN PAYMENT** by the Buyer is NOT a contingency, unless otherwise agreed in writing.

   C. **DEPOSIT** to be deposited ☐ with Escrow Holder, ☐ into Broker's trust account, or ☐ _____ $_____

      BY ☐ Personal check, ☐ Cashier's check, ☐ Cash, or ☐ _____,

      PAYABLE TO _____

      TO BE HELD UNCASHED UNTIL the next business day after acceptance of the offer, or ☐ _____

   D. **INCREASED DEPOSIT**, within _____ calendar days after acceptance of the offer, to be deposited ☐ with Escrow Holder,

      ☐ into Broker's trust account, or ☐ _____ $_____

   E. **BALANCE OF DOWN PAYMENT** to be deposited with Escrow Holder on demand of Escrow Holder .... $_____

   F. **FIRST LOAN IN THE AMOUNT OF** .... $_____

      ☐ NEW First Deed of Trust in favor of ☐ LENDER, ☐ SELLER; or

      ☐ ASSUMPTION of existing First Deed of Trust; or ☐ _____ ;

      encumbering the Property, securing a note payable at approximately $_____ per month (☐ or more), to include ☐ principal and interest, ☐ interest only, at maximum interest of _____% ☐ fixed rate, ☐ initial adjustable rate, with a maximum lifetime interest rate increase of _____% over the initial rate, balance due in _____ years. Buyer shall pay loan fees/points not to exceed _____.

   G. **SECOND LOAN IN THE AMOUNT OF** .... $_____

      ☐ NEW Second Deed of Trust in favor of ☐ LENDER, ☐ SELLER; or

      ☐ ASSUMPTION of Existing Second Deed of Trust; or ☐ _____ ;

      encumbering the Property, securing a note payable at approximately $_____ per month (☐ or more), to include ☐ principal and interest, ☐ interest only, at maximum interest of _____% ☐ fixed rate, ☐ initial adjustable rate, with a maximum lifetime interest rate increase of _____% over the initial rate, balance due in _____ years. Buyer shall pay loan fees/points not to exceed _____.

   H. **TOTAL PURCHASE PRICE**, not including costs of obtaining loans and other closing costs .... $_____

   I. **LOAN APPLICATIONS:** Buyer shall, within the time specified in paragraph 26B(1), submit to lender(s) (or to Seller for applicable Seller financing), a completed loan or assumption application(s), and provide to Seller written acknowledgment of Buyer's compliance. For Seller financing: (1) Buyer shall submit a completed loan application on FNMA Form 1003; (2) Buyer authorizes Seller and/or Broker(s) to obtain, at Buyer's expense, a copy of Buyer's credit report; and (3) Seller may cancel this purchase and sale agreement upon disapproval of either the application or the credit report, by providing to Buyer written notice within 7 (or ☐ _____) calendar days after receipt of those documents.

   J. **EXISTING LOANS:** For existing loans to be taken over by Buyer, Seller shall promptly request and upon receipt provide to Buyer copies of all applicable notes and deeds of trust, loan balances, and current interest rates. Buyer may give Seller written notice of disapproval within the time specified in paragraph 26B(5). Differences between estimated and actual loan balance(s) shall be adjusted at close of escrow by:

      ☐ Cash downpayment, or ☐ _____

      Impound account(s), if any, shall be: ☐ Charged to Buyer and credited to Seller, or ☐ _____

   K. **LOAN FEATURES: LOANS/DOCUMENTS CONTAIN A NUMBER OF IMPORTANT FEATURES AFFECTING THE RIGHTS OF THE BORROWER AND LENDER. READ ALL LOAN DOCUMENTS CAREFULLY.**

   L. **ADDITIONAL SELLER FINANCING TERMS:** The following terms apply ONLY to financing extended by Seller under this agreement. The rate specified as the maximum interest rate in F or G above, as applicable, shall be the actual fixed interest rate for seller financing. Any promissory note and/or deed of trust given by Buyer to Seller shall contain, but not be limited to, the following additional terms:

      1. REQUEST FOR NOTICE OF DEFAULT on senior loans.

      2. Buyer shall execute and pay for a REQUEST FOR NOTICE OF DELINQUENCY in escrow and at any future time if requested by Seller.

      3. Acceleration clause making the loan due, when permitted by law, at Seller's option, upon the sale or transfer of the Property or any interest in it.

      4. A late charge of 6.0% of the installment due, or $5.00, whichever is greater, if the installment is not received within 10 days of the date it is due.

      5. Title insurance coverage in the form of a joint protection policy shall be provided insuring Seller's deed of trust interest in the Property.

      6. Tax Service shall be obtained and paid for by Buyer to notify Seller if property taxes have not been paid.

      7. Buyer shall provide fire and extended coverage insurance during the period of the seller financing, in an amount sufficient to replace all improvements on the Property, or the total encumbrances against the Property, whichever is less, with a loss payable endorsement in favor of Seller.

      8. The addition, deletion, or substitution of any person or entity under this agreement, or to title prior to close of escrow, shall require Seller's written consent. Seller may grant or withhold consent in Seller's sole discretion. Any additional or substituted person or entity shall, if requested by Seller, submit to Seller the same documentation as required for the original named Buyer. Seller and/or Broker(s) may obtain a credit report on any such person or entity.

      9. If the Property contains 1 to 4 dwelling units, Buyer and Seller shall execute a Seller Financing Disclosure Statement (CAR FORM SFD-14) (Civil Code §§2956-2967), if applicable, as provided by arranger of credit, as soon as practicable prior to execution of security documents.

   M. **ADDITIONAL FINANCING TERMS:** _____

   _____

   _____

Buyer and Seller acknowledge receipt of copy of this page, which constitutes Page 1 of _____ Pages.

   Buyer's Initials (_____) (_____)   Seller's Initials (_____) (_____)

—— OFFICE USE ONLY ——

Reviewed by Broker or Designee _____

Date _____

BUYER'S COPY

REAL ESTATE PURCHASE CONTRACT AND RECEIPT FOR DEPOSIT (DLF-14 PAGE 1 OF 6)

SOURCE: Reprinted with permission, California Association of Realtors®. Endorsement not implied.

EXHIBIT 10.1   A Real Estate Purchase Contract from California *Continued*

Property Address: _____   _____ , 19_____

2. ATTACHED SUPPLEMENTS: The following ATTACHED supplements are incorporated in this agreement:
☐ _____ ☐ _____
☐ _____ ☐ _____

3. ESCROW: Escrow instructions shall be signed by Buyer and Seller and delivered to _____ , the designated Escrow Holder, within _____ calendar days after acceptance of the offer (or ☐ at least _____ calendar days before close of escrow). Buyer and Seller hereby jointly instruct Escrow Holder and Broker(s) that Buyer's deposit(s) placed into escrow or into Broker's trust account will be held as a good faith deposit toward the completion of this transaction. Release of Buyer's funds will require mutual, signed release instructions from both Buyer and Seller, judicial decision, or arbitration award. Escrow shall close ☐ on _____ , 19___ , or ☐ within _____ calendar days after acceptance of the offer. Escrow fee to be paid as follows: _____

4. OCCUPANCY: Buyer ☐ does, ☐ does not intend to occupy Property as Buyer's primary residence.

5. POSSESSION AND KEYS: Seller shall deliver possession and occupancy of the Property to Buyer ☐ on the date of recordation of the deed at _____ AM/PM, or ☐ no later than _____ calendar days after date of recordation at _____ AM/PM, or ☐ _____ . Property shall be vacant unless otherwise agreed in writing. If applicable, Seller and Buyer shall execute Interim Occupancy Agreement (CAR FORM IOA-14) or Residential Lease Agreement After Sale (CAR FORM RLAS-11). Seller shall provide keys and/or means to operate all Property locks, mailboxes, security systems, alarms, garage door openers, and Homeowners' Association facilities.

6. TITLE AND VESTING: Buyer shall be provided a current preliminary (title) report at _____ expense. Buyer shall, within the time specified in paragraph 26B(5), provide written notice to Seller of any items reasonably disapproved. (A preliminary report is only an offer by the title insurer to issue a policy of title insurance and may not contain every item affecting title.) At close of escrow: (a) Title shall be transferred by grant deed; (b) title shall be free of liens, except as provided in this agreement; (c) title shall be free of other encumbrances, easements, restrictions, rights, and conditions of record or known to Seller, except for: (1) all matters shown in the preliminary (title) report which are not disapproved in writing by Buyer as above, and (2) _____ ; (d) Buyer shall receive a California Land Title Association (CLTA) policy issued by _____ Company, at _____ expense. (An ALTA-R policy may provide greater protection for Buyer and may be available at the same or slightly higher cost than a CLTA policy. The designated title company can provide information, at Buyer's request, about availability and desirability of other types of title insurance.) For Seller financing, paragraph 1L(5) provides for a joint protection policy. Title shall vest as designated in Buyer's escrow instructions. **(THE MANNER OF TAKING TITLE MAY HAVE SIGNIFICANT LEGAL AND TAX CONSEQUENCES; THEREFORE, BUYER SHOULD GIVE THIS MATTER SERIOUS CONSIDERATION.)**

7. PRORATIONS:
   A. Real property taxes and assessments, interest, rents, Homeowners' Association regular dues and regular assessments, premiums on insurance assumed by Buyer, payments on bonds and assessments assumed by Buyer, and _____ shall be paid current and prorated between Buyer and Seller, unless otherwise shown in paragraph 7B or 7C, as of: ☐ date of recordation of the deed, or ☐ _____ .
   B. Mello-Roos and other Special Assessment District bonds and assessments which are now a lien shall be:
     ☐ paid current by Seller as of the date shown in paragraph 7A (payments that are not yet due shall be assumed by Buyer without credit toward the purchase price); or ☐ _____
   C. Homeowners' Association special assessments, which are now a lien, shall be: ☐ paid current by Seller as of the date shown in paragraph 7A (payments that are not yet due shall be assumed by Buyer without credit toward the purchase price); or ☐ _____
   D. County transfer tax or transfer fee shall be paid by _____ . City transfer tax or transfer fee shall be paid by _____ . Homeowners' Association transfer fee shall be paid by _____ .
   E. THE PROPERTY WILL BE REASSESSED UPON CHANGE OF OWNERSHIP. THIS WILL AFFECT THE TAXES TO BE PAID. Any supplemental tax bills shall be paid as follows: (1) for periods after close of escrow, by Buyer (or by final acquiring party, if part of an exchange), and (2) for periods prior to close of escrow, by Seller. TAX BILLS ISSUED AFTER CLOSE OF ESCROW SHALL BE HANDLED DIRECTLY BETWEEN BUYER AND SELLER.

8. CONDOMINIUM/P.D.: If the Property is in a condominium/planned development: (a) the Property has _____ assigned parking space(s); (b) the current regular Homeowners' Association dues/assessments are $_____ ☐ monthly, or ☐ _____ (c) Seller shall promptly disclose in writing to Buyer any known pending special assessments, claims, or litigation; and (d) Seller shall promptly request, and, upon receipt, provide to Buyer copies of covenants, conditions, and restrictions; articles of incorporation; by-laws; other governing documents; most current financial statement distributed (Civil Code §1365); statement regarding limited enforceability of age restrictions, if applicable; current Homeowners' Association statement showing any unpaid assessments (Civil Code §1368); any other documents required by law; most recent six months Homeowners' Association minutes, if available; and _____ . Buyer shall, within the time specified in paragraph 26B(5), provide written notice to Seller of any items disapproved. READ PARAGRAPH 7 FOR PRORATIONS AND TRANSFER FEES.

9. BUYER'S INVESTIGATION OF PROPERTY CONDITION: Buyer shall have the right to conduct inspections, investigations, tests, surveys, and other studies ("Inspections") at Buyer's expense. Buyer shall, within the times specified in paragraph 26B(2) and (3), complete these Inspections and shall notify Seller in writing of any item(s) disapproved. Buyer is strongly advised to exercise this right and to make Buyer's own selection of professionals with appropriate qualifications to conduct Inspections of the entire Property. If Buyer does not exercise this right to conduct Inspections, Buyer is acting against the advice of Broker(s). In any event, Buyer is relying upon Inspections made or obtained by Buyer. **BUYER AND SELLER ARE AWARE THAT THE BROKER(S) DO(ES) NOT GUARANTEE, AND IN NO WAY ASSUME(S) RESPONSIBILITY FOR, THE CONDITION OF THE PROPERTY. BUYER IS ALSO AWARE OF BUYER'S AFFIRMATIVE DUTY TO EXERCISE REASONABLE CARE TO PROTECT HIMSELF OR HERSELF, INCLUDING THOSE FACTS WHICH ARE KNOWN TO OR WITHIN THE DILIGENT ATTENTION AND OBSERVATION OF THE BUYER (Civil Code §2079.5).**
   Seller shall make the Property available for all Inspections. Buyer shall keep the Property free and clear of liens; shall indemnify and hold Seller harmless from all liability, claims, demands, damages, and costs; and shall repair all damages arising from the Inspections.
   No Inspections may be made by any building or zoning inspector or government employee without the prior written consent of Seller. Buyer shall provide to Seller, at no cost, upon request of Seller, complete copies of all Inspection reports obtained by Buyer concerning the Property.
   BUYER IS STRONGLY ADVISED TO INVESTIGATE THE CONDITION AND SUITABILITY OF ALL ASPECTS OF THE PROPERTY AND ALL MATTERS AFFECTING THE VALUE OR DESIRABILITY OF THE PROPERTY, INCLUDING, BUT NOT LIMITED TO, THE FOLLOWING:
   A. Built-in appliances, structural, foundation, roof, plumbing, heating, air conditioning, electrical, mechanical, security, pool/spa systems and components, and any personal property included in the sale.
   B. Square footage, room dimensions, lot size, and age of Property improvements. (Any numerical statements regarding these items are APPROXIMATIONS ONLY and should not be relied upon.)
   C. Property lines and boundaries. (Fences, hedges, walls, and other natural or constructed barriers or markers do not necessarily identify true Property boundaries. Property lines may be verified by survey.)
   D. Sewer, septic, and well systems and components. (Property may not be connected to sewer, and applicable fees may not have been paid. Septic tank may need to be pumped and leach field may need to be inspected.)
   E. Limitations, restrictions, and requirements regarding Property use, future development, zoning, building, size, governmental permits, and inspections.
   F. Water and utility availability and use restrictions.
   G. Potential environmental hazards including asbestos, formaldehyde, radon gas, lead-based paint, other lead contamination, fuel or chemical storage tanks, contaminated soil or water, hazardous waste, electromagnetic fields, nuclear sources, and other substances, materials, products, or conditions.
   H. Geologic/seismic conditions, soil and terrain stability, suitability, and drainage.
   I. Neighborhood or Property conditions including schools, proximity and adequacy of law enforcement, proximity to commercial, industrial, or agricultural activities, crime statistics, fire protection, other governmental services, existing and proposed transportation, construction and development, airport noise, noise or odor from any source, other nuisances, hazards, or circumstances, and any conditions or influences of significance to certain cultures and/or religions.
   J. Buyer is advised to make further inquiries and to consult government agencies, lenders, insurance agents, architects, and other appropriate persons and entities concerning the use of the Property under applicable building, zoning, fire, health, and safety codes, and for evaluation of potential hazards.
   K. Other: _____

Buyer and Seller acknowledge receipt of copy of this page, which constitutes Page 2 of _____ Pages.
   Buyer's Initials (_____) (_____)   Seller's Initials (_____) (_____)

OFFICE USE ONLY
Reviewed by Broker or Designee _____
Date _____

EXHIBIT 10.1   A Real Estate Purchase Contract from California *Continued*

Property Address: _____ _____ , 19____

10. CONDITION OF PROPERTY: (Initial ONLY paragraph A or B; DO NOT initial both.)

Buyer's Initials   Seller's Initials

____ / ____   ____ / ____   **A. SELLER WARRANTY: (If A is initialled, DO NOT initial B.)** Seller warrants that on the date possession is made available to Buyer: (1) Roof shall be free of KNOWN leaks; (2) built-in appliances (including free-standing oven and range, if included in sale), plumbing, heating, air conditioning, electrical, water, sewer/septic, and pool/spa systems, if any, shall be operative; (3) plumbing systems, shower pan(s), and shower enclosure(s) shall be free of leaks; (4) all broken or cracked glass shall be replaced; (5) Property, including pool/spa, landscaping, and grounds, shall be maintained in substantially the same condition as on the date of acceptance of the offer; (6) all debris and all personal property not included in the sale shall be removed; (7) _____ __

NOTE TO BUYER: This warranty is limited to items specified in this paragraph A. Items discovered in Buyer's Inspections which are not covered by this paragraph shall be governed by the procedure in paragraphs 9 and 26.
NOTE TO SELLER: Disclosures in the Real Estate Transfer Disclosure Statement (CAR FORM TDS-14), and items discovered in Buyer's Inspections, do NOT eliminate Seller's obligations under this warranty unless specifically agreed in writing.

OR

Buyer's Initials   Seller's Initials

____ / ____   ____ / ____   **B. "AS-IS" CONDITION: (If B is initialled, DO NOT initial A.)** Property is sold "AS-IS," in its present condition, without warranty. Seller shall not be responsible for making corrections or repairs of any nature except: (1) Structural pest control repairs, if applicable under paragraph 19, and (2) _____
Buyer retains the right to disapprove the condition of the Property based upon items discovered in Buyer's Inspections under paragraph 9. **SELLER REMAINS OBLIGATED TO DISCLOSE ADVERSE MATERIAL FACTS WHICH ARE KNOWN TO SELLER AND TO MAKE OTHER DISCLOSURES REQUIRED BY LAW.**

11. TRANSFER DISCLOSURE STATEMENT: Unless exempt, a Real Estate Transfer Disclosure Statement ("TDS") (CAR FORM TDS-14) shall be completed by Seller and delivered to Buyer (Civil Code §§1102-1102.15). Buyer shall sign and return a copy of the TDS to Seller or Seller's agent: (a). ☐ Buyer has received a TDS prior to execution of the offer, **OR** (b) ☐ Buyer shall be provided a TDS within _____ calendar days after acceptance of the offer. If the TDS is delivered to Buyer after the offer is executed, Buyer shall have the right to terminate this agreement within three (3) days after delivery in person, or five (5) days after delivery by deposit in the mail by giving written notice of termination to Seller or Seller's agent. DISCLOSURES IN THE TDS DO NOT ELIMINATE SELLER'S OBLIGATIONS, IF ANY, UNDER PARAGRAPH 10.

12. PROPERTY DISCLOSURES: When applicable to the Property and required by law, Seller shall provide to Buyer, at Seller's expense, the following disclosures and information. Buyer shall then, within the time specified in paragraph 26B(5) and (6), investigate the disclosures and information and provide written notice to Seller of any item disapproved pursuant to A-C and E1(b) below.

  A. GEOLOGIC/SEISMIC HAZARD ZONES DISCLOSURE: If the Property is located in a Special Studies Zone (SSZ) (Public Resources Code §§2621-2625), Seismic Hazard Zone (SHZ) (Public Resources Code §§2690-2699.6), or in a locally designated geological, seismic, or other hazard zone(s) or area(s) where disclosure is required by law, Seller shall, within the time specified in paragraph 26B(7), disclose in writing to Buyer this fact(s) and any other information required by law. (GEOLOGIC, SEISMIC AND FLOOD HAZARD DISCLOSURE (CAR FORM GFD-14) SHALL SATISFY THIS REQUIREMENT.) Construction or development of any structure may be restricted. Disclosure of SSZs and SHZs is required only where the maps, or information contained in the maps, are "reasonably available" as defined in Public Resources Code §§2621.9(c)(1) and 2694(c)(1).

  B. SPECIAL FLOOD HAZARD AREAS: If the Property is located in a Special Flood Hazard Area designated by the Federal Emergency Management Agency (FEMA), Seller shall, within the time specified in paragraph 26B(7), disclose this fact in writing to Buyer. (GEOLOGIC, SEISMIC AND FLOOD HAZARD DISCLOSURE (CAR FORM GFD-14) SHALL SATISFY THIS REQUIREMENT.) Government regulations may impose building restrictions and requirements which may substantially impact and limit construction and remodeling of improvements. Flood insurance may be required by lender.

  C. STATE FIRE RESPONSIBILITY AREAS: If the Property is located in a State Fire Responsibility Area, Seller shall, within the time specified in paragraph 26B(7), disclose this fact in writing to Buyer (Public Resources Code §4136). Disclosure may be made in the Real Estate Transfer Disclosure Statement (CAR FORM TDS-14). Government regulations may impose building restrictions and requirements which may substantially impact and limit construction and remodeling of improvements. Disclosure of these areas is required only if the Seller has actual knowledge that the Property is located in such an area or if maps of such areas have been provided to the county assessor's office.

  D. MELLO-ROOS: Seller shall make a good faith effort to obtain a disclosure notice from any local agencies which levy on the Property a special tax pursuant to the Mello-Roos Community Facilities Act, and shall deliver to Buyer any such notice made available by those agencies.

  E. EARTHQUAKE SAFETY:

    1. PRE-1960 PROPERTIES: If the Property was built prior to 1960, and contains ONE-TO-FOUR DWELLING UNITS of conventional light frame construction, Seller shall, unless exempt, within the time specified in paragraph 26B(7), provide to Buyer: (a) a copy of "The Homeowner's Guide to Earthquake Safety," and (b) written disclosure of known seismic deficiencies (Government Code §§8897-8897.5).

    2. PRE-1975 PROPERTIES: If the Property was built prior to 1975, and contains RESIDENTIAL, COMMERCIAL, OR OTHER STRUCTURES constructed of masonry or precast concrete, with wood frame floors or roofs, Seller shall, unless exempt, within the time specified in paragraph 26B(7), provide to Buyer a copy of "The Commercial Property Owner's Guide to Earthquake Safety" (Government Code §§8893-8893.5).

    3. ALL PROPERTIES: If the booklets described in paragraphs E1 and E2 are not required, Buyer is advised that they are available and contain important information that may be useful for ALL TYPES OF PROPERTY (Civil Code §§2079.8 and 2079.9).

  F. SMOKE DETECTOR(S): State law requires that residences be equipped with operable smoke detector(s). Local ordinances may have additional requirements. Unless exempt, Seller shall, prior to close of escrow, provide to Buyer a written statement of compliance and any other documents required, in accordance with applicable state and local law. (SMOKE DETECTOR STATEMENT OF COMPLIANCE (CAR FORM SDC-11) SHALL SATISFY THE STATE PORTION OF THIS REQUIREMENT.) Additional smoke detector(s), if required, shall be installed by Seller at Seller's expense prior to close of escrow.

  G. ENVIRONMENTAL HAZARDS BOOKLET: The booklet, "Environmental Hazards: Guide for Homeowners and Buyers," is published by the California Department of Real Estate, and contains information that may be useful for ALL TYPES OF PROPERTY (Civil Code §2079.7).

  H. LEAD BASED PAINT: Buyers obtaining new FHA-insured financing on residential properties constructed prior to 1978 are required to sign a lead paint disclosure form. (NOTICE TO PURCHASERS OF HOUSING CONSTRUCTED BEFORE 1978 (CAR FORM LPD-14) SHALL SATISFY THIS REQUIREMENT.)

  I. OTHER: _____

13. GOVERNMENTAL COMPLIANCE: Seller shall promptly disclose to Buyer any improvements, additions, alterations, or repairs ("Improvements") made by Seller or known to Seller to have been made without required governmental permits, final inspections, and approvals. In addition, Seller represents that Seller has no knowledge of any notice of violations of City, County, State, or Federal building, zoning, fire, or health laws, codes, statutes, ordinances, regulations, or rules filed or issued against the Property. If Seller receives notice or is made aware of any of the above violations prior to close of escrow, Seller shall immediately notify Buyer in writing. Buyer shall, within the time specified in paragraph 26B(7), provide written notice to Seller of any items disapproved.

14. RETROFIT: Compliance with any minimum mandatory government retrofit standards, including but not limited to energy and utility efficiency requirements and proof of compliance, shall be paid for by ☐ Buyer, ☐ Seller.

15. FIXTURES: All existing fixtures and fittings that are attached to the Property or for which special openings have been made are INCLUDED IN THE PURCHASE PRICE (unless excluded below) and are to be transferred free of liens. These include, but are not limited to, electrical, lighting, plumbing and heating fixtures, fireplace inserts, solar systems, built-in appliances, screens, awnings, shutters, window coverings, attached floor coverings, television antennas/satellite dishes and related equipment, private integrated telephone systems, air coolers/conditioners, pool/spa equipment, water softeners (if owned by Seller), security systems/alarms (if owned by Seller), garage door openers/remote controls, attached fireplace equipment, mailbox, in-ground landscaping including trees/shrubs, and

ITEMS EXCLUDED: _____

16. PERSONAL PROPERTY: The following items of personal property, free of liens and without warranty of condition (unless provided in paragraph 10A) or fitness for use, are included: _____
_____

17. HOME WARRANTY PLANS: Buyer and Seller are informed that home warranty plans are available. These plans may provide additional protection and benefit to Buyer and Seller. Broker(s) do not endorse, approve, or recommend any particular company or program. Buyer and Seller elect (Check ONLY ONE):

☐ To purchase a home warranty plan with the following optional coverage _____ , at a cost not to exceed $_____ , to be paid by _____ , and to be issued by _____ Company,

OR

☐ Buyer and Seller elect NOT to purchase a home warranty plan.

18. SEPTIC SYSTEM: (If initialled by all parties.)

Buyer's Initials   Seller's Initials

____ / ____   ____ / ____

☐ Buyer, ☐ Seller shall pay to have septic system pumped and certified. Evidence of compliance shall be provided to the other party before close of escrow.
☐ Buyer, ☐ Seller to pay for sewer connection if required by local ordinance.

Buyer and Seller acknowledge receipt of copy of this page, which constitutes Page 3 of _____ Pages.

Buyer's Initials (_____) (_____)   Seller's Initials (_____) (_____)

      OFFICE USE ONLY
Reviewed by Broker or Designee _____
Date _____

EXHIBIT 10.1   A Real Estate Purchase Contract from California *Continued*

Property Address: _____ _____, 19____

19. PEST CONTROL: (If initialled by all parties.)
Buyer's Initials   Seller's Initials
_____ / _____   _____ / _____

A. Seller shall, within the time specified in paragraph 26B(8), provide to Buyer a current written Wood Destroying Pests and Organisms Inspection Report. Report shall be at the expense of ☐ Buyer, ☐ Seller, to be performed by _____, a registered Structural Pest Control Company, covering the main building and **(If checked):**
☐ detached garage(s) or carport(s); ☐ the following other structures on the Property: _____
B. If requested by Buyer or Seller, the report shall separately identify each recommendation for corrective work as follows:
"Section 1": Infestation or infection which is evident.
"Section 2": Conditions that are present which are deemed likely to lead to infestation or infection.
C. If no infestation or infection by wood destroying pests or organisms is found, the report shall include a written Certification that on the inspection date no evidence of active infestation was found (Business and Professions Code §8519(a).)
D. Work recommended to correct conditions described in "Section 1" shall be at the expense of ☐ Buyer, ☐ Seller.
E. Work recommended to correct conditions described in "Section 2," **if requested by Buyer**, shall be at the expense of ☐ Buyer, ☐ Seller.
F. Work to be performed at Seller's expense may be performed by Seller or through others, provided that: (a) all required permits and final inspections are obtained, and (b) upon completion of repairs a written Certification is issued by a registered Structural Pest Control Company showing that the inspected property "is now free of evidence of active infestation or infection." (Business and Professions Code §8519(b).)
G. If inspection of inaccessible areas is recommended in the report, Buyer has the option to accept and approve the report, or request in writing within 5 (or ☐ _____) calendar days of receipt of the report that further inspection be made. BUYER'S FAILURE TO NOTIFY SELLER IN WRITING OF SUCH REQUEST SHALL CONCLUSIVELY BE CONSIDERED APPROVAL OF THE REPORT. If further inspection recommends "Section 1" and/or "Section 2" corrective work, such work, and the inspection, entry, and closing of the inaccessible areas, shall be at the expense of the respective party designated in paragraphs (A), (D) and/or (E). If no infestation or infection is found, the inspection, entry, and closing of the inaccessible areas shall be at the expense of Buyer.
H. Inspections, corrective work, and certification under this paragraph shall not include roof coverings. Read paragraph 9A concerning inspection of roof coverings.
I. Work shall be performed in a skillful manner with materials of comparable quality, and shall include repair of leaking shower stalls and pans and replacement of tiles and other materials removed for repair. It is understood that exact restoration of appearance or cosmetic items following all such work is not included.
J. Funds for work agreed in writing to be performed after close of escrow shall be held in escrow and disbursed upon receipt of a written Certification that the inspected property "is now free of evidence of active infestation or infection." (Business and Professions Code §8519(b).)
K. Other: _____

20. SALE OF BUYER'S PROPERTY: (If initialled by all parties.)
Buyer's Initials   Seller's Initials
_____ / _____   _____ / _____

This agreement is contingent upon the close of escrow of Buyer's property described as _____
situated in _____. Buyer's property is: ☐ Listed with _____ Company,
☐ In escrow No. _____ with _____ Company, scheduled to close escrow on _____, 19____.
A. (Check ONE:) ☐ Seller shall have the right to continue to offer the Property for sale, ☐ Seller shall NOT have the right to continue to offer the Property for sale (other than for back-up offers), ☐ Seller shall NOT have the right to continue to offer the Property for sale (other than for back-up offers) until _____ calendar days after acceptance of the offer.
B. If Seller has the right to continue to offer the Property for sale (other than for back-up offers) and Seller accepts another offer, Seller shall give Buyer written notice to (1) remove this contingency in writing and (2) comply with the following additional requirements _____
_____
If Buyer fails to complete those actions within _____ hours or _____ calendar days after receipt of such Notice from Seller, then this agreement and any escrow shall terminate and the deposit (less costs incurred) shall be returned to Buyer.
C. If Seller does not give the Notice above and Buyer's property does not close escrow by the date specified in paragraph 3 for close of escrow of this Property, then either Seller or Buyer may cancel this agreement and any escrow by giving the other party written notice of cancellation, and the Buyer's deposit (less costs incurred) shall be returned to Buyer.

21. CANCELLATION OF PRIOR SALE/BACK-UP OFFER: (If initialled by all parties.)
Buyer's Initials   Seller's Initials
_____ / _____   _____ / _____

Buyer understands that Seller has entered into one or more contracts to sell the Property to a different buyer(s). The parties to any prior sale may mutually agree to modify or amend the terms of that sale(s). This agreement is contingent upon the written cancellation of the previous purchase and sale agreement(s) and any related escrow(s).
(Check ONLY ONE of the following.)
☐ CANCELLATION OF PRIOR SALE: If written cancellation of the previous agreement(s) is not received on or before _____, 19____, then either Buyer or Seller may cancel this agreement and any escrow by giving the other party to this agreement written notice of cancellation. Buyer's deposit, less costs incurred, shall then be returned to Buyer.
☐ BACK-UP OFFER: This is a back-up offer in back-up position No. _____. BUYER'S DEPOSIT CHECK SHALL BE HELD UNCASHED until a copy of the written cancellation(s) signed by all parties to the prior sale(s) is provided to Buyer. Until Buyer receives a copy of such cancellation(s), Buyer may cancel this agreement by providing written notice to Seller. Buyer's deposit shall then be returned to Buyer. AS RELATES TO A BACK-UP OFFER, TIME PERIODS IN THIS AGREEMENT WHICH ARE STATED AS A NUMBER OF DAYS SHALL BEGIN ON THE DATE SELLER GIVES TO BUYER WRITTEN NOTICE THAT ANY PRIOR CONTRACT(S) HAS BEEN CANCELLED. IF CLOSE OF ESCROW OR ANY OTHER EVENT IS SHOWN AS A SPECIFIC DATE, THAT DATE SHALL NOT BE EXTENDED UNLESS BUYER AND SELLER SPECIFICALLY AGREE IN WRITING.

22. COURT CONFIRMATION: (If initialled by all parties.)
Buyer's Initials   Seller's Initials
_____ / _____   _____ / _____

This agreement is contingent upon court confirmation on or before _____, 19____. The court may allow open, competitive bidding, resulting in the Property being sold to the highest bidder. Buyer has been advised to be in court when the offer is considered for confirmation. Court confirmation may be required in a probate, conservatorship, guardianship, receivership, bankruptcy, or other proceeding. Buyer understands that the Property may continue to be marketed by Broker(s) and others, and that Broker(s) and others may represent other competitive bidders prior to and at the court confirmation. If court confirmation is not obtained by date shown above, Buyer may cancel this agreement by giving written notice of cancellation to Seller.

23. NOTICES: Notices given pursuant to this agreement shall, unless otherwise required by law, be deemed delivered to Buyer when personally received by Buyer or _____, who is authorized to receive it for Buyer, or to Seller when personally received by Seller or _____, who is authorized to receive it for Seller. Delivery may be in person, by mail, or facsimile.

24. TAX WITHHOLDING:
A. Under the Foreign Investment in Real Property Tax Act (FIRPTA), IRC §1445, every Buyer must, unless an exemption applies, deduct and withhold 10% of the gross sales price from Seller's proceeds and send it to the Internal Revenue Service, if the Seller is a "foreign person" under that statute.
B. In addition, under California Revenue and Taxation Code §§18805 and 26131, every Buyer must, unless an exemption applies, deduct and withhold 3-1/3% of the gross sales price from Seller's proceeds and send it to the Franchise Tax Board if the Seller has a last known address outside of California or if the Seller's proceeds will be paid to a financial intermediary of the Seller.
C. Penalties may be imposed on a responsible party for non-compliance with the requirements of these statutes and related regulations. Seller and Buyer agree to execute and deliver any instrument, affidavit, statement, or instruction reasonably necessary to carry out these requirements, and to withholding of tax under those statutes if required. (SELLER'S AFFIDAVIT OF NON-FOREIGN STATUS AND/OR CALIFORNIA RESIDENCY (CAR FORM AS-14), OR BUYER'S AFFIDAVIT (CAR FORM AB-11), IF APPLICABLE, SHALL SATISFY THESE REQUIREMENTS.)

25. RISK OF LOSS: Except as otherwise provided in this agreement, all risk of loss to the Property which occurs after the offer is accepted shall be borne by Seller until either the title has been transferred, or possession has been given to Buyer, whichever occurs first. Any damage totalling 1.0 (one) % or less of the purchase price shall be repaired by Seller in accordance with paragraph 10, if applicable. If the land or improvements to the Property are destroyed or materially damaged prior to transfer of title in an amount exceeding 1.0 (one) % of the purchase price, then Buyer shall have the option to either terminate this agreement and recover the full deposit or purchase the Property in its then present condition. Any expenses paid by Buyer or Seller for credit reports, appraisals, title examination, or inspections of any kind shall remain that party's responsibility. If Buyer elects to purchase the Property and the loss is covered by insurance, Seller shall assign to Buyer all insurance proceeds covering the loss. If transfer of title and possession do not occur at the same time, BUYER AND SELLER ARE ADVISED TO SEEK ADVICE OF THEIR INSURANCE ADVISORS as to the insurance consequences thereof.

Buyer and Seller acknowledge receipt of copy of this page, which constitutes Page 4 of _____ Pages.
    Buyer's Initials (_____) (_____)   Seller's Initials (_____) (_____)

OFFICE USE ONLY
Reviewed by Broker or Designee _____
Date _____

M-R-Jan-94

BUYER'S COPY
REAL ESTATE PURCHASE CONTRACT AND RECEIPT FOR DEPOSIT (DLF-14 PAGE 4 OF 6)

EXHIBIT 10.1   A Real Estate Purchase Contract from California *Continued*

Property Address: _____, 19____

26. CONTINGENCIES/COVENANTS: METHODS OF SATISFACTION/REMOVAL, TIME FRAMES, DISAPPROVAL/APPROVAL:
A. METHOD OF SATISFYING/REMOVING CONTINGENCIES: Contingencies are to be satisfied or removed by one of the following methods:
(1) **PASSIVE METHOD:** IF BUYER FAILS TO GIVE WRITTEN NOTICE OF DISAPPROVAL OF ITEMS OR OF CANCELLATION OF THIS AGREEMENT WITHIN THE STRICT TIME PERIODS SPECIFIED IN THIS AGREEMENT (except financing contingency, if paragraph 1A(2) is checked), THEN BUYER SHALL CONCLUSIVELY BE DEEMED TO HAVE COMPLETED ALL INSPECTIONS AND REVIEW OF APPLICABLE DOCUMENTS AND DISCLOSURES AND TO HAVE MADE AN ELECTION TO PROCEED WITH THE TRANSACTION WITHOUT CORRECTION OF ANY ITEMS WHICH THE SELLER HAS NOT OTHERWISE AGREED TO CORRECT. **OR**
(2) **ACTIVE METHOD:** IF BUYER AND SELLER INITIAL THIS PARAGRAPH, THEN PARAGRAPH A(1) SHALL NOT APPLY.

Buyer's Initials   Seller's Initials

_____ / _____   _____ / _____   BUYER'S DISAPPROVAL OF ITEMS OR REMOVAL OF CONTINGENCIES SHALL BE IN WRITING (except financing contingency, if paragraph 1A(1) is checked). IF BUYER FAILS TO REMOVE OR WAIVE ALL CONTINGENCIES IN WRITING WITHIN THE STRICT TIME PERIODS SPECIFIED IN THIS AGREEMENT, THEN SELLER MAY CANCEL THIS AGREEMENT BY GIVING WRITTEN NOTICE OF CANCELLATION TO BUYER.

B. TIME FRAMES: Buyer and Seller agree to be bound by the following time periods:

BUYER has the following number of calendar days to take the action specified, BEGINNING ON THE DATE OF ACCEPTANCE OF THE OFFER:

1. _____   Loan Application(s) (submit to lender(s) for new loan(s) and assumption(s), submit to Seller for seller financing, submit written acknowledgment to Seller (Para 1I)
2. _____   Buyer Inspections of Property (complete inspections, except GEOLOGIC, and give notice of disapproval) (Para 9)
3. _____   Buyer Inspections of Property (complete GEOLOGIC inspections and give notice of disapproval) (Para 9)
4. _____

BUYER has the following number of calendar days to DISAPPROVE the items listed below, BEGINNING ON THE DATE OF BUYER'S RECEIPT OF EACH ITEM:

5. _____   Existing Loan Documents (Para 1J),
            Preliminary (Title) Report (Para 6),
            Condominium/Planned Development Documents (Para 8),
            Geologic/Seismic/Flood/State Fire Zones/Areas (Para 12A-C),
            Governmental Notices Disclosure (Para 13)
6. _____

SELLER has the following number of calendar days to PROVIDE to Buyer, as applicable, the information listed below, BEGINNING ON THE DATE OF ACCEPTANCE OF THE OFFER:

7. _____   Geologic/Seismic/Flood/State Fire Zones/Areas Disclosures, if applicable (Para 12A-C), Homeowner's Guide to Earthquake Safety and/or Commercial Property Owner's Guide to Earthquake Safety (Para 12E)
8. _____   Pest Control Report (Para 19)
9. _____

The items listed below, as applicable, shall promptly be requested and upon receipt provided to Buyer:

10. _____   Existing Loan Documents (Para 1J),
            Preliminary (Title) Report (Para 6),
            Condominium/Planned Development Documents (Para 8),
            Mello-Roos Disclosure (Para 12D)
11. _____

C. DISAPPROVAL/APPROVAL OF ITEMS:
(1) If, within the time specified, Buyer provides written reasonable disapproval to Seller of any item for which Buyer has a disapproval right, Seller shall respond in writing within _____ calendar days after receipt of Buyer's notice. If Seller is unwilling or unable to correct the items disapproved by Buyer, then Buyer may cancel this agreement by giving written notice of cancellation to Seller within _____ calendar days (after receipt of Seller's response, or after expiration of the time for Seller's response, whichever occurs first), in which case Buyer's deposit shall be returned to Buyer. If paragraph A2 is initialled, then Buyer shall provide Seller with a written notice of either cancellation or election to proceed. If Buyer elects to proceed with the transaction without Seller's correction of items, Buyer shall assume all liability, responsibility, and expense for repairs or corrections, including the expense of compliance with governmental agency requirements. This does not, however, relieve the Seller of any contractual obligations to repair or correct items otherwise agreed upon.
(2) If a MELLO-ROOS DISCLOSURE notice under paragraph 12D is delivered to Buyer after the offer is executed, Buyer shall have three (3) days after delivery in person or five (5) days after delivery by deposit in the mail to give written notice of termination to Seller.

D. FOR ALL TIME PERIODS:
1. Buyer and Seller understand that time periods can be changed only by mutual written agreement.
2. If this is a back-up offer (paragraph 21), time periods which are shown as a number of days beginning on the date of acceptance of the offer shall instead begin on the date Seller gives to Buyer written notice that any prior contract(s) has been cancelled.

27. FINAL VERIFICATION OF CONDITION: Buyer shall have the right to make a final inspection of the Property approximately 5 (or ☐ _____) calendar days prior to close of escrow, NOT AS A CONTINGENCY OF THE SALE, but solely to confirm that: (a) Seller has completed alterations, repairs, replacements, or modifications ("Repairs") as agreed in writing by Buyer and Seller, and has complied with warranty obligations, if any, in paragraph 10, and (b) the Property is otherwise in substantially the same condition as on the date of acceptance of the offer. Repairs under this agreement shall be completed prior to close of escrow unless otherwise agreed in writing, and shall comply with applicable building code and permit requirements. Materials used shall be of comparable quality to existing materials.

28. MEDIATION OF DISPUTES: BUYER AND SELLER AGREE TO MEDIATE ANY DISPUTE OR CLAIM BETWEEN THEM ARISING OUT OF THIS CONTRACT OR ANY RESULTING TRANSACTION BEFORE RESORTING TO ARBITRATION OR COURT ACTION. Mediation is a process in which parties attempt to resolve a dispute by submitting it to an impartial, neutral mediator who is authorized to facilitate the resolution of the dispute but who is not empowered to impose a settlement on the parties. Mediation fee, if any, shall be divided equally among the parties involved. Before the mediation begins, the parties agree to sign a document limiting the admissibility in arbitration or any civil action of anything said, any admission made, and any documents prepared, in the course of the mediation, consistent with Evidence Code §1152.5. In addition, if paragraph 30 is initialled by Broker(s), Buyer and Seller agree to mediate disputes or claims involving an initialling Broker, as defined by that paragraph, consistent with this provision. The election by Broker(s) to initial or not initial paragraph 30 shall not affect the applicability of this mediation provision between Buyer and Seller and shall not result in the Broker(s) being deemed parties to the purchase and sale agreement. IF ANY PARTY COMMENCES AN ARBITRATION OR COURT ACTION BASED ON A DISPUTE OR CLAIM TO WHICH THIS PARAGRAPH APPLIES WITHOUT FIRST ATTEMPTING TO RESOLVE THE MATTER THROUGH MEDIATION, THEN IN THE DISCRETION OF THE ARBITRATOR(S) OR JUDGE, THAT PARTY SHALL NOT BE ENTITLED TO RECOVER ATTORNEY'S FEES EVEN IF THEY WOULD OTHERWISE BE AVAILABLE TO THAT PARTY IN ANY SUCH ARBITRATION OR COURT ACTION. However, the filing of a judicial action to enable the recording of a notice of pending action, for order of attachment, receivership, injunction, or other provisional remedies, shall not in itself constitute a loss of the right to recover attorney's fees under this provision. The following matters are excluded from the requirement of mediation hereunder: (a) a judicial or non-judicial foreclosure or other action or proceeding to enforce a deed of trust, mortgage, or installment land sale contract as defined in Civil Code §2985, (b) an unlawful detainer action, (c) the filing or enforcement of a mechanic's lien, and (d) any matter which is within the jurisdiction of a probate court.

29. ARBITRATION OF DISPUTES: Any dispute or claim in law or equity between Buyer and Seller arising out of this contract or any resulting transaction which is not settled through mediation shall be decided by neutral, binding arbitration and not by court action, except as provided by California law for judicial review of arbitration proceedings. In addition, if paragraph 30 is initialled by Broker(s), Buyer and Seller agree to arbitrate disputes or claims involving an initialling Broker, as defined by that paragraph, consistent with this provision. The election by Broker(s) to initial or not initial paragraph 30 shall not affect the applicability of the arbitration provision between Buyer and Seller, and shall not result in the Broker(s) being deemed parties to the purchase and sale agreement.
The arbitration shall be conducted in accordance with the rules of either the American Arbitration Association (AAA) or Judicial Arbitration and Mediation Services, Inc. (JAMS). The selection between AAA and JAMS rules shall be made by the claimant first filing for the arbitration. The parties to an arbitration may agree in writing to use different rules and/or arbitrator(s). In all other respects, the arbitration shall be conducted in accordance with Part III, Title 9 of the California Code of Civil Procedure. Judgment upon the award rendered by the arbitrator(s) may be entered in any court having jurisdiction thereof. The parties shall have the right to discovery in accordance with Code of Civil Procedure §1283.05. The following matters are excluded from arbitration hereunder: (a) a judicial or non-judicial foreclosure or other action or proceeding to enforce a deed of trust, mortgage, or installment land sale contract as defined in Civil Code §2985, (b) an unlawful detainer action, (c) the filing or enforcement of a mechanic's lien, (d) any matter which is within the jurisdiction of a probate or small claims court, and (e) an action for bodily injury or wrongful death, or for latent or patent defects, to which Code of Civil Procedure §337.1 or §337.15 applies. The filing of a judicial action to enable the recording of a notice of pending action, for order of attachment, receivership, injunction, or other provisional remedies, shall not constitute a waiver of the right to arbitrate under this provision.
"NOTICE: BY INITIALLING IN THE SPACE BELOW YOU ARE AGREEING TO HAVE ANY DISPUTE ARISING OUT OF THE MATTERS INCLUDED IN THE 'ARBITRATION OF DISPUTES' PROVISION DECIDED BY NEUTRAL ARBITRATION AS PROVIDED BY CALIFORNIA LAW AND YOU ARE GIVING UP ANY RIGHTS YOU MIGHT POSSESS TO HAVE THE DISPUTE LITIGATED IN A COURT OR JURY TRIAL. BY INITIALLING IN THE SPACE BELOW YOU ARE GIVING UP YOUR JUDICIAL RIGHTS TO DISCOVERY AND APPEAL, UNLESS THOSE RIGHTS ARE SPECIFICALLY INCLUDED IN THE 'ARBITRATION OF DISPUTES' PROVISION. IF YOU REFUSE TO SUBMIT TO ARBITRATION AFTER AGREEING TO THIS PROVISION, YOU MAY BE COMPELLED TO ARBITRATE UNDER THE AUTHORITY OF THE CALIFORNIA CODE OF CIVIL PROCEDURE. YOUR AGREEMENT TO THIS ARBITRATION PROVISION IS VOLUNTARY."
"WE HAVE READ AND UNDERSTAND THE FOREGOING AND AGREE TO SUBMIT DISPUTES ARISING OUT OF THE MATTERS INCLUDED IN THE 'ARBITRATION OF DISPUTES' PROVISION TO NEUTRAL ARBITRATION."

Buyer's Initials   Seller's Initials

_____ / _____   _____ / _____

Buyer and Seller acknowledge receipt of copy of this page, which constitutes Page 5 of _____ Pages.
Buyer's Initials (_____) (_____)   Seller's Initials (_____) (_____)

┌─ OFFICE USE ONLY ─────────┐
│ Reviewed by Broker or Designee _____ │
│ Date _____ │
└────────────────────────────┘

EQUAL HOUSING OPPORTUNITY

M-R-Jan-94

EXHIBIT 10.1   A Real Estate Purchase Contract from California *Concluded*

Property Address: _____ , 19____

30. BROKERS: (If initialled.) Any Broker who initials below agrees to (a) mediate any dispute or claim with Buyer, Seller, or other initialling Broker, arising out of this contract or any resulting transaction, consistent with paragraph 28, and (b) arbitrate any dispute or claim with Buyer, Seller, or other initialling Broker arising out of this contract or any resulting transaction, consistent with paragraph 29. However, if the dispute is solely between the Brokers, it shall instead be submitted for mediation and arbitration in accordance with the Board/Association of REALTORS® or MLS rules. If those entities decline to handle the matter, it shall be submitted pursuant to paragraphs 28 and 29. The initialling of this paragraph shall not result in any Broker being deemed a party to the purchase and sale agreement. As used in this paragraph, "Broker" means a brokerage firm and any licensed persons affiliated with that brokerage firm.

Selling Broker   Listing Broker
By: By:
_____   _____
(Initials)   (Initials)

31. LIQUIDATED DAMAGES: (If initialled by all parties.)

Buyer's Initials   Seller's Initials
____/____   ____/____   Buyer and Seller agree that if Buyer fails to complete this purchase by reason of any default of Buyer:

   A. Seller shall be released from obligation to sell the Property to Buyer.
   B. Seller shall retain, as liquidated damages for breach of contract, the deposit actually paid. Buyer and Seller shall execute RECEIPT FOR INCREASED DEPOSIT/LIQUIDATED DAMAGES (CAR FORM RID-11) for any increased deposits. However, the amount retained shall be no more than 3% of the purchase price if Property is a dwelling with no more than four units, one of which Buyer intends to occupy as Buyer's residence. Any excess shall be promptly returned to Buyer.
   C. Seller retains the right to proceed against Buyer for specific performance or any other claim or remedy Seller may have in law or equity, other than breach of contract damages.
   D. In the event of a dispute, Funds deposited in trust accounts or escrow are not released automatically and require mutual, signed release instructions from both Buyer and Seller, judicial decision, or arbitration award.

32. ATTORNEY'S FEES: In any action, proceeding, or arbitration between Buyer and Seller arising out of this agreement, the prevailing party shall be entitled to reasonable attorney's fees and costs, except as provided in paragraph 28.

33. MULTIPLE LISTING SERVICE: If Broker is a Participant of a multiple listing service (MLS), Broker is authorized to report the sale, price, terms, and financing for publication, dissemination, information, and use of the MLS, its parent entity, authorized members, participants, and subscribers.

34. OTHER TERMS AND CONDITIONS: _____
_____
_____

35. TIME OF ESSENCE; ENTIRE CONTRACT; CHANGES: Time is of the essence. All prior agreements between the parties are incorporated in this agreement, which constitutes the entire contract. Its terms are intended by the parties as a final, complete and exclusive expression of their agreement with respect to its subject matter and may not be contradicted by evidence of any prior agreement or contemporaneous oral agreement. The captions in this agreement are for convenience of reference only and are not intended as part of this agreement. **This agreement may not be extended, amended, modified, altered, or changed in any respect whatsoever except by a further agreement in writing signed by Buyer and Seller.**

36. AGENCY CONFIRMATION: The following agency relationship(s) are hereby confirmed for this transaction:

Listing Agent: _____ is the agent of (check one):
                         (Print Firm Name)

   ☐ the Seller exclusively; or ☐ both the Buyer and Seller.

Selling Agent: _____ (if not same as Listing Agent) is the agent of (check one):
                         (Print Firm Name)

   ☐ the Buyer exclusively; or ☐ the Seller exclusively; or ☐ both the Buyer and Seller.

(IF THE PROPERTY CONTAINS 1-4 RESIDENTIAL DWELLING UNITS, BUYER AND SELLER MUST ALSO BE GIVEN ONE OR MORE DISCLOSURE REGARDING REAL ESTATE AGENCY RELATIONSHIPS FORMS (CAR FORM AD-11).)

37. OFFER: This is an offer to purchase the Property. **All paragraphs with spaces for initials by Buyer and Seller are incorporated in this agreement only if initialled by both parties. If only one party initials, a Counter Offer is required until agreement is reached.** Unless acceptance is signed by Seller and a signed copy delivered in person, by mail, or facsimile, and **personally received by Buyer or by** _____ , who is authorized to receive it, by _____ , 19____ at _____ AM/PM, the offer shall be deemed revoked and the deposit shall be returned. Buyer and Seller acknowledge that Broker(s) is/are not a party(ies) to the purchase and sale agreement. Buyer has read and acknowledges receipt of a copy of the offer and agrees to the above confirmation of agency relationships. This agreement and any supplement, addendum, or modification, including any photocopy or facsimile, may be executed in two or more counterparts, all of which shall constitute one and the same writing.

Receipt for deposit is acknowledged: BUYER _____
BROKER _____   BUYER _____
                                                        Address _____
By _____   _____
                                                        Telephone _____ Fax _____

ACCEPTANCE

The undersigned Seller accepts the above and agrees to sell the Property on the above terms and conditions and agrees to the above confirmation of agency relationships (☐ subject to attached counter offer). Seller agrees to pay compensation for services as follows:

_____ to _____ , Broker, and
_____ to _____ , Broker,

payable: (a) on recordation of the deed or other evidence of title, or (b) if completion of sale is prevented by default of Seller, upon Seller's default, or (c) if completion of sale is prevented by default of Buyer, only if and when Seller collects damages from Buyer, by suit or otherwise, and then in an amount equal to one-half of the damages recovered, but not to exceed the above compensation, after first deducting title and escrow expenses and the expenses of collection, if any. Seller hereby irrevocably assigns to Broker(s) such compensation from Seller's proceeds in escrow. In any action, proceeding, or arbitration relating to the payment of such compensation, the prevailing party shall be entitled to reasonable attorney's fees and costs, except as provided in paragraph 28. The undersigned Seller has read, acknowledges receipt of a copy of this agreement, and authorizes Broker(s) to deliver a signed copy to Buyer.

Date _____ Telephone _____ Fax _____   SELLER _____
Address _____
_____   SELLER _____

Real Estate Broker(s) confirm(s) agency relationship(s) as above. (Real Estate Brokers are not parties to the purchase and sale agreement between Buyer and Seller.):

Real Estate Broker (Selling) _____ By _____ Date _____
Address _____ Telephone _____ Fax _____
Real Estate Broker (Listing) _____ By _____ Date _____
Address _____ Telephone _____ Fax _____

This form is available for use by the entire real estate industry. The use of this form is not intended to identify the user as a REALTOR®. REALTOR® is a registered collective membership mark which may be used only by real estate licensees who are members of the NATIONAL ASSOCIATION OF REALTORS® and who subscribe to its Code of Ethics.

┌─────────────────────────────────────┐
│   OFFICE USE ONLY   │
│ Reviewed by Broker or Designee ____ │
│ Date _____   │
└─────────────────────────────────────┘

EQUAL HOUSING OPPORTUNITY

Page 6 of _____ Pages.   M-R-Jan-94

BUYER'S COPY

REAL ESTATE PURCHASE CONTRACT AND RECEIPT FOR DEPOSIT (DLF-14 PAGE 6) OF 6)

n. Disclosures about the property, such as whether it is in a geologic hazard zone or a flood hazard area, and whether smoke detectors have been installed (required by law in California).

o. Government compliance—whether proper permits and approvals were obtained for any improvements made to the property.

p. A detailed list of any personal property included in the sale.

q. Information about any home warranty plans.

r. Pest control information—some states, including California, require a termite report; if the property is found to have termites, the seller is responsible for their removal.

s. Mediation, arbitration, and liquidated damages clauses.

Once the contract is signed by both the buyer and the seller, the buyer is said to have an **equitable interest** in the property; that is, the buyer has an ownership interest but not one that entitles him to possession of the property. That comes when the deed is transferred and the buyer obtains a legal interest in the property.

equitable interest
An ownership interest that does not entitle one to possession of the property, which occurs at the transfer of the deed when the owner obtains a legal interest in the property.

easement
A nonownership interest in land that gives its owner the right to the limited use of land owned by another.

7. **Title Insurance.** Before a deed may be issued, a title insurance company will check the title to the property to make sure that it is free of any liens, encumbrances, easements, or other items that might affect it. (A lien is a claim or charge against the property for payment of a debt, and an **easement** is the right of one property owner to use another's property, as when one owner must cross another's land to have access to his own.) The buyer and seller must agree on how these encumbrances will be removed before a clear title insurance policy will be issued.

Title insurance companies often employ paralegals and legal secretaries to check the title to property. Some firms conduct their own title searches; in that case, the paralegal may be asked to examine the records. In most states, these records are in the Office of the County Recorder. Find out how and where titles are checked in your own state and add this information to the State Specific Information box.

STATE SPECIFIC INFORMATION

In the state of _____, records are located at _____.

Titles are checked through the following procedures:

_____

_____

_____

abstract of title
A history of a property's ownership.

The buyer receives an **abstract of title** (or history of the property's ownership) that lists the results of the title search. Any liens against the property are indicated in the abstract. If a title insurance company has been hired and its search determines that the title is free of encumbrances, the company issues a title insurance policy, which insures that the buyer has received a clear title.

8. *Closing and/or Escrow.*   Once the buyer has obtained all the loans needed to purchase the property, title to the property has been cleared and a title insurance policy issued, the deed may be prepared and ownership of the property transferred. This procedure is known as a **closing** in some states and an **escrow** in others. A closing agenda for a fictitious commercial closing in New York is shown in Exhibit 10.2.

DEEDS

A deed transfers **legal title** (the right to possession) from the seller to the buyer. All deeds must comply with certain requirements, including the following:

- A deed must be a writing signed by the seller.
- The property being transferred must be described by metes and bounds, property address, plat map, or the legal name of the property (metes and bounds are discussed later in the chapter).
- Words indicating the intent to transfer the described property must be included.
- The buyer's name must be included.

Some states have additional requirements, which may include any or all of the following:

- The seller's signature must be witnessed.
- The seller must sign the deed before a notary public.
- The signature of the seller's spouse must be included.

Types of Deeds

Several different types of deeds are used. You will need to become familiar with warranty deeds, grant deeds, and quitclaim deeds.

Warranty Deeds.   Most states require a **warranty deed,** wherein the seller warrants to the buyer that the property is free of encumbrances and that she holds full and complete ownership in the property except for any which are specifically noted in the deed itself, such as mortgages or easements. The seller guarantees title to the property. In some states, the seller may guarantee the buyer's quiet enjoyment of the property. If the buyer learns after the transfer of the deed that the seller breached any of the warranties, the seller would be held liable for any damages. Exhibit 10.3 shows a warranty deed from North Carolina.

Grant Deed.   Some states use a **grant deed,** which is similar to a warranty deed. In this case, the seller warrants that the property is free of any encumbrances except those that have been previously disclosed to the buyer. In addition, the seller guarantees that he has title to the property and the right to convey it to the buyer.

---

title insurance policy
A policy issued by a title insurance company that insures that the buyer of property is receiving a clear title.

closing
A formal proceeding held in a lawyer's office where property documents and property are transferred from the seller to the buyer.

escrow
The time period during which a title search is conducted on property; extends up to the time the property is transferred from the seller to the buyer; used in some states instead of closing.

legal title
The right to possession of property; transferred through a deed.

warranty deed
A deed in which the seller guarantees that he holds full and complete ownership in the property and that the property is free of encumbrances unless specifically noted in the deed.

grant deed
A deed in which the seller guarantees that she has title to the property and the right to convey it and that the property is free of encumbrances except any that have previously been disclosed to the buyer.

EXHIBIT 10.2   A Closing Agenda

CLOSING AGENDA

AMERICAN NATIONAL BANK

$10,000,000 ACQUISITION MORTGAGE LOAN

TO

HOTEL INVESTMENT ADVISORS, INC.

Closing Date: NOVEMBER 29, 1996

<u>Parties and Miscellaneous Definitions:</u>

B&K	Korda & Levitz, counsel to Lender
Borrower	Hotel Investment Advisors, Inc., a California corporation
Closing Date	November 29, 1996
HS&M	Hart, Sanchez & Marx, counsel to Borrower
P&C	Point & Click, Lender's California local counsel
Lender	American National Bank
Premises	Oversleep Hotel 234 Fifth Street Los Angeles, California
Seller	Oversleep Hotels of the World, Inc.
Title Company	First American Title Insurance Company

Korda & Levitz
148 Eighth Avenue
New York, New York 10017
(212) 123-5555

Attention: Leslie Korda, Esq.

EXHIBIT 10.2   A Closing Agenda *Continued*

ITEM	DOCUMENT	RESPONSIBILITY
A.	**AUTHORIZATION DOCUMENTS**	
1.	Certificate of the Secretary of Borrower, dated the Closing Date, with respect to (and with the following items annexed):	HS&M
	(a) the Certificate of Incorporation of Borrower, together with all amendments thereto, all as filed with the Secretary of State of the State of California;	HS&M
	(b) the duly adopted by-laws of Borrower as in effect on the Closing Date;	HS&M
	(c) the duly adopted resolutions of Borrower authorizing the transaction; and	HS&M
	(d) a list of the officers of Borrower authorized to execute closing documents on Borrower's behalf, and their specimen signatures.	HS&M
2.	Certificate of the Secretary of State of the State of California, dated not more than 30 days prior to the Closing Date, stating that Borrower is in good standing under the laws of the State of California.	HS&M
B.	**LOAN DOCUMENTS**	
1.	Commitment Letter.	Lender
2.	Loan Agreement.	K&L
3.	Note.	K&L
4.	Mortgage, Deed of Trust, Assignment of Leases and Rents and Security Agreement.	K&L
5.	Security Agreement.	K&L
6.	UCC-1 Financing Statement for filing:	
	(a) in the Los Angeles County Real Estate Records; and	K&L
	(b) with the Secretary of State of the State of California.	K&L
7.	Assignment of Leases and Rents.	K&L
8.	Assignment of Contracts, Licenses, Permits, Agreements, Warranties and Approvals.	K&L
9.	Principals' Agreement.	K&L
10.	Environmental Indemnity Agreement.	K&L
11.	Replacement Reserve Agreement.	K&L

EXHIBIT 10.2   A Closing Agenda *Continued*

ITEM	DOCUMENT	RESPONSIBILITY
12.	Repair Escrow Agreement.	K&L
13.	Consent, Subordination and Recognition Agreement (Management Agreement).	K&L
14.	Franchisor's Comfort Letter.	Borrower
15.	Opinion of Borrower's local counsel.	HS&M (K&L form)
16.	Opinion of Lender's California local counsel.	P&C (K&L form)
17.	Closing Statement.	K&L
C.	**DOCUMENTS RELATING TO ACQUISITION & OPERATION OF THE PREMISES**	
1.	Purchase and Sale Agreement.	HS&M
2.	Deed to Borrower.	HS&M
3.	Franchise and License Agreements.	HS&M
4.	Management Agreement.	HS&M
5.	Certified Rent Roll and Occupancy Report.	HS&M
6.	Copies of all Commercial Leases.	HS&M
7.	Commercial Tenants' Estoppel Certificates.	HS&M (K&L form)
D.	**TITLE, SURVEY AND INSURANCE MATTERS**	
1.	Title Commitment.	Title Company
2.	Pro Forma Title Insurance Policy with all required endorsements.	Title Company
3.	Copies of all recorded documents that are exceptions to coverage.	Title Company
4.	Copy or other evidence of permanent Certificate of Occupancy for the Premises.	HS&M
5.	Municipality letter (or other evidence of compliance with zoning and subdivision ordinances and regulations)	HS&M
6.	Survey for the Premises.	HS&M
7.	UCC, Judgment and Tax Lien Searches against the Premises and Borrower.	Title Company
8.	Title Company Receipt of Documents and Recording Direction Letter.	K&L/HS&M/ Title Company

EXHIBIT 10.2   A Closing Agenda *Concluded*

ITEM	DOCUMENT	RESPONSIBILITY
9.	Original Fire and Casualty Insurance Policies.	HS&M
10.	Flood Hazard Certificate.	Title Company
E.	**MISCELLANEOUS**	
1.	Architectural and Engineering Report.	HS&M
2.	Environmental Audit.	HS&M
3.	Appraisal.	HS&M
F.	**PAYMENTS**	
1.	To Lender, the Closing Fee (1.0% of the original principal Loan amount).	Borrower
2.	To K&L, Lender's attorneys' fees and disbursements.	Borrower
3.	Payment of all title insurance premiums and survey charges, recording charges and filing fees, mortgage recording taxes and revenue stamps, if any.	Borrower

Quitclaim Deed.   From a buyer's perspective, the least advantageous type of deed is a **quitclaim deed.** In this case, the seller merely conveys to the buyer any interest he may have in the property, which may be all, a part, or none. No guarantees or warranties accompany a quitclaim deed. The seller in essence states to the buyer, "you may have any interest in the property that I might have." If the seller has no interest in the property, the buyer will have no recourse against the seller.

Sometimes a quitclaim deed is used to clear title to the property. For example, if the seller is divorced, his ex-spouse may be asked to sign a quitclaim deed giving up any claim she might have to the property.

quitclaim deed
A deed in which the seller conveys any interest that he may have in the property; the least advantageous form of deed; often used to clear title to property.

Property Descriptions

A deed must include a detailed description of the property so that all parties, along with the governing body, understand which piece of property is being transferred. Most states use a combination of metes and bounds and tract maps to describe property.

Metes and Bounds.   **Metes and bounds** measure the size of a piece of property from a permanent marker on the property itself. The distance from the marker is generally measured in feet. The direction from the marker is measured in degrees, minutes, and seconds. For example, 33°20'35" would be read as 33 degrees, 20 minutes,

metes and bounds
A method of describing property based on distance from a permanent marker.

EXHIBIT 10.3   A General Warranty Deed from North Carolina

| Excise Tax | Recording Time, Book and Page |

Tax Lot No. .... Parcel Identifier No. ....

Verified by .... County on the .... day of ...., 19 ....

by ....

Mail after recording to ....

....

This instrument was prepared by ....

Brief description for the Index ....

NORTH CAROLINA GENERAL WARRANTY DEED

THIS DEED made this .... day of .... 19 ...., by and between

| GRANTOR | GRANTEE |

Enter in appropriate block for each party: name, address, and if, appropriate, character or entity, e.g., corporation or partnership.

The designation Grantor and Grantee as used herein shall include said parties, their heirs, successors, and assigns, and shall include singular, plural, masculine, feminine or neuter as required by context.

WITNESSETH, that the Grantor, for a valuable consideration paid by the Grantee, the receipt of which is hereby acknowledged, has and by these presents does grant, bargain, sell and convey unto the Grantee in fee simple, all that certain lot or parcel of land situated in the City of .... ,

.... Township, ... County, North Carolina and more particularly described as follows:

EXHIBIT 10.3   A General Warranty Deed from North Carolina *Concluded*

The property hereinabove described was acquired by Grantor by instrument recorded in ....
....
A map showing the above described property is recorded in Plat Book .... page ....
TO HAVE AND TO HOLD the aforesaid lot or parcel of land and all privileges and appurtenances thereto belonging to the Grantee in fee simple.

And the Grantor convenants with the Grantee, that Grantor is seized of the premises in fee simple, has the right to convey the same in fee simple, that title is marketable and free and clear of all encumbrances, and that Grantor will warrant and defend the title against the lawful claims of all persons whomsoever except for the exceptions hereinafter stated.
Title to the property hereinabove described is subject to the following exceptions:

   IN WITNESS WHEREOF, the Grantor has hereunto set his hand and seal, or if corporate, has caused this instrument to be signed in its corporate name by its duly authorized officers and its seal to be hereunto affixed by authority of its Board of Directors, the day and year first above written.

....   USE BLACK INK ONLY   ....(SEAL)
      (Corporate Name)
By: ....(SEAL)
....President
ATTEST: ....(SEAL)
....
.........................Secretary (Corporate Seal)   ....(SEAL)

SEAL-STAMP   NORTH CAROLINA, ...County.
   I, a Notary Public of the County and State aforesaid, certify that
   ....Grantor,
   personally appeared before me this day and acknowledged the execution of the foregoing instrument. Witness my hand and official stamp or seal, this .... day of ...., 19 ....

   My commission expires: .... Notary Public

   Use Black Ink

SEAL-STAMP   NORTH CAROLINA, ... County.
   I, a Notary Public of the County and State aforesaid, that ....,
   personally came before me this day and acknowledged that ....
   he is .... Secretary of ....
   a North Carolina corporation, and that by authority duly given and as the act of the corporation, the foregoing instrument was signed in its name by its .... President, sealed with its corporate seal and attested by .... as its ....Secretary. Witness my hand and official stamp or seal, this .... day of ...., 19 ....

   My commission expires: ....Notary Public

   Use Black Ink

The foregoing certificate(s) of ....
....
....
is/are certified to be correct. This instrument and this certificate are duly registered at the date and time and in the Book and Page shown on the first page hereof ....REGISTER OF DEEDS FOR .... COUNTY

By ....Deputy/Assistant-Register of Deeds

SOURCE: This form is used with the permission of the North Carolina Bar Association who publishes this form and others on behalf of the Real Property Section of the NCBA.

and 35 seconds. Changes in the direction of the measurement are indicated by a semi-colon: for example, 33°20'35"; 25°18'30".

Tract Maps.   In most suburban areas, developers purchase a large plot of land and subdivide it into lots for houses. In those cases, the subdivider (developer) must file a **tract map** with the city in which the property is located. The map shows the size and shape of each lot. The city council (or other government agency) reviews the map. If the map is approved, the map is then filed with the county. The property description of an individual lot might be as follows:

> Lot 264 of Tract 33 of the Cordova Country Subdivision in the City of Cordova, County of Shelby, State of Tennessee, as recorded in Tract Map 22, page 102.

Consider how easy it would be to transpose a number when typing the description. Studies have found that a considerable percentage of property descriptions are incorrect. Therefore, the legal secretary and/or paralegal should proofread the descriptions carefully and plot them out on a piece of paper (if possible) to determine whether the lines actually intersect. In most cases, it is advantageous to have a private survey of the land taken by a surveyor to be sure the description is correct.

Recording Deeds

Most states require that all deeds be recorded in the county or state where they were issued. Recording gives notice to the world that the individual named in the deed is the true owner of the property. Any other documents concerning the property should also be recorded.

MORTGAGES OR DEEDS OF TRUST

In most states, a purchaser who obtains a loan against the property has a **mortgage** on that property. The borrower (or **mortgagor**) borrows the money from the lender (or **mortgagee**), usually a bank or other lending institution. The borrower signs a promissory note that makes her liable for payment of the debt. Title to the property remains with the borrower, and the lender has a lien against the property. If the borrower defaults on the loan, the property may be sold for the benefit of the lender, with any additional funds from the sale being returned to the borrower. An example of the mortgage form used in New York is shown in Exhibit 10.4.

Some states use a **deed of trust** instead of a mortgage. The only difference between a mortgage and a deed of trust is that with a deed of trust the lender retains title to the property until the mortgage is paid. (Exhibit 10.5 shows an example of a deed of trust.)

Mortgages on the property that are recorded take precedence over any previously obtained mortgages that have not been recorded. In the event that the buyer fails to repay any of the loans, the lenders are paid in the order the mortgages were recorded. Thus, if a bank issues a loan on a piece of property and immediately records the note (or mortgage), this loan will take precedence over all loans recorded later. In some states, however, the first mortgage always takes precedence over a second or subsequent mortgage regardless of which is recorded first.

Check with the County Recorder's Office to determine your state's requirements and list them in the State Specific Information box.

---

tract map
A map of a subdivision showing the size and shape of the lots; used in describing property in deeds.

mortgage
A written instrument creating an interest in property as security for a loan against the property

mortgagor
The person who obtains a mortgage; the borrower.

mortgagee
The person or entity, such as a bank, that provides a mortgage; the lender.

deed of trust
A written instrument used in some states as a mortgage; resembles a mortgage except that title to property remains with the trustee who issues the loan.

STATE
SPECIFIC
INFORMATION

In the state of _____, mortgages/deeds of trust are/are not

recorded in the Office of the _____.

The order of precedence for loans against the property is as follows:

1. _____

2. _____

3. _____

EASEMENTS

An **easement** is a nonownership interest in land that entitles its owner to a limited use of another's property. The most common easements are for utility companies to install telephone lines, electric poles, or underground equipment. Some easements involve a right of way across another's property, as in the case of land located on a golf course or public beach. Sometimes an owner whose land is not accessible from the public road will have an easement over the adjoining property for a driveway. Remember, though, that although an easement enables a property owner to use a portion of another's land, the easement owner does not actually own the land where the easement is located.

Most easements are created by a deed. Since easements constitute an interest in land, they must be in writing and signed by the owner of the property. An **easement by necessity** is an exception to the writing requirement. Such an easement is created when someone sells a portion of a tract that is not accessible except by passing over another lot in the tract (such property is said to be "landlocked"). Easements by necessity are justified by the intention of the parties and the public policy requirement of access to one's property. For example, suppose William sold the front and back portions of a tract of land to separate buyers, but only the front portion had access to a public road. An easement by necessity would be created for the purchaser of the rear portion of the land. Even though an easement by necessity does not have to be in writing, a prospective buyer should examine the property carefully and request that any necessary easement be written to prevent possible legal problems with future owners of the property where the easement is. An easement by necessity ends when the necessity ceases. Therefore, if a new road provides access to previously inaccessible land, the easement would end.

NUISANCE

A **nuisance** is an invasion of a person's interest in the use and enjoyment of her property. A **private nuisance** affects only close neighbors, while a **public nuisance** affects the general public. For instance, if your neighbor plays her radio so loud that you cannot sleep at night, the loud music would constitute a private nuisance, while a chemical plant emitting pollutants would probably constitute a public nuisance. Most

easement
A nonownership interest in land that gives its owner the right to the limited use of land owned by another.

easement by necessity
An easement that is created when land that is not accessible without passing over another's property is sold; does not have to be in writing.

nuisance
The disturbance of an owner's quiet enjoyment of property; unreasonable interference with the use and enjoyment of one's land.

private nuisance
A nuisance that affects only people in the immediate vicinity, such as the owners of adjoining property.

public nuisance
A nuisance that affects the general public and not just the people in the immediate vicinity.

EXHIBIT 10.4   A Mortgage from New York

682—Mortgage (First) Statutory From M.
Individual or Corporation.

JULIUS BLUMBERG, INC., LAW BLANK PUBLISHERS

THIS IS A LEGAL INSTRUMENT AND SHOULD BE EXECUTED UNDER SUPERVISION OF AN ATTORNEY.

THIS MORTGAGE, made the   day of   , nineteen hundred and

BETWEEN

herein referred to as the mortgagor,

and

herein referred to as the mortgagee,

WITNESSETH, that to secure the payment of an indebtedness in the sum of

dollars,
lawful money of the United States, to be paid on the   day of   19
with interest thereon to be computed from   day of   , 19   , at the rate
of

per centum per annum, and to be paid

according to a certain bond, note or obligation bearing even date herewith, the mortgagor hereby
mortgages to the mortgagee **ALL**

AND the mortgagor covenants with the mortgagee as follows:
1.   That the mortgagor will pay the indebtedness as hereinbefore provided.
2.   That the mortgagor will keep the building on the premises insured against loss by fire for the benefit of the mortgagee; that he will assign and deliver the policies to the mortgagee; and that he will reim-
burse the mortgagee for any premiums paid for insurance made by the mortgagee on the mortgagor's
default in so insuring the buildings or in so assigning and delivering the policies.
3.   That no building on the premises shall be removed or demolished without the consent of the
mortgagee.
4.   That the whole of said principal sum and interest shall become due at the option of the mortgagee:
after default in the payment of any installment of principal or of interest for twenty days; or after default
in the payment of any tax, water rate, sewer rent or assessment for thirty days after notice and demand;
or after default after notice and demand either in assigning and delivering the policies insuring the buildings against loss by fire or in reimbursing the mortgagee for premiums paid on such insurance, as hereinbefore provided; or after default upon request in furnishing a statement of the amount due on the mortgage and whether any offsets or defenses exist against the mortgage debt, as hereinafter provided.
5.   That the holder of this mortgage, in any action to foreclose it, shall be entitled to the appointment of
a receiver.
6.   That the mortgagor will pay all taxes, assessments, sewer rents or water rates, and in default
thereof, the mortgagee may pay the same.
7.   That the mortgagor within six days upon request in person or within fifteen days upon request by

SOURCE: Forms may be purchased from Julius Blumberg, Inc., NYC 10013, or any of its dealers. Reproduction
prohibited. Reprinted with permission.

EXHIBIT 10.4   A Mortgage from New York *Concluded*

mail will furnish a written statement duly acknowledged of the amount due on this mortgage and whether any offsets or defenses exist against the mortgage debt.

8.   That notice and demand or request may be in writing and may be served in person or by mail.

9.   That the mortgagor warrants the title to the premises.

10.   That the mortgagor will, in compliance with Section 13 of the Lien Law, receive the advances secured hereby and will hold the right to receive such advances as a trust fund to be applied first for the purpose of paying the cost of the improvement and will apply the same first to the payment of the cost of the improvement before using any part of the total of the same for any other purpose.

This mortgage may not be changed orally.

IN WITNESS WHEREOF, this mortgage has been duly executed by the mortgagor.

IN PRESENCE OF:

STATE OF NEW YORK,   }
COUNTY OF   }   ss.:

On the   day of   19   ,
before me came
to me known, who, being by me duly sworn, did depose and say that   he resides at
                                                    in
          ; that   he is the
of
the corporation described in and which executed, the foregoing instrument; that   he knows the seal of said corporation; that the seal affixed to said instrument is such corporate seal; that it was so affixed by order of the Board of   of said corporation; and that   he signed his   name therein by like order.

STATE OF NEW YORK,   }
COUNTY OF   }   ss.:

On the   day of   19
before me came

to me known to be the individual described in, and who executed the foregoing instrument, and acknowledged that he executed the same.

TO

Mortgage

Dated, ..., 19.....
Amount, $ ....
Due, ..., 19.....
Int. Payable ....

The land affected by the within instrument lies in

Record and return to

Reserve this space for use of Recording Office.

EXHIBIT 10.5   A Deed of Trust from North Carolina

SATISFACTION: The debt secured by the within Deed of Trust together with the note(s) secured thereby has been satisfied in full.

This the .... day of ...., 19 ....

Signed: ....

....

....

Mail after recording to:

....

....

....

This instrument prepared by:

....

Recording: Time, Book and Page

NORTH CAROLINA DEED OF TRUST

THIS DEED of TRUST made this .... day of ...., 19 ......, by and between:

GRANTOR	TRUSTEE	BENEFICIARY
		SOUTHERN NATIONAL BANK OF NORTH CAROLINA, a national banking association

Enter in appropriate block for each party: name, address, and, if appropriate, character of entity, e.g., corporation or partnership.

The designation Grantor, Trustee, and Beneficiary as used herein shall include said parties, their heirs, successors, and assigns, and shall include singular, plural, masculine, feminine or neuter as required by context.

WITNESSETH: The Grantor is indebted to the Beneficiary in the sum of _____

_____DOLLARS($ ....)

(the "Debt") for money loaned, as evidenced by promissory Note(s) of even date herewith, the terms of which are incorporated herein by reference.

NOW, THEREFORE, as security for the Debt, together with interest thereon, and as security for all renewals, extensions, deferments, amortizations and reamortizations thereof, in whole or in part, together with interest thereon whether at the same or different rates, and for a valuable consideration, receipt of which is hereby acknowledged, the Grantor has bargained, sold, granted and conveyed and does by these presents bargain, sell, grant and convey to the Trustee, his heirs, or successors, and assigns, the real property situated in the City of _____, _____Township, _____County, State of North Carolina, particularly described as follows:

DESCRIPTION SET FORTH HEREINBELOW AND ON SCHEDULE "A", IF ANY, ATTACHED HERETO AND MADE A PART HEREOF

TO HAVE AND TO HOLD said real property, including all buildings, improvements and fixtures now or hereafter, located thereon, with all the rights, privileges and appurtenances thereunto belonging, to the Trustee, his heirs, or successors, and assigns forever, upon the trusts, terms and conditions, and for the uses hereinafter set forth.

If the Grantor shall pay the Debt secured hereby in accordance with the terms of the note(s) evidencing the same, and all renewals, extensions, deferments, amortizations and reamortizations thereof, in whole or in part, together with interest thereon, and shall comply with all the covenants, terms and conditions of the deed of trust, then this conveyance shall be null and void and may be cancelled of record at the request of the Grantor. If, however, there shall be any default in any of the covenants, terms, or conditions of the Note(s) secured hereby, or any failure or neglect to comply with the covenants, terms, or conditions contained in this deed of trust, then and in any of such events, if the default is not made good within (15) days, the Note(s) shall, at the option of the Beneficiary, at once become due and payable without notice, and it shall be lawful for and the duty of the Trustee, upon request of the Beneficiary, to sell the land herein conveyed at public auction for cash, after having first given such notice of hearing as to commencement of foreclosure proceedings and obtaining such findings or leave of court as may be then required by law and giving such notice and advertising the time and place of such sale in such manner as may be then provided by law, and upon such and any resales and upon compliance with the then law relating to foreclosure proceedings to convey title to the purchaser in fee simple.

The proceeds of the Sale shall, after the Trustee retains his commission, be applied to the costs of sale, the amount due on the Note(s) hereby secured and otherwise as required by the then existing law relating to foreclosures. The Trustee's commission shall be five per cent of the gross proceeds of the sale or the minimum sum of $ .... whichever is greater, for a completed foreclosure. In the event foreclosure is commenced, but not completed, the Grantor shall pay all expenses incurred by Trustee and a partial commission computed on five per cent of the outstanding indebtedness or the above stated minimum sum, whichever is greater, in accordance with the following schedule, to wit: one-fourth thereof before the Trustee issues a hearing on the right to foreclose; one-half thereof after issuance of said notice; three-fourths thereof after such hearing; and the greater of the full commission or minimum after the initial sale.

And the said Grantor does hereby covenant and agree with the Trustee and with the Beneficiary as follows:

1. INSURANCE. Grantor shall keep all improvements on said land, now or hereafter erected constantly insured for the benefit of the Beneficiary against loss by fire, windstorm and such other casualties and contingencies, in such manner and in such companies and for such amounts as may be satisfactory to or required by the Beneficiary. Grantor shall purchase such insurance, pay all premiums therefor, and shall

EXHIBIT 10.5   A Deed of Trust from North Carolina *Concluded*

deliver to Beneficiary such policies along with evidence of premium payment as long as the Note(s) secured hereby remain unpaid. If Grantor fails to purchase such insurance, pay the premiums therefor or deliver said policies with mortgagee clause satisfactory to Beneficiary attached thereto, along with evidence of payment of premiums thereon, then Beneficiary, at his option, may purchase such insurance. Such amounts paid by Beneficiary shall be added to the Note(s) secured by this Deed of Trust, and shall be due and payable upon demand by Grantor to Beneficiary.

2. TAXES, ASSESSMENTS, CHARGES. Grantor shall pay all taxes, assessments and charges as may be lawfully levied against said premises within thirty (30) days after the same shall become due. In the event that Grantor fails to so pay all taxes, assessments and charges as herein required, then Beneficiary, at his option, may pay the same and the amounts so paid shall be added to the Note(s), secured by this Deed of Trust, and shall be due and payable upon demand by Grantor to Beneficiary.

3. PARTIAL RELEASE. Grantor shall not be entitled to the partial release of any of the above described property unless a specific provision providing therefor is included in this Deed of Trust. In the event a partial release provision is included in this Deed of Trust, Grantor must strictly comply with the terms thereof. Notwithstanding anything herein contained, Grantor shall not be entitled to any release of property unless Grantor is not in default and is in full compliance with all of the terms and provisions of the Note(s), this Deed of Trust, and any other instrument that may be securing said Note(s).

4. WASTE. The Grantor covenants that he will keep the premises herein conveyed in as good order, repair and condition as they are now, reasonable wear and tear accepted, and that he will not commit or permit any waste.

5. WARRANTIES. Grantor covenants with Trustee and Beneficiary that he is seized of the premises in fee simple, has the right to convey the same in fee simple, that title is marketable and free and clear of all encumbrances, and that he will warrant and defend the title against any lawful claims of all persons whomsoever, except for the exceptions hereinafter stated. Title to the property hereinabove described is subject to the following exceptions:

6. CONVEYANCE ACCELERATION: If Grantor sells, conveys, transfers, assigns or disposes of the hereinabove-described real property or any part thereof or interest therein, by any means or method, whether voluntary or involuntary, without the written consent of Beneficiary, then at the option of Beneficiary and without notice to Grantor, all sums of money secured hereby, both principal and interest, shall immediately become due and payable and in default, notwithstanding anything herein or in the Note(s) secured hereby to the contrary.

7. SUBSTITUTION OF TRUSTEE. Grantor and Trustee covenant and agree to and with Beneficiary that in case the said Trustee, or any successor trustee, shall die, become incapable of acting, renounce his trust, or for other similar or dissimilar reason become unacceptable to the holder of the Note(s), then the holder of the Note(s) may appoint, in writing, a trustee to take the place of the Trustee; and upon the probate and registration of the same, the trustee thus appointed shall succeed to all the rights, powers, and duties of the Trustee.

8. CIVIL ACTION. In the event that the Trustee is named as a party to any civil action as Trustee in this Deed of Trust, the Trustee shall be entitled to employ an attorney at law, including himself if he is a licensed attorney, to represent him in said action and the reasonable attorney's fees of the Trustee in such action shall be paid by Beneficiary and charged to the Note(s) and secured by this Deed of Trust.

9. PRIOR LIENS. Default under the terms of any instrument secured by a lien to which the deed of trust is subordinate shall constitute default hereunder.

IN WITNESS THEREOF, the Grantor has hereunto set his hand and seal or if corporate, has caused this instrument to be signed in its corporate name by its duly authorized officers and its seal to be hereunto affixed by authority of its Board of Directors, the day and year first above written.

(Corporate Name)

By: ....(SEAL)

....President   ....(SEAL)

ATTEST: ....(SEAL)

....Secretary (Corporate Seal)   ....(SEAL)

USE BLACK INK ONLY

SEAL-STAMP   *Use Black Ink*

STATE OF NORTH CAROLINA, COUNTY OF ....
I, ...a notary public of said county do hereby certify that ....Grantor, personally appeared before me this day and acknowledged the execution of the foregoing instrument. Witness my hand and official stamp or seal, this .... day of ...., 19 ....
My commission expires: ....Notary Public

SEAL-STAMP   *Use Black Ink*

STATE OF NORTH CAROLINA, COUNTY OF ....
I, ...a Notary Public of the County and State aforesaid, certify that .... , personally came before me this day and acknowledged that .... he is .... Secretary of .... , a North Carolina corporation, and that by authority duly given and as the act of the corporation, the foregoing instrument was signed in its name by its .... President, sealed with its corporate seal and attested by ....
.... as its...Secretary.
Witness my hand and official stamp or seal, this .... day of ...., 19 ....
My commission expires: ....Notary Public

The foregoing Certificate(s) of ....
is are certified to be correct. This instrument and this certificate are duly registered at the date and time and in the Book and Page shown on the first page hereof,
.... REGISTER OF DEEDS FOR ....COUNTY
By .... Deputy Assistant - Register of Deeds

SOURCE: This form is used with the permission of the North Carolina Bar Association who publishes this form and others on behalf of the Real Property Section of the NCBA.

states have passed statutes that protect the public from many forms of nuisance. City ordinances may prohibit residential property from being used for purposes that are noisy or offensive to neighbors. Thus, the neighbor's loud music may violate a municipal ordinance, and a call to the local police department might be helpful if talking to the neighbor does not solve the problem.

LEASES AND RENTAL AGREEMENTS

lease
A rental agreement between a landlord and tenant granting the tenant the right to possession of the property for terms prescribed in the lease. The tenant is known as the lessee; the landlord is the lessor.

lessor
A landlord; one who rents property to a tenant.

landlord
One who rents property to someone else; a lessor.

lessee
A tenant; someone who rents property from someone else.

tenant
One who rents property from someone else; a lessee.

A **lease** is a contract for the use of land or buildings, but not for their ownership. The **lessor** (the person who owns the property and rents it to someone else) is called the **landlord,** and the **lessee** (the person who rents the property from the landlord) is called the **tenant.** The tenant pays rent to the landlord for the use of the property.

Written Leases

The Statute of Frauds requires that all interests in land for one year or more must be in writing. Therefore, all leases or rental agreements for a year or more must be in writing and signed by both the landlord and the tenant. It is also advisable to put shorter term leases in writing to protect both parties' interests. The more specifically the rights and responsibilities of both parties are spelled out in the lease, the less likely there will be misunderstandings about the terms. The lease should include the following:

1. The names of the landlord and tenant. The landlord should require that the names of all tenants who occupy the premises be listed.

2. The lease term—inclusive dates.

3. The amount of the rent and when it is due.

4. Which party is responsible for utilities and insurance.

5. Whether the tenant may sublease the property. Most landlords prefer to prohibit subleases.

6. Persons other than the tenant who may live on the property.

7. The legal obligations of the tenant and landlord and the recourse each has for a breach of the lease terms. For instance, what is the landlord's recourse if the tenant does not pay rent? Are late payments subject to a flat fee, or is interest charged? If the latter, what is the interest rate?

8. Other fees charged, such as cleaning fees or a deposit. The landlord should be aware that any amounts deposited and not used are refundable to the tenant. While the tenant may be charged for damages to the premises, she may not be charged for ordinary wear and tear.

9. Which party is responsible for repairs to the premises. Some state statutes cover this area.

10. What the rented premises include, such as storage areas and/or garage space.

11. The landlord's right to enter the premises. Most states forbid a landlord to enter rented areas unless an emergency exists; other states allow entry by the landlord if it is specified in the lease.

Standardized leases are available on computer disk and in form books. Form leases where you merely fill in the blanks may be purchased in a stationery store. However, some attorneys prefer to use the standardized lease as a starting point and add their own clauses to suit the individual client's situation. Whenever a lease is prepared, the clauses should be written so that the particular client receives the maximum amount of protection. A sample lease is shown in Exhibit 10.6.

Oral Rental Agreements

Some landlords do not require a written agreement for a **month-to-month rental.** In this case, the tenant occupies the premises on a monthly basis and may be asked to leave with a month's notice. Rent is paid once a month. The tenant only has a right to occupy the premises for a month at a time. Other **periodic tenancies** may exist for various terms of less than a year, such as a week, three months, or six months.

Eviction or Unlawful Detainer

Landlords who wish to evict a tenant must use a summary eviction proceeding in some states and unlawful detainer in others. The basic procedures are similar, and the end result is the same—the tenant must vacate the premises. Tenants may be evicted for violating the terms of the lease agreement or for failing to pay rent.

Summary Eviction.   With the **summary eviction proceeding,** certain forms must be completed and filed with the court. The forms must specify the reasons for the **eviction.** After the forms are filed, the tenant must be served with the documents and has a set period of time in which to file an appearance. If no appearance is forthcoming from the tenant or the tenant appears but is unable to show why he should not be evicted, a court officer carries out the eviction proceeding.

Unlawful Detainer.   **Unlawful detainer** is a more complex system of evicting tenants that is used in California and other states. It requires that the tenant first be served with a Three-Day Notice to Pay Rent or Quit (see Exhibit 10.7). If no response is forthcoming from the tenant within three days, then the landlord's attorney prepares a Complaint for Unlawful Detainer, which is served on the tenant and filed with the court, along with a Summons for Unlawful Detainer (see Exhibits 10.8 and 10.9). The landlord must sign a verification for the complaint, which may be either a form or a pleading. All individuals occupying the premises must be served. The damages requested in the complaint will consist of possession of the premises, past-due rent, attorney fees, and, in some cases, **treble damages** (three times the actual damages). To collect treble damages, the landlord must prove malicious willfulness on the part of the tenant.

The tenant must reply to the complaint within five days of personal service. Note that this date differs considerably from the thirty-day requirement for other complaints.

If the tenant fails to respond, then the landlord can enter a **default judgment.** If the tenant responds by filing an answer within the allotted time, a court hearing will be held where each party can present his side. Then the court will issue a ruling.

In the case of a default judgment or if the landlord prevails in court, the court will issue (1) a judgment for the amount of rent due and (2) a Writ of Possession in favor of the landlord. The sheriff will serve the tenant with a Writ of Execution for Possession of Real Property (see Exhibit 10.10). If the tenant does not vacate the premises within five days, the sheriff may physically remove the tenant and his pos-

tenant at sufferance
A tenant who remains unlawfully on the premises after being served with a Writ of Execution for Possession of Real Property.

sessions from the premises. Tenants remaining unlawfully on the premises are called **tenants at sufferance.** Exhibit 10.11 illustrates the steps in the eviction process using unlawful detainer.

Find out what procedure is used for eviction in your own state, and describe it in the State Specific Information box.

STATE SPECIFIC INFORMATION

The following procedure is used for eviction in the state of _____:

_____

_____

_____

SUMMARY

The law of real property includes both the transfer of property and landlord/tenant relationships. Real property includes land, buildings, and items permanently attached to the land. Personal property consists of objects that are movable and not permanently attached to the ground.

Most property is owned in fee simple, which signifies absolute ownership. Property may be owned with others as tenants in common or joint tenancy. Spouses may hold property as community property, tenancy by the entirety, joint tenancy, or tenancy in common.

Condominiums and cooperatives are subject to special restrictions. A condominium owner owns the area inside the boundaries of the condominium unit and shares the use of the common areas with the other condominium owners. A cooperative owner owns a share of stock represented by a unit within the complex.

A transfer of real property begins with the location of a real estate agent and the preparation of a listing agreement. Once the seller has accepted an offer, a real estate sales contract is prepared. A title insurance company will determine title to the property and check to make sure there are no liens or encumbrances on it. At the closing (or escrow), a new deed will transfer title to the new owners.

Most purchasers do not pay cash for the property but obtain loans from banks or other lending institutions. The loan is known as a mortgage or deed of trust, depending on the state where the property is located.

Easements constitute nonownership interests in property. They entitle the easement owner to have limited use of another's property.

Leases and rental agreements for a year or more must be in writing. For the protection of both the landlord and the tenant, it is advisable to have all leases and rental agreements in writing regardless of the term. In the event that the tenant breaches the agreement or fails to pay rent, eviction proceedings may be instituted.

EXHIBIT 10.6   A Sample Lease

THIS LEASE, made this_____day of_____, between
_____, hereinafter called Owner, and _____
_____, hereinafter call the Tenant:

 WITNESSETH: Owner does hereby lease and rent unto Tenant, and Tenant does hereby take as tenant under the Owner the following property :_____
_____, to be used by Tenant during the term
only of _____ months, beginning _____, and ending
_____, inclusive.

 IN CONSIDERATION WHEREOF, and of the covenants hereinafter expressed, it is covenanted and agreed as follows:

 1.   Tenant agrees to pay to Owner as rent for said premises, the sum of $ _____ per _____, payable in advance.

 2.   Tenant shall not permit any unlawful or immoral practice to be committed on the premises, or to so occupy the premises as to constitute a nuisance.

 3.   Tenant shall not have the right or power to sublet the premises or any part thereof, or to transfer or assign this lease without the written consent of Owner.

 4.   Tenant has examined the premises, is satisfied with the physical condition and his taking possession is conclusive evidence of receipt of them in good order and repair, and Tenant agrees that no representation as to condition of repair has been made.

 5.   If the leased premises shall be abandoned or become vacant during the term of this lease, then in such case Owner shall have the right at his option, to take possession of the leased premises, re-enter the leased premises and annul and terminate this lease.

 6.   During the period of his tenancy Tenant agrees to maintain this property in as good state as he finds it, reasonable wear and tear excepted; and will have repaired, at his expense, any damage done to the water, gas, and electrical fixtures; replace all broken glass and burned out grates; keep sinks, lavatories, commodes, and sewer lines open; repair any plumbing or heating equipment that may be damaged by his negligence; replace all lost or broken keys.

 7.   In the event the leased premises are rendered untenantable by fire, rain, wind, or other cause beyond the control of Tenant, or are condemned and ordered torn down by the properly constituted authorities of the State, County or City, then in either of these events the lease shall cease and terminate as of the date of such destruction.

 8.   Owner shall not be held liable for any injury or damage whatsoever which may arise on account of any defect in the building or premises, or for rain, wind or other causes, all claims for such injury or damage being hereby expressly waived by Tenant.

 9.   Owner in person or by agent shall have the right at all reasonable times to enter the leased premises and inspect the same and to show the same to prospective tenants or purchasers. Owner may make such repairs and alterations as may be deemed by Owner necessary to the preservation of the leased premises or the buildings, but Owner is not required to do any repairing upon the premises leased unless so agreed in writing in this lease.

 10. Tenant shall deposit the sum of $ _____ as a security deposit, which deposit will be refunded to Tenant upon tenant vacating the property at the expiration of the Lease. Owner shall not refund the security deposit in the event Tenant vacates prior to the expiration of the Lease. Owner shall deduct from the security deposit any amount necessary to clean or repair the property. Owner may also retain the security deposit and apply it to any unpaid rent.

 11. Other conditions: _____
_____
_____
_____
_____
_____

 12. Should Tenant fail to pay the rent or any part thereof, as the same becomes due, or violates any other term or condition of this lease, Owner shall then have the right, at his option, to re-enter the leased premises and terminate the lease; such re-entry shall not bar the right of recovery of rent or damages for breach of covenants, nor shall the receipt of rent after conditions broken or be deemed a waiver of forfeiture. And in order to entitle Owner to re-enter it shall not be necessary to give notice of rent being due and unpaid or of other conditions broken to make demands for rent, the execution of this lease being signed by the parties hereto being sufficient notice of the rent being due and demand for the same.

 IN WITNESS WHEREOF, the parties hereto have hereunto set their signatures and seals, the day and year first above written.

_____	_____	_____	_____
Tenant	(date signed)	Owner	(date signed)
_____	_____	_____	_____
Tenant	(date signed)	Owner	(date signed)

EXHIBIT 10.7   Three-Day Notice to Pay Rent or Quit

3-DAY NOTICE

To Pay Rent or Quit

TO _____

TENANT(S) IN POSSESSION OF THE PREMISES AT

_____
(Street Address)

City of _____, County of _____, California

YOU ARE HEREBY NOTIFIED that the rent on the above-described premises occupied by you, in the amount of $ _____, for the period from _____ to _____, is now due and payable.

YOU ARE HEREBY REQUIRED to pay the said rent within THREE (3) days from the date of service on you of this notice or to vacate and surrender possession of the premises. In the event you fail to do so, legal proceedings will be instituted against you to recover possession of the premises, declare the forfeiture of the rental agreement or lease under which you occupy the premises, and recover rents, damages and costs of suit.

DATE:_____   _____
                               OWNER/MANAGER

EXHIBIT 10.8   A Complaint for Unlawful Detainer

ATTORNEY OR PARTY WITHOUT ATTORNEY (NAME AND ADDRESS): TELEPHONE:	FOR COURT USE ONLY

ATTORNEY FOR (NAME):

Insert name of court, judicial district or branch court, if any, and post office and street address:

PLAINTIFF:

DEFENDANT:

DOES 1 TO _____

COMPLAINT— Unlawful Detainer	CASE NUMBER:

1. This pleading including attachments and exhibits consists of the following number of pages: _____
2. a. Plaintiff is ☐ an individual over the age of 18 years.   ☐ a partnership.
       ☐ a public agency.   ☐ a corporation.
       ☐ other *(specify):*
   b. ☐ Plaintiff has complied with the fictitious business name laws and is doing business under the fictitious name of *(specify):*
3. Defendants named above are in possession of the premises located at *(street address, city and county):*

4. Plaintiff's interest in the premises is ☐ as owner   ☐ other *(specify):*

5. The true names and capacities of defendants sued as Does are unknown to plaintiff.
6. a. On or about *(date):*   defendants *(names):*

      agreed to rent the premises for a ☐ month-to-month tenancy ☐ other tenancy *(specify):*
      at a rent of $_____ payable ☐ monthly ☐ other *(specify frequency):*
      due on the ☐ first of the month ☐ other day *(specify):*
   b. This ☐ written ☐ oral agreement was made with
         ☐ plaintiff   ☐ plaintiff's predecessor in interest
         ☐ plaintiff's agent   ☐ other *(specify):*
   c. ☐ The defendants not named in item 6.a. are
         ☐ subtenants   ☐ assignees   ☐ other *(specify):*
   d. ☐ The agreement was later changed as follows *(specify):*

   e. ☐ A copy of the written agreement is attached and labeled Exhibit A.
7. Plaintiff has performed all conditions of the rental agreement.
8. ☐ a. The following notice was served on defendant *(name):*
         ☐ 3-day notice to pay rent or quit   ☐ 3-day notice to quit
         ☐ 3-day notice to perform covenant or quit ☐ 30-day notice to quit
         ☐ other *(specify):*
   b. The period stated in the notice expired on *(date):*   and defendants failed
      to comply with the requirements of the notice by that date.
   c. All facts stated in the notice are true.
   d. ☐ The notice included an election of forfeiture.
   e. ☐ A copy of the notice is attached and labeled Exhibit B.
                              (Continued)

Form Approved by the
Judicial Council of California
Effective January 1, 1982
Rule 982.1(90)

COMPLAINT— Unlawful Detainer   CCP 425.12

EXHIBIT 10.8   A Complaint for Unlawful Detainer *Concluded*

SHORT TITLE:	CASE NUMBER:

COMPLAINT—Unlawful Detainer   Page two

9. ☐ a. The notice referred to in item 8 was served
   ☐ by personally handing a copy to defendant on *(date):*
   ☐ by leaving a copy with *(name or description):*   , a person
   of suitable age or discretion, on *(date):*   at defendant's ☐ residence
      ☐ business AND mailing a copy to defendant at his place of residence on *(date):*
      because defendant cannot be found at his residence or usual place of business.
   ☐ by posting a copy on the premises on *(date):*   (☐ and giving a copy
   to a person residing at the premises) AND mailing a copy to defendant at the premises on
   (date):
      ☐ because defendant's residence and usual place of business cannot be ascertained OR
      ☐ because no person of suitable age or discretion can there be found.
   ☐ *(not for 3-day notice. See Civil Code section 1946 before using)* by sending a copy by certified or
   registered mail addressed to defendant on *(date):*
   b. ☐ Information about service of the notice on the other defendants is contained in attachment 9.

10. ☐ Plaintiff demands possession from each defendant because of expiration of a fixed term lease.
11. ☐ At the time the 3-day notice to pay rent or quit was served, the amount of rent due was $ _____
12. ☐ The fair rental value of the premises is $_____ per day.
13. Plaintiff is entitled to immediate possession of the premises.
14. ☐ Defendants' continued possession is malicious, and plaintiff is entitled to treble damages. *(State specific facts supporting this claim in attachment 14.)*
15. ☐ A written agreement between the parties provides for attorney fees.
16. ☐ Defendants' tenancy is subject to the local rent control or eviction control ordinance of *(city or county, title of ordinance, and date of passage):*

   Plaintiff has met all applicable requirements of the ordinances.
17. ☐ Other allegations are stated in attachment 17.
18. Plaintiff remits to the jurisdictional limit, if any, of the court.

19. PLAINTIFF REQUESTS
   a. possession of the premises.
   b. ☐ costs incurred in this proceeding.
   c. ☐ past due rent of $_____
   d. ☐ damages at the rate of $_____ per day.
   e. ☐ treble the amount of rent and damages found due.
   f. ☐ reasonable attorney fees.
   g. ☐ forfeiture of the agreement.
   h. ☐ other *(specify):*

. . . .   _____
                 (Type or print name)   *(Signature of plaintiff or attorney)*

VERIFICATION
(Use a different verification form if the verification is by an attorney or for a corporation or partnership.)

I am the plaintiff in this proceeding and have read this complaint. I declare under penalty of perjury under the laws of the State of California that this complaint is true and correct.

Date:

. . . .   _____
                 (Type or print name)   *(Signature of plaintiff)*

[982.1(90)]   Page two

EXHIBIT 10.9   A Summons for Unlawful Detainer

SUMMONS
(CITACION JUDICIAL)

982(a)(11)
UNLAWFUL DETAINER—EVICTION
(PROCESO DE DESAHUCIO—EVICCION)

NOTICE TO DEFENDANT: *(Aviso a acusado)*

FOR COURT USE ONLY
(SOLO PARA USO DE LA CORTE)

YOU ARE BEING SUED BY PLAINTIFF:
(A Ud. le está demandando)

You have **5 DAYS** after this summons is served on you to file a typewritten response at this court. (To calculate the five days, count Saturday and Sunday, but do not count other court holidays.)	*Después de que le entreguen esta citación judicial usted tiene un plazo de 5 DIAS para presentar una respuesta escrita a máquina en esta corte. (Para calcular los cinco días, cuente el sábado y el domingo, pero no cuente ningún otro día feriado observado por la corte).*
A letter or phone call will not protect you. Your typewritten response must be in proper legal form if you want the court to hear your case.	*Una carta o una llamada telefónica no le ofrecerá protección; su respuesta escrita a máquina tiene que cumplir con las formalidades legales apropiadas si usted quiere que la corte escuche su caso.*
If you do not file your response on time, you may lose the case, you may be evicted, and your wages, money and property may be taken without further warning from the court.	*Si usted no presenta su respuesta a tiempo, puede perder el caso, le pueden obligar a desalojar su casa, y le pueden quitar su salario, su dinero y otras cosas de su propiedad sin aviso adicional por parte de la corte.*
There are other legal requirements. You may want to call an attorney right away. If you do not know an attorney, you may call an attorney referral service or a legal aid office *(listed in the phone book).*	*Existen otros requisitos legales. Puede que usted quiera llamar a un abogado inmediatamente. Si no conoce a un abogado, puede llamar a un servicio de referencia de abogados o a una oficina de ayuda legal (vea el directorio telefónico).*

The name and address of the court is: *(El nombre y dirección de la corte es)*

CASE NUMBER: *(Número del caso)*

The name, address, and telephone number of plaintiff's attorney, or plaintiff without an attorney, is:
(El nombre, la dirección y el número de teléfono del abogado del demandante, o del demandante que no tiene abogado, es)

DATE: Clerk, by _____, Deputy
(Fecha)   *(Actuario)*   *(Delegado)*

[SEAL]

NOTICE TO THE PERSON SERVED: You are served
1. ☐ as an individual defendant.
2. ☐ as the person sued under the fictitious name of *(specify)*:

3. ☐ on behalf of *(specify)*:

   under: ☐ CCP 416.10 (corporation)   ☐ CCP 416.60 (minor)
   ☐ CCP 416.20 (defunct corporation)   ☐ CCP 416.70 (conservatee)
   ☐ CCP 416.40 (association or partnership) ☐ CCP 416.90 (individual)
   ☐ other:
4. ☐ by personal delivery on *(date)*:
   (See reverse for Proof of Service)

Form Adopted by Rule 982
Judicial Council of California
982(a)(11) [Rev. January 1, 1990]

SUMMONS — UNLAWFUL DETAINER

Code Civ. Proc., §§ 412.20, 1197

SOURCE: Reprinted from California Judicial Council Forms, published by West Publishing Company.

EXHIBIT 10.9   A Summons for Unlawful Detainer *Concluded*

PLAINTIFF:	CASE NUMBER:
DEFENDANT:	

PROOF OF SERVICE

1. At the time of service I was at least 18 years of age and not a party to this action, and **I served copies** of the *(specify documents)*:

2. a. Party served *(specify name of party as shown on the documents served)*:

   b. Person served: ☐ party in item 2a ☐ other *(specify name and title or relationship to the party named in item 2a)*:

   c. Address:

3. I served the party named in item 2
   a. ☐ **by personally delivering** the copies (1) on *(date)*:   (2) at *(time)*:
   b. ☐ **by leaving** the copies with or in the presence of *(name and title or relationship to person indicated in item 2b)*:

       (1) ☐ **(business)** a person at least 18 years of age apparently in charge at the office or usual place of business of the person served. I informed him or her of the general nature of the papers.
       (2) ☐ **(home)** a competent member of the household (at least 18 years of age) at the dwelling house or usual place of abode of the person served. I informed him or her of the general nature of the papers.
       (3) on *(date)*:   (4) at *(time)*:
       (5) ☐ A **declaration of diligence** is attached. *(Substituted service on natural person, minor, conservatee, or candidate.)*
   c. ☐ **by mailing** the copies to the person served, addressed as shown in item 2c, by first-class mail, postage prepaid,
       (1) on *(date)*:   (2) from *(city)*:
       (3) ☐ with two copies of the Notice and Acknowledgment of Receipt and a postage-paid return envelope addressed to me.
       (4) ☐ to an address outside California with return receipt requested.   ← *(Attach completed form.)* ➚
   d. ☐ **by causing copies to be mailed. A declaration of mailing is attached.**
   e. ☐ **other** *(specify other manner of service and authorizing code section)*:

4. The "Notice to the Person Served" (on the summons) was completed as follows:
   a. ☐ as an individual defendant.
   b. ☐ as the person sued under the fictitious name of *(specify)*:
   c. ☐ on behalf of *(specify)*:
       under: ☐ CCP 416.10 (corporation)   ☐ CCP 416.60 (minor)   ☐ other:
             ☐ CCP 416.20 (defunct corporation)   ☐ CCP 416.70 (conservatee)
             ☐ CCP 416.40 (association or partnership) ☐ CCP 416.90 (individual)

5. **Person serving** *(name, address, and telephone No.)*:
       a. Fee for service: $
       b. ☐ Not a registered California process server.
       c. ☐ Exempt from registration under B&P § 22350(b).
       d. ☐ Registered California process server.
           (1) ☐ Employee or independent contractor.
           (2) Registration No.:
           (3) County:

6. ☐ **I declare** under penalty of perjury under the laws of the State of California that the foregoing is true and correct.

7. ☐ **I am a California sheriff, marshal, or constable and** I certify that the foregoing is true and correct.

Date: ▶

_____
(SIGNATURE)

EXHIBIT 10.10   A Writ of Execution

ATTORNEY OR PARTY WITHOUT ATTORNEY *(Name and Address)* :	TELEPHONE NO.:	FOR RECORDER'S USE ONLY

☐ Recording requested by and return to:

☐ ATTORNEY FOR   ☐ JUDGMENT CREDITOR   ☐ ASSIGNEE OF RECORD

NAME OF COURT:
STREET ADDRESS:
MAILING ADDRESS:
CITY AND ZIP CODE:
BRANCH NAME:

PLAINTIFF:

DEFENDANT:

WRIT OF	☐ EXECUTION (Money Judgment) ☐ POSSESSION OF ☐ Personal Property ☐ Real Property ☐ SALE	CASE NUMBER: FOR COURT USE ONLY

1. **To the Sheriff or any Marshal or Constable of the County of:**

You are directed to enforce the judgment described below with daily interest and your costs as provided by law.

2. **To any registered process server:** You are authorized to serve this writ only in accord with CCP 699.080 or CCP 715.040.

3. *(Name)* :
   is the ☐ judgment creditor   ☐ assignee of record
   whose address is shown on this form above the court's name.

4. **Judgment debtor** *(name and last known address)* :

   ☐ additional judgment debtors on reverse
5. **Judgment entered** on *(date)* :
6. ☐ **Judgment renewed** on *(dates)* :

7. **Notice of sale** under this writ
   a. ☐ has not been requested.
   b. ☐ has been requested *(see reverse)*.
8. ☐ Joint debtor information on reverse.

[SEAL]

9. ☐ See reverse for information on real or personal property to be delivered under a writ of possession or sold under a writ of sale.
10. ☐ This writ is issued on a sister-state judgment.

11. Total judgment . . . . $
12. Costs after judgment (per filed order or memo CCP 685.090) . $
13. Subtotal *(add 11 and 12)* . . . . . $ _____
14. Credits . . . . $
15. Subtotal *(subtract 14 from 13)* . $ _____
16. Interest after judgment (per filed affidavit CCP 685.050) . . . . . . $
17. Fee for issuance of writ . . . . . . $
18. **Total** *(add 15, 16, and 17)* . . . . $ _____
19. Levying officer: Add daily interest from date of writ *(at the legal rate on 15)* of . . . . $

20. ☐ The amounts called for in items 11–19 are different for each debtor. These amounts are stated for each debtor on Attachment 20.

Issued on
(date) :   Clerk, by _____ , Deputy

— NOTICE TO PERSON SERVED: SEE REVERSE FOR IMPORTANT INFORMATION —

(Continued on reverse)

Form Approved by the Judicial Council of California EJ-130 [Rev. September 30, 1991*]	**WRIT OF EXECUTION**	Code of Civil Procedure, §§ 699.520, 712.010, 715.010 *See note on reverse.

EXHIBIT 10.10   A Writ of Execution *Concluded*

SHORT TITLE:

CASE NUMBER:

Items continued from the first page:

4. ☐ **Additional judgment debtor** *(name and last known address)*:

7. ☐ **Notice of sale** has been requested by *(name and address)*:

8. ☐ **Joint debtor** was declared bound by the judgment (CCP 989–994)
   a. on *(date)*:   a. on *(date)*:
   b. name and address of joint debtor: b. name and address of joint debtor:

   c. ☐ additional costs against certain joint debtors *(itemize)*:

9. ☐ *(Writ of Possession or Writ of Sale)*   **Judgment** was entered for the following:
   a. ☐ Possession of real property: The complaint was filed on *(date)*:   *(Check (1) or (2))*:
      (1) ☐   The Prejudgment Claim of Right to Possession was served in compliance with CCP 415.46.
             The judgment includes all tenants, subtenants, named claimants, and other occupants of the premises.
      (2) ☐   The Prejudgment Claim of Right to Possession was NOT served in compliance with CCP 415.46.
             (a) $ was the daily rental value on the date the complaint was filed.
             (b) The court will hear objections to enforcement of the judgment under CCP 1174.3 on the following
                 dates *(specify)*:
   b. ☐ Possession of personal property
      ☐   If delivery cannot be had, then for the value *(itemize in 9e)* specified in the judgment or supplemental order.
   c. ☐ Sale of personal property
   d. ☐ Sale of real property
   e. Description of property:

— NOTICE TO PERSON SERVED —

WRIT OF EXECUTION OR SALE.   Your rights and duties are indicated on the accompanying Notice of Levy.
WRIT OF POSSESSION OF PERSONAL PROPERTY.   If the levying officer is not able to take custody of the property, the levying
officer will make a demand upon you for the property. If custody is not obtained following demand, the judgment may be enforced
as a money judgment for the value of the property specified in the judgment or in a supplemental order.
WRIT OF POSSESSION OF REAL PROPERTY.   If the premises are not vacated within five days after the date of service on the
occupant or, if service is by posting, within five days after service on you, the levying officer will remove the occupants from
the real property and place the judgment creditor in possession of the property. Personal property remaining on the premises will
be sold or otherwise disposed of in accordance with CCP 1174 unless you or the owner of the property pays the judgment creditor
the reasonable cost of storage and takes possession of the personal property not later than 15 days after the time the judgment
creditor takes possession of the premises.
► *A Claim of Right to Possession form accompanies this writ (unless the Summons was served in compliance with CCP 415.46).*

---

* NOTE: Continued use of form EJ-130 (Rev. Jan. 1, 1989) is authorized until June 30, 1992, *except if used as a Writ of Possession of Real Property.*

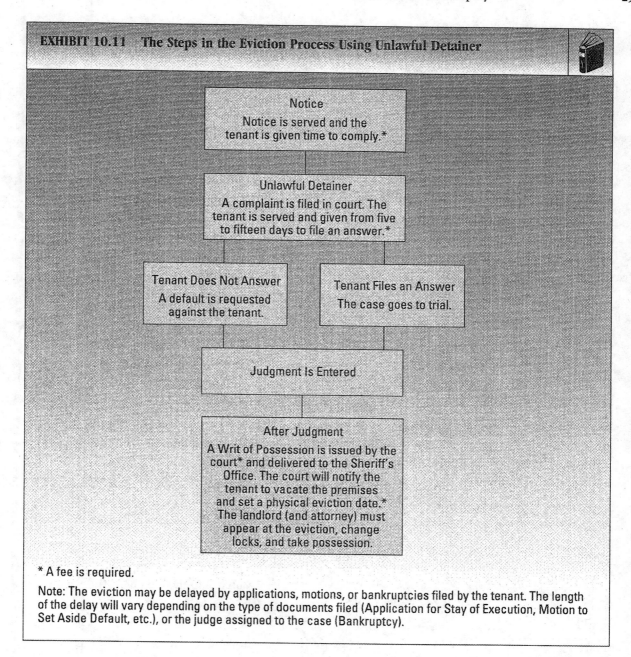

EXHIBIT 10.11   The Steps in the Eviction Process Using Unlawful Detainer

Notice
Notice is served and the
tenant is given time to comply.*

Unlawful Detainer
A complaint is filed in court. The
tenant is served and given from five
to fifteen days to file an answer.*

Tenant Does Not Answer
A default is requested
against the tenant.

Tenant Files an Answer
The case goes to trial.

Judgment Is Entered

After Judgment
A Writ of Possession is issued by the
court* and delivered to the Sheriff's
Office. The court will notify the
tenant to vacate the premises
and set a physical eviction date.*
The landlord (and attorney) must
appear at the eviction, change
locks, and take possession.

* A fee is required.

Note: The eviction may be delayed by applications, motions, or bankruptcies filed by the tenant. The length of the delay will vary depending on the type of documents filed (Application for Stay of Execution, Motion to Set Aside Default, etc.), or the judge assigned to the case (Bankruptcy).

KEY TERMS

SELF-TEST

A.   Indicate whether the following statements are true (T) or false (F):

_____ 1. Real property includes land and other items permanently attached to the land.

_____ 2. If you live in your car, it is considered to be real property.

_____ 3. Fixtures in a building are personal property.

_____ 4. Personal property is readily transportable from one location to another.

_____ 5. A light fixture permanently affixed to the ceiling of your home is real property.

B.   Circle the correct answer for the following questions:

1. The following items are examples of real property:

a. land, houses, in-ground swimming pools

b. portable microwave ovens, coffee grinders, houses

c. a chopped-down tree, a dog, a camper

d. none of the above

2. The following items are personal property:

a. a car

b. a truck

    c. a camper

    d. a and b

    e. all of the above

3. Absolute ownership of property is called

    a. fee tail.

    b. tenancy.

    c. fee simple.

    d. life estate.

4. Shared ownership in property is called

    a. tenancy in common.

    b. joint tenancy.

    c. community property.

    d. tenancy by the entirety.

    e. all of the above.

5. Individual ownership of a unit within a larger complex is known as a _____ form of ownership.

    a. cooperative

    b. condominium

    c. apartment

    d. tenancy

C. Fill in the blanks.

1. A _____ owner owns a share of stock represented by an

apartment unit.

2. An agreement with a real estate agent for the sale of property is known as

the _____.

3. A(n) _____ or history of the property's ownership is

provided to the buyer with the results of the search.

4. Transfer of ownership of property occurs at the _____.

5. The _____ transfers title from the seller to the buyer.

REVIEW QUESTIONS

1. What is the difference between a condominium and a cooperative? Discuss the advantages and disadvantages of each.

2. What is a closing? An escrow?

3. What are the advantages of a written lease or rental agreement?

4. Describe the steps in the unlawful detainer eviction process.

PROJECTS

1. Proofread and retype the cover sheet for the closing document in Exhibit 10.12. When retyping the cover sheet, add the names of counsel. The following information is pertinent: National Bank $2,000,000 mortgage loan to Marketing Investments, Inc. Closing date: September 1, 1996. Parties to the action include our office as counsel to the lender and James Roberts as counsel to the borrower. The remainder of the parties are the same as those shown in the Closing Agenda.

2. Using the facts provided here, prepare a lease using the format in Exhibit 10.6.

   - Client: Lynne Paltrow
   - Tenant: Ronald and Kirsten Shapiro
   - Rent: $1,000 per month
   - Address of property: 45 Sunset Drive; Your Town, Your State
   - Deposit: $1,000 plus one extra month's rent (the last month's rent)
   - Lease term: January 1, 1997, for one year
   - Rent payable: First day of each month

3. Assume the tenants in Project 2 have not paid their rent for the past two months. It is now June 1, 1997, and our client (Lynne Paltrow, the landlord) wants to initiate eviction proceedings against the tenants. Using the forms in Exhibits 10.8 and 10.9, prepare a Complaint for Unlawful Detainer and a Summons for Unlawful Detainer.

4. Locate a real estate document from the records in the courthouse or the County Recorder's Office by using the owners' names. Do this project for the property in which you live. Make a copy of the latest deed (deed of trust, warranty deed, grant deed, etc.) for that property.

5. List the steps required to transfer real property in your state and describe what happens at each stage.

6. What would you do in each of the following situations?

   a. Your next-door neighbor plays loud music late at night. You have asked her to turn the volume down, but she has ignored your request.

   b. A client, who is a tenant, complains that the roof of her apartment is leaking and that the landlord refuses to do anything about it. The attorney asks you to get more information about the problem. Where would you start?

   c. Our client lives next door to a toxic waste dump. He tells you that individuals in the neighborhood have been getting sick from the fumes. The attorney asks you to do some factual research on the problem. What is the first thing you would do?

EXHIBIT 10.12   A Closing Agenda

CLOSING AGENDA

NATIONL BANK

$22,000,000 MORTGAGE LOAN

TO

MRKG INC.

Closing Date: September 11, 1995

Parties and Miscellaneous Definitions

B&K	Bells, Lender
Borrower	Marking Inc.
HS&M	XXX, Counsel to Borrower
P&C	Point & Click, Lender's New York Local
Counsel	
Premises	Leap Hotel
	222 Main Street
	Your Town, Your State
Seller	Leap Hotel
Title Company	Ferrrst Amerkan Title Insrnce Compeny

Attorney Name here

Contract Law

CHAPTER OBJECTIVES

As a result of studying this chapter, you will learn the following material:

1. ***Elements of a Contract***   The elements of a contract will be presented. You will learn the roles that an offer, acceptance, and consideration play in a contract.

2. ***Bilateral/Unilateral Contracts, Express/Implied Contracts, Quasi-Contracts***   The characteristics of bilateral, unilateral, express, and implied contracts will be discussed. You will also learn the features of a quasi-contract.

3. ***Covenants and Conditions***   Covenants will be discussed, and the different types of conditions will be presented. You will learn how to distinguish conditions precedent, conditions concurrent, and conditions subsequent.

4. ***Parol Evidence Rule, Statute of Frauds, Uniform Commercial Code***   The implications of these rules and regulations will be discussed. You will learn which contracts must be in writing.

5. ***Breach of Contract***   The ways in which contracts can be breached will be examined. You will also learn remedies for a breach of contract.

6. ***Drafting a Contract***   The steps in drafting a contract will be discussed. You will learn how to draft clauses that commonly appear in contracts.

AN INTRODUCTION TO CONTRACTS

A **contract** is a legally enforceable agreement between two or more parties. This section will examine the elements of a contract, what is needed to make a valid contract, and what will make a contract void. Bilateral, unilateral, express, and implied contracts will be discussed, as will quasi-contracts. The importance of the Statute of Frauds, the Parol Evidence Rule, and the Uniform Commercial Code will be examined.

Elements of a Contract

The elements of a contract are the offer, the acceptance, and consideration. The **offer** is the manifestation by one party (the **offeror**) of the intention to enter into a contract. An offer may be as simple as the words, "I offer to sell you my car if you will pay me $400." The **acceptance** of the offer by the **offeree** is required for the contract to be valid. The third element of the contract (**consideration**) creates a bargained-for exchange. Each party gives up something of value and receives something of value in exchange. In the example, the offeror gives up his car and the offeree gives up $400. The offeror receives $400 and the offeree receives the car.

Valid and Void Contracts

A contract can be **valid** (legally enforceable) only if it is formed for a legal purpose. Thus, an individual may not enforce a gambling debt in the courts of most states because gambling is illegal. The gambling contract is considered **void** (not legally enforceable) at the outset.

Contracts made by minors are void and therefore not enforceable. In some states, however, if a minor makes a contract for the necessities of life (food, clothing, or shelter), the contract is enforceable in a court of law. In many states, the minor may enforce a contract even though the contract may not be enforced against the minor.

Intent of the Parties

Even if all of the elements of a contract are present, a contract will not exist unless the parties actually intended to enter into one. For instance, if you jokingly tell your friend that you will sell her your house for $5 and she accepts the offer, no contract would exist because neither party intended that there would be a contract.

Bilateral and Unilateral Contracts

Most contracts are **bilateral** (two-sided), in that each party to the contract promises to do or not to do something. At the point in time when the parties engage in this mutual exchange of promises, the contract is created. For example, in our earlier example, one party promised to give up his car, and the other party promised to pay him $400. The contract was created when the promises were made.

In a **unilateral** (one-sided) contract, only one party makes a promise; the promise is exchanged for the act itself. For instance, you might tell your teenage neighbor that you will pay him $50 if he mows your lawn. He does not promise to mow your lawn, but if he does mow it, then a contract is created at the time of the mowing, and he receives $50 upon completing the job.

Express or Implied Contracts

The contracts described in the preceding section are **express contracts** because the parties reached an explicit agreement, to which they mutually assented, and openly stated the terms of their contractual arrangement. An express contract may be either written or oral. As will be discussed later in the chapter, however, certain types of contracts must be in writing to satisfy the Statute of Frauds. Even express contracts must be written if they fall into the categories covered by the Statute of Frauds.

In an **implied contract,** the mutual assent of the parties is not manifested in words but in the actions of the parties. When a customer goes into a store and picks out a dress, the implication is that she will pay for the dress at the cash register. This contract is implied by the actions of the parties.

Quasi-Contracts

In some cases, an individual performs an act expecting to be paid even though no contract exists between the parties. In this case, the courts will provide an equitable remedy to prevent the unjust enrichment of the other party who has benefited from the actions of the first individual. To deal with such situations, the courts use a device called **quasi-contract,** which is essentially a legal fiction that allows a person to receive payment even though there is no contract because to deny payment would be unjust. To prevail in a suit in quasi-contract, the injured party must prove that the other party unjustly benefited from her actions, even though a mutual benefit was anticipated. In the classic example of a quasi-contract case, an elderly individual tells his young niece that if she will move into his home and take care of him, he will leave her certain property in his will. The niece relies on her uncle's statement, sells her own home and moves in and takes care of him until his death. However, he does not leave the property to her. She could sue her uncle's estate in a quasi-contract action in equity even though no contract existed between the parties. The court would probably award damages based on the reasonable value of the services provided.

> **quasi-contract**
> A legal fiction that allows a person to receive payment in a situation where there is, in fact, no contract but where circumstances are such that to deny payment would result in the unjust enrichment of the other party.

Contract Wording

The wording of an oral contract may be very simple, such as:

- "I promise to sell you my guitar if you will pay me $200." (statement by seller)
- "I accept your offer of your guitar for my $200." (statement by buyer)

A contract is created at this point.

Exhibit 11.1 shows an example of a formal written contract.

Statute of Frauds

The **Statute of Frauds** is a direct descendant of our ties to the common law of England and specifies that certain contracts must be in writing to be valid. Although different states have adopted different versions of this statute, it is most commonly applied to the following types of contracts:

> **Statute of Frauds**
> An English statute, adopted with variations by all the states, that requires certain types of contracts to be in writing.

1. Contracts for the sale of goods with a value of more than $500 (the amount may vary in a few states)
2. Contracts for an interest in real property (including a sale or lease)

EXHIBIT 11.1   A Formal Written Contract

This contract entered into this 20th day of October, 1996, between LENORE ARCINIEGA of 222 Main Way, in the City of Memphis, County of Shelby, and State of Tennessee and JOE M. YARDEN of 111 Electric Avenue, in the City of Whittier, County of Los Angeles, and State of California, consists of the following terms:

LENORE ARCINIEGA agrees to sell JOE M. YARDEN her 1992 red Toyota truck for the sum of $5,000, payable upon receipt of the truck.

IN WITNESS WHEREOF, the parties have hereby executed this contract on the 20th day of October, 1996, at Whittier, California.

_____
LENORE ARCINIEGA

_____
JOE M. YARDEN

3. Contracts in consideration of marriage (the "marriage contract" or prenuptial agreement)

4. Contracts that cannot be performed in one year (such as employment contracts for more than a year or leases for more than a year)

5. Promises to pay another's debts

Because these contracts must be in writing, if the parties perform on the terms of an oral contract in one of these categories, they cannot then sue the other party because the contract was oral. Some states will not allow a suit if the contract has been partially performed. For instance, if the Toyota truck in Exhibit 11.1 had been sold via an oral contract and the buyer had used the truck for several months, he could not then sue the seller based on the oral contract. Once the contract is performed (or partially performed in some states), the other party (not the one who performed) cannot seek to invalidate it later. Nor can the party sue for nonperformance.

Covenants and Conditions

covenant
The actual promise made by each party to a contract. The covenants create the terms of the contract.

The covenants of a contract form the essence of the contractual terms. More specifically, a **covenant** is the actual promise made by each party to the contract; the covenants create the terms of the contract. In Exhibit 11.1, the covenants involve the paying of $5,000 by one party and the giving up of the truck by the other party. The covenants create the contractual terms for both parties. If one party does not perform as promised, then the other party is not required to perform his side of the agreement. For example, if the seller does not provide the truck, then the buyer is not required to pay the $5,000. The seller in this case has **breached the contract** (failed to fulfill the promises made in the contract).

breach a contract
To fail to perform any promise that forms the whole or part of a contract.

In addition to covenants, a contract may include conditions. A **condition** is an event that creates a duty to perform on one or both parties. Conditions govern the timing of the performance of the contract and are of three types.

condition
An uncertain event on which an obligation is dependent.

1. Conditions precedent
2. Conditions concurrent
3. Conditions subsequent

The names indicate the point in time when the conditions occur.

A **condition precedent** is a condition that must occur before the contract will be performed. For example, the following words in a contract create a condition precedent:

condition precedent
A condition that must occur before the contract will be performed.

I promise to sell you my house for $250,000 if the house I am purchasing is completed by the signing of the deed.

Here the condition precedent is the completion of the purchased house. The contract may not be enforceable until the condition has occurred. Therefore, if the house being purchased has not been completed by the time the deed is to be signed, there is no contract.

Most employment contracts include examples of conditions precedent. For example, the following contract language establishes a condition precedent:

I, GLORIA ALVAREZ, agree to work as a paralegal for the RACHEL AVILEZ, ESQ. law firm for $2,500 per month, payable on the first day of each month.

In this case, Ms. Alvarez must work for Ms. Avilez for one month prior to receiving her $2,500 per month salary.

The most common type of condition is the **condition concurrent,** which creates an obligation on both parties at the time the contract is performed. For instance, the following contract wording creates conditions concurrent:

> I, SUSAN DAWOODI, agree to sell JENNIE KEIFER my 1990 Ferrari automobile for $200,000, upon delivery.

Susan agrees to surrender the car to Jennie at the time that Jennie delivers the $200,000 to her. If the money is not delivered, the car will not be given up.

As another example, Bill goes to the local coffee house and buys a cup of cappuccino. He pays the store clerk and receives the coffee at the same time. The promise and the act transpire concurrently.

A **condition subsequent** occurs "after the fact," that is, after the contract has been performed. If this type of condition occurs, it relieves the parties of their previous performance. For example, suppose you order merchandise from a catalog that states that if you are dissatisfied for any reason, you may return the merchandise for a full refund. If you subsequently return that merchandise, the catalog company is obligated to refund the purchase price. The basic terms of the contract were that the company would send you the merchandise and that you would pay for it. The condition subsequent was created by the company's statement that the merchandise could be returned for a full refund. Your dissatisfaction with the merchandise relieved you of your obligations under the contract. If the company did not have this refund policy and you did not pay for the merchandise, you would have breached the contract.

Parol Evidence Rule

During negotiations for a contract, individuals may make oral agreements before the contract is finally written. Under the **Parol Evidence Rule,** all previous oral agreements merge in the writing, and the written contract cannot be changed by any oral evidence unless the party can prove that mistake, duress, or fraud occurred when the written contract was being prepared. Therefore, the attorney should advise clients that any oral agreements made between the parties should be included in the written contract.

Uniform Commercial Code

The **Uniform Commercial Code (UCC)** establishes regulations for commercial transactions. Both parties must deal with each other fairly and in good faith. They must perform on their contracts in a timely fashion. They are also required to follow the customs of the industry and the community in which the contract is made, unless the custom is illegal or unsafe. For instance, suppose that the Service Department of a car dealer keeps your automobile overnight in an unlocked lot and does not lock the car. If your car is stolen, the dealer may not defend the theft by stating that it is the "custom" to leave cars unlocked in open parking lots. This custom is clearly unsafe.

Each state has adopted its own version of the UCC. Therefore, you should check your own state's statutes to determine the specific rules governing contracts in your state. The following are examples of some specific provisions of the UCC.

Sale of Goods.   Contracts for the sale of goods valued at more than $500 are governed by the UCC (Article II) and must be in writing. Contracts between merchants

condition concurrent
A condition that occurs at the same time as the contract is performed and creates an obligation on both parties.

condition subsequent
A condition that occurs after the contract has been performed and relieves the parties of their previous performance.

Parol Evidence Rule
A rule that holds that when a contract is written, all previous oral agreements merge in the writing and that the written contract cannot be changed by any oral evidence unless there is proof of mistake, duress, or fraud in the writing of the contract.

Uniform Commercial Code (UCC)
A set of regulations for commercial transactions that has been adopted, with variations, by all the states.

goods
Anything that is movable; may include merchandise, food, minerals, crops, oil, gas, electricity, and the like.

strictly liable
The condition of being legally responsible without regard to fault. Thus, if a product is defective and causes injury, the manufacturer and seller are held responsible even if they were not negligent.

merchant
An individual who is engaged in the purchase and sale of merchandise on an ongoing basis.

are also governed by this article. **Goods** are anything that is "movable" and include such things as merchandise, food, minerals, crops, oil, gas, and electricity.

Other provisions of the UCC hold the manufacturer and the seller **strictly liable** for any injuries caused to the buyer by a product that is defective. In other words, the plaintiff need only prove that the product was defective and caused her injuries in order to prevail in a lawsuit against the manufacturer or the seller. For example, Luis Gallardo purchased a bottle of juice from Gloria's Grocery. The bottle exploded, injuring Luis. He may sue both the manufacturer and the store for his injuries.

Contracts Involving Merchants.   Since the UCC is liberally construed, the definition of a **merchant** is very broad. Therefore, not only is the person who regularly deals in goods of this type (an individual who purchases and sells this type of merchandise on an ongoing basis) considered to be a merchant, but anyone who holds himself out as having specific skill related to the product is also included. Therefore, a collector of vintage automobiles may be considered a "merchant" under this provision if she has particular knowledge of the value of these automobiles.

For example, Stephanie Daniels is a collector of vintage automobiles and belongs to the Vintage Car Club. She has been buying and selling these cars for five years and currently owns four classic automobiles. She agrees to sell one of her cars to Michael Nicholson. In this situation, Stephanie would be considered a merchant under the UCC. If Michael is subsequently injured as a result of a defect in the automobile, he may sue her for damages, and she may be held strictly liable for his injuries.

Check your state's statutes to determine the specific rules governing contracts under the UCC in your state and add them to the State Specific Information box.

STATE SPECIFIC INFORMATION

The rules governing contracts under the UCC in _____ are as follows:

_____

_____

_____

warranty
A guarantee that goods are as promised.

implied warranty of merchantability
A guarantee by the seller that a purchased item is fit to be used for the ordinary purpose of that particular item.

implied warranty of fitness for a particular purpose
A guarantee by a seller that a purchased item is suitable to be used for a specified purpose.

Warranties

Warranties create guarantees in relation to the goods being purchased. Under the UCC, certain warranties may be implied. These implied warranties include (1) an implied warranty of merchantability and (2) an implied warranty of fitness for a particular purpose.

Under an **implied warranty of merchantability,** the seller is guaranteeing to the buyer that the item purchased is fit for the ordinary purpose of that particular product. If the buyer and the seller discuss how the buyer intends to use the product and the seller implies that the product is suitable (or fit) for that purpose, then the seller is making an **implied warranty of fitness for a particular purpose.**

For instance, Gloria Diaz purchases a lawnmower from Carlos Salaman Hardware Store. If she makes no specific inquiries about the lawnmower, then only the implied warranty of merchantability applies. However, if she asks the seller whether the lawnmower will cut grass that is five inches tall and he assures her that it will, then he has made an implied warranty of fitness for a particular purpose. The seller is guaranteeing that that particular lawnmower will cut grass that is five inches tall.

As another example, Azam Lavasani goes to Wendy Drew's Shoe Store to purchase shoes for her son to use for Little League baseball. The salesperson tells Azam that these shoes are the type used in that league and says specifically that the team coaches have given him this information. However, the shoes do not have cleats, and Azam's son is not allowed to wear them for his baseball game. Wendy Drew's Shoe Store has breached the warranty of fitness for a particular purpose because the salesperson knew of the use to which the shoes would be put and deliberately misled the customer in order to sell the shoes.

This example also involves a breach of an **express warranty** because the seller specifically told the buyer that the shoes could be used for a particular purpose. Express warranties are created by an explicit statement in the contract itself. In this case, an oral contract was made for the sale of shoes. The salesperson explicitly told the buyer that the shoes could be used for the boy's baseball games.

Express warranties may also be made in writing or in a catalog description. For instance, Francine Stinnett purchased a dress from Annette's catalog. The description of the dress stated that it was "machine washable." When the dress arrived, however, the label said "dry clean only." Thus, the express warranty in the catalog was breached.

express warranty
An explicit guarantee included in a contract.

Breach of Contract

If one of the parties to a contract fails to perform his obligations under the contract, the innocent party has an immediate cause of action for **breach of contract.** If a substantial portion of the contract has not been performed, a **substantial breach** has occurred. The plaintiff may sue to **rescind** (cancel) the contract or for **specific performance** to force the defendant to perform on the contract. Damages for **rescission** (cancellation of the contract) will amount to the monetary loss suffered by the plaintiff. In a suit for specific performance, the defendant will be required to perform his portion of the contract. In some cases, if the plaintiff has suffered other damages as a result of the defendant's lack of performance, she may sue for both specific performance and **money damages.** In most cases, however, the plaintiff may sue for either rescission of the contract and receive her money back or for specific performance and force the defendant to perform.

Suppose Teresa Alvarado hires a contractor to build a room onto her house. The contractor finishes half of the room and leaves. Teresa will sue for specific performance on the contract and force the contractor to complete the room. But suppose adding the room required the walls of her house to be removed and she cannot live there while the work is being done. The courts would likely award Teresa damages on the contract for her living expenses while the house was uninhabitable.

In the entertainment industry, suits for specific performance may be filed against actors who fail to show up for filming or fail to play the part called for in the contract. Other examples where specific performance would be sought include contracts for the sale of real property and contracts for the purchase of unique property, such as art objects or antiques.

breach of contract
The failure to perform any major part of a contract.

substantial breach
The failure to perform a substantial portion of a contract.

rescind
To cancel a contract and restore the parties to the positions they would have held if there had been no contract.

specific performance
Doing what was promised in a contract.

rescission
The act of canceling or abrogating a contract.

money damages
A monetary amount awarded as compensation for injuries.

DRAFTING CONTRACTS

To draft a contract properly, you must have a clear understanding of the wishes of both parties involved. Discuss the contractual terms thoroughly with the client to make sure you know exactly what he wants. Sample contract clauses can be found in form books and transactional guides. Computer software packages also offer sample clauses. Always check contracts that have been previously prepared in your law office to determine both the format and the sample clauses used. Do not rely too heavily on forms, however, because your client's contract may be different from earlier contracts. The following list provides examples of clauses that are likely to appear in a contract:

1. *Parties to the Contract.*　The first paragraph will contain the proper names of the parties to the contract, along with the date the contract is signed. For example:

   Agreement made between Marcelina Rodriquez (hereinafter referred to as "Buyer") and ANNETTE A. ARNESEN (hereinafter referred to as "Seller") this 20th day of October, 1996, at Whittier, California.

2. *Consideration.*　This paragraph constitutes the essence of the contract. It says what the parties are giving and receiving under the terms of the contract. For example:

   In consideration of the sum of Four Thousand Dollars ($4,000), Buyer agrees to purchase from Seller her 1982 Honda Civic automobile, #XYZ123.

3. *Time of Performance.*　Some contracts may indicate a future time at which the contract will be performed. Suppose that the parties in our example had agreed to pay the $4,000 and deliver the automobile on November 1. In that case, a clause such as the following would be included:

   Buyer agrees to pay the $4,000 to Seller on November 1, 1996, on which date the Seller will deliver the automobile to the Buyer's residence at 1111 Main Street, in the City of Prescott, State of Arizona.

4. *Signature Clause.*　A standard signature clause will have a line for the buyer's signature and a line for the seller's signature as follows:

   _____
   MARCELINA RODRIQUEZ
   Buyer

   _____
   ANNETTE A. ARNESEN
   Seller

Other clauses that might also be included in a contract include the following:

1. Conditions (as described earlier in the chapter).

2. UCC information. Some states have special forms that are utilized for all UCC contracts. Check your own state's rules in this regard.

3. Special warranties.

4. Special terms, such as installment payments or loan information.

SUMMARY

To be a valid contract, its elements must include an offer, an acceptance, and consideration. Some contracts must be in writing to satisfy the Statute of Frauds. Contracts that are void may never be made valid.

Contracts may be either express or implied. Express contracts explicitly state their terms within the contract. Implied contracts are based on the intent and performance of the parties.

Certain contracts are covered by the Uniform Commercial Code and must be written. Express and implied warranties are inherent in these contracts.

Specific clauses are required to make a valid contract. The following items must be included: the parties, the date, the consideration, and the parties' signatures.

KEY TERMS

SELF-TEST

A.   Indicate whether the following statements are true (T) or false (F):

_____ 1. A contract is a legally enforceable agreement between parties.

_____ 2. The offeree makes an offer to the offeror of the intention to enter into a contract.

_____ 3. In order for a contract to be valid, the offer must be accepted.

_____ 4. Contracts may be formed for both legal and illegal purposes.

_____ 5. A minor's contracts are usually not enforceable.

B.   Circle the correct answer for the following questions:

1. The elements of a contract are:

    a. the offer.

    b. the acceptance.

    c. the consideration.

    d. all of the above.

2. Consideration has been defined as:

    a. the manifestation of one party to enter into a contract.

    b. the offeree's acceptance.

    c. the bargained-for exchange.

    d. both (a) and (b).

    e. all of the above.

3. Void contracts include:

    a. illegal contracts.

    b. implied contracts.

    c. contracts made by minors.

    d. (a) and (b).

    e. (a) and (c).

4. A contract that requires each party to the contract to promise to do or not to do an act is

    a. a bilateral contract.

    b. a unilateral contract.

    c. an express contract.

    d. an implied contract.

5. In a/an _____ contract, the promise is exchanged for the act itself.

    a. bilateral

    b. unilateral

    c. implied

    d. express

C. Fill in the blanks:

1. In order to satisfy the _____, some contracts must be in writing.

2. The essence of the contractual terms is known as _____ .

3. The _____ establishes regulations for commercial transactions.

4. Courts provide an equitable remedy if an individual performs an act expecting to be paid even though no contract exists between the parties. This is called a/an _____ .

5. Contracts in which the mutual assent of the parties is not manifested in

   words but in the actions of the parties are _____ .

REVIEW QUESTIONS

1. What are the elements of a contract? Define each element.

2. What is the difference between express contracts, implied contracts, and quasi-contracts?

3. Are contracts made by minors legal? Explain the circumstances under which such contracts are enforceable.

4. What are the remedies for breach of contract?

5. Define the three types of conditions and discuss the circumstances under which each is used.

PROJECTS

1. Proofread and revise the Contract for Landscaping in Exhibit 11.2.

2. Draft a simple contract between Maria Guerrero and Linda M. Morales. Maria is selling her 1993 Jaguar XJS to Linda for the sum of $15,000. The automobile will be delivered on November 15 of this year and will be paid for at that time.

3. Write a contract with your instructor about reading the chapter, answering the questions, and completing any other projects required. Include a time line of when these items will be completed.

4. Go to the law library on your campus or the local law library and find a blank contract form or format for your state under its adaptation of the Uniform Commercial Code.

EXHIBIT 11.2   A Contract for Landscaping

Contrakt for Landscapping

THIS contract, made and enterred in to this _____ day of _____, 199 ___, by and betwean the CONNOR INVESTMANT CORORATION, a corporation organized and existing under and by virtue of the laws of the State of NY and having its offise and principle place of business at 3611 Gimore Ave., Utica, Oneida Co, NY, here in after refered to as the "Corporation", and Terrance W. Kroft, Jr., d/b/a Kroft contracting, of 231 Templeton Avenue, Utica, NY, hear in after referred to as the "Contractor",

WITNESSETH:

Wereas, the Corporation has agreed to hire the contractor and the Contractor has agreed to perform certain work, labor and services and furnish materials for the Corporation relative to certian landscapping and grading at premices hereinafter discribed and persuant to the plans, drawings and specivacations submited therefore.

NOW, THEREFORE, in consideratioon of there mutuel promises and covanants set forth herein the partys agreed as follows:

1. The Contracter shall provide all materials and laber for a landscaping project at 7887 Skyway Blvd., Utica, Oneida Co., New York. The Contractor shall bee responsable for the carrying out and the completion of said project in accordence witht he specifacations set out in the attach drawings, which have been prepared by Robert Urban, refered too herein as the Landscape Architect. All work shall be done in the mannor set fourth in the grading plan and specifications tharein.

2. The work on this contrakt shall began on or about the _____ day of _____, 199 ___, and will be completted on or abut the _____ dy of _____, 199 ___,

3. The agreed up on complension for the work and materials is Five Thousand Seven Hundred and no/100ths Dollars ($5,700)   Payment shall be maid to the contractor in accordance with the following schedule:

(A)   The Corporation shall pay to the Contractor the some of Twenty-seven Hundred ($2,700) Dollars up on the exacution of this contract.

(B)   The remaining balence of Three thousand and no/100ths Dollars ($3,000.00) shall be pay to the Contractor upon completion of all work discribed here under. Final payment shall e with-held untill all work has been inspected and approved by the Landscap Architact.

C.   Additionall or extraordinery expenses or changes to the original plans and specifacations must be submited to the Corporation and approved by the Landscape Architect prier to incuring such costs. Any bils for such extraordinary expenses shall be submitted, in duplicate, to the Landscape Archiect for his approval.

4. The entire contract between the partys is contained in this agreement. A copy of the drawings and specifications are attach hereto and marked Exhibit A and incorporated by referance as though more fuly set forth here in.

5. All materials and equipment necessery to completing this project shall be provided by the Contractor, in accordance with the specification set fourth in the drawings hearin. All work shall be comleted to confirm with sanderd building practice and the materials used shall be new. The quality of workmanship shall be first class.

6. Contractor shall provide Landscape Architect with a propose schedule of construction showing such ifnormation as required by him to make proper inspections.

This contract shall be binding upon the party and upon there hiers, successors, executers, administraters and assigns.

IN WITNESS whereof, the partys here to have set there hands and seals the day and year first above writing.

(SEAL)   Conner Investment Corp.

                                          By _____
                                          Richard Collins, Vice President

---

EXHIBIT 11.2   A Contract for Landscaping *Concluded*

_____

Terrance W. Croft, Jr. d/b/a
Kroft Contracting

STATE OF NEW YORK   )
                                    SS.:
County of Oneida   )

On this _____ day of _____ , 199 ___ , before me came RICHARD CONNOR, to me known, who, being by me dully swore, did depose and say that he resides in Utica, NY; that he is the Vice President of CONNOR INVESTMENT CORPORATION the corporation discribed in, and which eacuted the forgoing instrument; that he knows the seal of said corporation; that the seal affixed o said intrument is such corporate seel; that it was affix by order of the Board of Directors of said corporation; and that he signed his name theirto by like order.

_____

Notery republic

STATE OF NEW YORK   )
                                    ss.:
COUNTY OF ONEIDA)

On this _____ day of _____ , 199 ___ , before me came TERRENCE W. CROFT, Jr., to me known and known to me to be the same person described in and who eacuted the forgoing instrucment and he dully acknowlledged to me that he exacuted the same.

_____

Notery Public

SOURCE: Courtesy of Vicky Alexandra; Utica, New York.

The Job Search

APPENDIX OBJECTIVES

As a result of studying this appendix, you will learn the following material:

1. ***Winning Resume***   You will learn how to prepare a resume for a legal secretarial or paralegal position.
2. ***Cover Letter***   You will learn how to write an appropriate cover letter.
3. ***Seeking a Position***   You will learn the sources of employment.
4. ***Interview***   You will learn how to prepare for, dress for, and conduct an employment interview.

A WINNING RESUME

Preparing a winning resume takes time and effort. Since many employers will be screening hundreds of applicants, you must make sure that your resume stands out from the crowd.

The purpose of a resume is to enable you to get an interview for the position. When you prepare a resume, you are attempting to make a sale. Instead of a product, you are selling yourself. Therefore, you want to use persuasive words that will convince the prospective employer to "buy the product" (hire you).

Your resume should be one or two pages in length. Make sure it does not contain any typographical errors, misspelled words, or grammatical errors. Proofread your resume carefully. Do not depend on the "spell check" on your computer because it will not find misspellings that are actually other words (for example, *there* for *their* or *principal* for *principle*).

Law firms are very conservative. Therefore, use white or another neutral shade such as beige or gray for the paper. Never use bright-colored paper or colored printing.

If you do not feel comfortable preparing your own resume, it may be beneficial to hire a professional resume-writing service. These companies may be proficient in preparing winning resumes. Be sure to do some research before hiring the company, however. Ask to speak to former customers and discuss the services they asked the company to perform and the results they obtained.

The most common format for a resume is chronological. All items are listed in reverse chronological order with the most recent first. Exhibit A.1 shows an example of a **chronological resume.** If you have changed jobs often, you may prefer a **functional resume,** which groups positions together by the skills they involved without giving the chronological sequence (see Exhibit A.2).

Before you begin to prepare your resume, list your previous and present positions along with the duties and responsibilities each position involved. Try to relate those

EXHIBIT A.1   A Chronological Resume

JAMIE PAIGE

1234 Any Street
Your Town, Your State ZIPCODE
Telephone: (123) 456-7890

EDUCATION

Your Local University, Your Town, Your State, June 1995. BS Degree in English.
GPA: 3.8.

Paralegal Studies Institute, Phoenix, Arizona, June 1996. ABA-approved
Paralegal Program with emphasis in Civil Litigation. Civil Practice Certificate.
Member: Student Paralegal Association. GPA: 4.0.

SKILLS

- Speak, read, and write Spanish and Italian.
- Wordperfect 6.0.
- WESTLAW Training Certificate.

EXPERIENCE

Receptionist, Local Law Firm, Inc.—greeted clients and visitors; assisted
legal secretaries with overflow typing; telephone contacts. 4 years full-time;
4 years part-time while in college.

Paralegal intern, State Attorney General's Office—case management,
document production, summarized depositions, prepared pleadings and
legal documents.
1 year part-time.

PROFESSIONAL ASSOCIATIONS

Phoenix Paralegal Association
National Association of Legal Assistants

SEMINARS

Phoenix Bar Association Seminar on the Fast Track Rules in Civil Litigation.

EXHIBIT A.2 A Functional Resume

LEE KRUGER

1234 Any Street
Your Town, Your State ZIPCODE
Telephone: (123) 456-7890

EDUCATION

Your Local University, Your Town, Your State, June 1995. BS Degree in English. GPA: 3.8.

Paralegal Studies Institute, Phoenix, Arizona, June 1996. ABA-approved Paralegal Program with emphasis in Civil Litigation. Civil Practice Certificate.
Member: Student Paralegal Association. GPA: 4.0.

SKILLS

- Speak, read, and write Japanese.
- Wordperfect 6.0.
- WESTLAW Training Certificate.

EXPERIENCE

Legal secretarial and research positions in law firms and corporations; prepared documents and pleadings; case management; document production; discovery preparation; trial preparation—5 years.

chronological resume
A resume with education and experience listed in reverse chronological order.

functional resume
A resume that groups skills into functions.

duties to the paralegal or legal secretarial position for which you are applying. For instance, if you were formerly a bookkeeper, you might use words like "well organized" or "attention to detail" in describing your duties. Rewrite each duty you have performed in terms of skills required by the legal profession. Be realistic about your accomplishments. Employers will realize when you are magnifying your previous responsibilities.

After you have rewritten all of your previous duties and responsibilities, it is time to prepare the resume. It will include the following sections:

- *Heading.* The heading should include your name, address, and telephone number. You will need an answering machine to take messages at the number listed. Include your business telephone number only if you have a private telephone at work.

  The message on your answering machine should be professional. Prospective employers do not appreciate personal messages such as jokes, songs, or messages from children. State your name, say that you are not available to take the call, and indicate when you will be able to return the call. Remember that if the caller does not like your message, you may not get the interview.

- *Objective.* Some texts on resume writing suggest that you state your objective. If you do, however, you will have to change it whenever you apply for a different position. Therefore, this section is optional.

- *Education.* Only college-level education should be listed. In addition to the year you graduated, the degree, and the name and address of the college, list any honors received or special courses completed that would be valuable to the prospective employer. Indicate whether your paralegal program is ABA approved. If your grade point average (GPA) is 3.5 or above, mention this. The college you attended most recently should be listed first.

- *Special Skills.* If you have skills that would be valuable in a law office, they should be set apart under this category. List the following information here:
  1. Bilingual (and language)
  2. Computer skills and software usage
  3. Special legal knowledge
  4. Writing skills
  5. Knowledge of machines (dictation, etc.)

- *Employment.* Your work experience should be listed in reverse chronological order (most recent jobs first). Be sure to include any field work or internship experiences. Describe your duties and responsibilities in terms of the position for which you are applying. Try not to leave large gaps in employment.

- *Professional Organizations.* List any professional organizations of which you are a member. Do not include religious organizations or affiliations. Do not list organizations that would reveal your age, such as the American Association of Retired Persons (AARP).

- *Professional Seminars.* If you have attended continuing legal education seminars or classes, list the name and date, and include a short description.

- *Volunteer Experience.* If you have not held paying positions but have completed responsible volunteer work assignments, describe these jobs in a separate category or under Employment History with "Volunteer" indicated.

- *References.* The resume should mention that references are available on request. Contact at least three professionals who know you and are familiar with your work. Ask if they will allow you to use their names as references for employment. Ask former employers, doctors, lawyers, and former instructors. Your supervisor at your Internship Site would make an excellent reference. Prepare a separate sheet of references that includes names, addresses, and telephone numbers to bring to the interview.

THE COVER LETTER

A **cover letter** should accompany each resume. Employers expect to read a letter with your resume. Focus on the individual position for which you are applying and summarize the attributes and accomplishments that make you uniquely qualified for this position. Keep the letter brief, preferably two or three paragraphs.

cover letter
The letter that accompanies a resume.

A different cover letter should be sent with each resume. Never send a mass-produced letter that is designed to be used as an all-purpose letter for all situations. Each letter should be addressed to a named individual. If you are not sure of the name, call the law office and ask the full name and title of the individual who is responsible for screening resumes. Use the person's title in the inside address.

Let the reader know in the letter that you have done some research on the firm. Look the firm up in the **Martindale-Hubbell National Legal Directory** (a national directory of attorneys) or the local directory of attorneys for your area. Try to find information about recent cases handled by the firm. Let the reader know that you want this position. At the end of the letter, say that you are looking forward to an interview. Exhibit A.3 shows a sample cover letter.

Martindale-Hubbell National Legal Directory
A national directory of attorneys.

JOB FOLDER

Create a **job folder** or a notebook that lists all positions for which you apply. Keep track of all letters, follow-up telephone calls, research about the firm, and interviews. Make a cover sheet like the one in Exhibit A.4 to catalog all inquiries. If you have a personal computer, you may wish to set up a tracking system on your calendar.

job folder
A summary of positions applied for.

Keep the folder next to the telephone so that when a prospective employer calls to set up an interview, you can instantly find the information about the firm in your folder.

WHERE TO LOOK FOR A POSITION

Besides the local newspaper, many other resources are available. If your locality has a legal newspaper, read it daily for prospective employment.

EXHIBIT A.3   A Sample Cover Letter

555 Your Street
Your Town, State ZIP
Today's date

John L. Burns, Esq.
Vice President, Law
Legal Corporation
111 Main Street
Phoenix, AZ 96301

Dear Mr. Burns:

You may recall that we met at the Phoenix Bar Association Seminar on Civil Litigation on March 25. At that time you suggested that I contact you upon my graduation.

In June, I received my paralegal certificate from the ABA-approved paralegal program at the Phoenix Institute for Paralegal Studies. During this period I spent a year as a student intern in the State Attorney General's Office with responsibilities in civil litigation, including document discovery, legal research, case management, and deposition summaries.

I have used both Wordperfect and WESTLAW during school and at the Attorney General's Office. I also have experience with many legal software packages, such as LAW and LEGAL. A copy of my resume, listing my education and experience, is enclosed.

May I come in for an interview to discuss my qualifications further? Please call me at 444-1111 to arrange an interview.

Very truly yours,

Jonathan L. Washburn

JLW:ja
Enc.

EXHIBIT A.4   A Job File

Name and address of firm:

Contact Person & Title:

_____

_____

_____   Telephone:_____

DATE OF FIRST CONTACT:

RESUME SENT:

FOLLOW-UP CONTACT:

DATE OF INTERVIEW:
        Name of Interviewer:

THANK YOU LETTER:

FOLLOW-UP CONTACT:

SECOND INTERVIEW:
        Interviewer:

THANK YOU LETTER SENT:

JOB OFFER:

BACKGROUND OF FIRM FROM MARTINDALE-HUBBELL:

        Area of law:

        Size of firm:

        Major cases:

        Major clients:

        Other pertinent information:

Law Firms

Use the Martindale-Hubbell National Legal Directory to find law firms in your locality. Apply to those that are the size you want and that specialize in an area that interests you. This directory is an outstanding source for obtaining information about law firms, such as their size, names of attorneys, schools they attended, type of law practiced, professional affiliations, and other personal information. Some firms list their major clients.

Large Cases

Read the local and legal newspapers to keep track of large cases that are being litigated. Apply to those firms because they may need additional employees for these cases.

Government Offices

Positions may be available in federal, state, and county government offices.

Federal Government.   To apply for a position with the federal government, complete a standard Form 171, which is similar to an employment application. Obtain the form from your local Federal Office of Personnel Management (OPM). Make several copies of the form, with the specific position left blank. Then you can type in the position whenever you apply for an opening. A separate form must be completed for each position sought. By completing all information except the position desired, you will not have to complete a new form each time you apply for a position.

Before completing the form, obtain a copy of the Hiring Standards for each type of position from the Office of Personnel Management. Use these standards in your application so that it reflects the qualifications required for the positions you desire. Doing this also helps alleviate the need to complete a separate form for every position for which you apply.

To obtain additional information about positions in the federal government, contact the local office or write to the following address:

Office of Personnel Management
Room 5L45
1900 E Street, NW
Washington, DC 20415

State and County Governments.   Many state and county departments employ paralegals and legal secretaries in the criminal area in prosecution and defense. Paralegals assist in preparing cases for trial, do legal research, find and prepare witnesses for trial, and investigate cases. Legal secretaries may also assist in case preparation and do factual investigation to assist the attorney and paralegal.

On the defense side, usually called the Public Defender, paralegals and legal secretaries interview the accused and conduct background investigations. The Prosecutor (or District Attorney) may require the investigation of prior convictions, legal research, case preparation, and factual investigation.

County governments may employ paralegals and legal secretaries in a variety of departments. The Department of Consumer Affairs helps consumers with problems with merchants, landlords, tenants, and other organizations. The County Counsel handles lawsuits against the county.

Corporations

Go to your local library to obtain a copy of **Standard and Poor's Register of Corporations,** which lists corporate offices, officers, and their addresses. Call corporations that are located in your area to learn whether they hire paralegals or legal secretaries. If one of the corporate officers listed is "General Counsel" or "Vice President, Law," the corporation will have an in-house Legal Department that you can contact.

Standard and Poor's Register of Corporations
A national directory of corporations.

Professional Organizations

Networking with other professionals in your field is the best way to obtain a position. Join your local professional organization as a student member, attend the meetings, and network.

If you have already joined an organization, you will have obtained many business cards of individuals you met at the meetings. Write to each of them, reminding them of your meeting and inquiring about openings at their firms.

Some professional organizations have job banks for members. Members can send resumes to the job bank. Prospective employers who contact the organization are sent (or faxed) copies of resumes that match their requirements. These firms may not advertise their positions in the newspaper.

Seminars

Attend seminars of the local bar associations and other professional organizations in the legal field. Network with the attorneys at the seminars and let them know you are about to graduate. Bring copies of your resume and business cards to distribute at the seminar.

Volunteer Work

Government agencies, nonprofit organizations, and legal aid offices welcome volunteers to help with their legal work. Some courts also allow students to volunteer in the Clerk's Office or in the courtroom.

Advertising

Some people have obtained positions by placing advertisements in the local legal newspaper under "Positions Wanted." If there is a legal newspaper in your locality, ask about the cost of these advertisements. Call some telephone numbers in prior ads to learn if the individuals obtained results. If you place an ad, list any attributes or skills that make you unique and set you apart from other candidates. Be sure to include your telephone number.

Mass Mailings

Try to send out between ten and twenty resumes each week. If you are applying to firms in the Martindale-Hubbell Directory, start at the A's and fill out a 3 × 5 card for each firm in your area to which you will apply. Write the name, address, and telephone number of the firm. Call to ask who does the hiring and send that person a cover letter and resume. If you are interested in working in a corporation, follow the same procedure using Standard and Poor's Directory.

Some prospective applicants have found it effective to suggest that they will volunteer their time for a short period before actually being hired. In this way, the employer can learn that you would be a valuable employee.

Keep a comprehensive file of all firms to whom you send resumes. Keep responses in the file, along with interview information.

Follow-Up

Follow up all letters with a telephone call. Ask if your resume was received and whether the firm has any questions to ask or would like to schedule an interview. Be persistent but don't be a nuisance.

Informational Interviews

If a firm where you would like to work does not have any openings, try to arrange an informational interview with the hiring authority. Say that you would like to spend fifteen to twenty minutes of the person's time discussing a future career in the organization.

PREPARING FOR THE INTERVIEW

An interview is a form of two-way communication. Not only does the employer want to get information about you, but you must get information about the organization as well. The interview gives you the opportunity to learn whether this is a firm where you want to work. Therefore, you should make up a list of questions before the interview.

Practice the interview with a friend or in front of a mirror. Note any distracting or annoying mannerisms. Learn your questions from memory so that you don't have to refer to notes at the interview.

How to Dress

Dress conservatively. A woman should wear a neutral-colored suit, minimal makeup and jewelry, and neutral shoes and hose. A man should wear a dark suit, white shirt, conservative tie, polished shoes, and long socks. Clothing should be color coordinated in muted tones. Do not chew gum or smoke. Carry a small briefcase with extra copies of your resume, a list of references, letters of recommendation from your references, writing samples, and a list of questions.

A few days before the interview, check the clothes you plan to wear to be sure they are clean and pressed. Polish your shoes. Try your clothes on to be sure they fit properly. Lay your clothes out the night before the interview.

Punctuality

You must arrive at the interview site on time. One attorney I know will not conduct an interview if the individual arrives more than five minutes late. If you are not familiar with the traffic patterns or location, do a "dry run" from your home to the interview site at the same time of day your interview is scheduled. Check to see where you can park, especially if you are driving to a large metropolitan area.

If you do not know the location, ask the receptionist or the interviewer for directions and parking information when you arrange the interview. Do not ask if the firm will validate your parking, however.

THE INTERVIEW ITSELF

Try to arrive at the interview site about fifteen minutes early. Make a stop to check your clothes and appearance.

When you arrive at the office, give the receptionist your name and say you have an appointment with the interviewer. Be friendly but professional. If you must wait, choose a chair that is easy to get up from. Don't sink into a comfortable sofa that requires you to struggle to stand up.

In most cases, the interviewer will walk out to the reception area to greet you. Stand, introduce yourself, and shake hands firmly. Smile and establish eye contact.

If you must complete an application, write neatly and legibly using black ink. Use your resume as a reference source for dates and names.

When you enter the interviewer's office, sit in the chair indicated; if none is suggested, sit across from the desk. Be sure that you maintain eye contact and answer questions directly. Display self-confidence when discussing your accomplishments, skills, and education. Although you should be proud of your background and achievements, do not appear arrogant. Let the interviewer complete that portion of the interview before asking your questions. Never interrupt the interviewer during the interview.

Be prepared to answer questions about your resume, such as former employment, education, and skills. Open-ended questions like "Tell me about yourself" should be expected.

Prohibited Questions

Because of the Civil Rights Act, Title VII, employers may not ask about certain areas that may appear to be discriminatory. Questions about age, height, weight, marital status, children, ethnic background, religion, and other personal matters are not allowed.

Your Questions

Ask specific questions about any aspect of the position that is important to you. Do not ask questions that have already been answered. Do not ask questions about bonuses, salary, and overtime, unless they are major considerations in accepting a position.

Request a tour of the office and pay particular attention to the location of your prospective office. The size and decor of your office usually provide valuable information about the firm's opinion of your position. Compare your office with other offices in the firm.

Follow-Up

After the interview, prepare an evaluation of the firm and the position for your file. Write a thank you letter to the interviewer stressing your desire to work for the firm. Emphasize some attributes that would be of value to the firm.

SUMMARY

Winning resumes create a competitive edge in the employment marketplace. Most prospective employers like the resume to be no more than two pages in length. The resume is an opportunity to convince an organization to hire you; hence, persuasive words should be utilized. The resume should include a heading, objective, education, special skills, previous employment history, and professional organizations or seminars attended. Volunteer experience related to the legal profession may be included. A cover letter written specifically for each position should accompany the resume.

The interview is a critical stage of the job search process. The individual should be well prepared and dress professionally. After the interview, a follow-up letter should be written thanking the interviewer. Special attributes suited to this position should be emphasized.

KEY TERMS

Chronological resume   A–1
Cover letter   A–5
Functional resume   A–1
Job folder   A–5

Martindale-Hubbell National Legal
  Directory   A–5
Standard and Poor's Register of
  Corporations   A–9

PROJECTS

1. List your previous jobs and your duties at each. Reword the duties for your resume.

2. Prepare a resume for yourself using the format shown in Exhibit A.1 or A.2.

3. Prepare a cover letter to accompany your resume. Choose a law firm from the local legal directory or Martindale-Hubbell and address the letter to the hiring authority for that firm.

4. Prepare a list of questions that you would ask at an employment interview.

Answers to Self-Tests

Chapter 1

A. Matching
   a. 1
   b. 4
   c. 2
   d. 3
   e. 5
B. True/False
   1. False
   2. False
   3. False
   4. True
C. Fill-in-the-Blanks
   1. law office manager
   2. free-lance (or independent)
   3. Bar Exam
   4. receptionist
   5. a. law librarian; legal secretary
      b. legal secretary; law clerk; messenger
      c. bookkeeper; legal secretary
      d. legal secretary
      e. attorney; paralegal
      f. attorney; paralegal
      g. attorney; law office manager
      h. attorney
      i. attorney
      j. receptionist; legal secretary
      k. law office manager

Chapter 2

A. True/False
   1. False
   2. True
   3. True
   4. False
   5. False
B. Multiple Choice
   1. b
   2. d
   3. d
   4. b
   5. c
C. Fill-in-the-Blanks
   1. billable hours
   2. legal cap
   3. legal secretary
   4. tenths of hours
   5. project fee

Chapter 3

A. True/False
   1. False
   2. True
   3. False
   4. True
   5. True
B. Multiple Choice
   1. a
   2. c
   3. b
   4. a
   5. c
C. Fill-in-the-Blanks
   1. 51
   2. Venue
   3. Jurisdiction
   4. Municipal/Superior
   5. Municipal

Chapter 4

A. Matching
   1. c
   2. e
   3. b
   4. d
   5. a
B. True/False
   1. False
   2. False
   3. True
   4. False
C. Fill-in-the-Blanks
   1. written interrogatories
   2. 30
   3. Complaint
   4. Answer
   5. Request for Production (or Request to Produce)

Chapter 5

A. True/False
1. True
2. False
3. False
4. False
5. True

B. Multiple Choice
1. b
2. d
3. d
4. b
5. c

C. Fill-in-the-Blanks
1. subpoena
2. waiver
3. Motion to Suppress Evidence
4. plea bargaining
5. aiding and abetting

Chapter 6

A. True/False
1. True
2. False
3. False
4. True
5. False

B. Multiple Choice
1. c
2. a
3. d
4. c
5. e

C. Fill-in-the-Blanks
1. voir dire
2. prosecuting (or plaintiff's)
3. rebuttal
4. judgment; verdict
5. ¾ usually (some states may vary)

Chapter 7

A. True/False
1. False
2. True
3. True
4. False
5. True

B. Multiple Choice
1. d
2. c
3. e
4. c
5. d

C. Fill-in-the-Blanks
1. formal will
2. pretermitted heir
3. codicil
4. per stirpes (or by right of representation)
5. Letters Testamentary

Chapter 8

A. True/False
1. False
2. True
3. False
4. True
5. True

B. Multiple Choice
1. a
2. b
3. a
4. b
5. b

C. Fill-in-the-Blanks
1. Order to Show Cause Hearing
2. both
3. best interests of the child
4. Petition; Complaint
5. ancestors and descendants and when one spouse is already married

Chapter 9

A. True/False
1. False
2. True
3. True
4. False
5. True

B. Multiple Choice
1. a
2. d
3. b
4. a
5. e

C. Fill-in-the-Blanks
1. general and limited
2. general partner
3. form of business entity where one person owns all of the assets of the business
4. Articles of Incorporation
5. shareholders

Chapter 10

A. True/False
1. True
2. False
3. False
4. True
5. True

B. Multiple Choice
1. a
2. e
3. c
4. e
5. b

C. Fill-in-the-Blanks
1. cooperative
2. contract of sale
3. title
4. closing (or escrow)
5. deed

Chapter 11

A. True/False
1. True
2. False
3. True
4. False
5. True

B. Multiple Choice
1. d
2. c
3. a (can also be e except for necessities of life)
4. a
5. b

C. Fill-in-the-Blanks
1. Statute of Frauds
2. covenants
3. UCC (Uniform Commercial Code)
4. quasi-contract
5. implied contracts

GLOSSARY

abstract of title A history of a property's ownership.

acceptance An assent by the person to whom an offer has been made to enter into a contract.

administrator An individual appointed to administer an estate when the decedent did not have a will or did not name an Executor in the will.

adoption A legal proceeding where adoptive parents become the legal parents of an adopted child. The birth parents give up all legal rights and responsibilities for the child.

advance fees Fees paid before the services are performed.

affirmative defense A defense that sets forth a justification for the defendant's actions rather than denying the allegations.

agency adoption The adoption of a child through a public or private agency.

aiding and abetting Assisting someone in committing a crime; knowledge of unlawful purpose with intent to commit, encourage, or facilitate commission of the crime by act or advice.

annual report A yearly report issued by a corporation describing the past year's activities.

annulment The act of making a marriage void; also called nullity.

answer The defendant's response to the plaintiff's complaint.

appellant A litigant who appeals a case from a lower court.

appellate court A higher court to which a case can be appealed from a lower court.

appellee The individual or entity against whom the appellant appeals; the opposing party.

arbitration The settlement of a case by a disinterested third party; may be binding or not depending on the parties' agreement.

arraignment The step in the criminal justice process when the defendant is brought before a judge to hear the charges and enter a plea.

arson The intentional burning of another's home or building.

articles of incorporation The first document prepared during the formation of a corporation; include the corporation's name, its purpose, the name and address of the agent for process, and the corporation's stock structure.

assault Attempted battery.

associate A lawyer in a private law firm who is paid a salary and does not share in the firm's profits.

attorney An individual who has attended law school and passed the State Bar Examination; a **lawyer.**

attorney fees The fees that the attorney charges the client.

authentication A formal act that certifies that a document is correct so that it may be admitted into evidence; evidence proving a document is what it purports to be.

battery Harmful or offensive touching of another without consent.

beneficiary One who inherits from an estate.

best evidence rule A rule that requires that when a document is admitted into evidence at trial, either the original must be used or the attorney must show why it is not available.

beyond a reasonable doubt The standard of proof in criminal cases; a higher standard than the preponderance of the evidence standard used in civil cases.

bilateral contract A contract in which the contracting parties are bound to fulfill obligations reciprocally toward each other; a contract involving mutual promises between the parties.

billable hours The hours that are billed to the client.

binder Money given by a buyer to a seller to seal the bargain when an offer to purchase property is made; also called a deposit.

binding arbitration Arbitration in which the arbitrator's decision is final and cannot be appealed to the courts.

board of directors The individuals who oversee the running of a corporation.

bookkeeper An individual who is employed by a law firm to pay bills and keep accounting records.

breach An element of a negligence action; refers to the failure to fulfill duty of due care.

breach a contract To fail to perform any promise that forms the whole or part of a contract.

breach of contract The failure to perform any major part of a contract.

burglary The unlawful entry of a building belonging to another with the intent to commit a felony inside the building.

bylaws Rules that govern the day-to-day operations of the corporation.

calendaring The process of keeping track of appointments and deadlines on a desk or office calendar.

case law Decisions of appellate and supreme courts that establish precedents for other courts to follow.

causation An element of a negligence action; refers to the causal link between the breach of the duty of due care and the plaintiff's injury; to produce the effect that results in damages to another.

challenges for cause Dismissal of prospective jurors where bias or prejudice can be shown.

civil actions Lawsuits in which the plaintiff sues the defendant for money damages.

civil practice A law practice that deals with private lawsuits that are brought to enforce a right or gain payment for a wrong. One individual or company sues another, usually for money damages.

close corporation A corporation formed by a small number of people who manage and control the business.

closing A formal proceeding held in a lawyer's office where property documents and property are transferred from the seller to the buyer.

closing argument The summary of the case each attorney presents to the jury at the end of the trial.

codicil A change made to a will after it has been signed.

cohabitation Living together without a marriage contract and without the intent to enter a common-law marriage.

cohabitation agreement An agreement made between a couple who live together that sets out how their property is to be divided if the relationship ends.

commissioner A minor judicial position. In some states, commissioners are eligible to fill vacancies among the judges.

common area An area in a condominium complex that is owned by all the condominium owners as tenants in common.

common-law marriage When a man and woman agree to enter a marital relationship and live together as if married but never go through a formal marriage ceremony; not recognized in all states.

community property In certain states, property acquired by either spouse during marriage, except property acquired by gift or inheritance, is considered to be community property and to belong to both spouses equally; the concept applies only in community property states.

comparative negligence A system in which damages are assessed based on the degree (or percentage) of fault of each party.

complaint The first pleading filed in a lawsuit by the plaintiff.

condition An uncertain event

condition concurrent A condition that occurs at the same time as the contract is performed and creates an obligation on both parties.

condition precedent A condition that must occur before the contract will be performed.

condition subsequent A condition that occurs after the contract has been performed and relieves the parties of their previous performance.

condominium Ownership of a unit within a multiple-unit building.

condoning misconduct An affirmative defense to divorce; holds that the plaintiff accepted the defendant's misconduct.

connivance An affirmative defense to divorce; holds that the plaintiff lured the defendant into the misconduct that provides grounds for the divorce.

consent and agreement In adoption proceedings, the form in which the adopting parents obtain the approval of the biological parents.

consideration The bargained-for exchange created by a contract. Each party gives up and receives something of value as consideration.

consolidation The process in which two corporations dissolve and then join together to form a third corporation.

contingency fees Attorney fees that represent a per-centage of the award received by the client in a civil action.

contract A legally enforceable agreement between two or more parties; consists of an offer, acceptance, and consideration.

contributory negligence A system in which a defendant may be found to be not at fault if the plaintiff contributed at all to the injuries.

cooperative Similar to a condominium except that the unit is represented by a share of stock.

corporate law A legal specialty dealing with setting up corporations, securities, and corporate mergers.

corporate law department The department of a corporation that handles its legal matters.

corporation A business entity that exists separately and apart from its owners (shareholders) and has perpetual life.

counteroffer A higher price named by a seller after a would-be buyer has made an offer; may not be higher than the original listing price.

court arbitration Arbitration that is governed by local court rules.

court clerk A courtroom official who assists the judge, stores evidence introduced at trial, and administers oaths to witnesses; also, the official who runs the Clerk's Office where documents are filed.

court of appellate jurisdiction The court to which a case is appealed from a lower trial court.

court of original jurisdiction The trial court where an action is initiated.

court stenographer The person who records the testimony at a trial.

covenant The actual promise made by each party to a

contract. The covenants create the terms of the contract.

criminal law The area of law dealing with crimes and illegal conduct under which individuals accused of crimes are brought to trial and punished if convicted.

cross-examination The questioning of a witness by the opposing attorney.

damages Money or compensation paid to one who has suffered a loss or injury by the individual who actually caused the injury.

decedent A deceased person.

decree In adoption proceedings, a form issued by the court that states that the child may be adopted and indicates the child's new name.

deed of trust A written instrument used in some states as a mortgage; resembles a mortgage except that title to property remains with the trustee who issues the loan.

default judgment A judgment in favor of one party based on the failure of the other party to appear or plead at the appointed time; a judgment issued by the court in favor of the plaintiff when the defendant does not answer the complaint in the allotted time.

defendant The individual against whom a lawsuit is filed; the person or entity being sued by the plaintiff.

demurrer A defendant's pleading stating that there are no legal grounds for the plaintiff's complaint.

deponent The person whose testimony is taken at a deposition.

deposit Money given by a buyer to a seller as a pledge or down payment when an offer to purchase property is made; also called a binder or earnest money deposit.

deposition A pretrial examination of parties or witnesses to a lawsuit.

derivative suit A suit by shareholders against a corporation.

devise A gift of real property by will.

devisee A person who is left real property by will.

direct examination The questioning of a witness by the attorney who called that witness.

discovery The formal investigation stage of the lawsuit. Both parties share information using discovery documents.

dissolution Termination of the corporation; may be voluntary or involuntary; the term used for no-fault divorce in many states.

divorce Formal proceeding to end a marriage.

double jeopardy Being tried for the same crime twice.

duty An element of a negligence action; refers to a obligation to observe due care that the defendant owed to the plaintiff; legal obligation to another individual.

earnest money deposit Money given by a buyer to a seller to seal the bargain when an offer to purchase property is made; also called a deposit.

easement A nonownership interest in land that gives its owner the right to the limited use of land owned by another.

easement by necessity An easement that is created when land that is not accessible without passing over another's property is sold; does not have to be in writing.

embezzlement Taking property that is lawfully in one's possession with the intent to steal.

equitable interest An ownership interest that does not entitle one to possession of the property; the owner obtains a legal interest in the property at the time the deed is transferred.

equity suit A suit to force the defendant to do an act or stop doing an act; includes suits for restitution, injunctions, and restraining orders.

escrow The time period during which a title search is conducted on property; extends up to the time the property is transferred from the seller to the buyer; used in some states instead of closing.

estate The property a decedent owned at death.

estate planning The area of law that deals with ways to pass property upon one's death; includes wills, trusts, and probate.

eviction A formal proceeding by an owner of leased property to remove tenants.

examination of judgment debtor A formal court hearing where the defendant appears to answer questions about her assets.

executor An individual named in the will who is responsible for handling the decedent's affairs, including paying bills of the estate and distributing the property.

express contract An actual oral or written agreement between the parties.

express warranty An explicit guarantee included in a contract.

family law The branch of law dealing with divorce, support, custody, adoption, and related matters.

fax machine A machine that can be used to transmit information and written material instantly from one location to another.

fee simple Absolute ownership of property.

Felony Murder Rule A doctrine that holds that if a death occurs during the commission of a serious felony, all defendants who were involved may be convicted of first-degree murder, regardless of which defendant actually caused the death.

felony A serious crime punishable by incarceration in a state prison for more than one year.

Final Decree Nunc Pro Tunc A final dissolution of a marriage that is filed after the appropriate time for filing a final decree, but is effective as of the time the dissolution would have taken place if the final decree had been filed in a timely manner.

fixture An item of personal property that is permanently attached to land or to a building in such a way that it becomes part of the real property.

formal will A typed will signed by the testator in the

presence of at least two witnesses, who must sign the will at the same time.

franchise The right to market a company's goods or services in a particular territory. After purchasing the franchise from a franchise organization, an individual owns the business and leases the equipment and facilities from the parent organization.

garnishment A procedure that enables a creditor to obtain a percentage of the defendant's wages for payment of a debt owed.

general partner A partner who is involved in the management of the partnership and is personally liable for the actions of the other partners.

general practice A law firm that practices all areas of law and does not specialize.

goods Anything that is movable; may include merchandise, food, minerals, crops, oil, gas, electricity, and the like.

grant deed A deed in which the seller guarantees that she has title to the property and the right to convey it and that the property is free of encumbrances except any that have previously been disclosed to the buyer.

grounds for divorce Legal cause for divorce; required in some states.

holographic will A will entirely in the handwriting of the testator.

homicide The unlawful killing of another without justification.

implied contract A contract that is inferred from the conduct of the parties.

implied warranty of fitness for a particular purpose A guarantee by a seller that a purchased item is suitable to be used for a specified purpose.

implied warranty of merchantability A guarantee by the seller that a purchased item is fit to be used for the ordinary purpose of that particular item.

in-house counsel Attorneys employed by a corporation. They are employees of the corporation on salary.

indecent exposure The intentional exposure of private parts of the body in public.

independent adoption An adoption that is not carried out through an agency; usually carried out through an attorney who acts as a middleperson between the biological mother and the adoptive parents.

infraction A minor offense, such as a traffic violation, that is punishable by fine.

inter vivos (living) trust A trust established while the grantor (the person making the trust) is alive. All the grantor's property is put into the trust and he may serve as trustee for the beneficiaries, a device that enables him to have the use of the property during his lifetime and have it pass to the beneficiaries at his death. If the trust is revocable, the grantor retains control and can revoke it; if it is irrevocable, he cannot.

intestate Dying without a will.

involuntary dissolution The termination of a corporation against the will of the directors; must be initiated by the state, but shareholders or creditors may petition to begin dissolution proceedings.

joint tenancy Ownership of an undivided interest in property by two or more owners with a right of survivorship.

judge The individual who presides over a trial.

judgment A decision made by a judge without a jury; the decision in a civil case; may include money damages.

judgment notwithstanding the verdict (n.o.v.) A judgment in which the judge overrules the jury's decision.

jurisdiction The power of a particular court to hear a case brought before it.

jury instructions The instructions the judge gives to the jury before deliberations to explain the law the jury should apply.

justices Judges on the appellate or supreme court level.

kidnapping The transportation of an individual from one place to another against his will.

landlord One who rents property to someone else; a lessor.

larceny Taking and carrying away another's property with the intent to steal.

Last Will and Testament A heading that is often preprinted on the paper used for formal wills because it is the formal name for a will.

law clerk A law student working in a law firm part-time while attending law school.

law librarian An individual working in a law office or law library with responsibility for the law books.

law office manager An individual who handles the administrative functions in a law firm; may also be the **managing attorney.**

lawsuit Litigation; a civil action; occurs when a plaintiff sues a defendant.

lawyer An individual who has attended law school and passed the State Bar Examination; an **attorney.**

lease A rental agreement between a landlord and tenant granting the tenant the right to possession of the property for terms prescribed in the lease. The tenant is known as the lessee; the landlord is the lessor.

legacy A gift of personal property left in a will.

legal cap Lined and numbered paper that must be used for most documents filed with a court; used for legal pleadings and documents.

legal secretary A secretary to a lawyer or a law firm.

legal title The right to possession of property; transferred through a deed.

legatee A person who is left personal property by will.

lessee A tenant; someone who rents property from someone else.

lessor A landlord; one who rents property to a tenant.

letters of administration Forms approved by the Probate Court that authorize an administrator to administer an estate.

letters testamentary Forms approved by the Probate Court that authorize an Executor to administer an estate.

LEXIS A computerized legal research system.

limited partner A partner who invests in a partnership but is not involved in its management and is liable only for the amount invested.

listing agreement An agreement made with a real estate agent when property is put up for sale; sets out the agent's commission, the length of the agreement, and the rights and responsibilities of the parties.

mail log A record of incoming mail.

managing attorney An attorney who handles the administrative and management functions of a law firm.

mandatory arbitration Arbitration that is compulsory under a prior agreement of the parties.

marital settlement agreement An agreement made by a married couple contemplating divorce that sets forth the manner in which property is to be divided.

marriage The legal union of a man and woman as husband and wife.

mayhem The purposeful and permanent disfigurement of another.

mental impairment An affirmative defense to divorce; holds that the grounds for the divorce occurred as a result of a mental defect.

merchant An individual who is engaged in the purchase and sale of merchandise on an ongoing basis.

merger The process in which one corporation takes over another corporation.

metes and bounds A method of describing property based on distance from a permanent marker.

Miller v. California The case in which the U.S. Supreme Court defined obscenity.

Miranda v. Arizona The case in which the U.S. Supreme Court set out the rights of the accused during interrogation by the police. The rights are known as the *Miranda* rights.

misdemeanor A minor crime punishable by incarceration in a county jail.

mistake An unintentional omission or error in making a will.

modem A machine that uses telephone lines to connect one computer with another at a remote location; may operate as a fax machine for material prepared on a computer.

money damages A monetary amount awarded as compensation for injuries.

month-to-month rental A rental where the tenant occupies the premises on a monthly basis and may be asked to leave with a month's notice.

mortgage A written instrument creating an interest in property as security for a loan against the property.

mortgagee The person or entity, such as a bank, that provides a mortgage; the lender.

mortgagor The person who obtains a mortgage; the borrower.

motion for change of venue A request that a trial be moved to a location other than the one where it should ordinarily be held.

motion for summary judgment The plaintiff files a Motion for Summary Judgment if there is no defense that the defendant can claim. The defendant files a motion for summary judgment if the action has no merit.

motion to strike A motion filed by the defendant to strike legally objectionable language from the complaint.

municipal court A lower-level trial court that hears minor civil and criminal matters.

negligence Failure to exercise the degree of care that an ordinarily prudent person would exercise under the same or similar circumstances; must include the elements of duty, breach, causation, and damages.

network A series of computers connected together so that users can communicate electronically.

no-fault divorce A divorce available in many states that requires neither party to prove grounds. Either party desiring a divorce files a petition to commence the action; also called a dissolution.

nolo contendere Latin for "I will not contest it." A plea by which the defendant does not admit guilt, but also does not contest the charges.

nonbillable hours Hours spent working in a law office that cannot be billed directly to a client.

nuisance The disturbance of an owner's quiet enjoyment of property; unreasonable interference with the use and enjoyment of one's land.

nuncupative will An oral will.

obscenity Any material that appeals to the prurient interest, shows offensive sexual conduct as defined by applicable state law, and lacks serious literary, artistic, political, or scientific value.

of counsel A title used for an attorney who acts in an advisory capacity to a law firm and does not have an ownership interest or share in the profits.

offer A proposal or bid to purchase property at a particular price; the manifestation by the offeror of the intention to enter into a contract.

offeree The party to whom an offer to enter into a contract is made; the party who accepts the offer.

offeror The party who makes an offer to another party to enter into a contract.

opening statement The introduction to the facts of the case each attorney presents to the jury at the beginning of the trial.

order to show cause (OSC) A preliminary hearing in a dissolution action where the court issues temporary orders on such matters as support and child custody.

palimony Support paid to one party after a relationship ends based on an implied contract between the couple while they lived together.

paralegal A legal assistant; an assistant to an attorney; may not practice law but may perform tasks under the attorney's supervision.

Parol Evidence Rule A rule that holds that when a contract is written, all previous oral agreements merge in the writing and that the written contract cannot be changed by any oral evidence unless there is proof of mistake, duress, or fraud in the writing of the contract.

partner An attorney who is one of the owners of a law firm and receives a percentage of its profits.

partnership An association of two or more individuals who have joined together to operate a business for profit.

per capita A method of distribution in which each surviving child and grandchild receives an equal share of the estate.

per stirpes A method of distribution in which the children of a deceased parent receive the share of their grandparent's estate that their parent would have received if he were alive.

peremptory challenges Dismissal of prospective jurors without having to give a reason; may not be used to exclude jurors solely on the basis of race or ethnic background; limited number depending on the action.

periodic tenancy A rental where the tenant occupies the premises for a period of less than a year, usually without a written lease.

personal property Property that is not attached to the land.

petition The form filed to initiate a no-fault divorce or dissolution; also the form filed to initiate an adoption.

plaintiff The person or entity that brings a suit against the defendant.

plea bargaining Pleading guilty to a lesser offense with less jail time than the offense that was originally charged.

pleading A document setting forth the formal allegations made by a party to a suit.

prayer for damages The section of a complaint that indicates the damages the plaintiff is seeking.

predecease To die before another; often used in regard to spouses.

preliminary hearing A hearing in court to determine whether enough evidence exists to hold the defendant for trial in a criminal action.

prenuptial agreement An agreement made in contemplation of marriage that delineates the separate property of each party and sets out how property acquired during marriage will be divided if the couple separate.

preponderance of the evidence The burden of proof in civil suits. It means that the event in question is more likely than not to have happened in that manner.

pretermitted heir statute A statute that provides that if a child of the testator is not mentioned in the will, the omission is presumed to be unintentional, and the child receives the share he would have received if the testator had died intestate.

private arbitration Arbitration that is administered by a private organization.

private nuisance A nuisance that affects only people in the immediate vicinity, such as the owners of adjoining property.

probable cause A reasonable ground for believing that a person has committed a crime.

probate The court procedure used to validate a will, appoint a personal representative, and distribute property.

professional corporation A corporation formed by professionals, such as doctors or lawyers.

project fees Fees charged by an attorney for an individual project such as a will, trust, or divorce.

prostitution The provision of sexual favors in exchange for money.

public nuisance A nuisance that affects the general public and not just the people in the immediate vicinity.

quasi-community property Property in another state that would be community property if located in the state where the couple reside.

quasi-contract A legal fiction that allows a person to receive payment in a situation where there is, in fact, no contract but where circumstances are such that to deny payment would result in the unjust enrichment of the other party.

quitclaim deed A deed in which the seller conveys any interest that he may have in the property; the least advantageous form of deed; often used to clear title to property.

rape A forcible sexual attack; sexual intercourse without consent.

real estate sales contract An agreement prepared after the buyer and seller have agreed on a price for the property; sets out the rights and responsibilities of both parties.

real property Land and buildings, and items permanently attached to the land; the area of law dealing with real estate transactions and landlord/tenant relations.

receptionist The person who greets callers to the law office and answers the telephone.

recrimination An affirmative defense to divorce; holds that the plaintiff also engaged in misconduct.

request to enter default A document filed by the plaintiff after the defendant does not answer the complaint in the allotted time, usually 30 days. The plaintiff asks the court to rule in his favor.

rescind To cancel a contract and restore the parties to the positions they would have held if there had been no contract.

rescission The act of canceling or abrogating a contract.

residuary clause The clause in a will that distributes the residuary estate.

residuary estate The remainder of an estate after enumerated property.

retainer agreement A fee agreement between a client and an attorney.

retainer fees Fees paid in advance to obtain the attorney's services as needed.

robbery Taking another's property from her person by threat or force.

senior partner An attorney who is one of the major owners of a law firm and has a larger ownership interest than an ordinary partner has; often one of the firm's founders.

separate property Property acquired before marriage or during marriage through gift or inheritance. The concept applies only in community property states.

share of stock represented by a unit The ownership interest of a cooperative apartment owner.

shareholder An owner of stock in a corporation.

Shepardize Looking up a citation in Shepard's Case Citations to make sure the case has not been overruled; updating research by finding the latest cases and statutes.

small claims court A low-level court where litigants can pursue simple civil cases without an attorney; limited to matters involving small amounts of money.

sole proprietorship An unincorporated business, usually owned by one person, who is subject to unlimited personal liability.

Special Circumstances Rule A rule that holds that if a victim dies during the commission of a serious felony, as specified by statute, the defendant may receive the death penalty if he committed the felony, if he aided or abetted its commission with the intent to kill, or if he aided or abetted with reckless indifference to human life and was a major participant in the crime.

specific performance Doing what was promised in a contract.

spendthrift trust A trust in which the trustee retains control over the property, and the beneficiary receives a monthly income; the purpose of the trust is to prevent the beneficiary from wasting the property.

stare decisis The principle that holds that courts should follow the precedents set in earlier cases when deciding new cases.

Statute of Frauds An English statute, adopted with variations by all the states, that requires certain types of contracts to be in writing.

statute of limitations A statute establishing the time limit within which a particular type of case must be filed.

statutes Laws enacted by the legislature.

statutory law Law contained in statutes.

statutory rape The rape of a minor.

stepparent adoption The adoption by one spouse of the other spouse's child or children from a former marriage.

stipulation An agreement made between attorneys that is binding on the parties.

strict liability Liability that is imposed without proof of negligence because the defendant was engaging in an activity that is inherently dangerous.

strictly liable The condition of being legally responsible without regard to fault. Thus, if a product is defective and causes injury, the manufacturer and seller may be held responsible even if they were not negligent.

subchapter S corporation A corporation that is limited to twenty-five shareholders and to domestic operations; offers significant tax advantages because the income is reported on the owners' personal income tax returns. In size and structure, it is similar to a close corporation.

subpoena An order signed by a judge that requires an individual to appear at a specified time and place to testify.

subpoena duces tecum A subpoena that requires an individual to bring items to a proceeding.

substantial breach The failure to perform a substantial portion of a contract.

summary eviction proceeding A formal procedure for evicting tenants that is used in some states. The landlord files documents with the court listing the reasons for the eviction and serves the tenant with the documents. If the tenant fails to appear in court or is unable to show why the eviction should not be carried out, a court officer carries out the eviction.

summons A form accompanying the complaint that informs the defendant of the lawsuit and orders the defendant to respond within a specified time.

superior court A state trial court that hears major civil and criminal actions.

supreme court A name that is often used for the highest court in a state judicial system, also the highest federal court (U.S. Supreme Court).

tenancy by the entirety Joint ownership by a husband and wife of property acquired during the marriage; used in a minority of states. Neither party may sell or encumber the property without the express permission of the other party; on the death of one owner, the property automatically passes to the survivor.

tenancy in common Joint ownership of property with no right of survivorship.

tenant One who rents property from someone else; a lessee.

tenant at sufferance A tenant who remains unlawfully on the premises after being served with a Writ of Execution for Possession of Real Property.

testamentary capacity The mental capacity to understand the meaning of the material in the will.

testamentary trust A trust established in a will.

testate Dying with a will.

testator The person who makes a will.

title insurance policy A policy issued by a title insurance company that insures that the buyer of property is receiving a clear title.

tort A civil wrong or injury.

tortfeasor The individual who commits a tort.

tract map A map of a subdivision showing the size and shape of the lots; used in describing property in deeds.

transcript A typed record of a deposition or court proceeding; a writing made from the original. Usually prepared from a court reporter's notes of the proceeding.

treble damages An amount equal to three times the actual damages. A landlord must prove malicious willfulness on the part of the tenant to collect treble damages.

ultra vires acts Acts outside the scope of the corporation's powers as set out in the Articles of Incorporation.

undue influence Taking advantage of a testator's weakness, age, or distress to influence the asset distribution in the will.

Uniform Commercial Code (UCC) A set of regulations for commercial transactions that has been adopted, with variations, by all the states.

unilateral contract A contract in which one party makes a promise and the other party performs some act.

unlawful detainer An eviction process used in some states. It is used when the tenant stays beyond the time she has a right to occupy the property, or she has breached the terms of the lease.

valid Having legal efficacy or force; having been executed in the proper manner.

venue The proper geographic location where a case should be tried.

verdict The decision of the jury; must be unanimous in most states in criminal cases but only three-fourths in civil cases.

verification An addition to a complaint stating that the plaintiff knows or believes the allegations in the complaint are true.

void Having no legal force or effect.

void marriage A marriage that is not legal; includes marriages between close relatives and bigamous relationships.

voidable Capable of being adjudged void, but may also be made legal by taking certain steps.

voidable marriage A marriage that may be voided by one of the parties or may be made legal on the occurrence of certain events.

voir dire The process by which the judge and attorneys select a jury.

voluntary arbitration Arbitration that the parties accept without compulsion (e.g., no prior agreement requiring mandatory arbitration).

voluntary dissolution The termination of a corporation by the shareholders or the directors who act willingly and are not being forced to terminate by the state or creditors.

warrant An order issued by a magistrate authorizing the police to make an arrest, conduct a search, or carry out other procedures as part of the criminal justice process.

warranty A guarantee that goods are as promised.

warranty deed A deed in which the seller guarantees that he holds full and complete ownership in the property and that the property is free of encumbrances unless specifically noted in the deed.

WESTLAW A computerized legal research system.

with bond Refers to an Executor having to post a bond before administering an estate.

without bond Refers to an Executor being allowed to administer an estate without having to post bond.

writ of attachment A writ of execution.

writ of certiorari The writ used to ask the U.S. Supreme Court to hear an appeal.

writ of execution A writ filed against assets of the debtor to enable a creditor to satisfy a judgment. The assets may be sold to pay the debt.

INDEX